Hispanics and the Political System

To Mom and Dad,

Thank you this holiday season for moving closer to Anna and I, it has made Anna very happy to be near you. We are blessed with wonderful families, and I am very happy to have the two of you as mother and father in-laws.

Love your son,

Gabe

Hispanics and the U.S. Political System
Moving into the Mainstream

F. Chris Garcia, Ph.D.
The University of New Mexico

Gabriel R. Sanchez, Ph.D.
The University of New Mexico

PEARSON
Prentice
Hall

UPPER SADDLE RIVER, NEW JERSEY 07458

Library of Congress Cataloging-in-Publication Data
Garcia, F. Chris.
    Hispanics and the U.S. political system : moving into the mainstream / F. Chris Garcia,
Gabriel R. Sanchez.
        p. cm.
    Includes bibliographical references and index.
    ISBN–13: 978-0-13-061500-8
    ISBN–10: 0-13-061500-5
1.   Hispanic Americans—Politics and government.   2.   Hispanic Americans—Cultural
assimilation.   3.   Political participation—United States.   4.   United States—Ethnic
relations—Political aspects.   I. Sanchez, Gabriel R.   II. Title.
    E184.S75G366 2007
    323.1168'073—dc22

                                                              2007019147

Editorial Director: Charlyce Jones-Owen
Executive Editor: Dickson Musslewhite
Editorial Assistant: Synamin Ballatt
Production Liaison: Joanne Hakim
Senior Marketing Manager: Kate Mitchell
Marketing Assistant: Jennifer Lang
Operations Specialist: Mary Ann Gloriande
Cover Art Director: Jayne Conte
Composition/Full-Service Project Management: Kelly Ricci/Aptara, Inc.
Printer/Binder: RR Donnelley & Sons Company

Credits and acknowledgments borrowed from other sources and reproduced, with
permission, in this textbook appear on appropriate page within text.

Pearson Education LTD., London
Pearson Education Singapore, Pte. Ltd
Pearson Education, Canada, Ltd
Pearson Education—Japan
Pearson Education Australia PTY, Limited

Pearson Education North Asia Ltd
Pearson Educación de Mexico, S.A. de C.V.
Pearson Education Malaysia, Pte. Ltd
Pearson Education, Upper Saddle River,
    New Jersey

10 9 8 7 6 5 4 3 2 1
ISBN-13:   978-0-13-061500-8
ISBN-10:   0-13-061500-5

Dedicated to: ·

My parents, Flaviano and Crucita; my wife, Sandra; and my daughters, Elaine and Tanya

—*FCG*

My parents, Wilfred and Geraldine; my wife, Anna; and to Chris, who has blessed me with the opportunity to learn much from him while working on this book

—*GRS*

Contents

UNIT II: INPUTS INTO THE POLITICAL SYSTEM

List of Illustrations—Figures and Tables

Preface

"It's Hip To Be Hispanic!"—so headlined an article in a U.S. newspaper at the turn of the twentieth century. Many other similar media pronouncements were commonplace in the late 1990s and early 2000s. *Time* and *Newsweek* magazines both devoted cover stories to Hispanics and Latinos. The July 12, 1999 issue of *Newsweek* featured an article that proclaimed that "Hispanics Are Hip, Hot and Making History." Indeed, it was difficult to read any printed news source—magazine or newspaper—in the late twentieth century and not come across articles on what seemed to be a newly newsworthy ethnic group in the United States. Reportedly, this extensive recognition was brought about by the demographic changes that had been occurring in the 1980s and 1990s but that for various reasons were now coming to a head. One reason was obvious—the decennial U.S. Census of the year 2000 and the preparation for it. The Census pointed out that the Hispanic population was growing so fast that it could no longer be ignored in American society. In fact, some observers began to speak of the "browning of America," or its "Latinization" or "Hispanization." This population surge would likely mean some significant changes were coming to the United States in many areas of life—cultural, social, economic, educational, and political.

The political implications of this change in the ethnic composition of the American polity did not go unnoticed by politicians and public officials. It was evident that some major changes in the electorate and in their constituencies were in the wind, and they began to react accordingly.

This was most evident in the period leading up to the general elections of 2000. Early in the campaign, candidates and political party officials began to indicate that Hispanics were being perceived as major players in the campaigns. They were to become major demographic target blocs. In fact, some spokespersons labeled Hispanics as the most critical demographic segment in the presidential election—a "battleground" group—the "soccer moms" of the 2000 election. Latino spokespersons joined in, some even proclaiming that whoever wins the Hispanic vote wins the presidency in 2000.

So, at the turn of the twentieth century, Hispanics had been proclaimed not only as *the* demographic group to watch as far as social and cultural changes but also as the most critical political players in the nation's elections.

As it turned out, however, for a variety of reasons, Hispanics did not play a critical role in determining the outcome of the 2000 election. However, this period seems to have marked the beginning of a new era of accelerated political awareness and participation by Hispanics in politics. The widely publicized demographic changes, with their cultural, social, and economic implications, also spilled over into the political arena. Participation by the Hispanic public increased markedly. They were running for, and sometimes winning, offices in state and local races at an unprecedented rate and in places where they had not previously been noticeably involved.

No longer would Hispanics be labeled the "invisible minority," and many of the old, somewhat negatively tinged references to the "sleeping giant" would at least have to recognize this awakening. Some Latino spokespersons were so delighted with this new recognition that they began to term the 2000s as the "century of the Hispanic." A few exuberantly proclaimed this era to be the *"millennium* of the Hispanic!"

One need not go that far to realize that there is major change occurring in the United States that reflects the increased numbers, visibility, and influence of Hispanics. This dramatic increase in the Hispanic population, as well as the dispersal of Hispanics into areas in which they were largely unknown, are phenomena that have been increasingly recognized. It may not be that "demography is destiny," but it appears that the burgeoning numbers of Hispanics will continue to provide the potential for major cultural, economic, and political changes in this nation.

This book is primarily concerned with the *political* manifestations of Hispanics in the United States. In it, we explore the past and present status and roles of Latinos in the political system. Because so little is known about Hispanics in general, and because politics is greatly affected by a people's history, culture, psyches, attitudes, and economics, these are briefly examined before we turn to politics per se. Latinos have been in the United States since before this land became an independent nation, so the roots of Latino politics are deep, and historical experience continues to greatly affect current and future politics. However, in the early twenty-first century, Hispanics are moving into the mainstream of U.S. society and its politics as never before, and in doing so, it is also possible, perhaps even likely, that they may also move the mainstream itself. A group of previously largely excluded people will necessarily become more integrated into American life, although to what extent and under what conditions are not entirely clear. Although it is not clear how much the Latinization of this nation will change it, and most particularly how much the entry of Latinos into U.S. politics on an unprecedented scale will change mainstream U.S. politics—its institutions, its processes, its policies, and its culture—change they will.

Writing this book was fraught with difficulties for several reasons:

1. The systematic study of the politics of Hispanic Americans is of recent vintage. Not only are there a relatively small number of studies and scholarly writings on Latinos, but also some of these have produced contradictory conclusions. Therefore, little knowledge about Latino politics is based on solid and incontrovertible evidence that has stood the tests of time and replication. Much of the information provided in this book consequently must be considered as tentative and sometimes even hypothetical.

2. Ideological considerations are inevitably involved, thereby leading to as much or more heat as light being cast on observations about Hispanic politics. Among intellectuals, scholars, and activists who are engaged in Latino politics, there is often heated dialogue about which perspective or paradigm should underlie any explanations of the Latino situation in the United States, including the political aspects. A significant proportion of the academics, journalists, and activists approach explanations of Latino politics through a "radical" perspective, outside the mainstream of American political thought. The world views of many of these observers were strongly affected by the "Chicano movement" of the 1960s and 1970s, a time of radical challenges to many aspects of American society, and whose political philosophies and strategies were unconventional and unorthodox. Any "establishment" institutions, practices, or perspectives were highly criticized. This more confrontational perspective lives on in the actions and writings of some academics, journalists, and advocacy groups, and their leaders. Furthermore, the irreconcilable differences between these radical interpretations and more conventional approaches continue. So many basic disagreements in perspective exist that even the choice of the name that is applied to the group we are studying has been heatedly contended for decades.

3. It is not even entirely obvious that the group that is the subject of this book is a "real" ethnic group that constitutes a clearly defined and delimited political community. Is there enough commonality of interests and feelings among "Hispanics" to qualify them as anything more than a grouping created by government or the media or marketers as a matter of convenience?

4. Related to the foregoing point is the fact that Latinos palpably are the most heterogeneous, diverse ethnic group in the United States. There are so many distinctions in the historical experiences and so many differences in the demographic characteristics of individuals and groups subsumed under the labels of "Hispanics"

or "Latinos" that any generalization evokes challenges and exceptions. It is very difficult to establish any general facts about a group that is replete with so many exceptions.

5. There is often a significant personal and subjective element in any discourse about Hispanics. Many of the persons who study and write about this group are themselves Latinos or Hispanics, and the effects of their personal experiences are extremely difficult, some would say impossible, to remove from their perspectives, even as social scientists. That we, the authors of this book, are multiple-generation New Mexican Hispanics undoubtedly colors our observations and analyses, although we have made a consciousness and determined effort to be as objective and universal as possible.

6. The politics of Hispanic Americans are currently undergoing major and rapid changes. There is significantly more electoral activity and success than there has been over the past century. Hispanics are at long last being perceived as major players in American politics. Very importantly, the essence of Latino politics is itself morphing from a primary concern with the historical emphasis on the protection and promotion of civil rights to an agenda that is increasingly driven by the concerns of new arrivals to the United States—the incorporation of immigrants into the system and all that entails.

It is hoped that this volume will bring some awareness, as well as some enlightenment, to a wide range of readers. This book is intended primarily for undergraduates in colleges and universities, but it should also be useful and informative to anyone interested in learning more about an increasingly important aspect of life in the United States. Because some of the units and chapters deal directly with general concepts of politics, such as participation, representation, decision making, and leadership, this book has been designed to fit well as a supplement to the typical lower division course in American politics or government. A substantial portion of the book is devoted to the "essentials of American government and politics." Years of combined experience in the classroom have made it clear that many students have not yet mastered these essentials, so these are included along with the featured focus on Hispanics. This book is also ideally suited as the core text on courses on the politics of racial or ethnic groups, and, of course, on Latino/Hispanic politics. However, it should also be useful to any person wanting to know more about the fastest-growing population element in U.S. society in the context of the American polity.

The book is organized along the patterns in which most American government and politics courses are organized. Unit I begins with "background" contextual material about the United States and Latinos' places in it. This exploration of the setting for U.S. politics is followed by an examination of the various "inputs" that the American people in general and Latinos in particular have to their governments. Unit II focuses on participation through various means—public opinion, campaigns, and elections, including voting patterns, the role of political parties, and the activities of interest groups. This includes many of the ways that the people present their needs, wants, and demands, in short, their "interests" communicated to their representatives in government for consideration. Unit III looks at the "black box" of American governments—the public officials and decision makers, the representatives—those "authorities" who determine society's rules, regulations, and public policies. The phenomenon of representation and its relationship to reapportionment and redistricting is presented. The people and activities of all branches of government—executive, legislative, and judicial—are briefly examined at the national level, and even more briefly, at the state and local levels. Much of political activity is about the competition of ideas, issues, and policies, and in Unit IV, some public policies that are of special significance to Latinos are explored. Finally, we conclude with some overviews and speculations about the future of Latinos in U.S. politics.

Throughout the book, there are often comparisons with other groups in our society—most often the "Anglo" core culture or non-Hispanic whites, but also sometimes with other racial or ethnic groups such as African Americans or Native Americans.

As with any work of this nature, the volume is a product of a long, evolutionary process and the contributions of many individuals. Nearly forty combined years of studying and teaching about Hispanic politics at the college level has been an invaluable source of learning. Our students have continued to aid in our acquisition of knowledge—challenging many assumptions and broadening our intellectual horizons. An ever-increasing number of colleagues who follow or study Latino politics are major contributors, both directly and indirectly. Other associates and staff at the University of New Mexico have considerately provided their assistance toward the much-delayed completion of this volume. This includes Joann Buehler, Tali Gluch, Anna Hoefler, Scotty Shea, Maggie Toulouse, Jason Morin, and our illustrator, Sarah McGlothin. These individuals gave their time, talent, and effort toward the preparation or improvement of the manuscript. Of course, a special debt of gratitude goes to those associates at Prentice-Hall, including Celeste Nossiter, Ann Daniels, and Heather Shelstad, who first expressed interest in such a book and then continued to support its writing and publication through many delays. Later, Dickson Musslewhite, Charlyce Jones-Owen, Jennifer Murphy, Sinnamin Ballatt, and Lisa Iarkowski of Prentice-Hall; Donna Leik and Kelly Ricci of Aptara; and copy editor Kris Lynch, who worked with us through the long, complex, and sometimes tedious and frustrating processes of reviews, editing, and production. The following academics who reviewed the manuscript also provided us with some valuable feedback: Gilberto Garcia, Eastern Washington University; Harold W. Stanley, Southern Methodist University; Kenneth E. Fernandez, University of Las Vegas; Jason Casellas, University of Texas; Sybil Rhodes, Western Michigan University; Susan Hoffman, Western Michigan University; and Jamie Elizabeth Jacobs, West Virginia University. Finally, one cannot produce any substantial piece of work without strong familial support. For their continual, unwavering, and absolutely essential support, we owe a special debt of gratitude to our respective spouses, Sandra and Anna, and our respective parents, Flaviano and Crucita Garcia and Wilfred and Geraldine Sanchez. Even though those mentioned here were integral and essential to the conception and conclusion of this book, the responsibility for any errors or omissions rests solely with the authors.

In the end, after having read this material, it is hoped that readers will have a much better feel for the situation of Latinos with regard to U.S. politics. It is also possible that many will believe, as the authors do, that Hispanic Americans are inevitably and inexorably moving into the political mainstream. In addition, perhaps having been informed, stimulated, and possibly provoked by it, readers of this book will be better able to judge for themselves whether Latinos will be moving, however incrementally and almost gradually, into the U.S. political mainstream itself, hopefully toward the betterment of all.

F. Chris Garcia
Distinguished Professor of Political Science
The University of New Mexico

Gabriel R. Sanchez
Assistant Professor of Political Science
The University of New Mexico ·

April 2007

Hispanics and the U.S. Political System

Introduction

It is likely that many, if not most, people in the United States are not aware that the nation is undergoing one of the greatest demographic transitions in its history. Due to the tremendous influx of immigrants beginning in the 1980s and continuing into the twenty-first century, the culture of the nation is changing at an accelerated rate and is likely to continue to change for at least another generation. More immigrants came to the United States in the 1990s than were living here in 1970. In the year 2000, one in nine U.S. residents was foreign born. As immigrant cultures meet and mingle with existing cultures, both are inevitably transformed. Immigrant cultures eventually become "Americanized," and the overarching culture of the United States absorbs many aspects of the immigrant cultures. This absorption has many effects. Popular culture is altered and reflected in reconfigured forms of the food, music, clothes, toys, religions, holidays, and even languages of various immigrant groups. Eventually, cultural changes may also affect the social, economic, political, and governmental institutions and processes.

This book focuses on the *political* aspect of the interrelationship and dynamics between two cultures—the Hispanic (or Latino)[1] culture and the U.S. core culture. By far, the largest number of immigrants in the 1980s and 1990s came from Latin America, and the largest groups of immigrants from Latin America are from Mexico. It should be expected that the relationship between Latinos and the U.S. political system would be heightened, if for no other reason than that the numbers of a distinctive people dispersing throughout the United States make it imperative that their wants, needs, and interests be addressed. Marketers, business owners, and politicians have seen these new residents as opportunities for advancing their own goals—not merely for exploitation but also for utilization and incorporation.

Although Hispanics or Latinos have been residing in the United States for centuries, not much attention has been paid to them on the national scene until more recently. The major reasons for, and the driving forces behind, this new concern are *demographics*. The U.S. Latino population has expanded tremendously over the past few decades, particularly from 1980 to the present. Between 1980 and 1990, the Hispanic population in the United States increased by about 55 percent, and between 1990 and 2000, it grew by about 58 percent. This population increase has greatly

1

surpassed that of the white or African American populations. About half of the Hispanic increase was due to immigration; the other half due to natural increases, that is, an excess of births over deaths. Persons born in Latin America comprised more than half (51.7 percent) of all immigrants in the United States in the year 2000. Partly as a consequence of immigration patterns, a minority that for decades had been termed "the invisible minority" was now too large to overlook.

Population numbers are important in a democracy and in a market economy—as voters or consumers—so as the Hispanic population has increased, mainstream society has paid much more attention to them. Some have welcomed the "discovery" of Hispanics as an opportunity for new markets, new clients, new labor, and new voters. Others who are less opportunistic in nature simply welcomed a new, invigorating, and revitalizing element into this "nation of immigrants" that has historically benefited from the infusion of new hard-working, optimistic, achievement-oriented individuals. Some native-born residents have been apprehensive, anxious, or even upset by the latest influx of new residents. Among these, some have feared that the "foreignness" of these newcomers would swamp the American way of life, leading to unacceptably drastic changes in cultural lifestyles. Others have been most concerned that the economic impact would be negative—that additional public monies (through increased taxation) would be needed to provide public services, or that this new source of labor would provide unwanted competition for jobs.

Probably the greatest number of resident Americans held a mixture of beliefs and attitudes, incorporating both negative and positive aspects, or else they simply were unaware of the extent and implications of the tremendous changes occurring around them. Whatever the attitudes of U.S. residents, these new Americans needed to be accommodated and incorporated into the system. How could this best be done? There were no clear-cut answers because U.S. policies toward immigration and immigrants have always been a patchwork of decisions made in the short range to meet the latest crises or to solve the most pressing problem. One thing was clear—political decisions and actions were necessary.

As immigrant waves from Latin America entered into U.S. society, they were often lumped together with other Latinos already living in the country, some for many generations. Thus, the talk was about the dramatically increasing number of Hispanics or Latinos in the country and the many implications this had for society, including the politics of the land. Politics is one of the major ways that societies deal with challenging situations, and the politics that involved this new and largely unknown ethnic group called "Hispanics" began to emerge onto the public agenda. Besides, the mere existence of large groups of people with distinctive differences meant that there would be some degree of conflict, and the resolution of that conflict forms the essence of politics. As Edgar Litt (1970) so succinctly phrased it, "Whenever distinctions arise, there is the potential for conflict, and whenever conflict occurs, there is politics...to be sure, confronting and mediating the demands, interests and values of competing groups is the stuff of politics" (5).

Yet, much of the politics that included Latinos was a largely unexplored phenomenon. As far as most of society, including its politicians and political scientists, were concerned, until recently Latinos were indeed the "invisible minority." Little attention had been paid to Hispanic Americans by the major decision makers in society, particularly outside of the southwestern United States. There were some incidents that had briefly called national attention to this small, concentrated minority group earlier in the twentieth century. For example, there had been mass deportations or "expatriations" of Mexican laborers during the Great Depression and again during the 1950s, when their labor was no longer needed. During World War II, national publicity had been briefly focused on the so-called "Zoot Suit Riots" in Los Angeles, which actually involved the harassment and beatings of many Mexican Americans by rampaging sailors. But, at best, these were exotic and faraway items of curiosity for most Americans.

The greatest public notice of this increasingly significant ethnic group, especially in its political manifestations, occurred roughly between 1964 and 1974, during the *Chicano movement*. In general, this was a period of great turbulence in the United States, as the civil rights movement that began in the late 1950s heightened in intensity and grew from the African American experience to include Hispanic Americans, Asian Americans, Native Americans, women, and other minority groups. At the same time, the anti–Vietnam War movement was in full swing, with continuing high-profile protestations against U.S. involvement in that struggle. The women's liberation movement, seeking equality for half of the nation's population, was also in full force. The Chicano movement is discussed at length later in this book, but suffice it to say that it marked a significant turning point in the political status of Latinos. The nation's attention was drawn to the dramatic politics of the movement, and *el movimiento* had a profound and lasting impact on Hispanic Americans and on their relationship with the rest of American society, particularly its politics. The national media, public officials and politicians, and even some academics realized that the fabled "sleeping giant" had been aroused, and the implications of this revitalization were to reach across the country and touch all aspects of life in America.

Beginning in the late 1960s and early 1970s, there was a noticeable, if yet small, increase in the attention paid to Latinos and their politics, as evidenced by the writings of scholars and journalists. Most political research was of a limited scope that focused on one or a few political jurisdictions or had small samples that limited its generalizability. Many were by a new, first wave of scholars emerging from academic doctoral programs, whereas others only focused on one of the many Hispanic national origin groups. A major exception in terms of its scope and resources used was the comprehensive study of the Mexican American populations of Los Angeles and San Antonio conducted in 1965 and 1966 by a team of University of California, Los Angeles, researchers (Grebler, Moore, and Guzman 1970). Writing about "the forgotten minority" (another phrase used to describe Hispanics), the authors tell of a situation that summarized the Hispanic condition historically and even rings true today to a surprising extent:

> The general public has only recently become aware of the fact that the people of Mexican descent form a sizable and also a *permanent* part of our population, and this awareness has not penetrated deeply. School textbooks at both the secondary and college level tend to ignore them. (Grebler et al. 1970, 5)

This lack of awareness may have been ameliorated at a general and superficial level, but the *political* status, roles, attitudes, and activities of Hispanics in the early twenty-first century are still a little-known aspect of U.S. politics. There is a *sense* or a feeling that Latinos are greatly impacting U.S. life—*U.S. News & World Report* announced in 1999 that "Suddenly, Latino Culture Is Everywhere" (Robinson 1999)—but its specific effects in various aspects of society are just beginning to be explored and understood. This is certainly true of the impacts and interactions between the U.S. system of government and politics and the Hispanic populations.

This book attempts to cast some light on this relationship. Americans are not very knowledgeable about their governments or about Hispanics. The material herein aims to at least partially alleviate that situation. We examine the situation of Hispanics in U.S. politics from a broad perspective, not only surveying the major societal characteristics that affect Latino politics but also presenting the broad outlines of the U.S. political system itself. Our goal is to provide the reader with an overall understanding of Hispanic Americans, how they relate to American government and politics, and how the system operates to affect Hispanics. In doing this, a broad net is cast—it is the overview that is sought. Along the way, there are specifics and specific references that can be followed up for more specialized interests and deeper understandings.

Two questions permeate our presentation. Readers of this text should be able to discuss these questions with a more complete understanding and answer them with the information provided herein. (1) Are Latinos entering the mainstream polity, being incorporated into the churning mainstream channel of U.S. culture and politics, or are they remaining on the margins of the mainstream, separate and distinct? Are Latinos going to move into the mainstream of American culture, society, and politics? (2) Even if Latinos enter the mainstream, will they have an impact on the way government and politics are conducted in the United States? Will the cultural "browning of America" produce a corresponding change in the character and color of American government and politics? More succinctly, are Hispanics moving into the mainstream? If so, will they be moving the mainstream?

Before we can understand the relationship of Hispanics to the U.S. political system, we must at least have a working knowledge of who belongs to this group. We begin by looking at the people themselves to try to identify as precisely as possible who Hispanics are, how they identify and perceive themselves, and what makes them a potentially recognizable or viable political group.

Notes

[1] In this book, the terms *Hispanic* and *Latino* are used interchangeably. Although there has been a long debate over the labels applied to this group, we have chosen to employ the two major "umbrella" terms interchangeably. In general, these terms refer to those persons living in the United States who come from, or who have some ancestors coming from, countries in the Western Hemisphere that were significantly impacted by Spanish colonization.

THE CONTEXT AND SYSTEM ENVIRONMENT

1

The People, Politics, Power, and the U.S. Political System

HISPANICS/LATINOS: THE PEOPLE AND THEIR LABELS

Who are "Hispanics?" There is and has been considerable discussion over who exactly should be included under the label of "Latinos" or "Hispanics," and the terms themselves are subject to much debate and even controversy, as this book illustrates. In this chapter, the various names and labels used to refer to these people, as well as their associated connotations, diverse identifications, and political implications, are presented and discussed. Basic concepts, such as those of politics and the political system, and various competing models of political power, such as that of pluralism, are also introduced. Thus, the two most basic concepts in this book—the people (Hispanics) and a process (politics)—are introduced here and elaborated on throughout.

When referring to the group of people about whom this book is written, there has been a long, ongoing "name game" involved. For decades, raging debates and heated discussions have taken place over exactly what the best term is to describe the "Spanish heritage" people of the United States. In addition, the political implications of this labeling also continue to be important, as they have been for a long time.

Throughout U.S. history, most Hispanics in the United States have been of Mexican origin, but as the Hispanic population has grown, the national origins of "other" Hispanics have diversified. Although Mexican Americans still remain by far the largest group, other Latinos, including Central and South Americans, are beginning to make their presence known.[1] The 2000 U.S. Census indicated that 58.5 percent of Hispanics were of Mexican origin (Figure 1.1). However, subsequent studies led to adjustments of the 2000 Census data and calculated that the Hispanic population was comprised of a larger proportion (63.4 percent) of Mexican

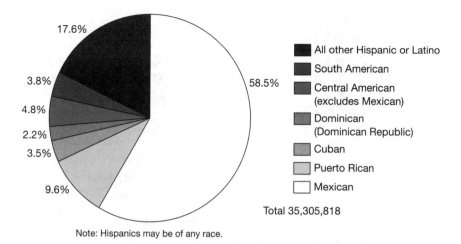

Note: Hispanics may be of any race.

Figure 1.1   Composition of U.S. Hispanic/Latino population, U.S. Census 2000. (From: U.S. Census Bureau, Census 2005 and Sung-Chang Chun, 2005. Latino-Origin Group Populations Revisited. Institute for Latino Studies, University of Notre Dame, Vol. 1, January 2005, pp. 12–13.)

Americans (Figure 1.2). This is only one illustration of the difficulties involved in identifying and enumerating the Hispanic population.

In this book, we define Latinos or Hispanics (the terms are used interchangeably) as those with ancestors from national origins in which Spanish is a significant and often dominant language. These are countries in which people from Spain have played a major role in their histories, and consequently, in their culture. The almost two dozen nations in the Western Hemisphere with a significant Spanish language or cultural background include Mexico, almost all of Central and South (Latin) America, and many of the islands in the Caribbean. Generally, this common definition excludes the "mother country" Spain itself; the largest country in Latin America, Brazil (because its colonial history is Portuguese rather than Spanish); and such Caribbean countries as Haiti, which is more French in its colonial background than Spanish. Excluding these countries (and not everyone thinks they should be) leaves us with twenty-two countries from which Hispanic Americans emanate or emigrate.

When they come to the United States, these Spanish origin populations are labeled "Latinos," "Hispanics," or a variety of other names. (There are no Latinos in Latin American countries, which is reflected in the relatively low level of support for panethnic self-identification among Latinos, a topic we expand on later in this chapter.) In fact, the particular label used has significant implications both for the perceptions of the majority culture

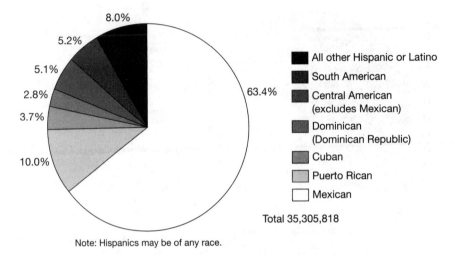

8.0%

5.2%

5.1%

2.8%

3.7%

10.0%

63.4%

- ■ All other Hispanic or Latino
- ■ South American
- ■ Central American (excludes Mexican)
- ■ Dominican (Dominican Republic)
- ■ Cuban
- ☐ Puerto Rican
- ☐ Mexican

Total 35,305,818

Note: Hispanics may be of any race.

Figure 1.2 Composition of U.S. Hispanic/Latino population (adjusted). (From: U.S. Census Bureau, Census 2000 and Sung-Chang Chun, 2005. Latino-Origin Group Populations Revisited. Institute for Latino Studies, University of Notre Dame, Vol. 1, January 2005, pp. 12–13.)

and for the psychology and politics of Latinos themselves. We discuss this further in Chapter 6.

Non–Hispanic Americans are often in a quandary as to what label they should use when referring to Spanish origin populations residing in the United States. Labels seem to be more easily applied to groups that are nonwhite, such as African Americans or Native Americans. There seems to be much less debate over the label of the "white" racial group in the United States, although this group is also quite diverse in national origins. In this book, the label "Anglo" is sometimes used to refer to the non-Hispanic, white racial group in the United States. However, Hispanics are not a racial group; they are an *ethnic* or cultural group. Their racial characteristics are diverse, and their skin color ranges from black, as that of some Cubans, Puerto Ricans, and other Caribbean Islanders, to a very light-skinned, white complexion, with blue eyes and blonde features. Most Latino people, however, are somewhere in-between; that is, they are of mixed racial characteristics. Usually this mixture includes the indigenous peoples of the Western Hemisphere, the "Indians," but it also sometimes includes the slaves brought from Africa, so that Latinos or Hispanics are a *mestizo*, or a mixed racial group, and skin color cannot be a precise basis for identification or an accurate identifying feature (Buriel 1987; Montalvo and Cordina 2001). This trend is reinforced by self-reported Latino racial identification data. For example, in the 2000 U.S. Census, approximately 42 percent of

Latinos chose "some other race" as their racial identification. This suggests that many Latinos do not think of themselves as a racial group.

What, then, should these people be called? Virtually every survey that has asked the people themselves for a preferred term of self-identification results in them first choosing labels that refer to their country of national origin (de la Garza 1993). That is, Americans whose ancestors first came from Mexico refer to themselves as Mexican Americans, those whose ancestors came from Cuba refer to themselves as Cuban Americans, and so on. So, the most common self referent is based on the country of national origin. As this book illustrates, these labels are important for politics. For example, if the primary or exclusive identification of Hispanics is with their country of national origin, then Hispanic or Latino politics is likely to be based on almost two dozen different identifications. However, if people of all Spanish heritage national origins identify with the same single term that transcends national origin, the implications of a potentially powerful cohesive or unified group cannot be ignored. For example, if spokespersons can claim that they are speaking for a large panethnic group of Hispanic Americans numbering approximately 45 million, this is much more impressive than if they are speaking for one national origin group of a few million, such as Cuban Americans.

Although Latinos or Hispanics identify themselves via their national origin as the first choice, there are also many secondary and even tertiary (third-level) identifications that also have political significance (Jones-Correa and Leal 1996). The most commonly used "panethnic" or "transnational origin" terms are Latino and Hispanic. Increasingly, these terms are used interchangeably, as they are in this book. However, there is a great deal of debate, discussion, and even controversy about which of these two names should be most properly applied to the people of Central and South America residing in the United States. This is an understandable if sometimes wearying exercise because the choice of terminology can have tremendous implications for politics. Let us examine each label in turn and then explore the implications.

Probably the most common term applied to the people who are the subject of this book is either Hispanics or Hispanic Americans. This is the term used by the U.S. government, by most state and local governments, and by much of the media and the business sector of the American economy. It is also most overwhelmingly chosen as the preferred panethnic term by the people themselves. This was first demonstrated in the Latino National Political Survey (LNPS; de la Garza, Falcon, Garcia, and Garcia 1990), and was later verified by survey studies conducted by the U.S. Census Bureau and by other national surveys.[1] Despite the fact that the people themselves overwhelmingly prefer Hispanic to Latino, the term Latino continues to be used in certain sectors—primarily by academics and by those who are more activist or even radical in their politics. Moreover, some media also have a policy of using the label "Latino." For example, the *Los Angeles Times* uses the label "Latino" exclusively.[2] There continues to be heated debate over whether the term Latino or Hispanic ought to be universally applied to people from almost two dozen nations, and both the proponents and opponents for each term sometimes become extremely agitated about the best umbrella label to use.

Those who prefer the term Latino argue that the term is a Spanish language word, which is seen as a positive characteristic, and that it clearly refers to residents of the Western Hemisphere (i.e., Latin America or the "new world"). It also emphasizes that a large part of the identity of the Latino community is tied to the indigenous peoples of the Western Hemisphere, the Native Americans, particularly the ancient cultures of the hemisphere. Those who prefer the term Latino say that the term Hispanic is undesirable, claiming that it is a term imposed on the people by the U.S. government or other centers of non-Latino power, and that it emphasizes the European or Spanish component of the people rather than the indigenous side.[3] This emphasis of the Spanish component is usually seen as objectionable because Latino advocates often value the indigenous native aspects of the culture and downplay, if not denigrate, the European, white component. In fact, some advocates of the term Latino claim those who prefer the term Hispanic American are refusing to see their true roots and are instead identifying with Europeans, who conquered and cruelly treated the indigenous peoples of the Western Hemisphere. The term Hispanic is seen as identifying with the oppressor, European Americans, and is a term of assimilation into the white American core culture with a consequent loss of "true" cultural identity.

One can see how the term Latino can be preferred by those who basically take a conflictual or confrontational position with regard either to the dominant power group in U.S. society or one of its major institutions—its government. In fact, there is a myth that the government imposed the name Hispanics on the people, when in fact there has never been, nor could there be, such an imposition. The term Hispanic was actually suggested by Hispanics or Latinos themselves at a meeting in Washington, DC, of Lyndon Johnson's Committee of Spanish Speaking Americans in the 1970s. So, it was suggested by Latinos (or Hispanics) themselves, and the people have remained free to accept whichever label they choose.

These umbrella, or panethnic, terms are important for the politics of Latinos or Hispanics because they imply that there is a large, somewhat cohesive, unified group of people in the United States with common backgrounds and common goals. When the 2000 U.S. Census reported in March 2001 that this group had become equal in size to, or perhaps even larger than, the previously largest distinctive minority ethnic group (African Americans), those coming from all twenty-two countries were included, regardless of their nationality or racial differences.[4] This view of a single ethnic group is a clever rhetorical position to be emphasized by spokespersons and "community leaders" of the Hispanic community because it implies that there is a cohesive, unified group with a distinctive interest and political agenda.

What do the members of these groups have in common, and where does meaningful variation exist? The most obvious feature of commonality for these groups is their Spanish heritage. Whether Latinos or Hispanics, they all come from countries that have been greatly influenced by the Spanish culture, for better or for worse. Indeed, the Spanish language may be the single most salient manifestation of the Hispanic/Latino culture and is one of the most important bonds of Hispanics and Latinos in the United States. Census figures indicate that the number of Hispanics who speak Spanish at home has increased from 10.2 million in 1980 to 24.7 million in 2000. Although not all Hispanics or Latinos speak Spanish, it is highly likely that they are very attached to the language and assign much symbolic importance to it. This is reflected by language policy being the issue/area that has the highest level of consensus among Latinos and that separates Latinos from other racial/ethnic groups (Uhlaner and Garcia 2002). Aside from the Spanish connections, there are some, albeit few, cultural similarities. Foods actually vary quite significantly from one national group to another, as do manners of dress, music, and history, although again there are some similarities. One example of cultural similarity often cited by scholars and pundits alike is the notion of a strong attachment of Latinos to Catholicism. Analyzing religious affiliation through the LNPS, we find support for this assumption because 77.4 percent of all Latinos identify as Catholics. Therefore, religious affiliation or religiosity has been identified as a point of cultural similarity, although this is becoming less intense today than it once was.

The similarities that the various Hispanic groups bring to the United States may be no more important than the way these groups are viewed and treated in this country. Throughout U.S. history, their general treatment has been discriminatory and quite negative. There has been little differentiation by the majority of society among members of a group often viewed as undesirable and given derogatory nicknames, such as "spics," "greasers," "wetbacks," or "beaners." Because these people are distinctive in their manners and behavior, cultural practices, and often in their appearance, they have been subject to the prejudice and discrimination that has been an unfortunate part of American history, not only for new immigrant groups but also for existing groups that have distinguishing physical or linguistic differences. Indeed, it may be that attempts to unify otherwise diverse Hispanics, more than anything else, are the cause of negative treatment by the host society in the United States. This is supported by research that indicates perceived discrimination among minority communities promotes a sense of group identity or group consciousness and influences political behavior

(Dawson 1994; de la Garza and Vaughan 1984; Uhlaner 1991). In addition, the increased use of terms such as Latino or Hispanic over time probably diminishes national origin differences, promotes identification with each other, and increases the likelihood that the host society will see these people as one Hispanic or Latino ethnic group rather than a variety of national origin groups. Again, this has substantial implications for politics in a democracy in which population numbers are an important resource.

It is important to determine whether, in fact, Latinos or Hispanics are a cohesive, unified group. Do they really have common interests, goals, and objectives—political and otherwise? Is there a common and distinctive political agenda? Can Hispanics or Latinos rally around certain leaders or issues that unify them and draw on their resources as a unified ethnic group? Are they a unified single political community, or are their differences such that it is stretching reality to refer to them as one community, when in fact they act more like several, if not many, different political communities? It is not difficult to see why there is so much importance attached to the labels applied to the Spanish heritage people of the United States. The political implications are great, depending on whether the people identify more with their unique national origins or with all other people of Spanish heritage, whether Latino or Hispanic, or indeed, whether most simply consider themselves to be Americans and not members of a distinctive ethnic group.

As mentioned previously, empirical studies such as the LNPS showed that the most preferred term of ethnic identification is that of national origin (e.g., Mexican American, Cuban American, Puerto Rican). The LNPS found that the second most preferred identification was American. This was particularly true of U.S.-born Hispanics. The least preferred terms were the umbrella, panethnic terms—Latinos and Hispanics. Of the two major panethnic terms, the term Hispanic was more greatly favored than Latino (de la Garza et al. 1990). This 1990 finding was reconfirmed in 1995 by a study that indicated that a majority of the same group preferred the term Hispanic (51 percent) to Latino (11 percent; Garcia F.C. 1995). Nevertheless, as both terms are used over time—particularly by the media and marketers—they will most likely be increasingly accepted by the people themselves.

The LNPS also asked its respondents to choose the name they most preferred as a panethnic or umbrella identity. Mexican American respondents' first choice was Hispanic, their second choice was American, and a distant third was Latino. This was particularly true of native-born Mexican Americans. Puerto Rican respondents' first choice, particularly those who were mainland born, was just American. Hispanic was a distant second and Latinos a distant third. Cuban respondents overwhelmingly favored American, with Hispanic as a second choice and Latinos, again, as a distant third.

In an analysis of only the Mexican American respondents in the LNPS residing in the southwestern United States, the overwhelming choice of the respondents was to refer to their national identity, that is, Mexican American (20.2 percent), followed by the panethnic term Hispanic (17.7 percent), followed by American (10.9 percent). This again illustrates the preference for national origin ethnic labels and for "Hispanic" as the preferred transnational label.

The people's preference for the panethnic term Hispanic over Latino was confirmed again in 1995 by the U.S. Bureau of Labor Statistics. In preparing for the 2000 U.S. Census, the Department of Labor conducted a special study of the preferred terminology of ethnic residents of the United States. This large survey of 56,000 households found that "Hispanic" was preferred by 57.8 percent of their respondents, followed by "Spanish Origin" (12.3 percent) and "Latino" (11.7 percent; U.S. Department of Labor, Bureau of Labor Statistics 1995).

Over the past several years, it is likely that the preference for Latino as an umbrella term has increased somewhat. The media, in particular, have often referred to Spanish origin people as Latin or Latino, even though Hispanic continues to be used as well. Although there is no empirical survey evidence to verify this, other than a probable increase in the preference for Latino, there is likely an increase in the acceptance of national origin terms as well as more than one umbrella or transethnic term.

To summarize, there is still a lot of ambiguity and even some confusion about what terms are most appropriate for the people that are having this great impact on the mainstream and are a major part of the "browning of America." The exact label that is used under certain circumstances can be politically important. The complexity of identification for the Hispanic population is heightened when one considers the growing literature indicating that identity, and therefore identification choice, for Latinos may be situational (Barvosa-Carter 1999; Padilla 1985). In other words, individuals have a set of social identities based on race, ethnicity, and gender that they emphasize or deemphasize based on the social context in which they find themselves. For example, a Hispanic American may see him- or herself both as a Latino and as a Puerto Rican, Mexican American, or Cuban. A respondent from Padilla's (1985) study describes this well: "When I talk to people in my community, I use Mexican, but I use Latino when the situation calls for issues that have city-wide implications" (62). Therefore, we must be aware that although previous data indicate that national origin may be the dominant identity for most Hispanic Americans, panethnic identity may be relevant when the situation or context calls for it. We examine some of these situations later in this chapter.

However loosely defined and heavily charged with feelings these names are, there is no doubt that over the past few decades major institutions in the

United States have become quite aware that there is a rapidly growing, culturally distinctive group that is having a significant impact on all aspects of life in the United States and its major institutions and that it will continue to do so increasingly in the future. Whether Hispanic, Latino, Mexican American, Cuban American, Puerto Rican, or any other national origin identification, these people are going to play an extremely important role in the future of the United States. As such, it is important for all U.S. citizens to be aware of this population and knowledgeable about their future role in American economic, social, cultural, and political systems. Because this book focuses on the *political* aspect of Latinos in the United States, it is to the political system that we now turn, with the presentation of some concepts, definitions, and explanations that provide the context for our discussion of Latinos' interaction with the political system.

WHAT IS POLITICS? WHY HISPANIC POLITICS?

Politics is all around us: it is one major aspect of human behavior that permeates society. Some contend that politics is everywhere, not only in government but also in schools, businesses, churches, and even families. Whether this is accurate depends on how one defines politics. In any case, politics is certainly an important aspect of human behavior, one that seems a natural and almost inevitable consequence of human interactions.

There are several ways to look at politics and also several definitions of politics. Here, it is important only to grasp the essential features of politics. Politics seems to arise whenever there is conflict or competition for resources—anything that is valued, whether tangible, material, or symbolic. When this conflict arises, a potentially political situation develops. The situation is further developed if such conflict or competition can be resolved by a person or persons who have the authority or power to decide how the conflict ought to be resolved.

Many assert that the central feature of politics is *power* (Dahl 1957). Power can be defined as the ability to control the behavior of others, that is, to be able to move behavior in a certain direction or to get people to act in a certain way. Some would define politics as the struggle to either become powerful, or to have powerful people act in such a way as to benefit one's own cause or advance one's own interests. Indeed, one of the most famous definitions of politics is by Harold Laswell (1936), who in the title of his book stated that "Politics is who gets what, when, and how." Others have defined politics as *decision making* that resolves conflicts (Leftwich 1984). The concept of *conflict resolution* embodies the idea of conflicting or competing interests trying to have their own desires, wants, or needs met and having this conflict or competition settled by an authority (typically governments) that determines the winners, that is, who will have their ways made official or be sanctioned.

Another famous definition of politics is David Easton's (1953) "authoritative allocation of values in a society" (146). This definition indicates that in society there are people or agencies that have the authority to choose from among competing or conflicting interests, then distribute or allocate what is wanted or valued by these competing interests. Easton (1965) also advanced his conceptualized schema of the *political system* in another work. We use the political system model in this book primarily to organize the various features of Hispanic politics and the interactions that take place in Hispanic politics in the United States (Figure 1.3). The integration of this political system model into our book is reflected in the organizing themes of the table of contents, which represent the major components of the system model.

In Easton's political system, the major components are (1) the *environment* or *context* in which politics operate; (2) the *inputs* to the system, consisting primarily of (a) supports and (b) interests, wants, and needs; (3) the *conversion* of inputs into outputs, which is the "black box" of governmental decision making; (4) the *outputs* of the system—decisions that become public policies such as laws, rules, and regulations; and (5) the *outcomes* and *feedback* that reflect the effects of political decisions as they change the environment and become new inputs into the system. The political system is an abstraction that represents the linkages and interactions of those activities that are political in nature. It is a dynamic process,

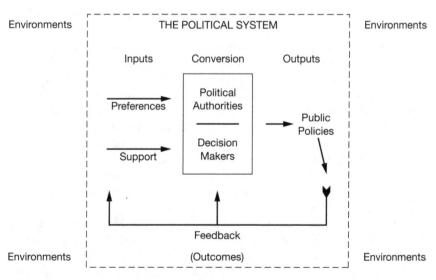

Figure 1.3   The political system.

always in motion, always changing, always seeking to carry out its major functions while maintaining a balance as it allocates resources through public decision making.

Of course, there are innumerable reasons why humans compete with and have conflicts with one another. Some people believe that it is simply human nature to be competitive or conflictual.[5] Others modify this idea by saying that differences within a society will inevitably lead to conflict and, consequently, to needs and wants that are based on these differences. One salient societal difference in the United States is that which occurs along racial and ethnic lines. The United States has a long history of conflict among various racial and ethnic groups and also, unfortunately, a long history of the majority ethnic or racial group controlling the decision-making apparatus and using government to control, exclude, or even discriminate against ethnic minority groups. Such conflict may be inherent in a society composed of a variety of ethnic and racial groups.

A political scientist, Edgar Litt (1970), captured the essence of this situation well when he stated that "Whenever distinctions arise, there is the potential for conflict, and wherever conflicts occur there is politics. To be sure, confronting and mediating the demands, interests, and values of competing groups is the stuff of politics" (5). So, in line with Litt's idea, the fact that there is a distinctive group in society called Hispanics or Latinos that is differentiated from non-Hispanics or non-Latinos means that inevitably there will be conflicts, and in turn, there will be politics; and this will lead to Hispanic (ethnic) politics. This means that Hispanics as an identifiable and distinctive group will be competing with other groups to have their values, needs, and wants accepted by the decision-making authorities in society and sanctioned in the form of governmental policies, perhaps by laws or other regulations.

Hispanics may want decisions, actions, and policies from government that are unique to their group but that are irrelevant to or opposed by other groups. These interests would comprise a distinctive and unique *Hispanic political agenda.* Or Hispanics may simply want some of the same valued resources that they see other groups having, but which they themselves do not have or have less of. Although this may not be unique to Hispanics, these items would also become part of the Hispanic political agenda. Thus, it is natural for Hispanics to be engaged in politics in the United States as Hispanics, as are so many other groups based on ethnicity, race, or other societal divisions, such as economics, class, religion, ideology, or other group interests.

Overall, this book examines the status of Hispanics in the U.S. political system today—that is, where they stand and how they reached their current status—to present the activities in which they are engaged within the political system in order to further advance their interests, goals, and objectives, and to judge how successful they have been and may be in the future. As we do this, we also attempt to separate fact from fiction, myth from reality, and truth from falsity. For it is only by knowing the truth of the situation (or as close as we can approach it) and by having accurate knowledge of Hispanics and of politics in the United States, that Hispanics can be successful in political activities. When this is done, they will no longer be at the margins of the polity; instead, they can become full-fledged, active, and successful players in the U.S. political game. Hispanics can move into the political mainstream, and in doing so, they can possibly also move the mainstream into a new course.

DISTRIBUTION OF POLITICAL POWER IN A POLITICAL SYSTEM: CONFLICTING THEORIES

We now have some working definitions of politics as well as a schematic diagram or model of the various components of this system and how they relate to one another. However, neither the definitions nor the model attempts to analyze how power is actually distributed in the system—particularly in the U.S. political system. So we now turn to the following questions: How is political power distributed in the United States? Is the distribution fairly equal; that is, does every individual or every group have equal or potentially equal political power? Is the system open and accessible to everyone regardless of individual or group characteristics? Is it possible for everyone or every group to present their interests or needs to the political system equally well, and will they all be equally well received by the authoritative decision makers? In short, is the political system a level playing field, or are there biases and inequalities in the system?

There have been many models put forth by political scientists and others who have developed their own ideas as to how the U.S. political system operates, and more particularly, who has the power in the system and how things get done. Here, we only look at two simplistic, archetypical (pure or ideal) models—one that is open and democratic, and one that is closed and undemocratic, or "elitist." Almost all other models of the distribution of power in the American political system are variations on these two basic themes.

DEMOCRATIC (AND PLURALISTIC) MODELS

The prevailing view of power in the American political system is that of *democratic pluralism*. The major characteristic of American government is that it is a *democracy*—the world's oldest large-scale democratic form of government. At the base of democratic theory is that the people are sovereign; that is, the public is the ultimate source of governmental power. The importance of the public is derived from the philosophy that every individual is an equally important member of the polity. In fact, governments were established to serve, protect, and preserve the individual rights of the citizenry. Foremost among those inalienable rights are liberty and freedom. Because no one individual is inherently superior to any other, all citizens are equal in their standing before the law and in their opportunities. The people may select some from among them to become their representatives in government, thus making the American democracy a *republic*—a representative democracy (Sidlow and Henschen 2004, 7).

As the American democracy operated, it was observed that much of the political activity and exercise of power was group based. Individuals tended to group together, or be grouped together, to the extent that groups seemed to be more significant in politics than the individuals that comprise the mass public.[6] This democracy retained its basic goals and values of individual rights and public sovereignty; however, in actuality, groups superseded individuals in most forms of political participation influence. This group-based form of democracy was termed *pluralism*. Various theories of pluralism have been put forth by scholars and philosophers and modified throughout the years.[7] There are also many variations of pluralism that have been given different names. Nevertheless, there are some basic, common features that distinguish pluralistic models from nonpluralistic models and nondemocratic forms of government. A democratic pluralist system must be more or less *open* and *fair*. It assumes either equality or potential equality of all players. Any citizen can participate in the political process and has the right to communicate with the decision makers, participate in elections, be engaged in the formation of public policy, and otherwise express his or her interests and have them heeded by government. If a person does not possess political influence or power, that person at least has the potential and the freedom to increase his or her resources so his or her interests and needs will be heard and possibly met. Few individuals have the kind of power by which they, acting alone, can influence government to give them what they want. However, individuals should at least have the freedom to organize, to seek common allies in their cause, and to attract other like-minded individuals to their cause—in short, to freely associate, communicate, and form groups, thereby multiplying their potential power and resources.

In fact, another feature of the pluralistic system is that it is basically a *group* political game rather than an individual one. The major actors in a pluralist system are groups and groupings of all sorts—neighborhood groups, student groups, educational groups, economic groups (e.g., labor unions, corporations), ethnic groups, ideological groups, religious groups, and many others. In short, a pluralist system encourages and rewards those who band together in attempts to influence government.

Individuals have *overlapping memberships* in this multitude of groupings and groups—ones based on religion, occupation, economic interests, race, ethnicity, education, and geography—an almost countless number of interests. The populace is not sharply divided into just a few groups whose members only have common interests with their fellow group members. Instead, people have *overlapping memberships* in many groups. Nor is there just one powerful elite group that is homogeneous in its composition. Elites, persons in positions of influence or power, have diverse characteristics— differing professions, religions, cultures, regional loyalties, and organizational memberships. The "less elite"—the masses or general populace—are at least as diverse, probably more so, and they share many characteristics with the more elite segments of society. Moreover, there may be a circulation of elites, so that some people at the top eventually lose their status and become downwardly mobile as some of the nonelites in society rise up and achieve higher, elite status.

In addition, the chances for success of any group being heard and their interests being heeded are good in a pluralist system because the *rules* of the political game are basically clear and fair to all participants and because there is a *multiplicity of access points* in such a system. By a multiplicity of points, we mean that there is a plenitude of individual offices and places where a group may make contact with officials and present their interests. For example, the United States has a *federal system*, which means that a group may present its preferred policies to officials in offices at the national, state, or local level, and citizens can try to access people in any and all of these levels. Furthermore, at each level there are many governments. For example, at the local level there are municipal or city governments; there are county governments, school board governments, and a whole variety of special district governments, such as pollution control, flood abatement, and fire fighting districts; the well-known school districts; insect abatement districts; irrigation districts; and dozens of others. In fact, in the United States, there are more than 88,000 local governments (U.S. Bureau of the Census 2002c). Another basic constitutional feature of the United States that also increases the number of access points is that at each level of government, there is also a *separation of powers*. This separation of governmental powers means that at any one level there will be opportunities to communicate with, and try to influence, people and agencies in the executive, legislative, and judicial branches. Thus, in a pluralistic United States, there are many thousands of access points for individuals and groups wanting to influence government.

Another feature of virtually all pluralist systems is that when any interest groups are successful and have their views accepted by government, and these in turn become laws or regulations, these policy changes are likely to be *incremental* (Dye 1992). A pluralist system is usually one in which change occurs gradually, so seldom, if ever, is there a radical change in policies or a major change in direction by governments. Typically, the status quo is modified only slightly with any new policy or regulation.

So, overall, a pluralist system is an open and democratic system—open to participation by all or virtually all, having rules of the game that are fair to all players, and in which there is a maximum opportunity for individuals (or more accurately for groups) to have their interests heard and perhaps accepted as government policy.

ELITIST SYSTEMS

Pluralist systems and their many variations can be contrasted with a variety of undemocratic or closed, *elitist* systems. These are political systems in which there is a significant amount of inequality between the players, usually divided into two major sectors—the rulers or ruling class and the masses, who are the ruled. This has been by far the most common form of government throughout the world's history. The ruling group (often termed an *oligarchy* or *autocracy*) dominates many, if not all, aspects of life and certainly regulates or even controls the political activities of the average citizen. Citizens have minimal opportunities to participate, and their participation is often meaningless, ineffectual, or, at most, only symbolic. The rulers do not allow meaningful participation by the masses for fear that there will be a change in their own advantageous, unequal relationship. Physical force, via the military or police, is often used to keep people in their places. Sometimes the ruling class holds its position much more subtly than through the outright use of force. Instead, the rulers will use propaganda and other persuasive techniques to educate or indoctrinate the citizens toward supporting the ruling regime. The goal of this practice is to ensure that the masses will accept their rulers as being rightfully in their positions of domination or power and accept the regime as is.

In a closed elitist system, there is little circulation between the ruling class and those who are ruled. There is little or no input from the citizenry; instead, the rulers decide what is best for them. Obviously, in a closed elitist system, the rulers are impervious to any wants or needs of a segment of the population. In a less forceful form, the ruling class will attempt to keep the masses from growing restive by either allowing them some meaningless form of participation or by manipulating their beliefs and thoughts through propaganda and indoctrination so the masses will not even think of wanting to change the system. Sometimes minor policies from or on behalf of the masses are accepted by the ruling class just to keep the citizenry content, that is, to forgo or preempt any kind of revolution. It is only through revolution or other kinds of radical action that significant change can occur; otherwise, the elites will resist and prevent it.

Communism is a typical and recent example of a closed, elite, and undemocratic system. The rulers were members of an elite segment of the Communist Party. Virtually all government officials were either members of the party or approved by the party. Authorities made decisions in a closed and secretive manner. The general public was excluded from decision making and often kept in the dark about what was happening in the higher councils of government. The role of citizens was to support the regime, not to provide input for policy direction. The elite class was privileged, while the masses often struggled in their day-to-day existence.

In a Communist system, the characteristics that define the ruling class from the masses are largely ideological; that is, the conflict was centered around party versus nonparty members. However, distinctions between the elite rulers and the ruled masses can sometimes be along other lines, for example, based on tribal differences, in which the members of one tribe will rule with a heavy hand while members of other tribes are excluded. Another distinction is between a hereditary royal elite and the mass of "commoners" who are not in the line of inherited privilege and power.

The distinction between the elite and the masses can also be economic, with those who have the wealth largely guarding their wealth and the means of production while preventing others from obtaining the same. This kind of government by the wealthy is known as a *plutocracy.* When the ruling elite are religious leaders, the government is a *theocracy*. An *aristocracy* has been a typical kind of elite rule of polities for centuries. Aristocrats are those who are born into the ruling class and inherit their titles of nobility (e.g., king, queen, prince, princess, czar, duke, earl). There also can be differences based on race or ethnicity. For many years in South Africa, the rulers were white, while the impoverished masses were blacks. This system of *apartheid* (an "apartness" of legal separation) lasted until international pressures and internal unrest and struggles resulted in radical changes in that government.

In closed, elite systems, there is usually little change, and when change comes about, it is often major or radical, involving the overthrow of the ruling elite government through physical force, such as via a revolution. Many of the nations of the world, even in the twenty-first century, still have closed or elite systems of government. But could this type of government exist in the United States? Some people believe that there already is a subtle form of closed or elite government in America, whereas others believe that non-Hispanic whites represent the ruling elite, with Latinos being among the excluded groups.

In an elite system, the leaders are all members of the ruling class, and it is virtually impossible for members of the outside masses to ever become true leaders. In fact, if the ruling elites recognize members of the outside masses who have special ruling talents, it is often the case that through a process of *cooptation* the rulers will allow persons from the masses to become members of the ruling group. Seldom, however, are these outsiders given full status and privileges. More often, they are allowed some of the trappings, but not all of the privileges, of the ruling elite. In all cases, these individuals are chosen from the nonprivileged mass

communities, thus depriving those communities of valuable leaders—
leaders who could possibly organize the masses and lead them against
the ruling class. Of course, these coopted leaders are often disowned by
the community from which they come and are seen as traitors to their
class or traitors to their race—in short, they are branded "sell outs" of
various sorts. (See Chapter 7 for a discussion of leadership as it applies
specifically to the U.S. Hispanic community.)

Many elitist models are based on ideology or economics, and often the
two go together. Of great interest to us in the study of Hispanic politics are
differences based on race and ethnicity (although economic and class differences should not be discounted). Indeed, there have been political theories developed that have analyzed the U.S. political system as being not
democratic but basically elitist and closed in nature, with members of one
racial/ethnic group being in control and members of other ethnic/racial
groups being controlled (Hero 1992a).

One of the most well known of these theories of a closed, elitist system
is that of *internal colonialism*. This is a theory most prominently laid out
by Robert Blauner (1969) as he offered an explanation of the disparities in
social position and political power between African Americans and the
white population in the United States. Professor Blauner took an elitist
system of governing that has existed throughout history, that of colonialism, and applied it domestically to the United States.

In a colonial system, a conquering power, usually an imperialistic one,
comes to an area that has resources it desires. The resources can be that of
additional space or raw materials, perhaps valuable minerals such as
gold, silver, iron, or petroleum; agricultural products; or the potential
labor provided by the inhabitants of the area. The colonialists or coloniz-
ers then conquer the native people of the area through force of arms and
subjugate them, keeping them in a state of oppression. Often, the native
people are enslaved, or they may even be exterminated. This process of
extermination of native people is termed *genocide*. If they are not exterminated, they may be enslaved and their labor controlled by the conquerors
to extract the minerals or produce the products that the conquering colonial power needs or desires. The native population's way of life is extremely disrupted or even eradicated. Their culture is discouraged or even
destroyed; this is called *cultural genocide*.

In a conquered colony, the people who have power are members of the
conquering nation, so that the masses of the native people—the colonized—
are ruled by the conquerors either through its representatives in the conquered area or through the government back home in the colonizing nation.
Colonized people are therefore *externally administered*. They do not have
their own system of government; they do not determine their own fate.
Their position is not one of self-determination; rather, it is one of *external
control* and external administration. The native people have no rights; the

only privileges they have are those that are granted to them by the conquering outsiders. The most well-known examples of classic colonialism are those in which European powers, largely in the sixteenth to nineteenth centuries CE, set out to conquer and control much of the world's land masses and peoples. A majority of the continents of Africa and Latin America were conquered and dominated by European powers such as the British, Spanish, French, German, Portuguese, and Dutch.

Professor Blauner applied this *classic colonialism* model to the United States. He believed that African Americans in the ghettos were internal colonies within the United States. They constituted a separate oppressed class, conquered by outsiders (in this case, African and white European slave traders) and put into slavery. Their culture was destroyed; families were torn apart; they were considered chattel, or personal property, and initially they had absolutely no human rights. In no way were they equal to the white European settlers. Moreover, this colonial legacy continued for 300 years in the United States. During this period, African Americans did gain some constitutional and legal rights so that by the 1960s, on paper, they were equal to white citizens. However, their segregated ghettos were administered not by their own representatives or their own leadership but by white people who occupied the important governmental offices and who maintained control of force and power in the society. Blacks had been deprived of their native languages, styles of dress, foods, and native religions, and were only allowed to use some of the cultural artifacts of the conquerors; the terms were set by the conquering, enslaving Europeans. Thus, Blauner argued, the situation of African Americans was similar to those of Third World colonized peoples throughout the world, except that this was a domestic, internal situation rather than an international, external one. Moreover, although American blacks appeared to have equality as citizens, they were, in fact, still largely oppressed and excluded.

A few years later, this analogy—the *internal colonial model*—was applied to the Hispanic population in the United States. In a well-known article entitled "The Barrio as an Internal Colony," some Latino social scientists argued that Mexican Americans or *Chicanos* were essentially in the same situation as many of the world's peoples of color in relationship to their white conquerors and oppressors (Barrera, Muñoz, and Órnelas 1972). In fact, their situation was even closer to that of African Americans in the United States. This model of internal colonialism was accepted by many Chicano activists—particularly those who were of a more radical bent during the heyday of the Chicano movement—as a very good, and perhaps the best, explanation of how power was structured in the American political system. It also provided the political strategies that needed to be employed if Chicanos were to be liberated and gain self-determination, that is, control over their own communities. Obviously, to change this kind of situation one could not just engage in conventional politics, such as voting or lobbying. First, the ruling classes would not allow any meaningful participation, and second, one could never get the kind of sweeping, radical changes that were needed to bring equality to Hispanics and African Americans in a slow-moving, pluralist system. More radical tactics and strategies would be necessary to truly change the system; some radical activists even called for revolutionary changes but many recognized that revolutionary change could not occur through the use of force simply because of the inequality in resources. Many called for a strategy of developing separate and equal institutions, often referred to as "parallel institutions" or "counterinstitutions," that were controlled and led by members of the Hispanic or African American communities. Thus, some Hispanics set about forming their own community institutions, including schools, colleges, police forces, and other institutions.

Some of the more radical activists in the Chicano movement even came up with the notion of a separate nation, the nation of *Aztlan*. For some, this was primarily a symbolic homeland, basically covering the American Southwest, the area where the ancient Aztec tribes originated before moving south on their venture in conquest. To a few, Aztlan was held forth as a real possibility, a geographical homeland for the Chicanos, with its separate government, flag, language, and borders excluding any non-Chicanos, a physical nation of self-determination and Chicano freedom and independence. Thus, one can see that any analysis of the way power is distributed in the United States has tremendous implications for the kinds of political strategies and tactics that a group should use to be successful politically.

These two extremely different and polarized ideas about the status of Latinos in the United States are reflected in a controversial treatise written by Peter Skerry (1993), entitled *The Mexican Americans: The Ambivalent Minority*. In this book, Skerry posits two very different models of the Mexican American in the United States today. On the one hand, he sees the Hispanic community as basically another "European immigrant ethnic group" that migrates into the United States. Over a period of generations, through hard work, smart political strategies, and learning and adopting the ways of the host country, Hispanics eventually succeed and become thoroughly integrated into the mainstream. He equates this model of the Hispanic American with such previous immigrants as the Italian Americans, Jewish Americans, or Greek Americans. This would be the most likely mode of operation in a pluralist system.

The opposing model is one of Hispanics being a "racially oppressed victim," analogous not to the ethnic immigrant but to racial peoples such as the African Americans or Native Americans, who were dealt extremely harsh discriminatory treatment and even forms of genocide by the host society. Skerry holds that Mexican American politics has started off on the wrong track. It is basically a politics of Hispanics as racial victims, claiming grievances, when instead it should be more similar to the politics of other ethnic immigrant groups. Furthermore, he holds that Latino spokespersons, leaders, or advocates most often operate from the much more radical stance of the Latinos as *racially aggrieved and discriminated victims*, thus demanding governments' special rights, privileges, and protections. The Latino leadership, Skerry believes, is badly out of touch with the masses of Mexican Americans and, consequently, is leading them along the wrong path if success is to be attained in the United States. Leaders and "spokespersons" are often more liberal, or even more radical, than the general Hispanic public. It is of critical importance that marginal groups are able to separate truth from reality and to select strategies that are based on reality and reason, not on myth and misconceived ideology. If the aim of Latinos is to become part of the U.S. political system, the Latino masses are being misled. To make matters worse, Latino leaders' opinions and values are very different from those of the rank-and-file Mexican American.

Obviously, Skerry's book was controversial because he drew a lot of attacks from other scholars of Latino politics. These strong criticisms of Skerry's analysis and position resulted in a symposium comprised of a panel of social scientists criticizing his scholarship and observations, and asking the question, "Are Mexican Americans really an ambivalent minority?" (Magana 1994). Although critics of Skerry's analysis do not necessarily embrace the internal colonial model or even a more general elitist model, their positions reflect some elements of these, and they most likely would hold that the pluralist model must be substantially modified if it is to be applied to Latinos.

Whatever argument carries the day, it is extremely important for Latinos to accurately assess their status in the U.S. political system and employ those strategies and tactics that will most likely help them achieve their goals. Accurate analysis can result in a smart and effective politics. However, if Hispanics are on the wrong track, based on the assumptions of incorrect analytical models, this would not bode well for their political or socioeconomic advancement.

It is quite possible that neither Skerry nor his critics are entirely correct in that Hispanic Americans are close to being one polar type or another, but instead they may be truly *in-between* these two extreme types. Although they have not suffered quite as much outright violence and legal discrimination as have African Americans or Native Americans, Latinos, particularly Mexican Americans, have endured a long history of injustices, oppression, and discrimination. They have been excluded and mistreated much more so and for a longer period of time than have the Italian Americans and Greek Americans. For example, laws were passed in California, Texas, and other parts of the Southwest to limit the rights of Mexican Americans in schooling, housing, public gatherings, and even marriages to

Anglos (Barrera 1979; Montejano 1986). Mexican Americans have also faced tremendous violence. Specifically, the lynching of Mexican civilians by duly commissioned Texas Rangers and self-appointed vigilante groups claimed the second largest group (after African Americans) of American ethnic-racial victims, with a documented 605 individual cases occurring between 1848 and 1928 (Horton 1999). Furthermore, records indicate 473 of every 100,000 Mexican migrant workers between 1848 and 1870 died as victims of lynchings (Carrigan and Webb 2003). Therefore, it is clear that Mexican Americans have suffered violence and discrimination similar to that of African Americans and Native Americans.

Moreover, many Hispanic Americans are more distinctly recognizable physically than are white ethnic European groups. Consequently, they are more subject to discrimination because, to a large extent, this cultural ethnic group has become *racialized* by the dominant society. In addition, unlike these other minority ethnic groups, most Latinos are not vast oceans apart from their homeland, but rather they are either directly adjacent along a 2,000-mile border in the Southwest or, if from the Caribbean Islands, across a small sea. Nor has the United States conquered or controlled the homelands and colonized the territories of European ethnics as they have those of many Latino groups. Hispanic Americans truly are an exceptional and unique case. Their culture is constantly replenished through continuing contact with their homelands. Many of them have not completely severed ties with their mother country; instead, they either hope to return at some point or are at least sending earnings back to their families.

It may be much more accurate to speak of Latinos as being in a unique and ambiguous position of a distinctive ethnic/racial minority that is somewhere *between* African Americans and Native Americans and the white, largely Mediterranean ethnic groups. Latinos' in-between status makes understanding and analyzing the political role of Hispanic Americans particularly difficult, yet it also makes it particularly intriguing.

MODIFIED PLURALIST MODELS

Most political scientists would reject the internal colonial model as an accurate interpretation of how power operates today in the United States for Hispanics, although a larger number would accept some of its features as helpful in explaining the history of Hispanics and the effects of that history on contemporary Hispanic politics. Some political scientists have tried to modify the pluralist model to account for the distinctive situation of Hispanics.

Rodney Hero provides one of the best examples of such a modified pluralist model. He appreciates the unique history and character of the Latino experience, which is characterized by its "betweenness"—neither truly analogous to that of whites or African Americans. Hero (1992a) created a

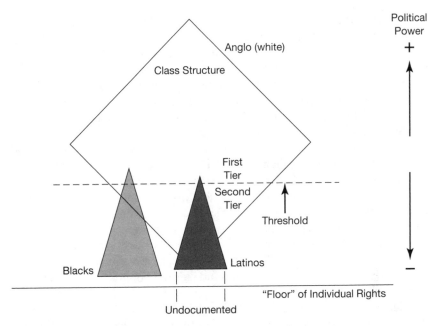

Figure 1.4   Hero's two-tiered pluralism (simplified). (From: Simplified version of "Two-Tiered Pluralism—A Schematic Presentation" from *Latinos and the U.S. Political System* by Rodney E. Hero. Used by permission of Temple University Press. © 1992 by Temple University Press. All Rights Reserved.)

model of the pluralist system that best illustrates the Hispanic role and perspective that he termed "two-tiered pluralism" (Figure 1.4). In this model, many of the elements of pluralism are present in our laws and institutions, but Latinos (as well as blacks) occupy a special second class or, in Hero's terms, "second tier" position in the pluralist system. Latinos are distinctive in their economic class position (lower than Anglo whites), are largely separate from most of society, and operate at a lower level of involvement in political decision making. Although Latinos have the legal and constitutional right of U.S. citizens, they are still largely marginal to politics.

In the dual pluralism model, the more powerful classes are shown at the top of Figure 1.4 and the least powerful at the bottom. The large diamond represents the mainstream Anglo (white) class with a small group at the top, a large middle class, and a small group at the bottom. Most of the mainstream class is above the dotted line—a policy-making threshold—and thus has political power and a role in making policy. They are largely "first tier." The two pyramids of blacks and Latinos at the bottom of the diagram represent smaller groups with little power. Their shape is pyramidal to illustrate how they have large bases comprised mainly of the lower socioeconomic classes. As the pyramids narrow and extend upward, they barely cross the threshold of policy making. Thus, although they have some political power, these two groups are almost entirely "second tier." Note that Latinos are more central in the figure and not as far removed from the Anglo (white) society as blacks, who are noticeably more marginalized. Additional undocumented Latinos extend even further below the "floor" of individual rights with no political power.

The perspective of this book would further modify the pluralist system. While preserving the essential ideas of the basic model and accepting Hero's modifications as a first step, some major changes would seem necessary to further refine pluralism as it applies to Latinos in the early twenty-first century. In addition to the dualism of the two tiers, our model would stress three major elements in the pluralist model that distinguish Hispanic Americans from others. The distinctiveness of Hispanics as an ethnic or cultural group should remain as in Hero's model, but with the understanding that there is a rapid acculturation process and even an assimilation occurring in which Hispanics are becoming more like non-Hispanics, and mainstream Americans are becoming "Latinized." The ethnic and cultural boundaries are becoming less hard and fast.

Second, the economic class of Hispanic Americans is also in a state of flux. Instead of representing almost all of the Latino population at the bottom of the socioeconomic ladder, the new pluralism must make way for a Latino population that is much more economically diverse. For example, although 20 percent of Latino household incomes are less than $20,000, just more than 30 percent of Latino households have household incomes of $50,000 or more (Welniak and Posey 2005). This apparent economic trend is reflected in a 71.2 percent increase in the Hispanic middle class from 1979 to 1999 (Pimental 2002). Latinos are no longer confined to the working class. There is a sizable and growing middle class among U.S. Hispanics, along with a larger (but still relatively small) upper economic class.

The third major modification that must be taken into account when attempting to characterize Hispanics in U.S. pluralistic politics is the significant role that Latino immigrants have had since the 1980s and will continue to have. How will the pluralist system accommodate the millions of new foreign-born residents? A sizeable portion of these residents are noncitizens, and thus do not have the rights and privileges accorded citizens. Moreover, another large segment has entered the United States without documentation, yet has a significant impact on the country's economy and public policy making. So, there are at least three dimensions that could substantially modify the already complex schema of a two-tiered political system.

We next examine the position of Hispanic Americans as they relate to the various components of the Eastonian political system model and are involved in the multitiered, multidimensional pluralist politics of the

United States. Using this political systems model, the organization of the book rather closely follows that of most standard American politics textbooks. It looks first at the environment or *contextual setting* in which the political system operates, including its history, demography, and economics. Then it moves into an examination of the *inputs* of the political system, including the *wants, needs,* and *interests* of the Hispanic people, plus the *supports* that they provide to the system. The focus then moves to the black box of authoritative decision making, the *conversion* of interests to public policies (or not). This part of the system includes those thousands of governmental offices and agencies in which countless decisions are made, which either help, hinder, or reflect the accumulation of power by Hispanics. Then we look at the effects of these inputs, including political participation, on the authoritative decision making (i.e., the politicians and public officials) and see how influential or powerful Latinos are in having their wants and needs converted to favorable public policies. We examine Latino representation and Latino leadership both within and outside the government. Finally, we examine some of the *public policies* and *policy outputs* that the political system has generated and that are of special interest and concern to Latino politics.

SUMMARY AND CONCLUSION

This chapter is largely dedicated to introducing the major concepts and principles that underlie this book, and to defining some of the critical concepts used in later chapters. Labels and ethnic-racial identifications and identities play a major role in American politics, a point that is made clear in the discussion of "Who are Hispanics?". Although most Hispanics choose to identify primarily with their national origin, factors such as language and treatment in the United States form the basis of commonality for all Latinos or Hispanics. Beyond establishing a working definition of the Latino or Hispanic population, this chapter also introduces the concept of politics. If politics involves the division of power and resolving of conflict among people, it is necessary to understand that there are many different theories used to explain how power is distributed and how public conflicts are resolved in the United States. We continue references to, and discussions of, the dominant theoretical interpretations of politics in the United States, especially a modified pluralist model, throughout this book in order to better understand how Latinos adapt to this political system and how the political system has, and will continue to, adapt to the greater involvement of Latinos.

Overall, the goal is to attempt to provide an overview of Latino politics in the United States so as to better understand the past, analyze the present, and think critically about what the future may bring for Latino politics as the group has become the largest ethnic minority group in the United States. Latinos are moving into the mainstream at an increasingly rapid pace. It is also possible that the mainstream itself will be moved, or transformed, as Latinos become major players in the system.

Notes

[1] National surveys that confirm the LNPS validity include the 1999, 2002, and 2004 National Survey of Latinos (Pew Hispanic Center 2002, 2004b), as well as the 1999 Washington Post/Kaiser Family Foundation National Survey of Latinos (*Washington Post* 1999).

[2] See, for example, the following recent article titles from the *Los Angeles Times*: "Latinos Souring on Governor and His Party," September 15, 2005; "Villaraigosa Aims to Make Most of 'Latino Mayor' Role," October 12, 2005.

[3] For example, author and poet Sandra Cisneros refused to be pictured in *Hispanic Magazine* due to her disgust with the term, and Celestino Fernández, a professor of sociology at the University of Arizona in Tucson, objects to the term Hispanic because he believes that the term was created by the dominant structure (*Hispanic Magazine*, "Hispanic vs. Latino," December 2000).

[4] The federal government defines Hispanic or Latino as a person of Mexican, Puerto Rican, Cuban, South or Central American, or other Spanish culture or origin, regardless of race (Ramirez 2004).

[5] The British political philosopher James Mill, for example, believed that members of societies are inherently self-interested and competitive.

[6] Books such as David Truman's (1951) *The Governmental Process: Political Interests and Public Opinion* argued that the activities of interest groups were the key to understanding how American public policies were formulated.

[7] See David Ricci's (1971) *Community Power and Democratic Theory: The Logic of Political Analysis* for a summary of several variants of pluralist theory.

2

Attitudinal, Constitutional-Legal, and Historical Settings

Politics is only one aspect of the totality of human behavior. It is pulled from the real world for analysis because it has special characteristics (as defined in Chapter 1) and because experts such as political scientists can more readily study and analyze one slice of the totality of people's "booming, buzzing" behavior if they separate out one segment. In this book, we focus on *politics* and the *political system*, and the relationship of Hispanics to them. However, we must also pay considerable attention to the environment, context, or setting in which Hispanic politics takes place in the United States. Politics is greatly affected by these factors. This chapter discusses the impact of the environment, context, or setting on the relationship between Hispanics and the political system.

The focus of this book is on the United States at the beginning of the twenty-first century of the Common Era, so we must examine the various characteristics of U.S. society as the third millennium begins. We look not only at this nation's politics but also at its social and psychological environment, its legal-constitutional context, its economic situation, its demographic condition, and some historical occurrences—all of which brought Hispanic politics to this point in time. These aspects of society impact politics and the political system at all points. They help shape the inputs to the system and greatly affect the actions of the government officials who make political decisions, as well as the policies and regulations that emerge from government. Most certainly, they seriously shape the eventual impact of these policies and the actual policy outputs, and reform and reconfigure them before these policy outputs, in their new form, once again affect politics and the political system.

THE SOCIAL PSYCHOLOGICAL OR ATTITUDINAL SETTING

We first look at the least tangible and yet perhaps the most important, environment in which Hispanic politics takes place in early twenty-first-century America—the social and psychological context. What is the social status of Hispanics in early twenty-first–century America? What is it like to be a Hispanic in the United States? Is it now, as some observers have cited, "hip to be Hispanic" (Granados 2003; Larmer 1999)? Are the Hispanic people admired, esteemed, respected, and valued as members of the American polity, or in contrast, are they devalued, denigrated, and not quite seen as full-fledged and respectable members of the American polity and community? If a group is to be a successful player in American politics, it is extremely important to be valued, for if a group is esteemed, people will listen to its interests and needs. If, however, a group is devalued and lacks status, then it is likely that it will be at best ignored and excluded, or at worst oppressed. Politically, it has been well documented that Latinos are garnering greater attention from both political parties; however, this attention may be focused on only small segments of the Hispanic population (Segal 2004).

In *Newsweek* magazine, it was asserted that "Hispanics are hip, hot and what's happening politically" (Larmer 1999, 48). But is this an accurate observation? Although it may seem that some Hispanics and some aspects of Latin culture are increasingly accepted by mainstream America, this may be a superficial acceptance—perhaps of select aspects of popular culture and certain celebrities (e.g., singers, dancers, actors, sports figures). It may be that only some of the food, music, and cultural styles have been taken over by mainstream culture. As evidence of this, it was often reported in the late 1990s that salsa had replaced ketchup as the most used condiment in American cuisine and that tortillas were rivaling white bread in sales (*Hispanic Business Magazine* 2004). But does this also mean that the Hispanic people themselves and the totality of their culture are valued and esteemed by the American polity? Fortunately, we do have a few solid studies that have taken an empirical and systematic look at the attitudes of Americans toward Hispanic Americans, and that provide us with a much more substantial (although certainly not the final or conclusive) measure as to the place and social status of Hispanics in the value rankings of the American people.

Perhaps tellingly, there is not a lot of empirical evidence on what Americans think of Hispanics, and it is only since the mid-1980s that we have had any solid social scientific evidence. Apparently, social scientists did not believe that this question was important enough to invest many resources in prior to the 1980s. Two major reports by the National Opinion Research Center (NORC) at the University of Chicago, however, do give us a good idea of how Americans viewed their Hispanic compatriots in the latter part of the twentieth century. Sponsored by the American Jewish Committee, the NORC General Social Survey conducted a repeat survey of a poll taken in 1964 (Tamor 1992). A nationally representative sample of American adults was asked to rate the social standing of several population (ethnic) subgroups in the United States. The ratings were scored on a scale of one (low) to nine (high).

When all cultural groups were ranked, at the top of the scale were "Native White Americans" scoring 7.25 in 1964 and 7.03 in 1989. In second place was "People of my own ethnic background" at 6.57. In the 1989 survey, these two groups at the top of the social standing ladder were followed by (in descending order) Protestants, Catholics, French, Irish, Swiss, Swedes, Austrians, Dutch, Norwegians, Scots, and Germans. These groups were mainly from northern and western Europe. In the middle of the social standing ladder were groups such as (again in descending order) "Southerners" (from the southern United States), Italians, Danes, French Canadians, Japanese, Jews, "people of foreign ancestry," Finns, Greeks, Lithuanians, Spanish Americans, Chinese, Hungarians, and Poles. Bringing up the bottom of the ladder were (again in descending order) the—at that time, during the cold war and prior to the fall of Communism—much-hated Russians, followed by Latin Americans, "American Indians," "Negroes," and "Wisians" (a fictitious group added by the poll takers to see how Americans would react to an unknown group). Dr. Tom W. Smith, the director of the study, said that his "explanation for the low ranking was that people probably thought that if they were foreign sounding, and if they never heard of them, they couldn't be doing too well" (Lewin 1992, A-12). But even below this fictitious and unknown group, at the very bottom, stood Mexicans, Puerto Ricans, and Gypsies. Although it was clear that tolerance toward diverse ethnicity seemed to be rising and anti-Semitism dropping, it was also evident that there was a pecking order with regard to the social standing of ethnic groups in the United States—with northern and western Europeans at the top, southern and eastern Europeans and some Asians and Jews in the center, and members of the country's major "distinctive" (racial) ethnic groups at the very bottom.

In an important but apparently still unpublished study, NORC prepared a topical report on ethnic images (Smith 1990). This report examined the attitudes that a representative cross-section of Americans had toward six groups of Americans—whites, Jews, blacks, Asian Americans, Hispanic Americans, and Southern whites. The study is really one of *stereotypes*. Stereotypes are, at best, simplistic images that Americans carry in their heads that condense and oversimplify the variation among members of any ethnic group. They are generalized concepts of an entire group, perhaps based on the appearances or actions of a single group member and applied to the rest. Participants were asked to describe six dimensions or character traits of each group. Each group was then compared with the benchmark group of "white Americans."

Overall (with the exception of Jewish Americans), minority groups were valued more negatively than were white Americans. The Jewish American population was rated more positively than whites on every characteristic but patriotism. The six characteristics that were studied were (1) the wealth that each group possessed, (2) their diligence or willingness to engage in hard work, (3) their proclivity toward violence, (4) their intelligence or lack thereof, (5) their being self-supporting or living off welfare, and (6) their patriotism. On every measure, Hispanics were judged more negatively than were white Americans. In other words, Hispanics were seen as poorer, lazier, more violent, less intelligent, more likely to live off welfare, and less patriotic. In fact, Hispanics were rated as the poorest (even poorer than blacks), as lazier than all but blacks, as the least intelligent, and, finally, as the most unpatriotic of the six groups. As NORC Director Smith wrote:

> Despite the demonstrable progress in inter-group tolerance over the last several decades, ethnic images are still commonplace in today's society. On the whole these images are neither benign nor trivial. Most Americans see most minority groups in a decidedly negative light on a number of important characteristics.... In particular Hispanic Americans and Blacks receive very low ratings. (Smith 1990, 8)

An interesting and reinforcing (if much smaller-scale) research project was reported in another research report (Jackson 1995). (The larger project was published in the *Journal of Personality and Social Psychology Bulletin.*) Professor Linda A. Jackson examined the stereotypic characteristics and values associated with Hispanics by Anglos and found that these included generally negative perceptions of Hispanics. For example, Hispanics were seen to be less productive and less intelligent, but more physically violent and more rebellious, than non-Hispanic whites. As the earlier studies also suggested, Jackson's review of the handful of studies that examined stereotypes of Hispanics found that perceptions are generally unfavorable. Jackson cited examples of Hispanics being viewed as lazy, cruel, ignorant, and pugnacious. For instance, she cited an older study by Marin (1984), who found that Anglos described each of three Hispanic groups— Mexican Americans, Chicanos, and Puerto Ricans—with negative characteristics, such as being aggressive, poor, and lazy. However, there are a few positive characteristics attributed to Hispanics in the Marin study, such as being family oriented and proud.

Jackson's (1995) own work, the group perception survey, measured stereotypic characteristics and values associated with Hispanics. She found that among the stereotypes of Hispanics by Anglos, only four were interpreted as positive characteristics—having strong families, being tradition loving, being religious, and being old fashioned; of the several remaining characteristics, many were unequivocally negative. To quote Jackson (1995):

> As specifically compared to Anglos, Hispanics were perceived by Anglos as being *less* productive, optimistic, ambitious, athletic and business wise, dependable, independent, self-disciplined, playful, efficient, intelligent, good looking, well adjusted, patriotic, industrious, prosperous, knowledgeable, and prompt. They were also perceived as *more* rebellious, physically violent, dirty/smelly, and criminally inclined. (4)

With regard to values, rather than characteristics, there were also negative perceptions because Hispanics were (compared to Anglos) stereotypically seen as placing *less* value on physical fitness, mature love, recognition by the community, a good life for others, national greatness, delaying pleasure to achieve success, the pursuit of knowledge, good health, economic prosperity, and financial independence. Hispanics were seen as placing greater value on salvation and religious or mystical experiences. Although most of the characteristics cited in Jackson's (1995) study were negative, some positive characteristics (e.g., strong families) and strong values (e.g., salvation) were attributed to Hispanics by the study's participants. The subjects in the study were 265 Anglo college students at a midwestern university. Jackson concluded that although perceptions were generally unfavorable, there was also a great lack of contact with and information about Hispanics by these participants. She concluded that Anglos must get their negative perceptions of Hispanics from such sources as the mass media. She also suggested that communities and educational institutions may also communicate such negative perceptions.

Obviously, the similar pattern of results from these various studies does indicate, at the least, that until the twenty-first century Hispanics were not valued or esteemed very highly in American society. To the contrary, it would appear that they were *de*valued. This has important political implications because society is not likely to listen to groups of people who are either not valued or judged negatively by the system. Moreover, the studies also have implications for the self-perception of Hispanics. For example, the "Ethnic Images" topical report (Smith 1990) revealed that 35 percent of Hispanics themselves believed that they were less intelligent than the average white American! This does not indicate a high level of self-esteem.

Political scientists recognize that low self-esteem is a psychological condition that is not supportive of participation in political activities. Feeling good about oneself and believing that one can affect one's own destiny (i.e., having a feeling of *efficacy*) are important to motivating oneself to act politically (Craig, Niemi, and Silver 1990). Moreover, to have a Latino *political community*, one must have a group in which people feel good about themselves and each other and are proud to identify with other members who bear the same labels or who have at least some of the same culture or customs. If Hispanics' "ideal types" are not other Hispanics, but instead are Anglos, Hispanics should be much less likely to identify with one another, support one another, and join together in a common cause— political or otherwise—to advance their interests or common concerns.

Throughout the 1990s and into the early twenty-first century, the attitudinal environment may be changing to be more positive and more supportive of Hispanics. Educational, commercial, and governmental institutions appeared to actually be eager to recruit or hire Latinos and Latinas. Sometimes they, along with other "minority" group members, were highly sought and even given preference over nonminorities. It may be that more than three decades of affirmative action have finally been integrated into the cultural values and norms of the dominant society. Or perhaps the dictates of demographics and the value of diversity are making inroads to American culture.

Bits of data from the 1998, 2000, and 2001 surveys by the Institute for Social Research at the University of Michigan hint that perceptions of Hispanic Americans have recently become more favorable. The National Election Survey of 2000 measured a positive rating for Hispanics by 58 percent of the American public, and a survey following the September 11 attack resulted in a 66 percent favorable rating for Hispanics. This was compared with a positive rating of 64 percent for Asian Americans, 70 percent for African Americans, and 79 percent for white Americans.[1] These developments of a more accepting and more valuing mainstream are so far mainly speculative and observational. If they are supported by research findings, the attitudinal setting for the success of Hispanic politics would certainly be enhanced. It is also possible that the great publicity given to immigrants and immigration in 2006 might affect the stereotypical image of Latinos held by Americans, perhaps in a more negative way. Exit poll data suggests, for example, that to the extent voters' views of Mexican immigrants shifted as a result of the immigration rallies, the impact tended to be negative (Marks et al 2006).

Moreover, the values of equality, justice, and freedom are inherent in the American system and embodied in documents such as the Declaration of Independence and the U.S. Constitution. These values are strongly held by the American public in its belief systems, and over the long run, these democratic norms have provided an attitudinal context that has assisted the advancement and acceptance of Hispanics into the mainstream.

THE CONSTITUTIONAL-LEGAL CONTEXT

Many things structure the politics and government of the United States, and one of the primary factors is the constitutional and legal frameworks in which they exist. Constitutions provide the most basic rules and norms of a political system, as well as the basic structures of government. Because the focus of this book is on politics and government, references to the U.S. Constitution and its principles are made throughout. At this point, we only examine a few of the more important features of the constitutional system of the United States—features that greatly affect the politics of Hispanics in this country.

LIMITED GOVERNMENT

The U.S. Constitution was written in an atmosphere of considerable distrust of a central or national government. The constitutional framers knew that a stronger union of states was necessary due to the many problems faced by the "loose bond of friendship" among sovereign states that had been their experience under the Articles of Confederation from 1781 to 1787. Yet, the suspicion of a strong, and possibly dictatorial, government still lingered from the War for Independence against Great Britain. Americans still believed that individual liberty was the foremost value and that governments were limited by the inalienable, divine rights of humans. The new federal government established only those institutions and laws that were considered absolutely necessary to conduct foreign affairs, promote the public safety, and protect the rights of individuals. The Constitution contains the most fundamental laws that safeguard individual liberties in its first ten amendments—the Bill of Rights. Although group rights in the form of civil rights are not explicitly found in the Constitution, some amendments form a basis for securing the rights of groups, classes, or people. For example, the Thirteenth Amendment prohibits slavery; the Fourteenth Amendment grants full citizenship, due process, and equal protection of the laws; and the Fifteenth, Nineteenth, and Twenty-Sixth Amendments protect the right to vote. These amendments, particularly the Fourteenth Amendment, have been of particular significance to Hispanics and other "minority" groups that have had a special need for constitutional and legal protection of their rights. State constitutions have also come to include these protections, and hundreds of laws have been enacted in accordance with the basic "civil rights" dictates of our constitutions.

At the national level, the most significant legislation safeguarding the rights of "minorities," such as Hispanics, included the Civil Rights Act of 1964 (prohibiting discrimination in places of public accommodation and employment), the Fair Housing Act of 1968, and the Voting Rights Act of 1965 (which brought the federal government into the protection of the franchise). Moreover, in the late 1960s, the U.S. government began to make affirmative action a policy through the first of many executive orders and federal regulations. Hispanics have used these and other protections written into our constitutions and laws to secure and gain their rights, sometimes through the moral persuasion, sometimes through constitutional and legal appeals in the courts, and sometimes through the enacting of laws and regulations based on these fundamental legal principles.

A REPRESENTATIVE DEMOCRACY

The writers of the U.S. Constitution disagreed over many aspects of the new national government. However, with a few exceptions, they agreed that classical "mass" democracy was dangerous. Although the people were to be the ultimate source of sovereignty, they were only to exercise their involvement in national government as their sentiments were filtered through more elite, educated, and experienced individuals who would temper the possible passions of the masses and make better decisions. It was these wise, educated, and land-owning persons (usually white, male property owners) who would represent the interests of the people. The main role left to the citizens was to be involved in the election of those who would make policies for them. Even the eligible electorate (mainly determined by state governments) mostly excluded women, persons younger than twenty-one, slaves, and those who did not own property. The new government was to be "republican" in nature; that is, it would be a representative democracy, not a pure democracy. In most cases, the people would select representatives to conduct most of their day-to-day governmental functions for them rather than participate directly themselves.

FEDERALISM

One of the most difficult problems facing the writers of the U.S. Constitution was how the states should be represented in the new national government. In fact, this was probably the most problematic of all the issues confronting the framers. Some of the colonies and states had existed for 100 years before the Constitutional Convention of 1787. Many had thriving, vital political systems that had governed for many generations, and their citizens and leaders jealously guarded their way of life and their "state's rights" to govern themselves as they chose. Few states were willing to surrender their sovereignty. The southern states, with their distinctive social, cultural, and economic systems, including a dependence on slave labor, were threatened by a union with the other states in any manner that would not safeguard their way of life. Moreover, the larger, populous, and prosperous states, such as Virginia, were hesitant to share representation in the national government with much smaller, less populous states. This dispute between states nearly broke up the constitutional meeting because a compromise over how states of varying size and population could be fairly represented seemed impossible. It took the invention of a new type of representative assembly through the "Connecticut compromise" or "great compromise" to salvage the new national government. The solution was to create two chambers or houses of the legislature. In the upper house or Senate, each state, regardless of size, would be equally represented. Its membership would be comprised of two persons selected in a manner to be determined by the legislature of each state. The other legislative chamber, the lower house, would be the most democratic of the new national institutions. The House of Representatives would be based on the population of each state and would be selected directly by the voters.

These debates illustrated the underlying basic tension between the state governments and the new central government. The end result, arrived at through a piecemeal and practical approach, was a new government that preserved individual state governments and also added a new national government of limited powers to the mix. Throughout the U.S. Constitution, there are many restrictions on the powers of the national government. One of the original amendments (the Tenth Amendment) explicitly states that those powers not expressly given to the national government are reserved to the states and to the people. This new dual-level system of government became known as a *federal* system—one of the United States' original contributions to the art of governing. The exact responsibilities of the states versus those of the national government in the U.S. system of *federalism* have continued to evolve throughout history and continue to do so even today. In any case, the existence of two parallel systems of government—that of the nation and those of each of the fifty states—continues to have major implications for Hispanic politics in the United States. Federalism provides multiple access points or inputs to government for the Hispanic community to use when seeking responses to their interests and concerns. Federalism also allows for state initiatives to be passed that have great impacts on Hispanics, including Proposition 187 in California and Proposition 200 in Arizona, which focus on the rights and access to government of undocumented populations.

SEPARATION OF POWERS

One other major feature of the U.S. Constitution that was uncommon for the time was the separation of governmental functions among what became the three branches of government. Because representative government was a key to the new system, it was the U.S. Congress—the Senate and the House of Representatives—that received most of the attention of the Constitution's architects. The first article of the new constitution, which specifies the powers, functions, and limitations of the new government, is actually devoted specifically to Congress. There is little doubt that Congress was to be the most important branch of government.

The framer's fear of a powerful individual—a dictator or a tyrant-king, such as they had perceived King George II to be—led them to create an executive (called the *president*) whose primary functions were that of administrator, diplomat, and military commander. As the top manager, he was to ensure that the laws passed by Congress were "faithfully executed." He was to represent the United States in its dealings with foreign powers, and he was to take command of the nation's armed forces when Congress declared war. The comparatively brief debate over the chief executive was tempered by the knowledge that George Washington would most certainly be the first president.

The third branch of federal government was the judiciary. The framers simply set up the U.S. Supreme Court to be the top body to settle disputes under law and to establish a system of lower national courts. Over time, the Supreme Court became the final interpreter of the laws of this nation and of the Constitution itself, and an entire system of national or federal courts was established, paralleling the court systems of the states. The separation of powers system has motivated the Hispanic community to channel their efforts toward the branch of government that they believe will best serve their interests. The courts, in particular, have been a critical access point to government for the Hispanic community. Organizations such as the Mexican American Legal Defense and Educational Fund have used the judiciary to improve the status of Hispanics in American society.

A brief review of the major elements of the U.S. Constitution is important because this basic structure provides the context for many of the legal and political battles involving Hispanics. It should be noted that these institutions were largely reflections of the political and legal philosophies and practices of Western Europe, primarily Great Britain. It has been in this largely Anglo American constitutional and governmental context that Hispanic politics take place in the U.S.

THE HISTORICAL SETTING

The historical experiences of a people are absolutely essential to understanding their current status. Historical experiences are certainly formative, if not determinative. History explains how and why a group has become what it has become, and how it has obtained what it has achieved. Important to the full realization of any group's history is understanding the conditions of its homeland or the area from which the group emanated, the reasons for its immigration, the conditions that existed in the new land into which the group came, and perhaps most important, the treatment that the group receives by the host society throughout the group's stay in its new home. Most assuredly, the history of an ethnic group forms an essential component of the contextual setting in which that group's politics take place in the United States. To better understand the current political status of Hispanics, it is essential to at least have some knowledge of the major events leading up to it. Hispanic history certainly has bequeathed a legacy to contemporary Hispanics that significantly affects their politics.

It is extremely difficult to encapsulate or present a brief history of the ethnic group referred to as Latinos. The major reason for this is that Latinos are arguably the most diverse and heterogeneous ethnic grouping in the United States today. With so much variation among members and even among the groups within this larger grouping, it is virtually impossible to summarize a single "history of Hispanic Americans."[2] As a result, it has been more common to present histories of each national origin group, with Mexican American history being cited most often (Acuna 2003; Gonzales 1999; McWilliams 1968; Meier and Rivera 1972; Samora and Simon 1993). Here, it is only possible to briefly review some of the main characteristics of some Hispanic groups' histories, and perhaps more important, to point out some commonalties or similarities, as well as some differences, in the histories that have been experienced by some major segments of the Hispanic population.

One of the things that makes discussing Latino history so difficult is that some Latinos claim that they are largely or even primarily "indigenous" people, that is, the original or aboriginal settlers of what is now the United States and the rest the Western Hemisphere. This would give them a history of some 15,000 to 30,000 years of residing in this area. However, much more common is an emphasis on Latinos being a *mixture* of peoples—most often a mixture between indigenous Native Americans, or Indians of the Western Hemisphere, and the European Spaniards. Less common, but also important, is the mixture between the Spanish colonialists and African Americans in the "new world," almost all of whom were slaves who had been brought by Europeans into the Caribbean area in the early 1500s.

The Spanish, along with other European explorers, sailed to the new world in the late fifteenth century. Columbus's voyages encountered the native peoples of the Caribbean, such as the Taino and Arawak Indians in the early 1490s, on the islands of what became Cuba and Puerto Rico. In the ensuing decades, much of the native populace was either enslaved or wiped out by disease or warfare. Slaves from Africa were later transported to these islands and the east coast of Latin America beginning in the early sixteenth century. Cortez first encountered the indigenous tribes of Mexico in 1519, and after warfare and conquest, expeditions of explorers or *conquistadores*, searching for land, gold, and religious converts, headed north into "North" America in the first half of the sixteenth century.

In any case, whether emphasizing their Indian, Spanish, or African roots, Latinos were among the first settlers in what was to become the United States, certainly preceding the formation of the United States as an independent nation. For example, the oldest "permanent" European city in the United States is St. Augustine, Florida, visited by Ponce de Leon in 1513 and founded at the site of the Timucuan Indian village of Seloy by the Spanish Admiral Mendez de Aviles in 1565. Santa Fe, New Mexico, is the oldest capital in the United States, founded in 1609.

It is little known but accurate not only that the Spanish were among the first European settlers of the territories that were to become the United States but also that they were involved in many of the early founding activities of this newly independent nation. Explorers and colonists from Spain, along with those from Great Britain, France, Holland, Portugal, Russia, and other nations, explored the Western Hemisphere. Beginning with the famous voyages of Columbus in the late fifteenth century and increasing during the sixteenth and seventeenth centuries, the Spanish explored the islands of the Caribbean, the coast of Florida, and other points along the Gulf of Mexico and the Gulf of California, and along the western coast of North America as far north as current-day Alaska. The most well-known expedition was Cortez's incursion into what is now Mexico in 1519; the establishment of the oldest European city in the United States, St. Augustine, Florida, in 1565; and the very early "permanent" settlement of Don Juan de Onate near Santa Fe, New Mexico, in 1598. Thus, the Spanish "side" of Hispanic American's lineage has roots going back more than 400 years. The Spanish side of Hispanics is emphasized here because it is the cultural and linguistic impact of the Spanish that is the major basis for the cultural commonality of Hispanics and Latinos today.

The African American and Native American roots of Latino culture are even earlier relative to American history. Black Africans were brought in bondage to this hemisphere beginning in the 1500s. These "racial" groups themselves were culturally diverse, mainly along tribal lines.

Great civilizations of the native indigenous peoples of the Americas, numbering from 60 to 100 million people, occupied this land from its southern tip to the arctic north. Best known are the majestic civilizations of Central and South America—the Aztecs, Mayans, Olmecs, Toltecs, and Incas—whose accomplishments in diverse fields rivaled those of the Europeans. In North America, scores of tribes were also thriving, with the Anasazi of the Southwest and the Iroquois confederation in the Northeast noted for their well-developed economic and political institutions.

Military conflict has had a major impact on the status of Hispanic Americans; therefore, much of the discussion of the histories of the various Hispanic communities will revolve around the various wars in which the United States has been involved. However, mainstream U.S. colonial history rarely mentions the involvement of the Spanish. This is largely because the centuries-long hostility between Britain and Spain, including decades of warfare, political and religious hostilities, and a general historical enmity between those nations carried over to the British colonies. Seldom taught in U.S. colonial history is that the Spanish played a significant role in the U.S. war for independence against Great Britain.[3] For example, it is not widely known that one of the naval heroes of the Revolutionary War, Admiral Jorge Farragut, was born in Spain. He commanded the ships of the new continental navy against the world's largest and most powerful navy, the British fleet. Spanish General Bernardo Galvez (after which the Texas city of Galveston is named) and his battalions of Mexicans, Puerto Ricans, and Cubans put together a string of victories over the British, including the British fortress and naval base at Pensacola, Florida. In addition, Spain sent major amounts of money to help the struggling American revolutionaries in their fight for independence against the British.

The Spanish and Spanish Americans were also very involved in the American Civil War, fighting on both sides. Spanish-born David G. Farragut, son of Jorge Farragut, was made the first admiral of the U.S. Navy in 1866, and he became one of the Civil War's biggest heroes with his bravery and leadership at the Battle of New Orleans.

It was World War II that was a major catalyst and turning point for Hispanics, mostly Mexican Americans, but also Puerto Ricans, to make their mark in the defense of the United States (as well as in politics). Many historians cite World War II as perhaps the most important historical point for Mexican Americans in the twentieth century because Mexican American soldiers, in defense of their country, engaged in many of the battle campaigns of World War II, including the famous Bataan Death March. Many Mexican Americans were awarded the Congressional Medal of Honor, the nation's highest recognition for valor in battle (Morin 1963). In fact, on a proportional basis, Hispanic Americans have been noted as one of the most decorated ethnic groups in U.S. combat history, serving valiantly not only in all the wars leading up through World War II, but also in Korea, Vietnam, and the Persian Gulf (Villahermosa 2002). Hispanics' willingness to volunteer, and their historical record of bravery and valor, is particularly notable and ironic given American society's misperceptions of a "lack of patriotism," as noted previously.

When the Second World War ended and Hispanic Americans returned to the United States with their compatriots after putting their lives on the line to defend this country, they found themselves still subject to considerable discrimination (Rivas-Rodriguez 2005). Yet, these were men who had traveled and grown more "worldly," who had served as equals among other ethnic groups, who had earned education and leadership roles, and who were no longer willing to be treated as second-class citizens. It was not just the men who served their country well; Hispanic women also took their positions along with those of other ethnic heritages in the factories and fields to do the hard work needed to keep the war economy going while many of the men were called to engage in combat.

Incidents such as the refusal of the town of Three Rivers, Texas, to bury a Second World War Mexican American veteran soldier in its segregated cemetery led to the strengthening of the recently formed American GI Forum in 1948 (Navarro 2004). Similar incidents across the American Southwest also spurred the newly revitalized Mexican Americans to organize and form various groups for the purpose of defending themselves against discrimination and improving their situation in the United States. Many believe that it was this cadre of World War II–experienced individuals who began the modern Latino civil rights movement, particularly in its political aspects. Political organizations were specifically designed to have an impact on state and national politics and policies, such as the Mexican American Political Organization in the 1950s, as well as to influence national elections, such as the "Viva Kennedy" clubs formed to help elect a presidential candidate in 1960 and the Professional Association of Spanish Speaking Organizations that emerged from this environment (Gomez-Quinones 1990). After World War II, Mexican Americans were never going to be the same politically.

The U.S.-Mexico War (1846–1848) is another event that was particularly significant for Hispanics, particularly those in the American Southwest. As the United States extended its boundaries in the name of "manifest destiny," more often than not through the use of force, it encountered in the West not only the Native Americans but also a significant number of Mexican/Spanish people well established in the vital communities of the area. These communities had been settled by the Mexican/Spanish coming north, usually along the Rio Grande, for more than 250 years. Now, the American government's drive to extend its boundaries across the continent to the Pacific made it necessary to deal with perhaps more than 100,000 Hispanics in long-established communities, often living on lands granted them by the king of Spain or the ruling authorities in Mexico.

After the briefly independent Lone Star Republic of Texas was incorporated into the United States in 1835, there still remained large areas of Mexican territory north of the Rio Grande, including what was to become New Mexico, Arizona, California, Colorado, Utah, and parts of Wyoming, that were desired as additions to the United States. President James K. Polk made no bones about wanting to incorporate these territories, with their rich lands full of agricultural soil, forests, minerals and other resources. President Polk needed little persuasion to send an army into the area under the pretext of keeping the peace, an army which then proceeded southward until Mexico City itself was captured. In 1848, the terms imposed on the defeated Mexican government forced them to cede half of what was then the entire country of Mexico, which in turn added about one-third of the existing land mass to the United States. The agreement, which was signed at the conclusion of the war, was the *Treaty of Guadalupe Hidalgo*. This treaty was signed on February 2, 1848, in the Mexican town bearing its name.

The people living in the newly acquired territory—approximately 100,000 to 150,000 or so, with more than half of them living *in Nuevo Mexico*, or New Mexico—were given a choice to either leave their ancestral lands and move to what was left of Mexico to the south, or remain and become U.S. citizens. For those who chose to stay, the U.S. government promised in the treaty to protect the cultural and linguistic rights of the residents and to honor most of the existing land grants. However, over the next several decades, as has so often been the case in the past, the U.S. government and private Anglo interests managed to renege on most of the provisions of assurance and protections, and much of the property believed to be protected was lost to the newly imposed, little understood, and harshly administered new legal system. Even now, the conflict over the status of these land grants is still a point of contention and has been the basis of much legal and political action among Hispanics in the Southwest (U.S. Congress General Accounting Office 2004).

Throughout U.S. history, a more or less conflictual relationship has continued between Hispanics and non-Hispanics (Estrada, Garcia, Macias, and Maldonado 1981). There has also been considerable discrimination by the majority society against Hispanics. In some places, particularly in Texas, the conflict was quite violent because Hispanics were treated similarly to African Americans, including the deprivation of legal and civil rights of these "people of color" up to the point of actual physical violence and even lynchings (Montejano 1986). In other parts of the Southwest, there were also incidents of violence. As Hispanic communities attempted to defend themselves and to protect their land, their families, and their culture from attacks, they were often branded as terrorists or bandits and were subject to the full force of the law and military actions as well as vigilantism and mob violence.

Since the late 1500s, Americans of largely Mexican ancestry have continued to migrate back and forth across what is seen by some as a largely artificial or arbitrary border. Because the Spanish/Mexicans had lived for centuries on both sides of the line drawn in 1848, the saying, "We didn't cross the border, the border crossed us," is often offered up to signify that the area was the ancestral homeland of Mexican Americans and that it is the Anglo Americans who, through conquest and colonization, have made Mexican Americans "foreigners in their own land" (Weber 2003). The history of 400 years of activity in this area, including emigration and immigration from different areas of Mexico and different parts of the United States, makes it difficult to summarize the history of even one of the component national origin segments of American Hispanics.

The history of the next two largest groups of American Hispanics, Cuban Americans and Puerto Ricans share some commonalties with those of Mexican Americans but are obviously also unique in their own right.[4] The history of Puerto Ricans' and Cuban Americans' relationships with the United States shares with Mexican Americans the fact that they came into the United States as a result of *conquest*, more specifically as a result of wars. In the case of Cuba and Puerto Rico, the conquests were the result of the war between Spain and the United States—the so-called "Spanish-American War," which only lasted for several months (April–December) in 1898. Again, American expansionism, this time worldwide under the doctrine of manifest destiny, employed what some consider a pretext in the sinking of the battleship *Maine* in Havana, Cuba's harbor, in order to expand its territory. A declaration of war with Spain was called, and in a few months of battle, the U.S. armed forces defeated those of Spain. This resulted in the United States gaining Spanish territory around the world, including the Philippines, Guam, Cuba, and Puerto Rico, all formerly Spanish colonies, in 1898. (Although Hawaii was not a Spanish possession, the stationing of U.S. troops there in 1898 had a great impact on its being annexed by the United States in that year.) Puerto Rico continued in its centuries of colonized status until 1952, when it became a commonwealth. The Jones Act of 1917 granted citizenship to the residents of Puerto Rico, so all Puerto Ricans are citizens of the United States whether they reside on the island or on the mainland.

Migration from Puerto Rico to the mainland United States has been constant due to the relationship established with the United States through the Jones Act. A small Puerto Rican enclave existed in New York since World War I, and that population grew to approximately 135,000 by the end of World War II. The Puerto Rican population increased significantly in the 1950s with the establishment of more frequent and readily available transportation by air between the mainland and the island. By 1960, more than 1 million Puerto Ricans were in the United States, and by 2000, almost as many Puerto Ricans lived in the fifty states (2.8 million) as on the island of Puerto Rico (Gonzalez 2000).

One of the continuing points of political conflict in Puerto Rico is the political-legal status of the island, with various groups on the island pressuring that Puerto Rico become an independent nation, the fifty-first state of the United States, or remain a commonwealth (Negron-Muntaner 2004). In plebiscite votes (a nonbinding election that expresses the will of the electorate) on the island during the 1980s and 1990s, the commonwealth option was favored by a plurality (i.e., with the most number of votes) of the citizenry, with independent nationhood being the least favored option. As commonwealth citizens of the United States, Puerto Ricans are, in a sense, second-class citizens. For example, they do not have voting representation in the U.S. Congress or votes in the Electoral College. Consequently, they do not vote in the presidential general elections of the United States, although they do have the right to vote in each party's presidential primaries. They are subject to service in the armed forces and have served valiantly in that capacity. However, Puerto Ricans on the island are not subject to federal income taxes. This question of political status often serves as the focal point for discussions of Puerto Rican history in the United States.[5]

There is a considerable amount of traveling back and forth between the island and the homeland. Most of the Puerto Ricans leaving the island for the continental United States have done so to seek economic opportunities. The economy of the island of Puerto Rico prior to U.S. colonization was based almost entirely on agriculture, with small coffee and tobacco growers being the backbone of the island's economy. U.S. sugar companies soon came in and purchased as much land as possible and brought with them the skills of industrialization. Although quite profitable for the U.S. companies, this resulted in less need for Puerto Rican manpower. As a result, wages for sugar cane cutters for a twelve-hour day were sixty-three cents in 1917, falling to fifty cents by 1932 (Gonzalez 2000). With no other options, but having U.S. citizenship status, many migrated to the mainland for a better life.

Most Puerto Ricans initially settled in the large urban areas in the United States, particularly in New York City, where they were subject to significant discrimination and prejudicial actions. As the number of Puerto Ricans flooding into New York City increased steadily, the tension directed toward Puerto Ricans also increased. The new Spanish-speaking population was often used as a scapegoat by political leaders for the city's economic problems, and consequently, they became disliked by Anglos and African Americans alike. Perhaps the most notable feature of the history of Puerto Rico and the United States is that, after 400 years as a colony of Spain, the island has also remained a kind of colony of the United States for so long without the self-government or self-determination equivalent to that of any one of the fifty American states.

The former Caribbean Spanish colony of Cuba was also a possession obtained through conquest in the war between the United States and Spain in 1898. Being very close to the continental United States (only about ninety miles away), Cubans had maintained a significant presence on the mainland, particularly on the gulf coast of Florida. Even in the 1800s, prior to the war, many Cubans were employed in the cigar industry in Florida, residing primarily on the state's west coast. Cuba's tenure as a U.S. colony was much shorter than that of Puerto Rico because it was granted independence as a legally independent republic in 1902. Nominally free in the political sense, it remained under control of powerful economic interests in the United States and ruled by U.S.-friendly dictators. In 1959, a revolution led by Fidel Castro overthrew the right wing, U.S.-controlled government of the island and established a leftist, socialist government. This takeover resulted in a large migration of middle and upper class, mainly white Cubans to the United States, primarily to the Miami-Dade County, Florida, area in the early 1960s. Approximately 215,000 Cubans left for the United States in the first two years following the revolution, and thousands more went to Spain and Latin America (Fagen, Brody, and O'Leary 1968).

These *political refugees* were welcomed by the U.S. government, given their strong pro-capitalistic and strong anti-Communist feelings in the era of the cold war with the Soviet Union. Hundreds of millions—even billions—of dollars in settlement aid and special benefits, such as expedited citizenship, were given to help the conservative and Republican-friendly refugees establish themselves quickly in their new temporary exile home in the United States under the 1966 Cuban Adjustment Act.

The state of Florida was also very welcoming to Cuban refugees, providing cash allotments for Cuban families (Gonzalez 2000). In addition, the University of Miami Medical School began special programs to assist Cubans in meeting licensing requirements. The next major wave of Cuban migration occurred in 1980, when Fidel Castro expelled "undesirables" to the United States. These were the so-called "Marielitos," composed of a heterogeneous group of people that included a significant number of Cubans of African ancestry, many impoverished working class people, and even some criminals (Grenier and Perez 2003).

Taking advantage of the resources provided them by the U.S. government, along with effectively employing their own business and technical skills, the Cubans have established a flourishing enclave in Miami-Dade County. This success was also the result of a tightly organized internal network. Cubans who were able to secure positions in Miami banks helped lend start-up funds to fellow Cuban refugees who could not secure credit from other lenders. They did this using a "character loan" system (Gonzalez 2000). A Cuban exile who did not posses either credit or collateral could secure a business loan from Cuban bankers based on his or her background or standing in Cuba.

Fueled by a steady flow of Cuban refugees arriving on the Florida coast in homemade rafts during the summer of 1994 that overwhelmed Florida's immigration centers, the long-standing favorable treatment of Cuban immigrants was halted. President William (Bill) J. Clinton reacted to a growing national debate over immigration by stating that Cubans attempting to reach the United States illegally would be detained and denied automatic entry just like any other immigrant group.

Although they have not garnered as much attention historically, Central and South Americans, America's "other Latinos," are becoming more relevant as a result of their increasing demographics in the United States. As indicated previously, the Central and South American population is the fastest growing among Latino subgroups and has the highest proportion of foreign-born persons. Hispanics that fall under the heading of "Central and South Americans" are those individuals whose lineage is traced back to the Central American countries of Guatemala, Honduras, Nicaragua, Panama, El Salvador, and Costa Rica, or any of the Spanish-speaking countries of South America.[6] Central and South Americans have histories with tremendous variation; however, the experience of fleeing oppressive political regimes is a common denominator for much of this population. Political revolutions and general instability in the countries of El Salvador, Guatemala, Honduras, and Nicaragua forced a plethora of Central Americans to leave their homes, many coming to the United States.[7]

One of the most notable aspects of this segment of the Latino population is that they are more dispersed throughout the United States. Contrary to the three largest subgroups that tend to be concentrated in particular regions, Central and South Americans are distributed more broadly, often in localities dominated by a preexisting Latino subgroup. Approximately half of all Guatemalans in the United States live in the Los Angeles area, as does a sizable segment of the Salvadoran population. Salvadorans are also the largest Latino subgroup in the Washington, DC, area (Wax 2001). The New York City metropolitan area is the area of greatest concentration for Colombians, Ecuadorians, and Peruvians, whereas the Gulf Coast (particularly the cities of New Orleans and Houston) has been a settling ground for Latinos from Honduras, Nicaragua, and the Dominican Republic (Farrington 2001; Paul 2001). The trend of Central and South Americans to move into regions already populated with Latinos from the three dominant subgroups (Mexican, Puerto Rican, and Cuban) has increased interaction among Latinos. It is not quite clear if this increased interaction will produce a greater sense of group consciousness among Latinos or greater competition. In either event, it will be critical for scholars of Latino politics to be aware of the growing presence of these "other" Latinos as the relationship between the Hispanic community and the American political landscape continues to be explored.

THE CHICANO MOVEMENT

The most visible, and probably also the most significant, period of contemporary Hispanic politics was the "Chicano movement." This era, lasting from approximately 1964 to 1974, was marked by Hispanics (mostly Mexican Americans but also Puerto Ricans and other Latino groups) becoming very visible actors on the American political stage. In general, the movement took place in a heightened era of political activity in the United States. Beginning with the southern civil rights movement by African Americans in the 1950s, through the women's liberation movement and the anti–Vietnam War protests well into the 1970s, the American "establishment" was confronted by a significant sector of heretofore low-profile political participants who, in often dramatic ways, confronted the political establishment. Much of the movement politics of this era would be considered "militant," "radical," or at least "activist" and certainly unconventional. At that time, these politics were of the dramatic and confrontational type, including marches, strikes, boycotts, demonstrations, walkouts, blow-outs, sit-ins, and other forms of confrontational "protest" politics. This type of politics was particularly suited to people who had either been excluded or ignored by the system and now needed to make their voices loudly heard. They lacked many of the usual conventional political resources such as money, well-established organizations, networks, or contacts with important individuals. Their primary political resources were their own bodies and their wills. They gave of themselves with heartfelt feelings and (sometimes) strong ideologies to make their points. Hispanic Americans had combated centuries of strong prejudice and discrimination, which not only included laws that were aimed at "keeping them in their place" but also a status that was inferior both materially and perceptually. They were combating inferior education, high unemployment, low wages, poverty, and other social ills.

The anti-Vietnam protesters of that era were primarily college students who let the government agencies know that they believed the war in Southeast Asia was a mistake, completely unjustified and morally wrong, and that they would have nothing to do with it other than trying to stop it. In so doing, they not only challenged one of the major national policies of the day but also most of the American lifestyles and establishment, including its economics, politics, mores, culture, dress, music, and ways of communicating—advocating almost anything that was anti-establishment. Hispanics, primarily Chicanos, also protested many of these same wrongs, including a lack of governmental attention to their plight of poverty, a lack of protective laws and policies, loss of their lands, lack of respect, police harassment, and a seeming invisibility to the governments of the nation and the states. At its heart were a strong cultural pride and a drive toward community control and self-determination.

These times brought forth many new organizations and many individuals who assumed leadership roles and who continued to play important roles in Hispanic politics long after the activist *movimiento* period had run its course. One of the earliest manifestations of the movement was the activity by Reies López Tijerina and his *Alianza Federal de Mercedes* in northern New Mexico (Blawis 1971; Gardner 1970; Jenkinson 1968; Knowlton 1967; Nabokov 1969). Tijerina was a fundamentalist preacher from Texas who came to northern New Mexico with a visionary plan, charisma, an extremely strong-willed motivation and determination, and a detailed, encyclopedic knowledge of the law. To help regain the way of life that was increasingly being destroyed in the villages of northern New Mexico, Tijerina and his followers confronted many governmental officials, including forest service officers, state police, and county law enforcement officials, both Anglo and Hispanic, and demanded that lands taken away from the rural Hispanic villagers be returned to them in accordance with the provisions of the Treaty of Guadalupe Hidalgo and other laws. After the famous Rio Arriba County courthouse raid in August 1967, Tijerina was taken prisoner and sent to a federal penitentiary for two years. The cause of returning to the communities those communal lands granted them by Spain and Mexico still continues for Hispanics even today. In early 2001, members of U.S. Congress from New Mexico ordered the U.S. Government Accounting Office to do a major study of the land grants in New Mexico and make recommendations as to how these cases could be settled (U.S. General Accounting Office 2004).

In California in 1964 and 1965, some migrant farm laborers, led by César Chávez, Dolores Huerta, and a small cadre of other migrant farm workers, joined together in organizing a strike against the agricultural industries in that state (Taylor 1975). At that time, farm laborers, mainly Filipinos, Mexicans, and Mexican Americans, were badly exploited and served as a cheap source of crop-harvesting labor. They had virtually no protection from the growers, including no right to unionize or bargain collectively for higher wages or better working conditions. The quietly determined César Chávez and the other leaders in the National Farm Workers Union, and later the United Farm Workers (UFW), managed against all odds to organize the farm workers into many strikes (*las huelgas*) up and down the central valley of California (Dunne 1971; Griswold del Castillo 1995; Matthiessen 1969). The UFW also engaged in various marches and protests, and even organized a nationwide economic boycott of grapes and lettuce. The farm workers' activities drew so much attention to their plight that many other types of people joined their cause (*la causa*), including U.S. Attorney General Bobby Kennedy, some state and national labor union leaders, various celebrities, and leaders of some religious organizations. This alliance managed to force many of the growers to the bargaining table, and consequently, many of the farm workers became unionized and were able to bargain for better working conditions.

Activities were also quite visible in the urban areas in California, and included walk-outs (or blow-outs) from several schools in the east Los Angeles area protesting the low level of education, lack of relevant curricula, and absence of Chicano teachers and administrators in the *barrios* of California. Student-led protests were also waged against the poverty and powerlessness of Hispanics. Organizations such as the *Movimiento Estudiantes Chicano de Aztlan*, United Mexican American Students, and Mexican American Youth Organization (MAYO) were formed to better structure and focus these activities (Munoz 1989). Hispanics demanded better education, better housing, an end to injustice and discrimination, more and better jobs, and the cessation of alleged police brutality; in short, the call was for self-determination and community control.

Similar activities were also occurring in urban Colorado, particularly in the Denver area. In Denver, former professional boxer and Democratic Party worker-activist Rudolfo "Corky" Gonzales organized the barrios into the "Crusade for Justice" organization (Marin 1977; Vigil 1999). The objective of the organization was to build pride and self-esteem, especially among Chicano youth, and to wrestle control from the dominant society of the institutions that Chicanos encountered in their everyday lives. Many of the cultural expressions of pride and much of the cultural ideology, as well as the art, symbols, and slogans used in the Chicano movement, came from the Crusade for Justice. In the name of self-determination, the crusade began to develop separate "counter" or parallel organizations independent of mainstream society, such as its own schools and social welfare organizations. In 1969, the Chicano Youth Liberation Conference produced documents about the pride of the new bronze nation of *Aztlan*, the mythical ancestral homeland of the Chicano people, and more particularly focused on their indigenous or Aztec side. The concept of Aztlan grew to be the major symbolic rallying point for much of the Chicano movement because it embodied all the principles of a proud nation such as heroic myths, its own flag, and its own set of institutions. Chicanos were members of a *mestizo*, or mixed nation, and were going to take a defensive posture that would no longer tolerate harsh and unjust treatment from the majority society. Paramilitary groups such as the Brown Berets and Black Berets were organized to defend their barrio communities from harassment and brutalization by what they viewed as the occupational troops of the white majority society, the police forces. A few activists took the notion of Aztlan so far as to call for an independent territorial nation in the American Southwest.

In Texas, much of the activity was more pragmatic and explicitly political in nature. José Ángel Gutiérrez and some of his colleagues began to organize college students in the form of MAYO and to pressure various establishment decision makers for a better life. From MAYO later sprung an independent all-Chicano political party, *El Partido de La Raza Unida*. The Raza Unida Party enjoyed some major victories in the 1960s by winning control over school boards, city governments, and local courts in such areas as Crystal City in the Winter Garden area of south Texas (Corona 1971; Garcia 1989; Gutiérrez 1998; Navarro 2000; Shockley 1974). Many of the towns in this area had huge majorities of Hispanic citizens but had a power structure that was almost entirely and exclusively white/Anglo.

The Chicano movement succeeded in revitalizing what often had been (and still is) labeled "the Sleeping Giant" of Hispanic Americans throughout the United States by calling the attention of the nation to the plight of a minority that had heretofore been largely invisible (or ignored).

El movimiento also developed several organizations that, in one form or another, continue to serve Hispanic Americans today. It also developed a cadre of leaders who then played, and even continue to play, a role in contemporary Hispanic politics. However, such activist movements are almost always self-limiting. Their participants grow tired of such demanding and stressful activities, especially because these activities are opposed and suppressed by the power establishment. In addition, as some of the initial goals are met with success, participants may believe that they have less to strive for and their motivation diminishes. For these and other reasons, movement politics are not readily sustained for a long period of time.

By the mid-1970s, few of these Chicano movement activities continued. The Raza Unida Party had held conferences to form a regional or even national party among its various ideological and geographical branches, but it was unable to do so because of disagreements and personal differences among the various leaders. Despite this decline, there remained a spirit among Hispanic Americans that they had some commonality of culture and some common experiences. Pride in a Chicano culture, or even in an emerging "pre-Latino" panethnic culture, became widespread and deeply ingrained among a significant number of people, regardless of whether they were active participants. Moreover, more people than ever became acutely aware of the widespread and deeply rooted discriminatory treatment by the dominant society. Perhaps most important, it was possible to move the political system and make it respond to the interests and needs of the Hispanic people. These militants, radicals, and ideologues had really laid the groundwork for the continuation and strengthening of conventional mainstream politics of "liberal reform" that was to grow from the late 1970s and into the 1990s.

COMMONALITIES OF HISTORY

In searching for a common history of Hispanics in the United States, it is difficult to find one that can be easily summarized. Even a cursory look at the brief history of the three largest national origin groups, as well as that of Central and South Americans, provides evidence of a great difference in historical circumstances among them. This does not even include the history of the other nineteen or twenty national groups of Latinos, all of whom have their own unique homeland histories and historical relationships with the United States. Undoubtedly, these historical differences make it more difficult for Hispanics to form a cohesive political community and share a common political interest or interests. Nevertheless, some commonalties can be found among many of these groups, and among the three largest groups in particular, which constitute some 78 to 80 percent of Latinos in the United States today.

One common feature is that of the *conquest* of the homelands of Mexican Americans, Cuban Americans, and Puerto Ricans—all were taken over by the United States through force of arms as a result of war. Unlike most "ethnic American immigrants," their history is not entirely rooted in voluntary immigration to seek their fortunes in the land of golden opportunity. In contrast, they initially became part of the United States, albeit as second-class members, as a result of forceful activities. Another common characteristic is that the home countries became colonized dependencies of the United States and in one way or another had their natural resources, including their labor, exploited by the United States. In addition, and more important, their people were never quite accepted as full and first-class citizens. Yet another common characteristic is that these homelands are not distant from the United States. Ocean voyages of thousands of miles, with the resultant psychological disconnection from the homeland, are not involved when Latin Americans come to the United States. Hispanic Americans either live on the same continent (and indeed, in Mexico, in an area immediately adjacent to the United States) or are only a relatively small distance across water or land from the mainland. Thus, immigration is nothing like the experience, either physically or psychologically, that ethnic minority groups such as the Italians, Poles, or Greeks experienced. Perhaps singularly significant in their common historical experiences is that Hispanic Americans were never fully accepted into this society, but instead were treated poorly and were discriminated against. This has remained a constant feature throughout their relationship with U.S. society.

Another commonality is *culture*. Although there is no denying some significant variations in cultures from one Latin American or Caribbean country to another, the one common cultural characteristic among these peoples is their Spanish heritage. Latinos are all from areas that were "Spain impacted"; that is, Spaniards had a profound and lasting impact on cultures of these regions in the new world. The most obvious manifestation is the Spanish language, plus some of the traditional values such as Catholic religiosity. Perhaps there is something in "Latin" music that is similar across these countries, but there is also noticeable variation in styles of dress, music, and architecture; kinds of food; holiday celebrations; and so on. A strong case can be made that it is the Spanish heritage of Latino Americans, along with the unfortunate prejudicial treatment by host Americans, that are probably the two most salient significant commonalties existing among Hispanic Americans.

SUMMARY AND CONCLUSION

The context or setting in which politics take place greatly affects the behaviors of the people engaged in them. This is as true for Hispanics as it is for anyone else. Some of the major aspects of the Latino political environment include the people's psychological conditions and histories, as well as the basic features of their governments. Throughout U.S. history, Latinos have often been disparaged, as evidenced by anti-Spain, anti-Indian, and anti-African behaviors and attitudes. The contributions of Hispanics have been little recognized, known, or credited. Anti-Hispanic stereotypes have emerged, even though over the past few years, some aspects of the Latino culture have become quite fashionable. The democratic values of equality and liberty have also supported and promoted Latinos' drives for full inclusion and equal status.

In addition to the cultural manifestations of Hispanics and their presence in the Americas, the constitutional and legal features of the United States, such as the division of powers between national and state governments (federalism), the separation of powers among the branches of government at any level, and the Bill of Rights and the "civil rights" amendments have significant implications for the political activities of Latinos. These contextual factors are often reflected on and referred back to as we move forward in the text because the historical and institutional frameworks described here provide the basis for our contemporary investigation of Hispanics and the American political system. How do these major institutions of U.S. government assist or hinder the movement of Hispanics into the mainstream? Will Latinos make any significant changes in the major institutions, processes, and policies of American governments and politics?

Notes

[1] Data were taken from "How America Responds (Part 2)." (2001).

[2] See Gonzalez (2000) for an exception.

[3] For more information on the role of Spain in the revolutionary war, see Chávez (2002).

[4] See Jennings (1977) and Jennings and Rivera (1984) for an in-depth discussion of Puerto Rican history in the United States. For an in-depth discussion of Cuban history in the United States, see Grenier and Perez (2003).

[5] For further reading on the sociopolitical status of Puerto Ricans, see Jennings and Rivera (1984).

[6] As we noted in the Introduction chapter, Brazil is generally excluded from countries associated with the Hispanic or Latino population.

[7] See Ricourt (2002) for an expanded discussion of the Dominican population.

3
The Demographic-Socioeconomic Setting

THE CONTEXT: DEMOGRAPHICS

The demographics, or socioeconomic characteristics, of the Hispanic people are an extremely important aspect of the environment in which Hispanic politics takes place for several reasons. First, the socioeconomic status of a group is strongly related to the **political resources** that the group possesses. It may be used to communicate with decision makers and to influence those decision makers to make decisions favorable to them. As such, these resources are important to shaping the input that Hispanics provide to governments. In fact, politics has often been conceptualized as an *exchange* behavior, one in which people or groups seeking things from politicians offer an exchange of something they possess for the politician's favor. The more "valued things" (resources) that people have to offer politicians and the more they have to exchange with them, the more likely it is that politicians in return will do what the petitioners want. So, the more socioeconomic resources Hispanics possess, the more likely it is that they will have the political currency for exchange in their dealings with politicians.

Second, the socioeconomic status or demographics of Hispanics is important in politics because these conditions also *shape the goals* of Hispanic politics. One goal Hispanics often mention that they are trying to attain is equality, or parity. Equality is such a broad concept, encompassing intangible aspects such as recognition, respect, and status, that sometimes the narrower word *parity* is used. Parity for Hispanics is typically a more measurable concept of the possession of tangible, material goods. Parity or material equality is relatively easily measured compared to the measurement of social status, respect, opportunity, discrimination, and other such qualities that are difficult to quantify. Consequently, Hispanics often present demographic or socioeconomic data to decision makers or to the public as a solid indication of how they are a "disadvantaged" group; that is, that they are, for example, below average in wealth or income; substandard housing; lower-prestige, low-paying jobs; less educational attainment; and so on. Thus, at the very least, it is important to know the demographics of Hispanics in order to measure the degree of distance from their objective of socioeconomic equality.

Third, Hispanic demographics are also important to political systems inputs in that they affect the *strategies* that Hispanics employ to influence the political decision makers. To have the most effective political strategy, groups must assess or calculate their resources—those resources available to them in order to maximize their effect. A group uses its most abundant socioeconomic resources to affect decision makers on the group's behalf. For example, a wealthy occupational group, such as physicians or chief executive officers of large corporations, would likely use their considerably above-average wealth to make large campaign contributions, hire lobbyists and other experts to represent their causes, and so on. If a group does not possess material wealth but has large numbers of people, they can use strategies such as voting, redistricting, or mass protests or demonstrations that will maximize that particular demographic characteristic.

Finally, demographics are also important because they can affect the *unity* or *disunity* of a group. If a group is relatively homogenous in many of its members' socioeconomic characteristics, then they are more likely to have similar interests than if the group has a wide range of socioeconomic characteristics. If, for example, a group is primarily comprised of low-income, working class individuals, then they are more likely to share economic interests. If they have common religious affiliations, then religion perhaps can be an additional unifying bond or source of unity or cohesion.

In contrast, if the group has a wide range and variety of demographic characteristics, then it is likely to have several "cross-cutting cleavages," that is, differing socioeconomic characteristics that tend to splinter or fragment the interests of the group. Thus, if Hispanics share many socioeconomic characteristics in addition to their Hispanic ethnicity, then they are more likely to be unified than if they have a wide range of demographic characteristics that consequently may make it more difficult for them to be unified.

A group's characteristics can also greatly affect the perception that people who are not group members have of that group. A group whose characteristics are deemed desirable or valuable by the larger society is, all else being equal, much more likely to have its way than a group that has characteristics that are not esteemed or valued, or that in fact may be disparaged. If a group has "valuable" characteristics, they are likely also to be perceived favorably by decision makers, and the appeals that they make to decision makers are more likely to be welcomed than rebuffed.

In this section, we look at several demographic or socioeconomic characteristics of Hispanics in the United States in order to get a better idea of how these factors can either strengthen or weaken their political influence. Such a perusal will also indicate whether Hispanics are legitimately complaining when they seek parity as a goal, that is, whether they are in fact *not* equal to non-Hispanics in terms of tangible social and economic characteristics. In addition, it will have strategic considerations because we can see whether Hispanics are a relatively homogenous group or whether their socioeconomic characteristics other than ethnicity are such that they will tend to be less unified in their political approaches. We may also see whether Hispanics have the kind of socioeconomic characteristics that can serve them well as political resources, as they attempt to influence the nation's political decision makers. This chapter's discussion of resources will make use of data collected primarily from official U.S. government sources, including the U.S. Census, the Department of Commerce, and the Department of Labor. We note the location of any data presented here that does not come from one of these primary sources.

POPULATION AND NUMBERS

Particularly in a governmental system based on the sovereignty of the people, sheer population *numbers* are extremely important in politics. Especially in a democracy, in a system where—at least theoretically—one person is potentially equal to every other person in political power or influence, the more persons a group can aggregate or amass, the greater its potential power. In a system of *majority rule*, groups that are "minorities" have to work to either become a majority or at least convince the majority that the minority's causes are right and just and should become enacted into public policy. If the process is open and fair, a minority can eventually become a majority.

Perhaps the most often and widely publicized fact about the Hispanic population has to do with its rapidly increasing size. During the late 1990s, it was repeatedly stated that Hispanics would become the largest ethnic minority group in the United States by the year 2005. (In the early 1980s, the projection for this milestone had been for the year 2010). Although these projections were estimated, by the late 1990s, almost all demographers agreed that Hispanics would surpass the number of African Americans in the United States around the year 2005, give or take a few years. Hispanics are a numerical minority nationwide, but they were the minority group in the United States that had been most quickly growing in terms of its numbers. To be the "number one" ethnic group was considered by many to be of extreme significance. If and when Latinos became *"numero uno,"* no longer could they be ignored or overlooked in the historically black and white picture of America. Latinos could not possibly continue to be the "invisible minority."

In early 2001, the U.S. Census Bureau released a preliminary report of the 2000 U.S. Census on a topic that had a galvanizing effect on many, that continues to be much discussed, and that continues to have tremendous effects on U.S. politics and culture (Guzman 2001). The bureau reported that the Hispanic population in the United States in the year 2000 had reached about 35.3 million people, or about 12.5 percent of the total

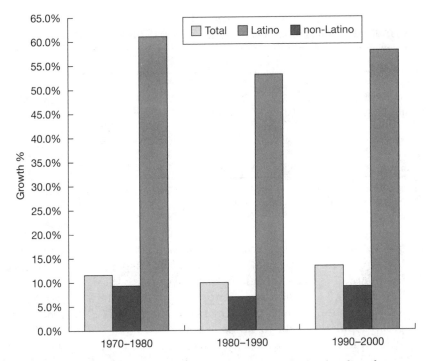

Figure 3.1   Comparative growth of population groups by decade (1970–2000). (From: Jorge del Pinal and Audrey Singer, "Generations of Diversity: Latinos in the United States," Population Bulletin 52, no. 3 [1997]: 13; Betsy Guzman, The Hispanic Population: Census 2000 Brief. C2KBR/01-3. [Washington DC: U.S. Bureau of the Census, 2001].)

population of 281 million (Figure 3.1). (If included, the commonwealth of Puerto Rico would have added another almost 4 million residents.) Major newspaper headlines in spring 2001 trumpeted that the Hispanic population had equaled or surpassed that of African Americans in the year 2000.

The fast-growing Hispanic population had increased by 58 percent between 1990 and 2000—a much higher rate than the general population increase of 13.2 percent. There were now officially 13 million more Hispanics than ten years earlier. From 1980 to 1990, the Hispanic population had increased by about 53 percent, much faster than the non-Hispanic population.

Furthermore, the Hispanic population of the United States had more than doubled between 1980 and 2000. According to the U.S. Census, within the Latino population in 2000 the size of subgroups varied significantly based on national origin (Tables 3.1 and 3.2).

Mexican Americans comprised about 58.5 percent of the Latino population, or about 20.6 million persons. The next largest sub-grouping is "Other Hispanic," which was 28.4 percent of the total who had identified

Table 3.1
GROWTH OF THE LATINO POPULATION IN THE UNITED STATES, 1970–2004 (GROWTH IN 1000S)

	1970	1980	1990	2000	2004[a]
Total	203,212	226,546	248,710	281,422	293,623
Total non-Latino	194,139	211,937	226,356	246,117	252,293
Hispanic	9,073	14,069	22,354	35,306	41,330
Mexican	4,532	8,740	13,496	30,641	NA
Puerto Rican	1,429	2,014	2,728	3,406	NA
Cuban	545	803	1,044	1,242	NA
Other	2,566	3,051	5,086	10,017	NA

[a]*Source:* Table 4: Annual Estimates of the Population by Age and Sex of Hispanic or Latino Origin for the United States: April 1, 2000 to July 1, 2004 (NC-EST2004-04-HISP): Population division. U.S. Census Bureau. Release Date: June 9, 2005.

themselves as Central American (4.8 percent), South American (3.8 percent), Dominican (2.2 percent), and "all other Hispanic" (17.3 percent). The next largest single national origin group, Puerto Ricans, increased by 29.4 percent to 3.4 million and comprised approximately 9.6 percent of the Hispanic population. Cuban Americans comprised 3.5 percent of the Hispanic population with 1.2 million people.

The rapid rate of growth of Hispanics continued into the twenty-first century. By 2002, the nation's Hispanic population was estimated to be at 38.8 million, an increase of 3.5 million over the April 2000 census count. Fifty-three percent of the growth was attributed to net international migration; the natural increase accounted for the remaining 47 percent (U.S. Bureau of the Census 2002a). It was estimated that the Hispanic population had increased to 41.3 million, or 14 percent of the U.S. population, in 2004 and to about 44 million in early 2007.

Table 3.2
GROWTH OF THE LATINO POPULATION IN THE UNITED STATES, BY NATIONAL ORIGIN, 1970–2000 (GROWTH %)

	1970-1980	1980-1990	1990-2000
Total	11.5	9.8	13.2
Total non-Latino	9.2	6.8	8.7
Hispanic	61	53	57.1
Mexican	92.9	54.4	52.9
Puerto Rican	40.9	35.5	24.9
Cuban	47.3	30	19
Other	18.9	66.7	96.9

Source: Jorge del Pinal and Audrey Singer, "Generations of Diversity: Latinos in the United States," Population Bulletin 52, no. 3 [1997]: 13; Betsy Guzman, The Hispanic Population: Census 2000 Brief. C2KBR/01-3. [Washington DC: U.S. Bureau of the Census, 2001].

In addition to the shock wave caused by the unexpectedly large number of Latinos, another surprise was the large proportion of Hispanics who classified themselves as "Other Spanish/Hispanic/Latino" (Grieco and Cassidy 2001). This has led to considerable speculation about the emergence of new transnational origin, panethnic identities, a loosening of national origin, homeland ties, and other psychological and sociological hypotheses. However, it may be that the major reason was the wording of the Hispanic origin identification in the Census questionnaire, which most likely caused considerable confusion and produced different results from both the earlier censuses and the interim Current Population Report surveys, all of which had used differently worded or ordered identification questions.[1]

Two other important factors that influence the level of political resources of the Hispanic community are nativity and citizenship status. Immigrants (i.e., foreign-born Latinos) accounted for 39.1 percent of the 35 million Latinos in America in 2000 (Ramirez 2004). However, despite the continuous immigration flow from Latin America, a larger portion of the Latino population increase described previously was due to a high birthrate rather than to immigration. Nativity is an important contributor to Latino culture because having a significant proportion of foreign-born persons perpetuates language, customs, and cultural traditions. This trend also impacts the policy goals of Latinos because the policy areas of immigration, bilingual education, and access to services are of great importance to this segment of the Latino community. Given the high percentage of foreign-born persons, naturalization is critical to this discussion of Latino political resources. In 2000, approximately 30 percent of Hispanics were noncitizens (compared to 10 percent for non-Hispanics). This statistic is critical as citizenship status has a direct link with electoral participation. In the United States, you must be a citizen to vote; therefore, the foreign-born segment of the Latino population that does not become naturalized citizens represent only an electoral or political potential. That is, the noncitizen segment of the Hispanic population lacks the political resource of voting power. This limits the bargaining power of Latinos because elected officials may not be as responsive to individuals who cannot hold them accountable through voting. Therefore, a low level of citizenship tends to offset the rapid growth rate that Latinos have experienced since the mid-1980s.

However, projections indicate that second-generation Latinos (the U.S. born children of immigrants) will emerge as the largest component of the Hispanic population over the next twenty years (Suro and Passel 2003). This has several important implications for the economic and political status of Latinos. The rise of the second generation will have an immediate impact on the nation's schools. Approximately one in seven of all new students enrolling in the public school system between 2000 and 2020 are estimated to be second-generation Latinos (Suro and Passel 2003). Second-generation Latinos are also projected to account for 23 percent of labor force growth over this same time period. These are positive trends for Latinos because the native-born segment of this population tends to have higher educational attainment levels, higher incomes, and are more proficient in English than their first-generation parents. This demographic change may also lead to an increase in political participation, primarily in regard to voting because second-generation Latinos have the advantage of being native-born citizens.

CONCENTRATION AND DISPERSION

The particular pattern of *distribution* of a population throughout the nation is also important, particularly in a political system in which geography forms the basis of many of its political constituencies. Under the rule of "one person, one vote," the primary consideration for determining electoral districts is an equal number of persons in each district. In fact, the reason the Constitution calls for a decennial census is primarily to provide a numeric basis for representation in the U.S. House of Representatives. Today, the census numbers not only provide the official basis for reapportionment and redistricting of electoral districts but also for the allocation of many federal dollars. These grants from the national government to states and localities were estimated at about $185 billion in 2000.

Hispanics continue to be somewhat concentrated in several regions of the United States, although they are quickly dispersing throughout the nation. In fact, the dispersal of Latinos into areas that previously had few if any Hispanics may be one of the most significant aspects of the "Latinization" of the United States. Roughly 80 percent of Hispanics live in nine states—California, Texas, New York, Florida, Illinois, Arizona, New Jersey, New Mexico, and Colorado. Seven states each have more than 1 million Hispanics residing in them. California has about 12 million; Texas, 8.3 million; Florida, 3.3 million; New York, 2.9 million; Arizona, 1.7 million; Illinois, 1.5 million; and New Jersey, 1.2 million. Three states, California, Texas, and New York, are home to almost two-thirds of the Hispanic population; and two states, California and Texas, have almost a majority (more than 50 percent) of the total Hispanic population (Guzman 2001).

As important as these total numbers are, perhaps even more important is the proportion or population *density* of Hispanics in any given geographical area. The highest proportion of Hispanic residents is in the state of New Mexico, whose population is approximately 44 percent Hispanic. California has an approximately 35 percent Latino population; Texas, 35 percent; Arizona, 29 percent; Nevada, 24 percent; Florida, 20 percent; and Colorado, 20 percent. This has significant political implications. For example, given the workings of the Electoral College and the location of relatively high proportions of Latinos in states with a large number of electoral votes, Latinos are strategically positioned to play an important role in presidential elections. Even more important, the concentration of Latinos provides an excellent potential power base for them to exert considerable control or influence over local governments, such as those of counties, cities, and towns, and school districts, and as the populations increase, the corresponding influence will be experienced at the state level of government. This state level influence is reinforced by Latino concentration in specific counties within several states. For example, nearly 75 percent of the Latino population in Nevada is concentrated in Clark County (Las Vegas).

Although Latinos are still concentrated regionally, they are also becoming increasingly dispersed throughout the United States. Probably the most dramatic population trend with regard to Latinos during the 1990s was that they moved into areas in which there had previously been few. There has been a dramatic move out of the central cities into the suburbs. Although Latinos remain perhaps the most urban of all peoples, with some 96 percent residing in urban areas, the movement from the inner cities to the suburbs is increasing at a rapid pace. At the same time, Latinos are still predominantly moving into the large metropolitan melting pots. For example, Hispanics (27 percent, 2.1 million) now outnumber blacks in New York City; and Los Angeles is now 47 percent Latino. Chicago's loss of population was stemmed by the huge influx of Latinos (to 26 percent of the city's population), which actually resulted in a citywide gain in population from 1990 to 2000 (Guzman 2001). This certainly belies the stereotype of the rural Hispanic living in the small villages and towns of the country, in the *campos* of the agricultural areas, the small *colonias* of Texas, or the small rural villages or *pueblos* in northern New Mexico.

Another major manifestation of this movement within the United States is that, increasingly, Hispanics, particularly immigrants, are moving into states, counties, and towns where there have previously been very few Hispanics. In 1990, the Hispanic population comprised less than 2 percent of the inhabitants of twenty-two states. Most of these states were in New England, in the central part of the nation, and in the South. By 2000, there were only eleven states left in which Hispanics were 2 percent or less of the population. Hispanics are now found in numbers greater than 1,000 in every one of the fifty states. While, in 1990, Hispanics comprised between 4 percent and 42 percent of the population in sixteen states, Hispanics now reside in those proportions in twenty-eight states. Much of this new movement has been into new areas of the Midwest, and most strikingly, into the southeastern part of the United States. In the Midwest, the Hispanic population grew from 1.7 million in 1990 to more than 3 million in 2000. In the South, Latinos almost doubled in that region's population—from 6.8 million to almost 12 million (Guzman 2001).

The rise in Hispanic population growth in almost every growing county was greater than the overall population growth in those counties—from Alaska to Georgia, from Maine to Utah, and from Wisconsin to the Mississippi delta. Some observers contended that perhaps never before in U.S. history has such a geographically dispersed in-migration taken place. In the 1990s, in five states, the Hispanic population more than doubled. The five states in which the Latino population grew the fastest were North Carolina, whose Hispanic population increased by 394 percent; Arkansas, 337 percent; Georgia, 300 percent; Tennessee, 278 percent; and Nevada, 217 percent.

The growing trend of dispersed Latino population has implications for the political resource base of this community. As Latinos continue to move into areas traditionally not associated with Hispanics, a greater national presence is provided for Latinos. Although the southern, upper Midwest, and northwestern regions of the country have had virtually no contact and little awareness of the Latino community, this will undoubtedly change as Hispanics continue to settle in these localities.

There have also been some significant social and economic repercussions due to the "cultural shock" from this migration of Hispanics into the southern region such as the states of North Carolina, Georgia, and Tennessee. Along with presenting surprising opportunities in the small towns of these areas, new ethnic tensions have become evident. The traditional racial polarities of black and white societies are now being altered by a new "in-between" presence—a mixed race ethnic group—and it undoubtedly will take some time for the new interactions to reach a balance. The fact that most of the immigrants are young, male, and poorly educated will undoubtedly have an effect. However, it is also noteworthy that there has not been a white flight out of the South; instead, both the white and black populations have increased along with the Hispanic growth. Moreover, economic growth in the region has continued to be robust, widespread, and diversified (Kochhar, Suro, and Tafoya 2005).

In summary, perhaps the most important of the demographics discussed in this section is population size. The Hispanic population in the United States is estimated to be growing by as much as 1 million people each year. It is difficult to obtain an accurate count because only an estimated percentage of these numbers are comprised of illegal and undocumented migrants into the United States. In any case, just the sheer size of the burgeoning Hispanic population and its dispersal into new areas are pre-eminent factors contributing to the "browning" of America and of Latinos moving into the mainstream. This growth certainly has tremendous implications for politics in the United States, a politics that in many respects is based on numbers, the number of people in groups and the number of groups in particular geographical areas.

FAMILIES AND HOUSEHOLDS

In general, Latino families tend to be larger than those of non-Hispanic whites. In 1998, Latino families averaged almost four members per family, while non-Hispanic whites averaged a family size of slightly less than three. Household size (which may include persons who are unrelated) averaged 3.4 among Hispanics and only 2.5 among non-Hispanic whites. Compared to 11.6 percent of Hispanic households that were comprised of six persons or more, only 2.3 percent of non-Hispanic whites had that number in the house. Thirty-one percent of Hispanic households consisted of five or more persons compared to 12 percent of non-Hispanic white households. These trends continued through 2002. For example, in 2002, 26.5 percent of Hispanic family households consisted of five or more people, compared to only 10.8 percent for Anglos. Among Hispanic family households, Mexican family households were most likely to have five or more people (30.8 percent), while Cuban family households were most likely to have only two people (43.1 percent) (Ramirez and de la Cruz 2003).

Hispanic households are more likely to be in *urban* areas than are those of non-Hispanics. Ninety-two percent of Hispanic households are in urban areas, and only 8 percent are rural, with only 1 percent of those being farm-rural residences. Non-Hispanic households were 73 percent urban at the same time. Furthermore, most Hispanics live within metropolitan areas; in 2002, nearly half of all Hispanics lived in central cities within a metropolitan area compared with approximately one-fifth of Anglos. Another 45.7 percent of Hispanics live outside central cities, but still within metropolitan areas. That leaves only 8.7 percent of the Hispanic population who live in non-metropolitan areas, which is considerably smaller than the 22.1 percent of Anglos who live outside metropolitan areas (Ramirez and de la Cruz 2002).

AGE

Another interesting characteristic of the Hispanic population is that it is very young. The average age of Hispanics is about twenty-six years, and this is approximately nine years younger than the average age of all Americans. In 2002, with respect to the politically important voting age of eighteen, 34 percent of Hispanics were under that age, while only 23 percent of non-Hispanic whites were younger than eighteen (U.S. Bureau of the Census 2003a). Although the youthfulness of the Latino population may represent an electoral disadvantage now, this could signify the coming potential for a greater Hispanic electorate as the larger cohort under eighteen reaches voting age.

ECONOMIC STATUS

Income, money, and wealth are all extremely important in politics (Verba and Nie 1972). Although population numbers are perhaps the most important political resource theoretically, many would say that, in reality, financial conditions at least rival population numbers as the most influential political resource. With money and wealth, one can enhance communication to political decision makers, or make significantly large campaign contributions to candidates for public office. Money can buy expertise, which then can be provided by hired lobbyists to the decision makers in attempts to influence their decisions. In fact, money can hire the very best "interest representatives" or lobbyists to present a group's case. Money is such an important political resource that a former speaker of the California State Assembly uttered the oft-quoted words that, "money is the mother's milk of politics."[2] Even ardent pluralists would admit that there is a bias in our pluralistic system and that it is an economic one. As E.E. Schattschneider (1960) so vividly put it, "the flaw in the pluralist heaven is that the heavenly chorus sings with a strong upper-class accent" (34–35).

Measurements of wealth are also important politically because they bring to statistical light the comparative socioeconomic position of individuals and groups in our society as perhaps no other figures do. Are any distinct ethnic or racial groups really "disadvantaged" economically? If so, how great is this inequality? Data on income, wealth, and occupations can lend statistical credence to the answers to these questions.

In addition, levels of wealth are an important indicator of the status that an individual or group enjoys in the capitalistic American society, which places great emphasis on monetary wealth as an indicator of one's success, or indeed even of one's worth as a human. People with a lot of money enjoy high status in this society; in general, people with little money have low status. This can constitute a double disadvantage because, as indicated previously, status itself can be a major political resource.

Moreover, whether groups have an abundance of financial resources is extremely important in their calculations of political tactics and strategies. If a group has money, it can use this resource in the ways mentioned previously, as well as in others, to buy political access and influence. If a group does not have money, it must use any and all other resources available to influence decision makers.

Finally, measurements of wealth speak dramatically as to how close to one important form of equality—economic equality or "parity"—a particular group comes in comparison to other groups in U.S. society. Groups significantly below average can rightly claim that their situation is one of inequality and can, with added justification, make claims on the political system for policies, laws, and regulations that at least can help them work toward the achievement of financial equality.

How do Hispanics measure up with regard to their economic status? In general, the most accurate statement is that Hispanics as a whole are significantly below average in their monetary and material possessions; they are, in fact, an *economically disadvantaged* group.

INCOME

One measurement of financial equality is income. In 1997, based on the Current Population Survey of March 1998, the median family income of the total Latino population was $28,141; that of whites was $46,754. In 1998, the median household income was $28,330, or 66.8 percent of non-Latino whites' median household income of $42,439. So, in 1997 and 1998, Hispanic income was overall about 60 percent of that of non-Hispanic whites.[3] In 2000, the median income for all U.S. households was $42,187, with non-Hispanic whites exceeding that figure with a median income of $45,904. Both Hispanics and blacks trailed the national median considerably; the median household income for Hispanics was $33,447, and $27,910 for blacks. Overall, in the year 2000, Hispanics were less likely (23 percent) to have earnings of $35,000 or more than were non-Hispanic whites (49 percent). Hispanic family income in 2000 had reached 72 percent of white family income, which is a reflection of income disparity since the 1970s (U.S. Bureau of the Census 2001a). In fact, throughout the 1970s, 1980s, and most of the 1990s, using various measures, Hispanic income was almost always between 60 and 70 percent of that of non-Hispanics. Some saw this leveling off as a lack of progress due to discrimination; certainly, the numbers were not reassuring. However, there is reason for optimism; Hispanic household incomes in 1997, 1998, 1999, and 2000 did show increases of slightly more than 5 percent—a real and significant increase.

As with other data about Hispanic Americans, one should also recognize that there is considerable variation among the various national origin groups. For example, as a percentage of white household income in 1998, Mexican Americans had 64.5 percent of white median household income; Puerto Ricans, 62.1 percent; Cubans, 76.3 percent; Central and South Americans, 74.5 percent; and other Latinos, 71.8 percent. Among Hispanics, Cuban Americans had the highest household incomes, followed closely by Central and South Americans. Mexican Americans' household incomes were about $5,000 less, and Puerto Ricans had even lower household incomes.

Looked at another way, comparing the earnings of year-round full-time workers, in 2001, 53.8 percent of non-Hispanic whites earned $35,000 or more compared to only 26.3 percent of Hispanic workers. Making $50,000 or more annually were 31.8 percent of non-Hispanic whites and 12.4 percent of Hispanics (U.S. Bureau of the Census 2002a).

Another example of the disturbing demographics of financial disparity dealt with the "net worth" of households, that is, the difference between the total assets of a family and the total debts and liabilities. From 1995 to 1998, the median Latino household net worth fell by 24 percent—from $12,170 to $9,200 (adjusted for inflation). In stark contrast, white households' net worth increased from $81,243 to $95,610. (Black household net worth rose from $10,620 to $15,000.) A 2005 report by the Pew Hispanic Center updated these data and calculated them in 2003 dollars. In 2002, the median net worth of Hispanic households was $7,932; for non-Hispanic whites, it was $88,651 (Pew Hispanic Center 2005, 82). These dramatic differences caused observers to speculate about the reasons for such large discrepancies. One of the major suspected factors in this decrease seemed to be the continuing and increased arrival of more and poorer immigrants from Latin America who are significantly less likely to have financial assets.

Another way of looking at income, or the lack thereof, is by examining the *poverty* rate. The general conclusion is that Hispanics are considerably more impoverished than are non-Hispanic whites. The percentage of Hispanics below the federal poverty level in 2000 was 21.2 percent, compared to 11.0 percent for whites, although it has been decreasing the past few years. The poverty rate for Hispanic married couples with children in 2000 was 16.9 percent, about three times higher than the comparable rate for white families (3.8 percent) and about twice as high as for similar black families (6.3 percent).[1] In 2002, the poverty rate for Hispanics rose slightly; 21.4 percent of Hispanics were living in poverty compared to 7.8 percent of non-Hispanic whites (U.S. Bureau of the Census 2001b). These figures have remained nearly constant, as the Hispanic poverty rate in 2005 was 21.8 percent compared to 8.3 percent for non-Hispanic whites. Finally, we must mention perhaps the saddest economic statistic of all—the poverty rate for children. In 2000, the poverty rate for children (younger than eighteen years) among Latinos was 28.0 percent—more than one-fourth of the population of young Latinos. For non-Latino whites, it was 9.4 percent, and for black children, it was 30.9 percent. In 1998, among Latinos, the rate of children's poverty was greatest for Puerto Ricans—43.5 percent of the children of Puerto Ricans were impoverished, as were 35.4 percent of Mexican Americans and 16.4 percent of Cuban Americans. In 2002, 28 percent of Hispanic children were still living in poverty, as were 9.5 percent of non-Hispanic white children.

This national origin variation in these measures of economic well-being has revealed a typical pattern of indicators of well-being among Hispanics, with Puerto Ricans usually being the poorest, the least financially well off, and Cubans being exceptionally high, the most financially well off. Mexican American income and wealth is usually in-between, but much closer to that of Puerto Ricans than to that of Cubans. However, this ranking seems to be changing over the past few years, with Mexicans becoming the poorest group. This probably reflects the large influx of poor immigrants from Mexico. Some data reported in 2002 on annual earnings showed Mexicans as having the lowest earnings, with Central and South Americans just above them; Puerto Ricans, Cubans, and "other Hispanics" had relatively higher earnings and were closely grouped together.

We also see this differential pattern in the poverty statistics for 2001. The percentage of Puerto Ricans under the poverty level for individual persons was 26.1 percent; for Mexicans, 22.8, percent; and for Cubans, 13.6 percent. For non-Latino whites, the poverty rate was 7.8 percent.

Another way of viewing economic conditions is to examine the data on home ownership. As of 1998, 73 percent of non-Latino whites and 67 percent of the total U.S. population owned or were buying their homes. This was compared to 57.6 percent of Cubans, 48.7 percent of Mexicans, and 32.8 percent of Puerto Ricans (U.S. Bureau of the Census 1999).

Employment statistics are also an indication of economic condition. In 1998, the unemployment rate for white Americans was 3.9 percent; for Cubans, 6.0 percent; for Mexican Americans, 7.3 percent; and for Puerto Ricans, 8.3 percent. In the third quarter of 2004, the Hispanic unemployment rate was 6.8 percent for Hispanics and 4.3 percent among whites (Pew Hispanic Center 2005, 78). Although Latinos tend to be unemployed at a greater rate than non-Latinos, there is an overall greater percentage of Latinos in the labor force (i.e., those who are working or who are actively seeking jobs), than there are non-Hispanic whites. For example, in 1998, 67.9 percent of the total Latino population was in the labor force compared to 67.3 percent of the white population. Among Mexican Americans, 68.8 percent were in the labor force, and among Central and South Americans, the number was 72.9 percent. In 2004, 69.1 percent of Hispanics were in the labor force, as were 66.8 percent of non-Hispanic whites (Pew Hispanic Center 2005, 78). Based on these data, Latinos want to work but are unable to find as much employment as are non-Hispanic white Americans.

OCCUPATION

Another interesting way to look at economic well-being (and its potential as a political resource) is to look at the occupations and professions in which Hispanics and non-Hispanics are found. In general, Latinos occupy much lower-paying, lower-status jobs than do non-Latinos. As classified by the U.S. Census Bureau, the top rung of jobs is called "Managerial/ Professional," and the lowest level is "Operators/Laborers." In 2002, Hispanics (14.2 percent) were much less likely than non-Hispanic whites (35.1 percent) to work in managerial/professional occupations. Among Latinos, Mexican Americans were the least likely to work in these occupations (12 percent). Conversely, Hispanics were almost twice as likely to be employed as operators and laborers (22 percent versus 12 percent of whites) and also were more likely to work in service occupations (19 percent versus 12 percent of whites). Among non-Latino white males, 31.7 percent are in managerial/professional positions. Among the total population of Latino males, only 11.8 percent are in this higher socioeconomic occupational group. Even this number is greatly inflated by the Cubans, 27.3 percent of whom are in managerial/professional positions compared to 15.4 percent for Puerto Ricans and only 8.9 percent for Mexican American males. Looking at the lowest-level occupation, that of operators and laborers, in 2002, 10.9 percent of non-Latino white males were in this group, compared to 20.8 percent of total Latino males, including 22.8 percent of Mexican Americans, and 20.1 percent of Central and South Americans. Among females who are non-Latina whites, 35.0 percent are in managerial/ professional jobs; only 17.8 percent of Latinas are in that same higher occupational bracket.

A recent report from the Pew Hispanic Center reinforces these trends regarding Hispanics in education and suggests that the gap in occupational status between Hispanics and whites widened throughout the 1990s. Overall, the occupations in which Hispanics are concentrated have low wages, educational requirements, and socioeconomic indicators. A measure of occupational dissimilarity used in the report reveals an increasing degree of separation between Hispanics and whites from 1990 to 2000. Whites increased their representation in professional occupations while Hispanics tended toward construction and service sector jobs (Kochhar 2005).

Jobs and professions are very important politically. They are important not only for the financial resources that they bring to their holders and for the status that they either bestow or take away from their holders, but also because of the opportunities and skills that are associated with various types of jobs. Persons in high-status jobs such as the "professions"—physicians or lawyers—or managerial positions, such as high-level executives, have many opportunities and skills that lower-level jobs lack. Higher-level professionals and managers are able to use their time flexibly, including making time for political activities. Lower-level job workers, usually in hourly, wage-paying jobs, must be on the job and working during certain predetermined hours, usually punching in and out of a time clock with their time strictly supervised. Their time schedule does not allow them to make phone calls or communicate with others outside the job situation as they want, nor is it as easy for them to take off time to actively engage in politicking, whether lobbying, supporting candidates, or running for office. Moreover, persons in lower occupational ranks must usually work long hours and engage in demanding physical labor, which often leaves them dirty or exhausted at the end of the day. Often, they have yet an additional job (or two) to which to attend.

Also important is that people in the higher occupational/professional positions have developed skills that allow them to communicate with others, including political decision makers, effectively. They can write effective letters, make effective phone calls, and organize groups and hold meetings on their behalf. In short, they have the kind of communication, organizational, and leadership skills that accrue to their advantage in their political activities. People who spend the day waiting on others, serving others, cleaning facilities, or doing other hard manual labor do not learn the kinds of on-the-job skills that can be transferable to political activities. Thus, persons at the bottom of the occupational ladder not only have fewer financial resources but also fewer general skills that can be applied to helping them politically. They lack the communication and social networks, the contacts, that people in upper-level jobs have because the latter attend training sessions; participate in conferences and seminars; meet a variety of people; engage in networking; and, in general, improve their leadership, communication, and organizational skills.

In summation, an overall examination of the income, wealth, occupations, and other measures of financial status all point to the same general conclusion—that Latinos are at a considerable economic disadvantage in U.S. society; that is, they truly are an economically disadvantaged group, with all the attendant *political* disadvantages this brings to them.

It must be noted, however, that there are signs that this situation is improving for some Latinos—perhaps dramatically so. In March 2000, the U.S. Census Bureau reported that the growth in household median income from 1995 to 1999 was higher for Hispanics (23 percent) than for all other ethnic groups (U.S. Bureau of the Census 1999). Another study conducted by the Tomas Rivera Policy Institute indicated that there is a growing Latino middle class, particularly among U.S. native-born and second- and third-generation Latinos (Bean, Trejo, Capps, and Tyler 2001). From 1979 to 1998, the Latino middle class ($40,000-plus income) grew by 80 percent—a rate three times higher than among non-Hispanic whites. Also, these studies indicate that much of the depressed economic condition of Latinos (but not all) is due to the fact that many immigrants and foreign-born Latinos have typically been included in the overall statistical measures. Because Mexican and other Latino immigrants tend to be quite poor, the averages for these statistics are depressed considerably by the inclusion of immigrants. The remarkable growth in the middle class was concentrated among U.S.-born Latinos. Almost 42 percent of native-born Latino households had achieved middle class status in 1998—still lower than non-Hispanic white households, but impressive. In contrast, among foreign-born Latino households, those who were poor (income less than $20,000) increased almost three times—from about 600,000 in 1978 to 1.6 million in 1998. Overall, an economic gap was evident between Latino households and all U.S. households, and it widened from $12,000 in 1976 to $16,000 in 1998. About 60 percent of Anglo households had achieved middle class status, but only 35 percent of all Latino households had attained that level.

This achievement came at some cost. A 2000 study by the Economic Policy Institute reported that from 1989 to 1998, middle class Hispanic families worked five hours more per week than their white counterparts. Upper-income Hispanic families worked the most of any group in any economic class, putting in an average of 12.9 hours more per week than whites.

Yet, even when some financial data are controlled for nativity and generation, Latinos are still in a below-average economic condition, even after more than a few generations in this country, compared to non-Hispanic whites in the United States. One might conclude that Latinos' progress is on a track similar to those of other ethnic immigrant groups, and it is just a matter of time before economic parity is achieved. Alternatively, those favoring a racially based, "elitist" perspective of the U.S. system would contend that discrimination has severely retarded the advancement of Latinos, and unless government takes special actions to prevent this and to afford additional opportunities, the depressed condition of Latinos will continue. There is evidence that both perspectives contain some truths.

EDUCATION

The quantity and quality of schooling is certainly one of the most important socioeconomic characteristics of a population. Education is highly correlated with many other indicators of social well-being, as well as with levels of participation in politics, such as voter turnout. Education is a valuable political resource. For one thing, it provides information and knowledge to those who attain a high level of education. They are thus able to understand their situation and that of the American political system, as well as the relationship between them. The political system of the United States is extremely complex and takes a substantial amount of knowledge in order to understand even its basic operations. A proper political education can certainly be useful in this regard. Even a general education is highly desirable. In fact, education is almost always mentioned by the American public as one of the top two or three public policies that need to be addressed by government. For Latinos, it is particularly important. Even though it is often said that Latinos do not value education, much empirical data contradict this. Surveys, such as the Latino National Political Survey, show that (contrary to some conventional wisdom) Latinos highly value education as a goal.[4] Mexican Americans, in particular, seem to be particularly interested in education, often ranking it as the number one problem or public policy of importance to their community. In addition, Latinos appear to have high expectations for their children's educational futures. Family surveys conducted by the education department show that more than nine of ten Hispanic parents expect their children to attend college (Schmidt 2003, A8).

Despite recognizing the tremendous benefits of educational attainment, it is true that being lower on the socioeconomic ladder, Latinos must often sacrifice higher education, especially at the college level, in order to get a job and bring additional income to the family, and this is particularly true for immigrants and persons from traditional, rural small towns. Some of the children, particularly females, have been discouraged from continuing into higher education and encouraged to resume the familiar domestic role of helper, wife, or mother. Nevertheless, Mexican Americans believe that it is extremely important for their children to obtain a quality education, and often state that it is through education that most progress—economic social and political—can be made.

What are the levels of educational attainment achieved by Latinos compared to others in the United States? What particular obstacles do

Latinos face in attaining higher levels of education and better quality education? As with the other socioeconomic indicators, Latinos once again have less than do non-Hispanic whites. As of March 2002, for example, among persons twenty-five years and older, 57 percent of U.S. Hispanics had obtained a high school diploma compared to 88 percent of non-Hispanic whites (Ramirez and de la Cruz 2003). Again, there is significant variation among the various national origin groups of Latinos. At 73 percent, Cubans have the highest proportion of adults who have finished high school. The Cubans are followed by the "Other Hispanic" group at 72 percent, Central and South Americans at 64 percent, Puerto Ricans at 64 percent, and Mexican Americans at 51 percent. This pattern among Latino national origin groups is notably different for education than it is for many of the other socioeconomic indicators. Usually, the Cubans are at the highest level and the Puerto Ricans at the lowest. However, in the area of education, Mexican Americans are farthest down the ladder.

The same picture emerges at the level of attaining a college bachelor's degree or higher. In March 2002, 29.4 percent of non-Hispanic whites (twenty-five years or older) had obtained a bachelor's degree, compared to only 11.1 percent of Hispanics. Among Latino national origin groups, Cubans were by far the most highly college educated, with 18.6 percent of their population having a college degree, compared to 17.3 percent of Central and South Americans, 19.7 percent of other Hispanics, 11 percent of Puerto Ricans, and only 7.6 percent of Mexican Americans (Ramirez and de la Cruz 2003). The level of educational attainment is increasing for all groups, and Hispanics continue to make steady gains in the area. Younger Hispanics have completed more schooling than have older Hispanics. The high school completion rate is increasing at a steady rate. For example, among native-born Hispanics, 40 percent finished high school in 1970; by 2000, 70 percent had done so. Especially for Hispanic men, college enrollment has been increasing over the past few decades, as it has for other minority groups and for women. From the high school class of 1992, 70 percent of Hispanics went on to college; of the graduating classes of 1972, only half had matriculated in college. Furthermore, Hispanics' share of all bachelor's degrees awarded has risen from about 2.3 percent in the mid-1980s to about 6.2 percent in 2003. However, although Latinos represent about 18 percent of the college-age population, they account for just 9.5 percent of all students at the nation's higher education institutions (Schmidt 2003). College attendance, however, is progressing much more slowly for Hispanics than for others. Indeed, there is some evidence that even high school graduation rates are declining for Mexican Americans. The most stubborn problem seems to be the dropout rate, as Mexican Americans have a much higher dropout rate than African Americans or non-Hispanic whites. For example, in 1991, the high school dropout rate for Latinos was 35 percent compared with 13 percent for all students, 9 percent for whites, and 14 percent for African Americans. According to the 2000 U.S. Census, the high school dropout rate for Latinos was 21.1 percent among sixteen- to nineteen-year-olds compared to 6.9 percent for whites. The 59 percent high school completion rate in 2006 for Hispanics compares to 81 percent for non-Hispanic African Americans. Even in the younger age group of persons from twenty-five to twenty-nine years old, 93 percent of whites and Asian Americans, 89 percent of blacks, and only 60 percent of Hispanics had completed high school.

The dropout problem is magnified when applied to Latino immigrants, particularly those of Mexican origin. The President's Advisory Commission on Educational Excellence for Hispanic Americans indicates that the high school completion rate for Hispanic citizens born in the United States is 81 percent, compared to only 40 percent of foreign-born Latinos. The dropout rate for Mexican immigrants is a robust 61 percent, nearly twice the rate of other Latino subgroups. The education deficiency does not end at high school completion.

Another issue that impacts the degree attainment of Latinos, particularly Mexican Americans, is concentration in two-year institutions. Among eighteen- to twenty-four-year-olds, 44 percent of Hispanic undergraduates are enrolled at two-year universities (Fry 2002). This is considerably higher than the 30 percent enrollments of both whites and African Americans in two-year universities. This trend seems to be more apparent among Mexican Americans than other Latinos. Approximately 46 percent of Mexican college students (eighteen- to twenty-four-year-olds) attend two-year universities, compared to 31 percent for Cubans and Puerto Ricans. Unfortunately, the heavy concentration of Latinos in these types of higher educational institutions may have a negative impact on their chances of attaining degrees because statistics indicate that Latino students are more likely to drop out of college if they begin their college careers at two-year universities (National Center for Education Statistics 2000). This trend may have an impact on Latino representation in graduate and/or professional schools. As of March 1997, 8.3 percent of non-Hispanic whites had earned a master's degree, a professional degree, or a doctorate. This compared to only 2.9 percent for Hispanics.

It is apparent that the high school dropout rate for Latinos, particularly Mexican Americans, is going to have to be addressed if Hispanics are to approach educational parity with non-Hispanic whites or even members of other ethnic groups. The problem of Latino high school dropouts is compounded by the large number of immigrants coming to the United States from Latin America, particularly from Mexico. Often, immigrant parents from Mexico have very low incomes and very little education. This affects the preparedness of their children, and as they encounter the American public school system, they have to learn an entirely different language, as well as learn about life in the United States in general. Some enter the system with a significant education gap because they are not fully literate in either their native language or English, come from homes in which English is not the primary language, and attend schools without bilingual education programs. These factors alone place them at a tremendous disadvantage. Indeed, the Pew Hispanic Center has emphasized that when examining educational statistics, it is important to distinguish between native-born and foreign-born Hispanics (Fry 2005; Lowell and Suro 2002; Pew Hispanic Center 2005). In 2004, only 62 percent of all Latinos completed high school, but 84 percent of the native-born twenty-five- to twenty-nine-year-old Hispanics had finished high school. This compared to 93.6 percent of non-Hispanic white young adults (Pew Hispanic Center 2005, 84). The presence of a large number of many poorly educated immigrants greatly affects the average statistics.

In addition, although schools are slowly changing, for most of our history, U.S. public schools have been basically middle class, Anglo American cultural institutions and have had many institutional features that have not been a comfortable fit for children who are not of this group.

Not only is the Hispanic population of the United States growing, but also the younger age group is growing in greater numbers. In several states, minority children, largely Latino children, will become the majority of grade school children in the next few years. This is already true in California and New Mexico. In many school systems, Latino children will become the majority of the public school attendees in the next several years. Therefore, a great challenge is presented to the U.S. public educational system to continue to educate its citizenry to the point where virtually all of them can become productive citizens with a decent income and a real and equal opportunity for participation in community and political activities. This challenge is not only an educational one but also a political one because public schools are political institutions in some ways and are governed by political bodies, the local school boards. Not only will the quantity and quality of education received by Latino children affect their status and participation in the economy and politics, but it will also greatly affect the future of U.S. society in general.

Students learn not only basic facts about government and politics (and sometimes about participation in politics), but also, especially as they enter college, they pick up many other resources that can serve to further their political objectives. For example, networking is important, and the connections with colleagues and classmates one has in college often continue into post-educational economic and political life. Also, many of the skills that are learned in school, particularly skills involving analysis, critical thinking, reading, and communication, are important for political activities. Thus, for many reasons, it is important for Latinos to pursue parity in the quality and quantity of education that they receive in the United States.

SUMMARY AND CONCLUSION

Although we have presented discussion and data on national demographics, for many Hispanics the politics of their states and localities are at least, and perhaps even more, important. It cannot be stressed enough that the socioeconomic environments of these regions and localities are at least as critical to the political situation in each as national demographics are to Latinos' involvement in national politics. Unfortunately, the presentation of data for analysis of fifty states and thousands of municipalities is beyond the scope of this book. However, it is important for the student of Latino politics to pay as much attention as possible to the socioeconomic and demographic situation in various states and localities because that is where much of the action will be taking place. Indeed, in many of these localities, Latinos are a significantly large part of the population, and increasingly, this is the case. Many municipalities and counties already have large minority or even majority populations of Latinos, and this is usually even more so in school districts. At least three states already have large populations of Latinos approaching majority status. Some preliminary and important work has been done on the socioeconomic environment of those states in which a significant number of Latinos reside, such as works by Rodney Hero, most notably his book *Faces of Inequality: Social Diversity in American Politics* (1998).

In a prior book, *Latinos in the U.S. Political System: Two Tiered Pluralism,* Hero (1992a) briefly explored the effects of the socioeconomic environment and the political cultures of each state. He came to some conclusions about the implications of these for the probable political success or lack of political success of Latinos in these various states. He also examined major political variables in these states and then compared the policy outputs with the varying socioeconomic environments, political cultures, and political institutions of each state. Hero (1992a) concluded that with the exception of New Mexico, Latinos lacked proportionate political influence and presence in state decision-making bodies, and political influence and political outcomes did not seem to be particularly responsive to Latino concerns. There was some "descriptive" representation in the states but not much success in terms of helpful policies being passed ("substantive" representation). The contextual environment of each state that Hero examined, again including the socioeconomic and political culture and political institutions of each state, explained the policy outcomes in each state as much or more than did any other factors. Hero concluded that patterns of correlation between various characteristics of the states and political outcomes were "difficult to explain" (1992a, 114).

In any case, it is crucial to be familiar with the demographic characteristics (i.e., the socioeconomic qualities) of the Latino population in the nation, in the states, and in various localities because there doubtless is a close, if not precisely defined, relationship between these and Latinos' political strategies, objectives, and opportunities for success in the political arena. It should be indisputably clear that Latinos are generally below parity in several areas. Most notably, their financial and educational well-being is lower than those of non-Hispanic white Americans. Thus, one item on the Latino political agenda is the attainment of that long elusive socioeconomic parity. Moreover, the political strategies and tactics that Latinos use to achieve their goals must take into account the relative scarcity of factors that can often be used as political resources, and they must adapt their tactics accordingly. Hispanics lack several of those traditional political resources, such as numbers, money, and education that can and are used by groups possessing more of these. However, there are notable changes, almost all positive, in most of these demographic indicators that suggest that not only are Latinos increasingly moving into the mainstream, but also that they will increasingly have the resources to move the mainstream. Surely, the social, cultural, and economic aspects of the United States have been and are being greatly affected by the demographics of Hispanics. Will this also be true for the U.S. political system?

Notes

[1] For a discussion of how question wording was changed in the 2000 U.S. Census, see Ramirez (2004).

[2] A phrase coined by Jesse Unruh, speaker of the California Assembly from 1961 to 1968.

[3] Income statistics for the years of 1997, 1998, and 1999 were taken from U.S. Census Bureau Current Population Surveys for those years.

[4] In addition to the Latino National Political Survey, the Pew National Survey of Latinos (2004) and *Washington Post* (1999) National Survey of Latinos indicate education is a high priority for Hispanics.

4

Supports, Interests, and Resources

The context in which politics takes place in the United States is crucial because it shapes and conditions the attitudes and behaviors of political players. The psychological, cultural, historical, constitutional, economic, and demographic features of the United States may even be said to be determinative of the way in which politics in this country operates. In system terms (including the Eastonian political system presented in Chapter 1), the environment in which Hispanic politics takes place determines the *inputs* of the system. The operation of the political system greatly depends on the inputs it receives from the environmental context in which it operates. Inputs into the system are often conceptualized into two major groups: (1) supports, and (2) interests, such as preferences, needs, wants (or demands). In Chapter 2, we discuss some supports of the political system. The political system, just like any other system—respiratory systems, circulatory systems, and so on—needs certain supportive inputs before it can do its job, or the function for which it is designed. The political system is designed to take competing interests in U.S. society and resolve them in an authoritative, legitimate way by deciding who wins a particular conflict. To do this, like any other system, the political system needs resources, and its fuel is supplied primarily by its citizenry. For example, our political system needs personnel. It needs people who participate in government—in selecting, forming, and running the government. Thus, people who participate in campaigns and elections, as well as those who are elected to public office and who are in appointed or even civil service merit positions in governments at all levels, are part of the system's support system or inputs.

In addition, the system also requires money or financial resources to survive. American citizens pay taxes to its various governments (local, state, and/or federal) to support their operations. Moreover, the system sometimes calls on individuals to make the supreme sacrifice—to give their lives for their country—or to at least defend their country from foreign enemies who are attempting to attack and destroy the U.S. political system and the way of life or society in which it operates. Thus, military service can be seen as another political system support function.

The system also needs *socialization* support for its new citizens. That is, future citizens must be socialized to support the system; that is, they must have inculcated in them a basic loyalty and proper democratic attitude toward it. Yet, they should also be taught to question the system and to challenge authority whenever and however it is deemed appropriate in a democracy. When one thinks of fundamental attitudes, the first attitude that comes to mind is patriotism, or pride in one's country. However, there are other psychological attitudes besides these basic attitudes that must be instilled in citizens. These include feelings of political efficacy—the feeling that one's actions can have an effect on government, political trust—the feeling that government is basically honest and carrying out the will of the people, and civic duty—the feeling that one is obligated to participate in government and politics.

We have already seen that Hispanics are supportive of the American political system in the sense that they have certainly done their share, and perhaps even more than their share, of providing money, labor, and even their lives when the occasion called for it. We have also seen that Hispanics are extremely patriotic and possess a trust that makes them prone to being even more supportive of government than non-Hispanics. In fact, research has indicated that Mexican Americans are more likely, in many cases, to express support for the American values of individualism and patriotism than are Anglos (de la Garza, Falcon, and Garcia 1996).

It is interesting that there is also a physical manifestation of support for the U.S. system in the behavior of Hispanics, in the sense that they have consciously decided to remain in the United States. The ancestral homelands of many Hispanics are easy to return to because they are in the same hemisphere. Indeed, Mexico is adjacent to the United States along a 2,000-mile border to its south. Yet, few Hispanic citizens leave the United States to permanently live in Mexico or other Latin American countries. Indeed, most migrant flow is from the rest of the Western Hemisphere into the United States rather than the other way around. The fact that few Hispanics actualize the opportunity to leave the United States in favor of ancestral homelands indicates that there is widespread support for U.S. social and political institutions.

INPUTS: INTERESTS—PREFERENCES, NEEDS, WANTS, AND DEMANDS

Throughout this book, a lot of time is spent looking at the other major types of inputs into the political system—the wants, needs, and demands of Hispanics, otherwise called Hispanic *interests*, or the "Hispanic agenda." This is really the essence of politics. Without effective input into the system by Hispanics, it is most certain that their interests will not be heard, heeded, or converted into public policy. Whatever the Hispanics interests are (and we discuss this further later in this chapter), they need to be effectively communicated to the authoritative decision makers, who need to have the potential to decide in favor of Hispanic interests. However, before Hispanic interests can be presented or communicated to decision makers, they must be aggregated and then clearly defined. The aggregation, definition, and articulation of these interests are done through *political participation.* Participation is the key. Without participating in politics, it is unlikely that Hispanic interests will effectively become public policy.

THE POLITICAL INTERESTS OF HISPANICS

If Hispanic interests are to be presented, then they must be understood. That is, we must know the Hispanic policy agenda. To put it bluntly, what do Hispanics want or need? What is the Hispanic agenda? Are there Hispanic interests that are distinctive from that of other groups in U.S. society, or do Hispanics simply want what others have and they do not yet have? The answers to these questions have all kinds of implications for the shape of Hispanic politics.

What are some possible Hispanic interests? Some seem to be intangible or symbolic. For instance, Hispanics want to be valued and respected in U.S. society. We know that Hispanic pride and self-esteem can take a beating in a society that for most of its history has devalued and denigrated things and people that are Hispanic. Hispanics want to be recognized and accorded the same respect that is given to members of other ethnic groups. Hispanics want to see people like themselves in positions of high visibility and power; they want to see some brown faces in governmental offices, all the way from city hall to the presidency. They want to see people from their own culture in positions of influence and power throughout society, including in the military, the police, the media, the educational systems, the entertainment industry, and various public offices. Having Hispanics in such positions of power and/or visibility makes other Hispanics believe that their interests are being represented, and that they have a voice in the crafting and maintenance of our society.

One should not underestimate the importance of this so-called "recognition" or "symbolic" politics. For example, it is important that the U.S. government simply recognize the Hispanic population in the United States and its many contributions because, as we discussed previously, Hispanic Americans have contributed much to what is now present-day society. For example, there is now a national governmental policy for having an officially proclaimed "Hispanic Heritage" month each year from September 15—the Independence Day of five Central American countries

(Mexican Independence Day is September 16)—to October 12, the encounter of the Europeans, Christopher Columbus, and crew with the indigenous people of the new world. This recognition started out as a week-long festivity in 1968, and now a full month is devoted to the celebration of Hispanic culture and heritage. This seems a right and proper awareness of the people who comprise such a major segment of U.S. society. It shows recognition of and respect for their culture.

In the early 2000s, various states in the Southwest began to be pressured to declare March 31 (César Chávez's birthday) a state holiday. This day would honor Chávez, one of the great leaders of the Chicano movement, and more particularly, of the UFW. As of mid-2005, seven states—Arizona, California, Colorado, Michigan, New Mexico, Texas, and Utah—and dozens of cities and counties throughout the United States had declared the day an official state holiday. In fact, Representative Joe Baca of California introduced a bill to make March 31 a national holiday honoring the Chicano civil rights activist. This bill has been referred to the House Government Reform Committee for potential revisions and consideration for passage. This recognition is another example of Hispanic culture being recognized and respected by U.S. society.

It is important to place Hispanics in positions of visibility and in key decision-making positions not only for the effects that they may have on public policy but also for the sheer sake of recognition or pride in seeing one's own in positions typically held by members of other ethnic groups. Thus, part of the interests of Hispanics has always been to place Hispanics into public office, almost as an end unto itself, as if just having them there as role models or as symbolic representatives of the Hispanic people was sufficient. Certainly, this has been important, but again one should not underestimate the importance of these intangible Hispanic cultural interests that indicate societal respect for the Hispanic culture and people. Much of Hispanic politics, indeed all politics, involves symbolic or recognition politics.

THE HISPANIC AGENDA   Of course, when people indicate what they want from government and public officials, they most often refer to tangible or material interests that will substantially impact and improve the well-being of those involved in politics. Much like most other people, Hispanics are interested in improving their socioeconomic status—their jobs, income, health, housing, and education—in short, their *quality of life*. We have already examined the socioeconomic status of Hispanics in U.S. society, and we have seen that on virtually every measure Hispanics are lower on the socioeconomic scale than are non-Hispanic whites. So, one of the interests of many Hispanics is to seek *parity* (parity being a measure of being on the same tangible level with non-Hispanic whites). Sometimes this discussion is framed using the word "equality" instead of parity, but parity is a narrower, more measurable type of equality usually applied to tangible objects rather than including subjective or conceptual comparisons. So, in discussions about what Hispanics want, one often hears that Hispanics want "a bigger slice of the American pie." They want their proportionate share of resources, which they have not had throughout their history in the United States. So, how do Hispanics get to parity through government, and is this the best way to go?

Certainly, politics is one route to take, so one major Hispanic interest is to pressure government for public policies that will benefit Hispanics in a way that will enhance their economic, educational, and material well-being. Indeed, there is some evidence that Hispanics are more likely to look to government for help in providing services that will promote the Hispanic community than are other ethnic groups (de la Garza, DeSipio, Garcia, Garcia, and Falcón 1992). Hispanics are more likely, for example, to believe that the government should be responsible for providing job opportunities, public housing, quality schooling, and other social welfare benefits than are non-Hispanics. Yet, these kinds of material improvements are almost universally desired by all ethnic groups, indeed by all individuals.

Therefore, one might ask whether Hispanic interests are just the same as non-Hispanic interests. But this is not an easy question to answer. There is considerable debate about what the Hispanic agenda is or should be. There is no doubt that a large part of the Hispanic agenda is comprised of issues that are shared by many other groups in society. Indeed, this commonality of issues may form the basis for various coalitions of interests, as we discuss later in this chapter. However, one might ask whether there is a truly *distinctive* and *unique* Hispanic political agenda. Are there issues or policies supported by a significant majority of Hispanics that are distinctive to them (i.e., not also supported by other segments of society)? The answer seems to be that there are some, but it is a much smaller group of concerns than one might think. Typically, when confronted with the possibility of some items on the Hispanic political agenda, people often mention such issues as immigration, affirmative action, and bilingual education. These are certainly not unreasonable issues because they are all related to Hispanic ethnicity. However, these issues must be examined further to determine whether they are the peak items comprised of distinctively Hispanic policies that top off the large iceberg of symbolic and tangible interests that Hispanics share with various other ethnic groups in American society. So, the Hispanic agenda (i.e., those issues that are on the public policy priority list for Hispanics) should be clearly defined before the interests comprising it can be presented to government as a significant input for public policy making. After Hispanic wants, needs, and desires have been defined as clearly as possible, they must be aggregated or collected for presentation to government because an individual acting alone is unlikely to pressure government into responding favorably and positively. There must be some mechanisms in society for taking these individual interests and bringing them together so that some sort of coherent presentation can be made to governmental policy makers. Again, this process leads to various forms of political participation because there are many ways in which individuals' interests can be strengthened and presented more effectively. For example, meetings can be held, petitions signed, and organizations formed or joined. In these forms of aggregation, however, the quality and quantity of political participation is once again the key to success.

Individuals can and do participate in politics, and individual participation is important. Certainly, the most common and well-known form of participation in politics is the act of voting. Although it can be argued that the act of voting sends a message of public policy preferences and interests to government officials or incoming government officials, this idea of a policy "mandate" is arguable, to say the least. In its most direct form, voting is the political act of an individual who is involved in choosing the public authorities and government officials who will be making decisions on his or her behalf. Voting preferences for individual candidates are a "blunt measure" of policy preferences. The selection of some candidates over others has an *indirect* effect on policy, but one that may take a little expected shape.

Of course, at the state and local levels, particularly the former, there are some elections in which an individual can vote directly on the issues of public policy. These are known as *referenda*. Referenda are usually placed on the ballot by the legislature or by citizens directly; then voters have a choice of approving these referenda and making them official policy in the form of a law or constitutional amendment. Or sometimes they involve choices of whether a bond should be issued by a certain level of government, or a tax imposed. In these cases, the act of citizens voting can be conceptualized as a direct representation of their interests. In fact, there have been examples of state initiatives or referenda highly salient to Latino communities, including Proposition 187 in California and Proposition 200 in Arizona. Both propositions dealt with issues of undocumented populations' access to government services and benefits. As important as these referenda are, they are much less common than the typical election in which one votes for competing candidates.

In addition, there is the occasional individual who is so powerful or influential that a communication from that individual to a public official will result in his or her having that interest fulfilled. However, this is fortunately not too common in a democracy, nor are there many individuals of this stature who are of Hispanic origin. Far more common is that the interests of individuals are brought together or "aggregated" in various ways so that the interests can be said to represent those of a larger proportion of the population.

The pluralist system, as noted previously, is a model of *group politics*, and it is these groups that are the main players in the U.S. political system. The United States is full of groups, organizations, and associations of all kinds—literally tens of thousands of them. People belong to these groups (i.e., join into either a formal or informal membership with other persons) because they share similar interests at some level. People may join an *interest group* that is a formal organization, such as the League of Latin American Citizens, or they may just get together temporarily to push forth legislation, such as the *Recuerda a César Chávez Committee*, to push for a state holiday commemorating that American leader's exemplary dedication and accomplishments. Joining with others in a cause multiplies an individual's influence many times over. If the group is strongly united in its purpose, with its members being very cohesive and strongly bound to one another, and has effective organization and leadership, it is quite likely that it will succeed in exerting some influence on government in the United States. Such groups are called *interest groups,* or when they try to exert influence on government, they are sometimes called *pressure groups.* There are also "latent" or potential interest groups.[1] People may feel a common bond or have a "linked fate" that only needs a catalyst to precipitate participation in the form of organization or action.

Are Hispanics an interest group in the United States? Perhaps so. If a substantial proportion of Hispanics have the same interests, and these interests can be brought together in some measure of unity or cohesion, then they could be called an interest group, or at least an interest "grouping" (or a "latent" interest group) because certainly there is no formal organization that encompasses them all, and we know there are many differences within this diverse group along socioeconomic, historical, regional, and national origin lines. If one can specify or define the Hispanic interest, then there can be an Hispanic interest group. Short of that, one has to look deeper into the situation, and try to define and understand several various Hispanic interest groups and groupings. These include everything from neighborhood associations that are primarily Hispanic community organizations of various sorts, to associations operating at the city, county, state, or even national levels. These groups and/or groupings can range from highly structured and formalized organizations with officers, constitutions, by-laws, formal memberships, and dues, to informal get-togethers for the purposes of advancing a particular issue. They can be as large and inclusive as political parties, or they can be small and private exclusive interest groups. In any case, they all serve to aggregate and coalesce interests.

Actually, there have been some expressions of interests, including Hispanic interests, that have been larger and perhaps less organized than political parties. Take the example of *social movements* such as the Chicano movement of the late 1960s and early 1970s (*el movimiento*) discussed previously. Here was a loose collection of various leaders, ideologies, submovements, and activists in various geographical areas, all working sometimes more or less in concert toward the general goal of advancing the betterment of Chicanos in American society. It would be difficult to tell if a person was or was not a member of the Chicano movement. Many people participated; many did not. Some participated for brief periods of time; others for most of the movement. Some were very involved and major activists in the cause (*la causa*); others participated only minimally. Nonetheless, it cannot be denied that the Chicano movement as a social movement brought together many of the interests of Hispanics and effectively influenced government toward enacting public policies that would enhance their well-being.

Another way—actually, a quite passive way—that interests can be aggregated is through public opinion polls. In fact, surveying the opinions, beliefs, and attitudes of Americans seems to be increasing to the point where both public policy makers and citizens are inundated with the results of public opinion polls. Although these polls typically look at the opinions of people as defined by geographical areas, such as American citizens or residents of the state of New Mexico, they sometimes look at subgroups within our society, such as when they examine the opinions or attitudes of women, or ethnic or racial minorities, or senior citizens, likely voters, students, or any other demographic subgrouping. Unfortunately, until recently, the public opinions of Hispanics as a separate group were little known. In fact, the first survey focused on the political attitudes of Latinos was not conducted until 1979, and that data only included Latinos of Mexican origin (Arce 1979). This trend is also reflected in the title of a book on Hispanic public opinion, *Ignored Voices*, which aptly describes the way that American society overlooked Latino public preferences until more recently (de la Garza 1987). It was not until the 1980s and 1990s that a significant amount of information on Hispanic public opinion was collected, and that public officials and decision makers started paying attention to the opinions of Hispanics as a significant group in society. As we move into the twenty-first century, it seems that the expression of public opinion interests by Hispanic people has finally been incorporated into the considerations of those who make decisions for the American people.

THE COMMUNICATION OF HISPANIC INTERESTS

Once the Hispanic agenda has been defined and clarified (if it can be), and these interests have been aggregated and brought together among various groups and organizations throughout U.S. society, then the next task will be to present those interests to the decision makers in the system as effectively as possible. This task of *"interest articulation"* or communication is not as easy as it may seem. During the Chicano movement, the protest politics of the time were given considerable coverage by the media; thus, the messages of the protesters were conveyed to the government and the general public using this method. Individuals, of course, can communicate directly with their representatives and other decision makers through the use of such devices as letters, telephone calls, and e-mail messages. However, knowledge and skills in these forms of communication are required for them to be effective. Lower education levels and the "digital divide" (the reality that Hispanics, along with other ethnic groups such as Native Americans, have less access to computers, the Internet, and e-mail than non-Hispanics) would seem at first glance to put Hispanics at a disadvantage in this kind of communication. For example, recent public opinion data indicate that approximately 71 percent of whites and 60 percent of African Americans go online, compared to only 56 percent of Latinos (Fox and Livingston 2007). Language is critical to this dynamic, as only 32 percent of Spanish-dominant Latinos go online. In addition, Hispanics are less than proportionally represented among the persons who control the media in the United States (Pachon, DeSipio, Noriega, and de la Garza 2000). Few, if any, Hispanics are in the upper echelons of ownership or management of television stations, radio stations, or major newspapers or magazines. It should be noted that the increase in the Spanish language media has been striking in the 1990s and early 2000s. However, how effective Spanish language media are in communicating the message of Hispanic constituents to decision makers is still an open question, particularly because this mode of communication is different than that currently used or understood by most decision makers.

As each of these system input functions has been examined, several things have become clear: (1) Hispanics seem to be at a disadvantage in aggregating and representing their interests to decision makers, and (2) participation is essential for these functions to operate as they should. Participation in politics does not guarantee success for an individual or a group, but without participation it is inevitable that an individual or a group will not be heard and will not have political success.

RESOURCES   Before we proceed with an application and examination of these functions with specific regard to Hispanics, let us quickly review another important component of politics, that of *resources.* To have any success in politics, whether it is in forming or presenting one's interests effectively, people must have resources at their disposal. Resources are things that are valued by others and that consequently can be used in exchange for other desired goods, such as takes place in politics, or resources can be used to barter or bargain for what a person wants. With resources, one person has something that another wants, and that person is willing to be influenced or persuaded to gain those resources.

Sometimes politics is defined as the *exchange of resources* whereby the citizenry has certain resources that politicians or public officials want, such as their vote, their money, or their support in other ways. In turn, politicians are willing to exchange their support for, or on behalf of, a particular piece of legislation. A quick survey of the major resources, particularly those useful in politics, will give an early indication of whether Hispanics are at a disadvantage in their political relationships with decision makers.

1. Economic resources (money). Of course, money is an important political resource; many would contend that it is the most important one in U.S. politics. A famous politician (Jesse Unruh, speaker of the California Assembly) once said that "money is the mother's milk of politics." With money, a candidate can give major campaign contributions to candidates; he or she can hire the best, most skilled experts to represent his or her interests in city hall, the state capitol, or Congress. These representatives of interests, or "lobbyists," are important players in American politics. A professional lobbyist costs a lot of money. Money also can buy time on the media through which one can represent his or her views. There are many ways in which money is an important resource—in fact, it is perhaps the most important political resource.

2. Contacts. It is important to know people and to be able to establish a network of communication among them. To effectively increase these network resources, one must find out what others are doing and let them know how your common interests can be advanced. To have friends in high places acting on your behalf can greatly help influence decision makers to your side. Contacts or social networks can also be valuable tools for political participation and can increase the likelihood that you will be mobilized to participate. Those who have expansive social networks will have an easier time running for office or organizing activities focused on persuading policy makers or government. These folks are also more likely to be contacted by public officials, parties, organizations, and so on because it is assumed that they can have some influence over those within their networks. The importance of social networks in politics is reflected in the growing literature focused on the concept of social capital.[2]

3. Knowledge. A person must have knowledge of politics and the political system to engage in it effectively. It is necessary to know the structure of the system and its various institutions. It is also important to know how the political system works—where can pressure be most effectively applied, in which arenas can a political battle best be fought, how is public policy made, and at what points can it best be affected? This kind of knowledge can be gained through formal education or through a more applied and practical learning outside the classroom (and in the political system itself).

4. Time. Every human activity takes time, and politics is no exception. In addition to earning a living and carrying out responsibilities to family and friends, a potential candidate, for example, needs additional time to engage in politics. People who are too busy earning a living, trying to find a job, or working night and day at two or more jobs do not have the time to participate in politics. Hispanics, in particular, are more likely to have the kind of job that takes more time and is less flexible, allowing them little, if any, time to participate in politics.

5. Numbers. This resource rivals money in significance and might be the single most important resource that Hispanics possess. In a democracy, each individual is an important political unit. When individuals comprise more than half of a population, they are a majority, and majority rules. Even in the case where majority does not rule, in a democracy, the more people that can be attracted to a cause, the better. Voting is important, and obviously, a candidate wants to attract the most voters possible. Everything else being equal, a large group will be paid much more attention than will a smaller group. This certainly puts Hispanics at a disadvantage at the national level because indeed Hispanics are a national minority group, having almost 15 percent of the population in 2007. It is also true that at each state level in 2005, Hispanics were a minority. The state of New Mexico is the only state in which Hispanics have comprised half of the population (and, not coincidentally, New Mexico is also the only state in which Hispanics approach parity in terms of representation in government). So, when numbers are important, as they are in U.S. democratic politics, it is most likely that on the basis of that resource alone, much of the effective political action by Hispanics will be in areas where they make up a substantial and significant portion of the population (e.g., in a school district, in a city or town, or at the county level).

That numbers are extremely important symbolically was made evident (as presented previously) by the announcement that, in spring 2001, Hispanics had equaled and probably surpassed the number of African Americans in the United States. This announcement had tremendous symbolic implications not only for Hispanics but also for African Americans and the general American public because the claim of being the largest ethnic minority—*numero uno*—carried great symbolic weight and had many profound political implications.

6. Organization. One major way to multiply resources is through *organization*—creating an institution that has a membership, rules and procedures, regular meetings, and recognized leaders multiplies its resources tremendously. It is probably true that the sum of the parts exceeds the whole when it comes to individuals organizing. That is, when they are organized, individuals can do so much more politically and be so much more effective than they could be in the same number acting as individuals.

Hispanic organizations have existed throughout the history of the United States. The conventional wisdom is that Hispanics have lacked organization or have been difficult or hesitant to organize, but this is not entirely accurate. Research has shown that throughout history there have actually been a large number of organizations in Hispanic communities (Navarro 2004; Tirado 1970). However, most of these organizations have been multipurpose organizations rather than specifically political, often operating in a style that is not easily recognized by Anglo American society. Historically, many of these organizations were *mutualistas*, multipurpose organizations that were set up to help members of a community, often new members of that community, such as immigrants, to feel at home and to provide them with services that they needed to become established (as well as to get them acquainted with the local political landscape).

7. **Leadership.** Undoubtedly, an organization with excellent leadership will be more effective than an organization with poor leadership. It is also true that leaders by themselves can make a difference regardless of the condition of their organization or constituency. Strong leadership requires leaders to have charisma and the ability to encourage others to admire and support them, take pride in them, and follow their direction. Hispanics have had many leaders, but many have been in the local communities—in the *barrios*; in the *pueblocitos*; in the *colonias*; and in the neighborhoods, small cities, towns, and villages, rather than at the state or national levels. Hence, the conventional wisdom has held that Hispanics lack leadership. Certainly, the Chicano movement and the subsequent decades have demonstrated that Hispanics have been able to develop effective leaders among their own. Some of the major efforts of Hispanic organizations have been to provide leadership training for their members, particularly for the young, who will be the future leaders of society. For example, the National Association of Latino Elected Officials sponsors major conferences for the training and skill improvement of Latino public officials. The Hispanic Congressional Caucus Institute and the Hispanic Leadership Institute offer seminars in training to develop leadership skills in young potential leaders.

8. **Motivation.** If people have the will or determination to get something done, if they feel strongly about an issue, if they will persevere in their actions, and if they will keep trying until success is achieved, then they possess an extremely important political resource. This kind of determination or willpower (termed *ganas*) can take people a long way, even if they do not have many of the other traditional resources mentioned. If Hispanics have the determination to better their position, to exert themselves, and to keep trying until they succeed, they will go a long way in politics, as will any people who approach the challenge of influencing the American political system.

SUMMARY AND CONCLUSION

Now that the major components of the input side of the political system have been laid out, we will examine each component in detail, with particular reference to Hispanics in the United States. Although Hispanics have always been involved in politics, they have often been at a disadvantage.

Resources that can be used to political advantage have been in relatively short supply. However, so far in the early twenty-first century, Hispanics are making strides toward increasing their resources, improving their lives, and achieving many goals, including political goals. As the population increases and Hispanics become increasingly aware not only of their own situation but also of the big picture in American politics, they are participating in ways that are likely to advance the Hispanic agenda. Unfortunately, progress has been slow and there are some aspects of participation that remain problematic for Hispanics, in particular, their participation in the electoral process.

In the following chapters, we begin by examining the most elemental and individualistic form of participation—voting—and proceed to look at forms of participation that involve group activity, including the activities of political parties and interest groups. As these organizations and associations are examined, we also discuss the topic of leadership in the United States, particularly as it applies to Hispanic politics. Moreover, because Hispanics are a numerical minority in many areas of the United States, and certainly nationwide, we look at the politics of coalition and alliance— a politics that is absolutely essential if Hispanics are to make the major gains in politics that they seek to achieve.

Notes

[1] For classic work on interest groups, see Truman (1951). Also see Hudson (2004) for a good review of interest or potential interest groups.

[2] The seminal work on social capital and the role of social networks in politics is Putnam's (2000) *Bowling Alone: The Collapse and Revival of American Community.*

5

Latino Public Opinion, Political Socialization, and Political Culture

To some extent, every type of government—whether it is pluralist democratic, elitist-authoritarian, or internal colonial—depends on the feelings and attitudes of its citizens. Every government rests on a psychological foundation of attitudes, beliefs, and values that requires a certain degree of support. Of course, a democracy such as the United States is much more dependent on the citizenry's psychological support for successful government than nondemocratic forms of government. Modern democracies theoretically reflect the will of the people, or at a minimum, rest on the consent of the governed. Therefore, what people think about government, how they feel about the people in government, how they believe government operates, and how much they are willing to support it are extremely important. Moreover, citizens of a democracy must believe in the basic rules of the game, that is, how politics is supposed to operate. They must accept the purposes of government—its goals and ideals, and its major values. In the American democracy, government is supposed to protect individuals' freedoms and rights, and promote equality and a feeling of shared responsibility.

In a democracy, people must have a basic sense of commonality. Ideally, they should not only tolerate each other but also respect each other's rights. They should experience feelings of community with each other and common pride (or patriotism) in the country's ideals. In the United States, this means that people should feel that Americans share a common bond, and this should involve at least a minimal level of shared attachment, if not affection. For these reasons, it is important to look at public opinion, political socialization, and political culture, particularly as they apply to Latinos.

In the United States, the government is supposed to be a government of the people, by the people, and for the people. To reflect this popular sovereignty, and to reflect the will, needs, and concerns of the citizens, these must be known to government. That is why in democracies, and most particularly in the United States, *public opinion* and its measurement have become so important. Public opinion can be defined as "the expression of ideas on matters of general importance by a significant number of people" (Hennessey 1981, 4). Although public opinion can be defined in many other ways and, in fact, is a slippery concept when one tries to pin it down, the term is commonly used by the media, by public officials, politicians, and by the general population. To say that public opinion supports one position or another on a public issue is to bring a heavy basis of support on behalf of that position because the public is theoretically the ultimate arbiter of any argument in a democracy (with the exception of some civil liberties and individual rights).

Hundreds, if not thousands, of public opinion polls or opinion surveys are conducted in the United States every year. Public officials—from the president to members of Congress to state and local officials—are constantly measuring their constituents' opinions to determine what the public thinks about them and their issue positions. To keep or win public support, candidates running for office spend tens or hundreds of thousands of dollars trying to discern what various segments of the electorate think about them, their personal characteristics, and their issue positions, as well as that of their opposition, so they can make the appropriate adjustments in order to maximize the number of groups that can be put together to enhance the chances of an electoral victory. The Clinton administration raised the use of public opinion polls to a new level; Clinton spent nearly $2 million conducting surveys and focus groups in his first year in office alone (Bardes and Oldendick 2007, 34). Polling, however, is not restricted to the presidential level; Senate and House members spend about 3 percent of their sizable campaign war chests on polling their constituencies (Fritz and Morris 1992). The media and academic research organizations are also continually plumbing the psyches of the American public, both for entertainment and human interest purposes and as an attempt to influence public policy. For the latter, and particularly for purposes of understanding why and what the public thinks about public issues, much demographic analysis is done, dissecting the opinions of the larger body politic into various demographic subgroups or subgroupings, including gender, age, race, ethnicity, income, occupation, religion, party affiliation, political ideology, and other subcategories. Often, it is these smaller "publics" that are examined as much as or even more than the overall public.

People's opinions on political and governmental issues do not spring full blown into their minds. They are the result of a lifetime of development and experiences that affect each person's opinion formation differently. Every individual also has a different genetic composition and physical character, and every individual experiences a unique upbringing—having different experiences with their parents and other family members; with their friends; during their years in school when their peer groups become of primary importance; with various organizations to which they belong; and with the all-important, all-pervasive media, particularly television, in this society. Each individual's political personality develops in a unique way, such that he or she develops a unique set of ideas, attitudes, and values about politics, government, and other topics.

This lifelong developmental process is called the process of *political socialization.* This is the process of political learning, or the development of political attitudes, beliefs, and values, that every individual undergoes in a society. Although each individual's socialization is unique, people also share much in common with other individuals, particularly persons living in the same society. For example, many individuals undergo similar political socialization—direct and indirect—in the American public schools. So, there is a commonality and uniqueness to this socialization, and society must attempt to civilize and socialize each new member of its system, whether it is a child or an immigrant, to share certain attitudes and values that hold the system together. It is much easier in a dictatorship, a totalitarian system of government, to control this socialization process than in a democracy, which is much freer, more open, and less controlled. Still, even in a democracy, it is believed that some common and basic values, ideas, and attachments must be inculcated in most individuals, or else the political system cannot hold together and will collapse (Easton 1965).

The result of the development of individuals in a polity over a period of time is an overarching set of shared values, attitudes, and beliefs that form a community's political culture. The *political culture* consists of the manifestations—all the outward signs of a group's attitudes and behaviors—that make one group distinct from others. Thus, Americans have a political culture that is distinctive from that of other countries in that Americans have a shared cluster of beliefs, such as support of democratic ideas, that distinguish them from the Chinese or Cubans, who believe in different goals for government, those reflecting a socialistic system and a different economic system than exists in the United States. Obviously, they also have loyalty to their own nations over other nations. This is a basic patriotism or nationalism that is instilled by virtually every nation to help maintain its existence. But within the greater American political culture with its identifiable set of beliefs, there are many smaller *political subcultures,* each of which has some variation of beliefs from that of the larger society. Typically, most of these groups share most of the basic values of other Americans. However, to be a distinctive political subculture, they must have some variation in their beliefs—some distinctions that make them unique and different from the larger group and from other subgroups.

In this chapter, we explore the political socialization, public opinions, and, to a lesser extent, the political culture of the ethnic subgroup called Hispanics or Latinos. Even though the knowledge of Latino public opinion is recent and still relatively minimal, we also look at the political socialization process of some Latinos in an attempt to gain some insight into how Latinos' public opinions are formed. In addition, we speculate some about Latino political culture. If there is a paucity of information about Latino public opinion, and even less is known about Latino socialization, almost necessarily there must be less known about Latino political culture. Latinos' political culture is the end result of the political socialization process and the sum of their public opinions, beliefs, attitudes, and values. It is true that there is very little, if any, solid knowledge about Latino cultural values in general, much less political culture. Nevertheless, we try to suggest some of its content and some of its parameters.

Because they underlie the behavior of Latinos, the psychological components of Latino politics give us clues into Latinos' past political behavior and how they may behave in the future. This will also help us understand where Latinos fit into the American political system, how they feel about it, and where they want to go with it. Such an examination will also help us jettison some of the myths and misconceptions held by non-Latinos about the way Latinos think and what they believe. While we survey these topics, it is important to remember that Latinos are an extremely diverse group, and although we must often speak in terms of generalization, there are often significant variations within the Latino community, particularly along such lines as national origin and socioeconomic status. It is also important to point out that community leaders and activists tend to have political views that are more extreme than the general public. For example, Latino organizational leaders tend to have more liberal views on immigration policy than Latinos generally. With these warnings and caveats in mind, we can proceed to at least explore, in a preliminary way, the public opinions, the political socialization, and the political cultures of Latinos.

LATINO PUBLIC OPINION[1]

One of the salutary effects of the increased recognition of the Latino population in the United States has been a commensurate interest in what Latinos think about various matters, including politics and public affairs. Until the 1980s, there were virtually no representative national opinion survey research studies that reported reliable and valid opinions of Latinos across the nation (de la Garza 1987). In fact, prior to 1990, there were no adequately sized, nationally representative opinion polls of Latinos focusing on politics and public affairs. Since the late 1960s, there have been a few studies of Latino opinions in cities in which they are concentrated, such as San Antonio or Los Angeles (Grebler et al. 1970). There were also some studies of one or another national origin groups, such as Mexican Americans or Puerto Ricans (Arce 1979). But measurements of political opinion that could be generalized to all or most of the Latino population in the United States simply did not exist prior to the Latino National Political Survey (LNPS) of 1989 and 1990 (de la Garza 1987).

In the 1990s, there was heightened interest in knowing what Latinos thought about various public matters, and increasingly, major opinion polling organizations began to report the results of Latino subsamples in their ongoing polls. However, these samples were quite small, usually comprised of about 100 to 200 respondents; therefore, their validity was questionable. With the approaching election in the year 2000 and the talk about Latinos being one of the most critical "battleground" voting blocs in the national elections, a few major nationally representative surveys of Latinos were taken by reputable organizations.[2]

As the twenty-first century progresses, it seems that regular polling of Latino populations is becoming a standard feature of the measurements of this nation's public opinions. However, several caveats about Latino opinion must be given before we examine some of what we know about the attitudes, beliefs, and values of Latinos on government and politics.

As with any measurement of public opinion, including those of the American public in general, one must be cautious about interpreting or accepting the results. All public opinion surveys are estimates of opinion and include variability due to the way the sample of people who are surveyed is selected and drawn, the wording of the questions, and the placement of the questions within the questionnaire. One should also be aware of what organization is conducting the survey and who is paying for it or sponsoring it. The details of the survey should be provided by those reporting it, and media interpretations should be supplemented by providing the exact wording and results of the questions in their reports. In addition to these cautions, such surveys that report the opinions of either the American public or the Latino public are gross generalizations.

Within this umbrella of aggregated opinion lies a tremendous variation due to the wide socialization experiences of individuals within the group and the base reflecting the various socioeconomic and demographic variations within these larger "publics." So, when Latino public opinion is reported, one must realize that this is an average, and there are probably substantial differences within those opinions based on such factors as different national origins, different regions of the country, varying levels of income and education, the number of foreign-born or native-born generations in the United States, and other demographic characteristics.[3] In fact, a major problem of most Latino public opinion polls has been that they have taken fairly restricted samples measuring opinion in six or seven cities with large Latino populations and reported this as "Latino public opinion"—without describing the limitations of the sample and without analyzing by socioeconomic status, nativity, or generation those variables that produce significant variations in opinion. Whether one is interested in overall general national Latino public opinion or whether one is interested in dissecting that opinion and understanding the various elements that can contribute to the overall opinions depends on the researchers' objectives in surveying Latinos. Typically, the media are only interested in general Latino public opinion, whereas social scientists, and sometimes campaigns and candidates, are more interested in some of the variation that exists within the Latino populations. Such finer differentiation allows political scientists to better explain the variations of political behavior within the Latino population and gives politicians information that helps them tailor their messages to targeted segments of the Hispanic electorate.

Given that there is only a relatively small and recent body of sound empirical data on Latino public opinion, the data that are reported in this chapter must be considered tentative and preliminary. However, it can be said that the major studies that have been conducted in the 1990s and later have been fairly consistent in their findings. At the least, what Hispanics think about government, politics, and public affairs seems to be important enough to warrant their inclusion in major studies and to even be the subject of separate studies. Latino voices are no longer silent or unheard as they were for many generations; instead, they have been added to the multitude of public preferences with which political decision makers must now contend. Latino public opinion is now often a significant political input.

One of the primary questions that the area of research on Latino attitudes has addressed is whether there is a distinctive Hispanic political community; that is, is it meaningful to talk about a "Latino public?" Answering this question involved examining how Latinos identified themselves, what they called themselves, with whom they associated, and with whom they shared feelings and values. When Hispanics are asked what label they prefer when referring to their group identity, they have consistently preferred to be identified first by their national origin (e.g., Mexican American, Puerto Rican, Cuban American). However, they are also very accepting of a variety of labels. A significant portion accepts "American" as a label, although that may not be their primary identification. In addition to their national origin names, a sizable proportion will also accept the terms that have been used over the years to refer to the collective two dozen or so groups this book is about. The two most commonly used names are "Hispanic" and "Latino." As described in Chapter 1, when the people themselves are asked which of these terms is preferred, the majority vastly and consistently prefers Hispanic to Latino. However, activists, academics, and some of the media substitute their own preference for "Latino" over the people's preference.

What seems to tie this group together more than anything else is their culture, primarily the Spanish language; some less well-defined commonality of feeling about ancestry; and their typically similar treatment in the United States. The various Latino national origin groups seem to believe that they are tied together more closely culturally than they are politically, and, in fact, shared political values or goals at a national level are difficult to perceive, other than those that are against discrimination and for respect and fairness. In questions of identification and community, there are significant differences between Latinos who are foreign born and have migrated to the United States, and those who are native born, particularly those who have resided in the United States for two or three generations. The native born have been socialized by the pervasive agents of political socialization in the United States. Typically, these generational differences are not reported, but there are often major variations in opinion among Latinos, particularly Mexican Americans, largely based on nativity, generation, and, to a lesser extent, socioeconomic status.

One of the widespread myths about Latinos is that they are foreign to the United States (e.g., "alien"), and they are often suspected of harboring foreign values and being less loyal and patriotic to the United States than other Americans. However, actual opinion research has provided results to the contrary. Latinos are extremely patriotic to the United States, particularly those who have resided here for a generation or more. Second- or third-generation Latinos want their children to be taught U.S. history and to learn English. They strongly believe in basic American values of freedom, liberty, and equality. In fact, their support for core American values of individualism and patriotism has been found to be higher than Anglos (Citrin et al. 2007; de la Garza et al. 1996).

Latinos overall are more likely than non-Latinos to favor a strong and active government that provides services to the people. Latinos as a group would prefer that government provide more public services, such as job training and opportunities, public housing, income support, health benefits, and other such collective goods. There are variations among the national origin groups, with Puerto Ricans being the most in favor of governmental support and activity and Cuban Americans the least so (de la Garza et al. 1992, 85–86).

This may be a reflection of another major point—an important feature of Latino public opinion that perhaps reflects an underlying cultural value—and that is that Latinos appear to be more "collectivist" or "communalist" in orientation than non-Latinos. They tend to place more emphasis on their group's advancement than on individual achievement. This is probably tied also to Latinos' strong emphasis on family and family values. For example, 82 percent of respondents to the *Washington Post* (1999) National Survey indicated that relatives are more important than friends, compared to 57 percent of Anglos. In addition, however, individual advancement is also supported, and Latinos' values also include perseverance, diligence, and a notably strong work ethic.

Surprisingly to some, particularly given their often less than favorable treatment by U.S. society, Latinos tend to be measurably more optimistic about government than non-Latinos (Uhlaner and Garcia 2002). They are also more trusting and less cynical about government officials (de la Garza et al. 1992, 81). As Hispanics live in the United States through succeeding generations and are exposed to the socialization experiences of Americans, their opinions increasingly resemble those of other Americans. In the case of attitudes toward government, as Hispanics become more aware and knowledgeable of politics in the United States, they unfortunately also become less trusting and optimistic (Michelson 2003; Wenzel 2006a).

So, Latinos' broad attitudes, values, and beliefs are much more like non-Hispanic whites' orientations than was believed before survey research demonstrated this to be the case. Latinos support democratic ideals and norms, including civil liberties and civil rights, and generally show considerable respect for public authority and satisfaction with public authorities. Some aspects of their public opinion become more similar to that of the general American public the longer they are in the United States.

Public opinion is one of the major inputs of the American political system. There is probably no better way for public officials to hear the will of the people than through regular and reliable sounding of American public opinion. With new attention being paid to Latino public opinion, Latinos now have an additional voice to express their needs, wants, and concerns to decision makers—what is it that Latinos want from government, what policies do they favor, and which do they oppose? Again, as we present the answers to these questions, it is important to remember that these are generalizations based on national samples, and there are significant variations within the Latino population from state to state, region to region, among national origin groups, and along other demographic lines, especially generational differences.

With regard to Latinos' basic political attitudes and beliefs, we also find many similar results regarding the Latino political *agenda* (i.e., what Latinos want or do not want government to do). Overall, this is very similar to non-Latino whites' policy preferences. For example, when Latinos are asked in open-ended questions what is the most important problem facing this country or "their communities," the answers provided are usually similar to those given by non-Hispanics. Almost always, education is at or near the top of the list, with concerns about the economy also being a top item (Uhlaner and Garcia 2002). Education seems to be the highest priority for Mexican Americans. We should recall that the educational difficulties faced by Mexican Americans are great, including their having the lowest level of educational attainment and the highest dropout level of any of the Latino groups, even higher than that of African Americans. Economic considerations are often high on the agenda because Latinos are typically much lower on the economic ladder than non-Latinos. Another concern that is often near the top of the list is that of crime, particularly drug-related crime. Latinos are urban people, and the problems of the central city are of direct and immediate concern to many of them.

With regard to *political ideology,* which is a system of interrelated beliefs, we have seen that Latinos overall do not vary much in their self-identified ideology from non-Hispanic whites. In fact, Mexican Americans' political ideologies are almost exactly the same as those of non-Hispanic whites, Cubans are somewhat more conservative, and Puerto Ricans (when self-identified) are conservative. However, when ideology is constructed from the groups' positions on various issues, Puerto Ricans are the most liberal, followed by Mexican Americans and Cuban Americans. Most Latinos are liberal in the sense that they support an active, service-oriented government; the protection of minority groups; and governmental endeavors that promote the material well-being of a group.[4] Latinos also hold some issue positions that are more conservative than non-Hispanics. For example, Latinos tend to be more in favor of the death penalty than whites and are slightly more opposed to abortions and homosexuality (Leal 2004; Uhlaner and Garcia 2002). Again, one must be careful about these generalizations because there is considerable variation among national origin groups as well as along generational and socioeconomic lines.

It is in the area of cultural issues that one finds the greatest difference in opinions between Latinos and non-Latinos. One might expect this because Latinos are a culturally distinct ethnic group. However, given that Latinos are spoken about as being such a different and distinctive group, perhaps their varying orientations toward culturally related issues may not seem as great as they could be. We do know that on many race-related issues, as well as on some other policy issues, there are significant differences between African Americans and white Americans. For example, African Americans are much more likely than white Americans to believe that government needs to continue to assist African Americans in achieving equality. African Americans also perceive many greater problems and obstacles facing them than their white compatriots (Dawson 1994; Tate 1993).

On many issues involving race, ethnicity, and culture, there is often a gap between black and white Americans, with the positions of Hispanics being in-between the black and white publics. This "betweenness" is a common pattern of Hispanic public opinion. For example, a 2001 Gallup poll (Saad 2001) reported that 42 percent of black Americans and 54 percent of non-Hispanic whites were very satisfied with their lives, whereas Latinos were in-between, with a 49 percent level of satisfaction. The same national survey reported that only 18 percent of black Americans believed that racial minorities have job opportunities equal to those of whites; 53 percent of non-Hispanic whites believed that there was equality of job opportunity; and Hispanics were in-between, with 46 percent agreeing with equality of job opportunity in this survey. Seventy-six percent of blacks said they felt discriminated against because of their race, while 64 percent of Hispanics said they occasionally felt discriminated against because of their ethnicity. Given that whites consistently maintain lower levels of perceived discrimination than racial and ethnic minorities (Tropp 1997), once again, the in-between pattern is found. In that survey's questions about each groups' community, 42 percent of blacks were very satisfied with their community as a place to live compared to 61 percent of whites. Fifty-three percent of Hispanics were very satisfied with life in their community (Saad 2001).

The same pattern is found on issues of discrimination and affirmative action. These issues are usually of little continual concern to white Americans, unless they are subject to some less common kind of discrimination or are opposed to affirmative action. The generally low-level priority given to these issues is in marked contrast to that of Latino spokespersons or leaders who are strongly in favor of affirmative action programs. In general, it is true that Latinos as a whole tend to be more supportive of affirmative action–type programs than whites and less supportive of them than blacks (F.C. Garcia 1997, 368–400; Lopez and Pantoja 2004). However, Latino opinions on affirmative action are complex, and their opinions vary greatly, depending on the specific wording of the question and the personal characteristics of the Latinos expressing their opinions on this matter. When Latinos are simply asked about whether they support affirmative action programs, support is usually quite high.

At this general level, one can find support for affirmative action from a substantial proportion of white Americans and very high support from black Americans as well. However, as one begins to probe deeper into Latino attitudes toward affirmative action, various complexities and subtleties emerge. For example, Puerto Ricans tend to support affirmative action more than Mexican Americans, and Cuban Americans support it less than either of these other two Latino groups and have attitudes more in line with those of Anglo Americans. When asked about specific items of affirmative action, such as using race or ethnicity as a criterion for admission to colleges and universities or in employment, one finds substantial variation: Puerto Ricans are very supportive, Mexican Americans are ambivalent or very opposed, and Cuban Americans and Anglos are highly opposed (de la Garza et al. 1990). Opposition to preferential or special treatment among Latinos is also least among those with higher education and greater income.

Although all surveys report that Latinos believe that they have been discriminated against more than non-Hispanic whites, answers to items concerning the amount and type of discrimination against Latinos vary tremendously. Cuban Americans in the Untied States seem to feel least discriminated against, but this is probably because most of them are less physically distinctive and many live in ethnic enclaves that are replete with Cuban American institutions. Recent measurements of Latino opinions on discrimination that include newly immigrated Central and South Americans, almost all of whom are foreign born, show that they perceive a significant level of discrimination. Puerto Ricans also seem to perceive more discrimination against members of their group (Pew Hispanic Center 2002). However, surprisingly low levels of discrimination have been reported in some surveys of Mexican Americans, particularly among those who have been in the United States for several generations. So, although it can be said that perceptions of discrimination do exist among Latinos, these perceptions vary greatly, depending on each persons' or groups' history and experiences with American society.

Immigration is another culturally relevant policy area that features much more complexity in Latino opinion than is generally supposed. Because Latino spokespersons and organizational leaders are usually very liberal in their positions on immigration, often advocating open borders, the eradication of borders between Mexico and the United States, and favorable treatment or amnesty for undocumented immigrants, the popular perception is that this is the position of Latino mass opinion.

However, several studies of Latino mass public opinion demonstrate that support for a more relaxed immigration policy is mixed at best. One finds some support for more liberal immigration policies and some opposition to it. For example, the LNPS indicated that 75 percent of Mexican Americans, 79 percent of Puerto Ricans, and 70 percent of Cuban Americans agreed with the statement that there are too many immigrants coming to the United States (de la Garza et al. 1992). In addition, it may be a surprise that in a list of Latinos' most pressing concerns, immigration policy is often far from the top. Immigration does appear on the Latino political agenda, but it does not have as high a priority as those other items mentioned previously that are common to all Americans. This situation may have changed, at least for the short term, in 2006. A Pew Hispanic Center (2006) survey reported that 14 percent of Latinos believed that immigration was the second "most important problem facing this country," following the war in Iraq.

Several surveys subsequent to the LNPS validated and elaborated on its findings on immigration. For example, the 2006 National Survey of Latinos: The Immigration Debate (Pew Hispanic Center 2006) reported that two-thirds of Latinos nationally believed that the number of immigrants allowed into the United States should be kept the same or decreased. The National Latino Voter Poll 2000 (Knight Ridder News Organization 2000) reported that 43 percent of all Latinos nationwide believed that the U.S. government was not doing enough to stop illegal immigration. However, Pew surveys beginning in 2002 have reported that almost half of Latinos surveyed favor increased *legal* immigration from Latin America, whereas about one-third would allow the same number to enter legally. Again, there is variation within the Latino population on this issue. Later generations favor a more restrictive policy than more recent arrivals (Binder, Polinard, and Wrinkle 1997; Knight Ridder News Organization 2000). For example, the National Latino Voter Poll 2000 (Knight Ridder News

Organization 2000) showed that support for curbing illegal immigration increases from 37 percent among foreign-born Latinos to 45 percent of first-generation U.S.-born Latinos and up to 50 percent for second-generation Latinos. That survey also found national origin differences, with Cuban Americans being most concerned with illegal immigration, and Mexican Americans being much less concerned about government intervention with illegal immigration. In addition, scholars have found that wealthier, more educated, and older Latinos are also more likely to support more restrictive immigration policies (Hood, Morris, and Shirkey 1997). There are also differences in Latino opinion on immigration from state to state. California Latinos tend to be more open to immigration than Latinos in Texas, New York, and Florida.[5] The picture of the attitudes of low-income Latinos is mixed because many of them are immigrants or first-generation descendants of immigrants and are supportive of freer immigration policies. But those who are personally impacted by competition for jobs are more concerned about the potentially harmful economic impact that more liberal immigration could have on them (de la Garza 1998; Wrinkle 1997).

It is necessary to separate the feelings of Latinos toward immigration, which sometimes include reservations, from sentiments toward immigrants. Many Latinos have positive and supportive attitudes about immigrants themselves and sympathize with their plight (de la Garza 1998). For example, Latinos are more likely than whites, African Americans, or Asians to support amnesty for illegal immigrants (Cain and Kiewiet 1987). Furthermore, Mexicans, in general, are more likely to support policies that facilitate the political and social integration of Mexican immigrants, such as bilingual education and immigrant access to services and citizenship (de la Garza 1998). Harsher discriminatory treatment against immigrants may remind later generation, U.S.-born Latinos of the treatment that they or their ancestors received in the United States and may work to help them create even closer bonds with new residents from Mexico and other countries.

The one issue that seems to be both the most distinctive from that of the black and white publics in the United States and also the most consensual among Hispanics involves language policy, including bilingual education. All major national surveys, including the LNPS, the Pew Hispanic Center (2002, 2004) surveys, and surveys in Texas and California, have found that Latinos are overwhelmingly supportive of bilingual education and, more particularly, of protecting and promoting the Spanish language. This is most true at a very general level in that Hispanics believe that it is important to preserve their culture, and the Spanish language is one of the most important, if not the most important, element in that (Houvouras 2001). Also, bilingual education means at minimum not preventing or inhibiting the speaking of Spanish but rather treating the language with respect while also teaching the unofficial but dominant language of the United States, which, of course, is English.

There is some variation in opinions on bilingual education and official English along lines of national origin, nativity, and citizenship, but in virtually every case the variation is just within the high levels of support (Uhlaner and Garcia 2002).

Although Latinos strongly support the Spanish language, particularly at a symbolic level, Latinos also exhibit a very strong desire to learn English as quickly as possible while preserving their native language. For example, the LNPS found that 70 percent of Mexican Americans, 74 percent of Puerto Ricans, and 77 percent of Cuban Americans agreed that the objective of bilingual education was to learn two languages. More than 90 percent of each group agreed or strongly agreed that those U.S. citizens and residents should learn English. Furthermore, less than 10 percent of Latinos believed that the primary purpose of bilingual education should be to maintain Spanish language or culture (Schmidt 1997).

In summation, although it has only been recently that major studies of Hispanic opinion on politics and public affairs have been conducted, we have now at least begun to establish some basic parameters of Latino public opinion. With the advent of this increased polling, some basic facts have emerged that should serve to dispel some of the myths and incorrect, off-base conventional wisdom that has been attributed to Latino orientations. Accurately knowing what Latino public opinion is should give the leaders of Latino organizations, spokespersons for Latino communities, and American public officials at all levels of policy making a much clearer idea of what an increasingly important segment of the American public thinks. This is very important because policy issues play an important role in shaping the voting preferences of Latino voters (Alvarez and Garcia-Bedolla 2003; Nicholson et al. 2006).

First, the stereotype of unpatriotic, disloyal Latinos with primary allegiance to their homelands has been continually contradicted by the findings of opinion surveys. Latinos are extremely patriotic; they love and support the United States. In fact, on measures of optimism and political trust, they are more positive than non-Latinos (de la Garza et al. 1996). Hispanics do share an affinity for their homelands and other Latinos, but not particularly for the government or public officials or the political systems of those ancestral lands. As with most other Americans, Hispanics believe in the American dream of liberty and equal opportunity. They also embrace the American ethos of hard work, integrity, and success. Although when self-professed, Latino ideologies overall are quite similar to those of most other Americans, when operationalized on particular issues Latinos tend to be a bit more in favor of an active, positive government, which would most typically be classified as a liberal position (Uhlaner and Garcia 2002). This is not true of all Latinos; Cuban Americans (and this demonstrates another major characteristic of Latino public opinion that it is not homogenous but instead is extremely diverse internally) often differ significantly along the lines of national origin, nativity, generation, region, and socioeconomic status.

The generalization that Latino public opinion is similar to that of the rest of America has been measured and found accurate. The Hispanic political agenda is also similar to that of most Americans. The major differences are on culturally related issues, most particularly on topics that embody the very soul of their culture, such as language policies, in which Latinos are fairly united and distinctive from those of non-Latinos. When Latino opinions are contrasted with those of non-Hispanic whites and African Americans, the Hispanic positions are often in-between the black and white polar extremes. Another myth that has been destroyed is with the discovery that Latinos are not at all consensual in their opinion on such issues as immigration and affirmative action. Latino elites, such as leaders of advocacy organizations whose assertions tend to be reported in the media, do not reflect the variation within the Latino community and the complexity of opinion below the general surface.

With their inclusion in the study of public opinion and the reporting thereof, Latinos now have another method and a significant one at that, of providing input into the political system—another important way of participating in politics by expressing their opinions to governmental decision makers.

POLITICAL SOCIALIZATION

As mentioned in the previous section, Latinos, just like non-Latinos, are not born with a full constellation of attitudes, beliefs, and values in their heads. Their political orientations are learned. They are formed as each individual develops from a newborn infant into an adult. These psychological orientations are the result of the interactions that individuals have with the environment around them. This process of the learning of political orientation is called *political socialization.*[6] Because Latinos are a distinctive ethnic group, it follows that Latinos are distinctive in some prominent ways—one of these most certainly being the cultural manifestations of their ethnicity. For the purposes of looking at Latino political socialization, this means that most Latinos would grow up in a subcultural environment, that is, a cultural environment that is different from the majority mainstream environment in some ways that are distinctive enough to qualify it as an ethnic group. These differences could include the way families rear their children; the mode and style of their interactions; the power relationships within the family; the values that are imparted by parents and other caregivers to the children; the kinds of food, clothing, architecture, music, interpersonal social discourse, and interactions; the experiences with schooling and modes of interaction with peers; styles of communication; contacts with the content of various media; religious experiences; treatment by members of other groups in society; relationships to government and its officials; treatment by authority figures; and many other experiences too numerous to mention. All of these influence each individual in complex ways. However, when enough individuals share a common experience, they tend to share a common culture, and this culture is the result of a socialization that includes sharing many of its features. To understand *why* Latinos think and believe the way we do, we need to examine the process of Latino political socialization because it is interactions between the individual and the polity that ultimately produce political orientations and opinions.

We have seen that our understanding of Latino public opinion is relatively new and sparse. Knowledge of Latino political socialization, that is, the process of developing those opinions, is even considerably less robust. Political socialization research was a popular area of research, study, and teaching for academics in the 1960s and 1970s. However, it has been out of vogue since the 1970s or so, and few studies of political socialization have been conducted since then, even among the general population. At the turn of the twentieth century, there seems to be a bit of a revival of interest in political socialization. This might be partly due to the fact that the United States is becoming so diversified, particularly with regard to its immigration, that once again people want to understand what experiences lead to certain orientations and behaviors, especially among its new citizens. Traditionally, the process of socialization has been focused on new citizens—those newly born into a society and those who migrate into a society. It is quite possible that the large-scale immigration of the 1980s and 1990s will prompt more studies of "the making of citizens" among the nation's newest residents.

Unfortunately, there is a great paucity of research on the socialization of Latinos, both children and adults. A few studies were done of Hispanic children in the 1960s and 1970s (Garcia 1973; Lamare 1975). Although they were limited in scope, they gave us some ideas on how political attitudes of Latinos may be formed and how they compared with those of non-Latinos. Much of the following is based primarily on the few early works that exist, plus some hypothesizing or even speculation about how and why opinions, attitudes, values, and beliefs of Latinos are formed and what implications they may have for Latino politics. The research is largely based on Mexican Americans, and unless otherwise stated, it is this largest group of Latinos that is being discussed.

One way to approach the socialization of Latinos or any other group is to look at the major "agents" of political socialization, that is, those people and institutions with which the developing citizen interacts. The first agent of socialization for most people, including Latinos, is the family, and most particularly the parents. One of the major principles of political socialization is that early socialization is one of the most important periods of development; this is the period in which basic orientations underlie, channel, shape, and otherwise affect later orientations. Children learn their most basic values and some beliefs from their parents or other caregivers, such as feelings of efficacy or being able to affect the environment, a sense of general trust or distrust of others, patterns of authority and power relationships, and basic morals, including the right and wrong ways to behave and to treat others. These general orientations have implications for their later political attitudes.

Children also seem to pick up some specifically political orientations a little later in childhood. Even though they do not fully realize cognitively what these are, they still develop a positive or negative affect toward such things as political authorities, political parties, and various groups in society. In effect, they are learning who are members of the "in group" and who are members of the "out group," or who are "we" and who are "they?" Latinos are widely known to traditionally have strong families and to place greater emphasis on familial relationships than most non-Hispanics in the United States (Garcia-Bedolla 2005). Moreover, many Latinos have an extended family, including aunts, uncles, grandparents, godparents, and others with whom they have close relationships. There are also lower incidences of divorce and separation and a lower incidence of nonfamilial child care among Latino families than among non-Latino families. Therefore, from what we know, it can be inferred that families are probably more important agents of political socialization for Latinos than they are for non-Latinos in the United States.

Thus, Latino political socialization probably reflects the influence of the family more heavily than non-Latino socialization. We know that African American children are less likely to be raised in a home with two parents than Latino children and that non-Hispanic white children are more likely to be given a substantial amount of their child care by nonfamilial agents, such as child care centers and nursery schools. The traditional Latino family has a reportedly fairly controlled environment, with strictly defined roles for each member of the family, including gender-assigned roles. The traditional Latino family is also viewed as being more hierarchical in nature, with more decisions being made by the parents exclusive of children's input. The traditional Latino family is more patriarchal, or ruled by the father, than modern American households. There has been some research that has cast doubt on this latter assumption, giving the mother a key decision-making role on domestic matters within the household. But in outside-the-house activities such as politics and public affairs, the male would be much more expected to be a participant than would be a traditional female. This pattern of political socialization could affect the way that Latino women and men view their respective roles in politics, which is a major arena outside the household.

Historically, the next major agent of political socialization children encounter would be the schools. In America, for the Hispanic population, this would mainly be the public (and some parochial) schools. The public schools are governmental agencies, and as such they are charged with inculcating particular values, skills, and knowledge in our future citizens. They are charged with instilling patriotism; teaching the country's often aggrandized history; promoting the superiority of this country's way of life; instilling the democratic creed and the so-called American dream in children; and preparing these future citizens with the basic skills for effective citizenship, such as voting, communicating with representatives, and other means of participation.

Previous political socialization studies have shown that public schools in higher socioeconomic areas impart different socialization training to their children than the schools of working class or poor families. The latter are much less involved in preparing future leaders, and instead emphasize the importance of becoming good law-abiding citizens, paying taxes, serving one's country, and similar "subject" rather than participant or leadership styles of political activities. Knowing what we do about the education of Latinos—that by and large there still exists secondary-level discrimination and that Latinos certainly are receiving less education than non-Latinos, and in many cases are receiving education inferior in quality to that of non-Latinos, does not bode well for their preparation as successful participants in politics (Meier and Stewart 1991). Education, in general, and a good civic education that teaches the skills of successful political involvement is essential for successful Latino political participation. It is much less likely that Latinos are receiving this kind of socialization than non-Hispanic whites, particularly those of the middle and upper socioeconomic classes in the public schools, not to mention the private schools. The private schools that most Latinos attend are denominational schools—overwhelmingly Catholic schools, and the Catholic tradition has been one of teaching its church members to be good followers, and to be humble, accepting, and unchallenging of authority—again, generally a more "subject" orientation than a participant or leadership orientation.

From what we have said about Latino political socialization so far, largely based on general knowledge about Latino society, one would expect that as Latinos develop in their traditional societies they would not be expected to be very active, competitive individuals in the political process.

Another important agent of socialization is the peer group. Peers are particularly important in adolescence, but they are also important sources of social interaction throughout adult life, such as in work groups and friendship groups. Because peer groups are difficult to study, little is known about their influence on political socialization. For Latino adolescents, growing up in a society in which they were generally devalued and that has different cultural values than their own, this must be an even more difficult time.

As adolescents try to figure out who and what they are, they must deal with relationships with adults, relationships with members of the opposite sex, questions about their own manhood or womanhood, questions of authority, and relationships to rules. For Latinos, added to this are additional questions of identity in a society that has not valued and has in fact devalued them. With whom will they identify? Will they identify with their Latino peers only? Do they try to bridge the gap between Latinos and non-Latinos, or do they identify with the superordinate whites rather than the subordinate Hispanic groups? They learn valuable lessons in power relationships both in and out of schools.

By the time they are in middle school, Hispanics have developed cognitive abilities to the point where they are better able to understand and make sense of what is going on in the world around them. They see that most of the people in positions of power and influence in the United States, particularly in the top levels of government, are not Hispanic. They have relatively few role models in public life to emulate, so they must look elsewhere for their role models. They may now learn more about the United States, its system of government, and its economic successes. They may compare and contrast these with the governments, economies, and societies of Mexico, Cuba, Guatemala, El Salvador, and other Latin American countries. It would not be difficult to conclude that interactions with peer groups among Latinos are not particularly conducive to promoting participation in politics and government.

A decade or so after the apex of emphasis on studying childhood political socialization, a few researchers came to the conclusion that there is another period that is of significant importance to the formation of political selves, and that was the period of adolescence and young adulthood—probably from about the ages of fifteen to twenty-five, with an average age of about eighteen to twenty (Shiraev and Sobel 2006, 98–99). It seems that at this point "generations" may be formed—that youth now have the background plus the cognitive and mental abilities to be aware of what is going on around them, they are not yet settled into the routines or the ruts of adulthood, and they are open to developments in the outside world. Major and sometimes dramatic events such as depression, wars, or major social movements have had impacts on people of all ages, but they seem to have the largest impact on people of this particular age group—so much of an impact that this often forms the basis for the reputed "generations" that are given labels and are treated as unique groups—such as the World War II generation, the Baby Boomers, or Generation X or Y.

For many older Latinos, probably the most significant political event that affected their political orientation during this time in their lives would be the Chicano movement of the mid-1960s to mid-1970s. During that heyday of Latino activism, the media was full of reports of active, even aggressive, Latinos engaged in conventional and even unconventional "radical" political activities such as demonstrations, marches, and protests, challenging authorities and the political system, and even establishing their own counterinstitutions. The media was replete with reports of heroes and role models such as César Chávez, Rodolfo "Corky" Gonzales, Reies López Tijerina, and José Ángel Gutiérrez. These were very dramatic and exciting times that would, according to most socialization theories, have great impact on the youth of that time. Indeed, research on the orientations of Hispanic political leaders has shown that one of the major factors accounting for those Latino leaders who believe that they have a special obligation to help other Latinos is that they were greatly affected in their youth by the Chicano movement (de la Garza and Vaughan 1984). As youth mature, they become more settled in their ways and focus on finding an occupation or a profession, getting married, establishing residence, and so on. Because there have been so many years of socialization experiences by the time of adulthood, changes that occur in later adulthood are much less influential and more incremental than the basic orientations that were established earlier in their lives. Indeed, it is the early orientations that shape and channel later orientations. Barring traumatic or dramatic events, adults usually do not change their basic political orientations, yet socialization continues to be important. Socialization never ends; people continue to interact with society. Their feelings, emotions, and knowledge continue to be affected by external events and relationships with other people. As mature citizens or residents, Latinos are aware of what is going on around them. They pay some attention to politics and public affairs. They discuss these and other matters on the job with their coworkers, spouses or significant others, and children, and they continue to be treated somewhat differentially by Latinos and non-Latinos. All of these experiences affect their opinions and attitudes.

The last and perhaps the most significant agent of socialization, after the family in contemporary times is the media. It is extremely difficult to generalize about the media because there are so many different forms. Yet, much of what is learned about the world outside the family is brought to us through the media. Most of what is learned about government, politics, and public affairs comes to us not through direct experience but through the media. Regrettably, throughout most of America's history, Latinos have usually been negatively stereotyped by the media, particularly the visual media, such as movies and later television.

Although the most blatant examples of the stereotyped Mexican—the violent "greaser"; the lazy, good-humored, serape-clad Mexican; the treacherous, cruel *bandito*—are largely gone, the visual media is still negligent in presenting many positive role models to the Latino communities. As mentioned previously, few of the news stories carry positive images of public officials who are Latino; instead, crime, drugs, and gangs, along with welfare recipients, are often emphasized when reporting news stories about Latinos. In addition, there are few Latino newscasters on major network television stations and in national television programming. Fortunately, the burgeoning numbers of Latinos in the United States have led to a corresponding major increase in the number of alternative Spanish language media outlets, including radio stations, television stations, magazines, and newspapers throughout the country. A few celebrities, particularly in the music and sports areas, have led some observers to the somewhat overstated and certainly premature conclusion that in the first year of the twenty-first century it was "hip to be Hispanic" (Granados 2000).

In addition to considering what political and governmental effects Latino experiences with these agents of socialization might have, we also have some data on the result of these experiences. Although not directly tied to them, a few studies measured the content of the orientations of Latino children. In a way, these early orientations could provide a window to the political attitudes and opinions of adult Latinos. These studies found that, for example, Mexican American children simply were less aware of their membership in their political communities, such as the nation, their state, and their cities than were their Anglo cohorts in the early grades of school, but by the beginning of high school, they were equally able to name the political communities in which they lived.

By the ninth grade, socioeconomic class seemed to be at least as important as ethnicity in affecting the youths' abilities to recognize and name their political communities and recognize symbols of those communities, such as flags of each nation. The degree of Spanish language usage and length of residency in the United States was a significant factor in this recognition. The roots of Latino pride in being an American are found in these studies, as young Mexican American children evidenced high pride in being American. These children are proud of being Americans because of such things as freedom—the preeminent value of liberty in this country. There are almost no differences in affection for the United States between Mexican American and Anglo American children. The only significant differences between the two ethnic groups appeared on questions relating to Mexico. On these questions, the cultural pride of the Mexican American children was evident. Even though they were as or more patriotic than the Anglo Americans, they still felt a special attachment to the country of their ancestral origin—a kind of "dual patriotism" (Garcia 1973, 24–50).

With regard to participation in government, it is interesting to note that Anglo American children became increasingly aware of, and impressed with, the importance of voting, but that Mexican American children's appreciation of the importance of voting among very young adults was almost the same as it was in the third grade. With regard to attitudes toward government, it was also interesting to note that the Mexican American children became more quickly disillusioned with governments' helpfulness and abilities and perceived a lack of responsiveness. Mexican

American children in California were much more favorably impressed with the national government than they were with their state or local governments. Economic class was also a major factor in evaluating governments, with the lower economic classes of both Anglos and Mexicans (but particularly Mexicans) being the most disillusioned with the government.

With regard to the basic norms and ideals of the American system, both Mexican Americans and Anglo children become disillusioned with the reality of democracy compared to its theory over their years in school. With regard to the component values of democracy, such as freedom of expression, equal opportunity, civil liberties, and civil rights, Mexican American and Anglo attitudes were similar throughout the years. However, Mexican American students were apt to observe that they were not treated the same as their Anglo counterparts. This was not true in the earlier grades, but by the time they were teenagers, Mexican Americans were well aware of this discrepancy.

With regard to participation, the Mexican American children were generally not sure about expanding participation in government. The young Mexican Americans were more likely to view democracy in "subject" rather than in "participant" terms. However, on questions dealing with mass participation, Mexican American youngsters did evidence a higher level of participant orientation than did their Anglo classmates. (It is important to recall that these studies were conducted during the height of the activist Chicano movement.) Overall, there was no significant attitudinal cleavage between Mexican Americans and Anglo Americans with respect to the democratic goals of the United States.

In the area of democratic norms of behavior, Mexican American children generally trust the American government about as much as their Anglo cohorts, but the cynicism level of both groups was high. Rural, lower class, mainly Spanish-speaking Mexican Americans were the most distrustful, although they seemed to enter the schools with a similarly high level of trust. Mexican American youth did manifest lower levels of a sense of participating in elections than did Anglo Americans. This was particularly true among the lower class Mexican American youth. However, during adolescence, Mexican American youth evidenced significantly lower levels of internal political efficacy (the ability to affect government) than did Anglo Americans. They were substantially less confident than Anglos that their activities as citizens would affect governmental decisions. Mexican Americans at that time, particularly those from rural areas and of the lower class, believed that much political activity was irrelevant or inapplicable to their own experience and that other forms of political activity such as strikes, boycotts, walkouts, and demonstrations might be necessary to have an effect on government.

In the study of Mexican American children in California, there were slightly different patterns of socialized orientations for Latinos and Anglos, and from that, one could infer different socialization experiences (Garcia 1973). There was also considerable variation within the opinions of Mexican American children, with socioeconomic class and Spanish language ability (a good measure of cultural integration) often being the two most important sources of differentiation. It is important to note that this was a study bound by time and space, as are all studies. It was conducted at the height of the Chicano political movement and in one of the most active areas of unconventional political activism—the state of California. Yet, other studies of the orientations of Mexican American youth, such as those taken in the state of Texas, produced similar results. One study did show that those Mexican American children who identified themselves as Chicano rather than as Mexican American or Hispanic also tended to be much more participatory in their orientations and much more aggressive in their behavior— much more willing to challenge the establishment (Hirsch and Gutiérrez 1977).

Surely studies thirty to thirty-five years later could be much improved in design and scope, and could provide some valuable insights into the sources of the political opinions of Latinos. In particular, studies of the way that immigrant Latinos of all ages become socialized to the American system of politics and government not only would be fascinating but would also have much practical importance for politicians and for people charged with providing good representative government for all U.S. citizens. Because a larger proportion of the population is comprised of foreign-born Hispanics, socialization research would be helpful in understanding whether and how Latinos might influence the political mainstream in the United States. Fortunately, there are signs that the socialization literature is moving in this direction, as a few recent studies have investigated the political socialization of Latino immigrants (Garcia-Bedolla 2005; Tam-Cho 1999).

POLITICAL CULTURE

If Hispanics are any kind of a "real" authentic ethnic group, and not just a loose conglomeration of distinctive national origin groups brought together mostly by the perception, treatment, and labeling by "out-group" persons and organizations, they are a group distinguished primarily by their culture. Hispanics are not a racial group, having the entire spectrum of physical characteristics, even though many or most are physically distinctive from persons of northern European ancestry. They are first and foremost an *ethnic* group whose primary ethnic characteristic comes from their connection with the Spanish culture and to a secondary extent their Indian and/or African roots. The Spanish language is the most salient and predominant characteristic of this culture, but there are other elements of the Hispanic culture that are also widely shared, such as their religion, which is primarily Catholic. So, underlying the bonds that tie Hispanics together in many ways, including politically, is the Hispanic culture. If there is no common Hispanic culture, any talk of a distinctive Hispanic political culture and consequently a distinctive Hispanic politics would be virtually meaningless. If Latinos are not distinctive in their culture, how can they be recognized, and how would their relationship to the mainstream majority culture be of any significance if it were the same?

Culture is one of the broadest concepts in the study of human societies. There are literally hundreds of acceptable different definitions of culture. Common to most of these definitions is that culture is the sum "way of life" of a people. It is produced by humans; that is, it is not carried in the genes but must be transmitted through learning from generation to generation. It includes virtually everything that a group of people produces— their language, building styles, foods, clothing, music, and other arts. There is also a psychological side to culture because people who share a culture generally share basic values; they have similar "world views," and these ways of thinking and beliefs are distinctive enough to give them a separate identity from other groups that have a different common configuration of attitudes, beliefs, and values. Of course, there are many individual variations within any large group, but there must be enough similarities to warrant a group's being recognized as a separate ethnic or cultural group.

For an idea as common and universal as culture, it is surprisingly difficult to use it precisely. Anthropology is the social science that most studies cultures, but culture in one form or another is also an important concept in other disciplines, including political science. However, for political scientists, culture—or more specifically, political culture—has usually been a problematic concept. For our purposes, we can simply define *political culture* as those aspects of a culture that are related to government and politics. This would include the ways that a certain group of people think and act about politics. For example, in the American political culture, the major ideal is democracy, which includes values such as freedom, self-government, equality, and individual liberty. U.S. political culture also includes norms such as participation, the rule of law, majority rule and minority rights, tolerance, trustworthiness, and obeying the rules. The U.S. political culture has been compared and contrasted with the political cultures of other nations and has been shown to be distinctive (Almond and Verba 1969).

Within the U.S. culture and political culture, there are many subcultures, groups whose ways of life or outlooks on life are so distinctive as to warrant special attention. Some are regional; for example, the regional cultures of the New England "Yankee" and the southern United States are substantially different from one another. Although the United States is supposedly a classless society, many would detect a significant difference between the lifestyles of the wealthy and those of the economic under-class, including a "culture of poverty." Because Hispanics are generally recognized as an ethnic/cultural group, almost by definition, one would expect to find a distinctive set of values, reflected in political values, among Hispanics compared to non-Hispanics. Although this may seem to be a mundane observation, there is actually a great amount of debate and controversy over Hispanic culture in general and Latino political culture in particular.

The subject of the political culture of Hispanics is a highly contro-versial one. There are several reasons for this. First, the general culture of Hispanics (or Mexicans, Mexican Americans, or Puerto Ricans) itself has been the subject of intense feelings and controversy. Throughout U.S. history, an extremely negative and derogatory view of the Spanish and Mexican cultures has prevailed. Many negative characteristics have been attributed to these cultures. They have been characterized as dis-honest, authoritarian, deceptive, slothful, dirty, violent, secretive, hate-ful, and treacherous—and these are just a few of the many pejorative features found in Anglo American pronouncements, writings, "stud-ies," and even official declarations by public authorities. Although many of these were obvious manifestations of prejudice and/or igno-rance, several social scientific studies of the early twentieth century bol-stered the public view that the Hispanic or Latin American culture was inferior and undesirable, if not completely dysfunctional. Many of these cultural traits have been attributed to Mexicans, for example, many of which were antithetical to the "American norm" (F.C. Garcia 1995).

However, many of these supposedly scientific findings were the result of flawed methods of research. Some studied only one small, traditional, rural village or one urban barrio and then generalized this to all Mexicans or Mexican Americans. Usually, these studies consisted of one individ-ual's personal observations, influenced by the observer's own personal characteristics, and were thus unable to be replicated or verified for their validity. Because so many of these "findings" painted Latinos in such an unfavorable light, they later became (and continue to be) intensely criti-cized by mainly Latino writers and social scientists. Some of them see the negative presentations of Hispanic culture as another tool of discrimina-tion and domination by the power holders in a system of internal colo-nialism. Almost all rightfully question the near universal negative stereotyping that has resulted in part from the commentaries on Latino cultures and their politics. There is considerable consensus that up until quite recently, a distorted picture of Latinos has been prevalent. Since the mid-1960s, mainly since the Chicano movement, several attempts have been made to correct and rectify this demeaning picture and to present a more positive, or at least a more accurate, picture of the behaviors, values, beliefs, and attitudes of Latinos. All these taken together would constitute a more accurate understanding of Latino culture and Latino political culture.

Several studies have begun to counter some of the conventional cultural stereotypes and provide some clues to aid in the understanding of Latino politics by better understanding Latino values. Yet, they have only scratched the surface. The student of Latino politics will continue to find references to cultural explanations of Latino political behavior that often rest on shaky ground. Not enough research has yet been conducted on Hispanic political culture to be able to use cultural explanations of Latino political thought and behavior. Moreover, with the notable exception of some political scientists who have conducted comparative, cross-national empirical research on political cultures, the use of political culture as an explanatory variable in political science research has itself been out of vogue for more than three decades (although there seems to be some renewed interest in it).

In this book, we can only look at a few examples of some aspects of Hispanic political culture to give an idea of how it has been typified and what has been learned about it. We have already taken a close look at some of the attitudinal components of Hispanic political culture in earlier sections, such as the foregoing section on public opinion. Although, this topic deserves much more exploration, in this section, one or two examples will have to suffice.

If we are interested in any differences that Hispanics might make in American politics, one essential bit of knowledge would be whether, or to what degree, Hispanic political orientations differ from those of the mainstream U.S. political culture. We know that some aspects of Hispanic culture differ from that of the mainstream culture or there would not be an ethnic group called Hispanics or Latinos. But will these values manifest themselves in *politics* in a manner that will substantially affect the way politics is conducted in the United States or in the public policies that are pursued and enacted? Will Latinos move into the political mainstream by bringing different values and goals to the system, or will these values either be excluded or perhaps included but then engulfed in the acculturation process of American mainstream politics? Culture is not static; it is dynamic and constantly changing as diverse peoples interact. There is no doubt that the core American culture has been and will increasingly be "Hispanicized." Conversely, the Hispanic culture or cultures in the United States are being acculturated to the U.S. mainstream every day. This continual cultural churning is an inevitable process that over generations results in a new culture for everyone.

We cannot leave a discussion of Hispanic political culture without recounting the fable of the "Hispanic crabs." This story illustrates how an alleged (negative) Hispanic cultural value is used to explain some purported political behavior of Hispanics:

> A person enters a store alongside a beach. Among the items in the shop are various seafoods, including a barrel of crabs. The shopper notices that there is no lid on the barrel and inquires of the clerk: "Aren't you afraid that those crabs will climb out of the barrel and escape?" The clerk responds: "No problem. You see...those are Hispanic crabs. Every time one of them climbs up and is about to reach the top, the other crabs reach out and pull it down!"

This story has been used for decades to explain why Latinos do not succeed in the U.S. society and how their culture holds back any individual who seeks to "make it" as an individual in this society. It attributes Hispanics' lower levels of political and economic success to themselves and their culture, not to exclusion or discriminatory practices and institutions of the dominant culture.

The allegedly dysfunctional cultural value usually tied to this story is that of *envidia* or envy. From this perspective, the Hispanic culture is supposed to be one that works to the detriment of any individual that attempts to climb the ladder of success. Hispanic communities will hold back or pull down anyone who tries to get ahead; in this sense, they are their own worst enemy. Another alleged cultural value that is sometimes found in this story is that of *familism*. According to the negative view of this cultural value, the primary (or only) obligation of an individual Latino family member is to the family (or community group). It is wrong for an individual to leave the family to seek individual achievement. Success must be for or with the family.

Several points about this political cultural story bring out its weaknesses. Is *envidia* actually a cultural trait of Hispanics? Empirical studies have provided evidence to the contrary about the existence of political *envidia*. The LNPS showed that Latinos hold opinions contrary to the Hispanic crabs story. For example, Latinos expressed the opinion that when any one Latino person succeeds, it helps the entire community. In addition, although envy is widely held to be an undesirable trait, concern for the family and its preservation is viewed from many perspectives as a highly desirable value. Why cast it in a negative light in this story? Even if some cultural traits are validated, how are they manifested in political behavior? There is very little, if any, knowledge about this.

Yet, the political culture of Latinos is important to understand both because it is the sum total result of the socialization process and because it is the overall structure on which Latino public opinion and socialization processes rest. Few persons have tried to explain Latino political behavior by references to political culture; most often it is used as a "residual" explanation, that is, when other measurable factors cannot explain a particular political behavior of Latinos, it is attributed to possibly being the result of the political culture of Latinos. This is saying that a particular political behavior (or nonbehavior) is rooted in the more general social behavior of a culture, but that so far its exact configuration has not been discovered or revealed. For example, after many other explanations have been offered and not all is accounted for, the often lower levels of participation of Latinos in elections may be attributed to the fact that theirs is a "fatalistic" political culture. This means that Latinos, due perhaps to their religious socialization as Catholics, are simply resigned to whatever happens to them on earth as good humble subjects. The purpose of their life is not to change things here but to lead a good, quiet, dignified life, and they will be rewarded in the hereafter. Again, little or no empirical evidence has been found to support this simplistic but widespread explanation. Another example of the use of political culture as an explanatory variable is found in some attempts to explain the relatively low political and socioeconomic standing of Latinos in the United States. Rather than looking at the historical experiences of discrimination and lack of opportunity, a political cultural explanation might attribute them to a general lack of achievement orientation, particularly on an individual basis. There does seem to be some evidence that Latinos are more concerned with the community and the group than with individual advancement and that in traditional Latino cultures helping the group is more important than success through individual competition. In contrast, American politics is a highly competitive and often individual-versus-individual kind of competitive game. Therefore, Latinos do not fare as well in the U.S. political arena. As indicated previously, lack of individual success may also be attributed to the reported political cultural values of *envidia* or familism. The high value that Hispanics place on the family may be seen as somewhat dysfunctional in a society in which family life is often subordinated to individual success—economic or political.

However, little, if any, empirical evidence has been gathered through systematic survey research to validate this or most other observations about Latino political culture. Nevertheless, or perhaps because of this, much of the conventional wisdom, usually negative, sometimes continues even in the folklore of Latinos themselves, many of whom would swear that *envidia* exists and is a major problem for Latinos, as well as being accepted by non-Latinos who are reaching for a facile explanation that absolves them of any responsibility and places all the blame for any negative or unfavorable situation on Latinos themselves. Although political cultural explanations are appealing because they are intuitive and not easily subject to scientific analysis, they must be approached with great caution. Well-designed and scientifically valid studies of political culture can potentially offer major insights, more subtleties, and a more completely developed picture of the attitudes, opinions, and the behaviors of Latinos in U.S. politics.

SUMMARY AND CONCLUSION

In this chapter, we explore the political socialization, public opinions, and political culture of the ethnic subgroup called Hispanics or Latinos. One of the primary methods of providing input to the American political system for both individuals and groups is through public opinion. Although until recently the Latino population has been virtually ignored by public opinion polls, we have been able to assess the various opinions that Latinos have regarding political and policy issues. After reviewing the extant literature on Latino public opinion, we conclude that Latino public opinion is very much like the opinions of the rest of America and the Hispanic political agenda is very similar to that of most Americans. However, significant differences exist on culturally related issues, most particularly on topics that embody the essence and soul of Hispanic culture, such as language policies, in which Latino opinions exhibit solidarity and are very distinctive from those of non-Latinos. As the Latino population continues to grow and become more prominent in American politics, we will have greater opportunities to assess the way Latinos think about politics across a number of issue areas. More important, with Latinos now included in the reporting of public opinion, they have a new and meaningful method of providing input into the political system.

In this chapter, we also look at the political socialization process of Latinos in an attempt to gain some insight into how Latinos' public opinions are formed. This investigation is critical because it is the interactions between the individual and the political system that ultimately produce the political orientations and opinions of the Hispanic community. It is clear that Latinos have different experiences and interactions with American political institutions from that of non-Latinos and that these experiences influence their political attitudes. In particular, family is more prominent in the socialization process for the Latino community, and negative portrayals of Latinos in the media may influence how Hispanics view themselves and the world around them. Finally, the study of the socialization process could be advanced tremendously by analyzing how the Latino foreign-born population becomes socialized into the American political system.

Arguably the most interesting aspect of this chapter and the entire text for that matter is the investigation of the political culture of the Hispanic community. Latinos' political culture is the end result of the political socialization process and the sum of their public opinions, beliefs, attitudes, and values. Therefore, determining the political culture of Latinos can provide a summary of the experiences, opinions, and values that drive Latino political behavior. We present several components of Latino political culture that have negative connotations and that have been used to suggest that the disadvantaged status of Latinos in the United States is the result of their own cultural norms and values. Although we attempt to dissect and discredit these notions, to a large extent, current social science data do not allow for empirical investigation of Latino political culture.

Knowledge of the attitudes, beliefs, and values of Hispanics is extremely important in helping answer the questions of whether they will be entering the mainstream rather easily, without a major clash between Hispanic orientations and those of the core culture. Moreover, these orientations could also play a major role in determining whether any differences will move American mainstream thought, practices, and institutions in a significant way.

In any case, by focusing on three important and unfortunately understudied aspects of Latino politics, this chapter advances our knowledge of the Hispanic community by introducing the public opinion, socialization, and political culture of Latinos to a new generation of students and scholars. At the least, this discussion might generate more interest in and research on these important aspects of an increasingly salient population.

Notes

[1] This section draws heavily on Uhlaner and Garcia (2002).

[2] Examples of these surveys include National Latino Voter Poll 2000 (Knight Ridder News Organization 2000), National Survey of Latinos 2002 (Pew Hispanic Center 2000), and National Survey of Latinos: Education 2004 (Pew Hispanic Center 2004a).

[3] A recent study asserts that there is a great homogeneity in Hispanic opinions and that socioeconomic differences do not reveal any significant variations of opinion within the Latino community. However, this study is based on only six issue-positions and does not include some demographic cleavages that are known to cause significant variations of opinion within the Hispanic population. See Claassen (2004).

[4] See Uhlaner and Garcia (2002) for a discussion of Latino ideology.

[5] These data are taken from the Tomas Rivera Policy Institute Survey (2000) of 2,011 Latino registered voters from the five largest states prior to the 2000 election.

[6] See Shiraev and Sobel (2006). A basic and comprehensive work on the topic is Dawson, Prewitt, and Dawson (1977).

6

Participation—Voting and the Electoral Process

As noted previously, much of the effective political activity in the United States is *group based* in this pluralistic system. However, there is still plenty of room for *individual* political activity. Perhaps the most elemental and basic individual level of political activity is that of *voting*. Indeed, if one asked a group of middle school civics students how citizens are supposed to participate in the political process, it is most likely that they would say through the act of casting a ballot (Jennings and Niemi 1974).

The idea of voting is implanted early in our socialization as one of the most important norms of political activity in a democracy; in fact, it is the way in which most citizens actively engage in politics (Verba, Schlozman, and Brady 1995). Other than reading about or discussing political activities, voting is probably the most common mode of participation. This individual political input activity has probably been studied and written about more than any other aspect of politics that is researched by political scientists. There is even an ever-expanding body of literature on the topic of Hispanics and their roles and activities in the electoral process (Barreto and Munoz 2003; Barreto, Segura, and Woods 2004; de la Garza and DeSipio 1997; DeSipio 1996; Garcia and Sanchez 2004; Leal, Barreto, Lee, and de la Garza 2005; Sanchez 2006; Shaw, de la Garza, and Lee 2000; Suro, Fry, and Passel 2005).

There is no doubt that voting is important. Voting is one of the most basic ways that citizens have of controlling their public officials. Every so often, elected officials must come to the populace to request that they be returned to their positions as the people's representatives. This act of legitimizing popular government is essential to a democracy. However, it is not the end all and be all of political activity. In some ways, it is a necessary but insufficient condition for political effectiveness; that is, even though citizen input through voting is far removed from producing a policy result that a citizen may want, it is still an important act. Although voting may not *directly* get a person what he or she wants with regard to public policy preferences, as many have stated, if one does not vote, one can be sure that he or she will be ignored by the politicians. This is also true for groups. If identifiable segments of the population do not vote or have a very low voting rate, campaigners, politicians, and public authorities are much less likely to pay them attention than they will those who have a higher rate of electoral participation. This notion underlies this chapter's focus on the political participation of the Latino community relative to other groups in American society.

LATINO VOTING TURNOUT AND REGISTRATION

Regarding Hispanics or Latinos at the beginning of the twenty-first century, the most accurate generalization that one can make about their rate of electoral participation is that it has been and remains strikingly lower than most other demographic segments of the U.S. population, including being lower than other identifiable ethnic and racial groups. Indeed this has produced one of the major questions for scholars who study Latino politics: Why do Latinos participate at noticeably lower rates in elections than other ethnic and racial groupings?

Earlier in our nation's history, there were several institutional and structural features that explicitly kept Latinos from the polls. For example, monolingual English ballots were often discouraging to predominantly Spanish-speaking Latinos. In some states, most notably Texas, registration procedures were particularly onerous, requiring long periods of residence at one address, thus discriminating against more mobile occupations, such as migrant farm laborers. Moreover, registration hours were set at times that made it very difficult for working people to register in only one designated place, such as the county courthouse, thus again imposing a particular burden on working class or migrant Latinos. In many respects, the Civil Rights Act of 1964 and the Voting Rights Act (VRA) of 1965 were policy attempts to remedy institutional practices that impeded participation by minority populations. The practices of literacy tests, limited registration periods and locations, poll taxes, and economic and physical intimidation were prohibited, and voting activities were monitored by federal officials. VRA, especially as extended to "language minorities" in 1975, is seen by many as being the single most important national legislation protecting and promoting the political status of Hispanics. VRA has been the basis for numerous court actions that sought to advance the franchise for Latinos. Provisions included the entrance of direct federal protection of Latinos' full rights at the ballot box by requiring preclearance and approval of changes to elections, including redistricting of constituencies, by the states. It also provided for the provision of bilingual ballots in places where they were needed. Perhaps most important, it provided a strong statutory basis for the redrawing of electoral districts so persons such as Hispanics who had experienced "minority vote dilution" due to gerrymandering could now have districts redrawn in a manner that gave them a large majority in those districts—the so-called majority-minority districts.

The courts have also been vital contributors in this area, as case law such as *Smith v. Allwright* (1944; which eliminated white primaries) and *White v. Regester* (1973; which challenged at-large election systems), as well as constitutional amendments that prohibited the poll tax and gave eighteen-year-olds the right to vote, served as examples of legal remedies designed to remove structural obstacles to participation. To implement VRA, election officials provided bilingual materials and assistance for elections to benefit linguistic minorities, including Latinos. Therefore, this long history of structural and institutional barriers for Latino political participation has been eradicated through federal legislation, court cases, and constitutional amendments.

Some of the other reasons for the notably low participation of Latinos in elections are presented in this chapter, but our research at this point does not satisfactorily or completely address this issue. Table 6.1 provides a graphic illustration of comparative voting rates between a few major ethnic and racial groups in U.S. presidential elections over the past nine presidential elections. Immediately, the very low numbers for Hispanics stand out, and there is a relatively easy, first-level explanation for much of the lower rate. That is the fact that a large and increasing proportion of Hispanics are not citizens. Indeed, in 1990, about 20 to 25 percent of Hispanics in the United States were not citizens. In the year 2000, roughly 40 to 50 percent of the Hispanic population was noncitizen, and by the year 2010, it is estimated that as much as 70 percent of the Hispanic population will be noncitizen. Obviously, because noncitizens cannot vote, this immediately and greatly lowers the pool of eligible voters and consequently the number of those who are legally able to vote (*Eligible* voters are citizens who are at least eighteen years of age).

The voter participation figures historically provided by the U.S. Bureau of the Census have been based on a percentage of the voting age population (VAP) of residents in the United States who claim they have turned out at the polls. Because of the large number of Latino noncitizens (estimated at between 40 and 50 percent in 2006), the Latino voter participation rate seems much lower than it actually is. In its report of voting patterns in the November 2000 election, the U.S. Bureau of the Census (2002b) made a major change in its reporting. It changed its historical method and began to adjust its numbers by taking citizenship into account.

When adjusting for citizenship and using the number of *registered* voters (i.e., persons who are eligible to vote) as a base for Latino voter turnout, one finds that approximately 44 percent of Latinos who were citizens and were registered turned out to vote in 1996. This compares with 53 percent of African American registered voters and 60 percent of white Americans. Again, controlling for citizenship, the Latino *registration rate* was 59 percent of the voting age population, which was somewhat lower than for African Americans (67 percent) and thirteen percentage points below that of white citizens (72 percent).

Table 6.1
REPORTED VOTING BY RACE: U.S. PRESIDENTIAL ELECTIONS, 1972–2004 (PERCENTAGE)

	2004		2000[d]		1996	1992	1988	1984	1980	1976	1972[c]
	Citizen	VAP	Citizen	VAP[a]							
Total voting age (in 1000s)	215,694		202,609		193,651	185,684	178,098	169,963	157,085	146,548	136,203
Voted	63.8	58.3	59.5	55.0	54.2	61.3	57.4	59.9	59.2	59.2	63.0
Race											
White	67.2	65.8	61.8	60.4	56.0	63.6	59.1	61.4	60.9	60.9	64.5
Black	60.0	56.3	56.8	53.5	50.6	54.0	51.5	55.8	50.5	48.7	52.1
Hispanic origin[b]	47.2	28.0	45.1	27.5	26.7	28.9	28.8	32.6	29.9	31.8	37.5

Source: Current Population Report Series P20, nos. 192, 253, 322, 370, 405, 440, 466, 542; November 1996 Current Population Survey.
[a]Civilian, noninstitutional.
[b]Hispanics may be of any race
[c]Prior to 1972, data for people 21–24 years of age, with the exception of those 18–24 in Georgia and Kentucky, 19–24 in Alaska, and 20–24 in Hawaii.
[d]Prior to 2000, data are based on voting age population (VAP), including noncitizens. Beginning in 2000, data are reported for both citizens and VAP.

In the 2000 national election, these percentages or proportions changed very little. The Hispanic citizen registration rate was at 57 percent compared to 68 percent for African Americans and 70 percent for white Americans. Hispanic citizens' voting turnout in 2000 was 45 percent; that of African Americans was 57 percent; and for whites it was 61 percent (U.S. Bureau of the Census 2002b). In both the 1996 and the 2000 national elections, the turnout rate for Hispanic citizens was 15 percent lower than the national average. So, even controlling for citizenship, Latinos turned out at a much lower rate.

In July 2005, the U.S. Census Bureau released some results from the 2004 elections based on its November 2004 Current Population Survey. These percentages for Hispanics looked much the same as they had over the past several elections. Of the total VAP in the United States, 65.9 percent were registered to vote; for Hispanics, the rate was 35.3 percent. Among eligible (citizen) persons, 58 percent of Hispanics who were citizens and of age were registered compared to 75 percent of non-Hispanic whites and 69 percent of African Americans. (In 1996, the registration rate was 59 percent; in 2000, it was 57 percent.) Of the total population in 2004, 58.3 percent reported voting compared to 28.0 percent of the Hispanic population older than eighteen years. These numbers include noncitizens, which comprised about 9 percent of the total population and 41 percent of the Hispanic population. Among persons eligible to vote, 47 percent of eligible Latinos actually voted, as did 60 percent of African Americans and 67 percent of whites. As a percentage of registered voters, voter turnout in 2004 was 89 percent for whites, 87 percent for African Americans, and 82 percent for Latinos. Hispanics were more likely than most non-Hispanics to cite being "too busy" or having "registration problems" as reasons for not voting.

Still, in some ways, the participation of the Hispanic electorate was impressive, mainly because of its growth in raw numbers compared to the rest of the population. For example, there was a 23 percent increase in the number of Latino votes cast from 2000 to 2004. This more than doubled the voting growth rate of the total electorate (Suro et al. 2005). Yet, as other observers have also noted, the increase in voters was notably low compared to the growth rate of the Hispanic populace in general (Leal et al. 2005). Latinos comprised half of the increase in the total U.S. population between 2000 and 2004 but only 10 percent of the increase in total votes cast. Approximately one-third of the increase was adult immigrants who came to the United States during that time, whereas approximately two-thirds were illegal immigrants. Births have contributed a large proportion of the population increase, but about one third of those were still too young to vote. Because such a large proportion of the Latino population is young, and because it will at best be a lengthy period of time before those who were legal immigrants and who will be naturalized will be eligible to vote, it is expected to be some time before even those who are eligible to vote are any reflection of the political *power* potential inherent in the general increase in the Hispanic population.

There are variations within and exceptions to the general pattern of Latino voter participation. For example, Cuban Americans vote at a rate that is comparable and sometimes even greater than that of non-Hispanic whites (de la Garza et al. 1992). Most likely, their higher socioeconomic status is a major factor here. In addition, they have been in a situation of relative empowerment and community of interests and culture within their ethnic enclave in the Miami-Dade County area. Puerto Ricans vote in considerably lower numbers than other groups while on the mainland, although interestingly enough, on the island of Puerto Rico, they vote at a rate of 80 to 90 percent. Their status as a somewhat excluded, alienated, lower socioeconomic ethnic group on the mainland compared to their "mainstream" status on the island greatly contributes to this. Mexican Americans also illustrate a low level of voter participation. Because there is variation among national origin groups in electoral participation, there is also considerable variation between different areas of the country. For example, Hispanics in New Mexico have a relatively high voting rate (40 percent of the voting age population in 2000) as compared to Hispanics in California (25 percent), so regional differences also exist (Garcia and Sierra 2004). These mainly have to do with the unique historical circumstances of each region. In addition, a large proportion of the Latino electorate of New Mexico is comprised of native-born, English-speaking Hispanics, a far greater proportion than is found in the Hispanic population as a whole.

REGISTRATION

Granted these variations, why is the average turnout still so low? When we look at the registration numbers, this starts to give us some clues (Table 6.2). For several years, Hispanic *voter registration* had been closer to the level of non-Hispanic whites than was the level of actual voter turnout. One of the reasons for this is that there has been a great emphasis placed on registration drives aimed at Hispanics throughout the United States. One of the foremost organizations that has engaged in massive voter registration drives over the years is the Southwest Voter Registration and Education Project (SVREP). SVREP has been engaged in voter registration drives across the Southwest, in the *barrios, colonias,* and *campos* throughout the region, for several decades. Other organizations, such as the Midwest-Northeast Voter Registration Project (which lead to the National Hispanic Leadership Agenda in 1996), the National Association of Hispanic Elected and Appointed Officials, the Mexican American Legal Defense and Education Fund, and the Puerto Rican Legal Defense and Education Fund, have also been engaged in extensive and expensive voter

Table 6.2

Reported Voter Registration by Race: U.S. Presidential Elections, 1972–2004 (Percentage)

	2004		2000		1996	1992	1988	1984	1980	1976	1972[c]
	Citizen	VAP	Citizen	VAP[a]							
Total voting age (in 1000s)	215,694		202,609		193,651	185,684	178,098	169,963	157,085	146,548	136,203
Overall registered	72.1	65.9	69.5	63.9	65.9	68.2	66.6	68.3	66.9	66.7	72.3
Race											
White	73.6	67.9	71.6	70.0	67.7	70.1	67.9	69.6	68.4	68.3	73.4
Black	68.7	64.4	67.5	63.6	63.5	63.9	64.5	66.3	60.0	58.5	65.5
Hispanic origin[b]	57.9	34.3	57.3	34.9	35.7	35.0	35.5	40.1	36.3	37.8	44.4

Source: Current Population Report Series P20, nos. 192, 253, 322, 370, 405, 440, 466, 542; November 1996 Current Population Survey.

VAP, voting age population.

[a]Civilian, noninstitutional.

[b]Hispanics may be of any race.

[c]Prior to 1972, data for people 21–24 years of age, with the exception of those 18–24 in Georgia and Kentucky, 19–24 in Alaska, and 20–24 in Hawaii.

registration and voter protection efforts in the courts. Consequently, the registration figures for Latinos had been raised to a level almost as high as those of non-Hispanic whites when based on citizen numbers only. Yet, there was a considerable drop-off from registration to the voting act, and this drop-off is significantly greater for Latinos than for non-Latinos. For a long time, the rule of thumb was that about 80 percent of non-Hispanic whites who are registered actually turn out to vote. Among Latinos, the number ranges from 67 percent to a little more than 75 percent of those registering actually going to the polling places.

The 2000 and 2004 registration rates were significantly lower for Latinos than for others. In 2000, 57 percent of eligible Hispanics and 72 percent of whites were registered to vote (U.S. Bureau of the Census 2002b). In 2004, only 58 percent of Latinos were registered compared to 69 percent of blacks and 75 percent of whites (U.S. Bureau of the Census 2005). These numbers were in spite of continued major campaigns by various organizations or increasing Latino participation.

There have been several studies that have examined this lower rate of Latino voter registration in order to try to explain the lower rate of voter participation by Latinos. Some studies have focused on *socioeconomic factors* and have found that demographic variables that depress the level of voting among non-Hispanics also do so among Hispanics (Leighley and Vedilitz 1999; Verba et al. 1995). In fact, among Hispanics these vote-lowering factors are even stronger and more abundant, thus further depressing the rate of voter participation. For example, low levels of income; low levels of formal education; and low-paying, low-prestige occupations are all correlated with lower voting in general, and Latinos are concentrated in the lower levels of all these socioeconomic groupings (Chávez 2004).

Moreover, *age* is an important demographic variable in voting because younger voters have a greatly reduced rate of voting compared to persons in older age groupings. Those in the eighteen- to twenty-four-year-old age group, for example, voted at only half the rate of sixty-five- to seventy-four-year-olds in 2000. Because the Latino population is on average about nine to ten years younger than the non-Latino population, this is another demographic feature that is associated with the lower voting rate of Latinos. In addition, research has found that factors that indicate a longer- or greater-standing stake in U.S. society tend to raise voting levels. Thus, as with people from other ethnic groups, Hispanics who have been in the United States a longer period of time, or who have established residence and are home owners, for example, tend to vote at higher rates than people who have not done these things. As these "negative" socioeconomic indicators that depress voting continue to slowly diminish, it is likely that their improvement will also be correlated with higher rates of voting for Latinos.

The characteristic of being either born in the United States or being an immigrant also has some interesting effects on the electoral participation of Latinos, as does the act of naturalization itself. In 2004, foreign-born Latino citizens were more likely to register (60 percent vs. 57 percent) and vote than were the U.S. born. Eighty-seven percent of the registered foreign-born Latinos reported that they voted compared to 80 percent of the native-born adult Latinos (Suro et al. 2005). However, there has been extensive research discussing the obstacles that Latino immigrants face when trying to become active participants in American politics, including the attainment of citizenship (Jones-Correa 1998). Although there are contrasting viewpoints on the matter, the Pew Hispanic Center concluded that the naturalization process itself increases the enthusiasm of Latinos for participating in U.S. elections (Suro et al. 2005, 8). This trend may help explain why other research has found that foreign-born Mexicans are no less likely to participate in American politics than their native-born counterparts (Barreto and Munoz 2003). Finally, recent analysis has found that naturalization associated with the Immigration Reform and Control Act did not spur the recent increases in Latino political participation as many have suggested (Barreto, Ramirez, and Woods 2005). This study sheds light on the potential of currently debated proposals in U.S. Congress to legalize many of the undocumented individuals living in the United States to impact the electorate.

Another approach at understanding lower Latino voting participation has been to look at some *psychological* or *attitudinal* features. Of course, such sociopsychological factors have been found to be important determinants of voting behavior among all people (Almond and Verba 1963; Liu 2001; Verba et al. 1995). With regard to Hispanics, the results of these studies are more mixed. Some investigators have found that Hispanics, or at least Mexican Americans, often have attitudes such as a sense of civic duty or high levels of political trust and corresponding low levels of cynicism, optimism, and feelings of efficacy. These are generally correlated with higher levels of voting (J. Garcia 1997; Garcia and Arce 1988; Michelson 2003c). Yet, other studies show that Latinos have some attitudes such as lower self-esteem, feelings of being excluded from the society (i.e., discrimination), and less interest and knowledge about public affairs— characteristics that are correlated with a lower level of voting (J. Garcia 1995; Hero 1992a). So, it is not yet clear which attitudinal factor or combination of factors leads to the lower voting rate of Latinos.

It is important to note some other features of Latino voting turnout patterns. One is that the actual raw *numbers* (which are what count in elections rather than percentages) of Latinos voting in national elections have continued to grow significantly over the years. Another is that Latinos as a portion of the total electorate (i.e., people who actually participate in the elections) have also continued to increase steadily (if less dramatically) throughout the years. These numbers have risen to the point where in the 2004 general election, Latinos comprised about 8 million voters (estimated by the National Council of La Raza at 7.6 million and calculated by the Pew Hispanic Center at 7,587,000) voters or 6 percent of the total electorate, compared with 5.5 percent in the 2000 election, 5 percent in the 1996 election, and 4 percent in the 1992 election (Pew Hispanic Center 2005). (Other studies of the 2004 and earlier elections have reported the Hispanic share of the electorate to be greater, including as high as 8.4 percent in the 2004 election.) This would be about a 23 percent increase from the 2000 race. Although Latinos are still a relatively small proportion of the electorate, many elections, and certainly the 2000 presidential election, are won or lost by a much smaller margin than several percentage points. Perhaps most important, all agree that the Latino electorate is recognized as one social group that has been continuously and dramatically expanding in numbers and is projected to continue doing so.

Moreover, Latinos are located and distributed in such a way that they can be key voting blocs in elections, particularly presidential elections. Latinos are concentrated in some states that have the largest numbers of presidential electoral votes, such as California, Texas, New York, Illinois, and Florida. Because the presidential candidate who wins the popular vote in any of these states (by no matter how slim a margin) wins *all* of that state's electoral votes, Latinos are strategically located to be major players in the presidential politics of the Electoral College. However, for their influence to be maximized, the election must be competitive (i.e., very close between the contenders) so the relatively small Hispanic vote can make a difference. The lack of competitiveness in recent presidential elections within states that have the greatest Latino concentrations may minimize the influence of Latino voters. For example, California and New York have been overwhelmingly Democratic and Texas heavily Republican, and thus they were not seen as contested or competitive states. Moreover, to play a strategically important role, Hispanics must also be *swing voters*—that is, to maximize their potential influence at the polls, Latinos must be able to switch back and forth among parties and candidates, depending on which individual or group is most likely to advance Latino interests. In a close election, the movement of one "bloc" of voters toward a candidate may just be enough to give that candidate the winning margin. In presidential elections, whichever candidate wins the vote in a state, even by a margin of a single vote, is awarded *all* the electoral votes of that state. If it is perceived that a recognizable group of voters is up for grabs, this group becomes a "target" group, and their vote highly courted. When added to the known "base" of supporters, the targeted group's vote can make the difference between winning and losing all the electoral votes of any state.

Although strategically located, Latinos historically have not been major players in *national* politics. One reason is because of their relatively small numbers. The second is they have *not* been swing voters; instead, they have been strongly committed to one party or another in presidential elections (Table 6.3). This commitment has been to the Democratic Party and the Democratic presidential candidates. On average, since this has been measured, about 67 to 68 percent of the Latino vote has gone to the Democratic presidential candidate over the years. (As indicated previously, Cubans are the exception to this trend.) When a Republican candidate garners 37 percent of the Hispanic vote, as Ronald Reagan did in 1980, or perhaps even 35 percent of the vote, as George W. Bush did in 2000, Republicans have been known to declare this as a moral victory. In the 2004 presidential election, when estimates were that the Latino vote

Table 6.3
DIRECTION (PARTY CHOICE) OF LATINO VOTE IN PRESIDENTIAL ELECTIONS, 1960–2004

Year	Democrat Vote (%)	Republican Vote (%)	Other Vote (%)
1960	75–85	15–25	
1964	90	10	
1968	87	10	3
1972	64	36	
	80	20	
	56	15	
1976	82	18	
1980	56	37	7
1984	66	34	
	68	32	
	56	44	
1988	70	30	
	70	30	
	69	69	
	62	62	
1992	62	24	14
	53	31	16
1996	72	21	
2000	67	31	2
	62	35	3
2004	53	44	2
	53	45	2
	68	32	

Data are derived from estimates, including exit polls. Results from 1960 to 1972 are for Mexican Americans only. When more than one result is given for any election, it is because more than one estimate (or exit poll) was reported that year.

Sources: Compiled by the authors from media exit polls, including ABC, CBS, CNN, Fox, NBC, *Los Angeles Times*, *New York Times*, Voter News Service (VNS), and the National Election Pool (NEP); and also from Mark R. Levy and Michael S. Kramer, *The Ethnic Factor: How America's Minorities Decide Elections*, p. 228.

for George W. Bush was about 38 to 40 percent, some observers believed that this was a very significant breakthrough for the Republican Party. However, it is not certain that the 2004 vote was actually indicative that Hispanics had been transformed into a swing voting bloc. (Indeed, the percentage of the Hispanic vote for Bush, based on exit polls, has been questioned and intensely debated.[1])

It may be that this movement of some three to six percentage points was almost entirely due to the particular circumstances of that election and did not portend anything more significant in terms of long-range Hispanic voting patterns. The particular appeal, or non-appeal, of the candidates themselves was undoubtedly a major factor, as were the state of the nation and world at that time and the effectiveness of each party's campaigns and mobilization efforts. The style and personality of incumbent President Bush seemed to be more compatible with the social and personal style of many Latinos than was the perceived more elite, less folksy, and more northeastern Yankee character of his opponent, John Kerry. Moreover, the nation was at war in Iraq and Afghanistan and under the threat of attack by terrorists at home. This played to the advantage of the incumbent president, who is the commander-in-chief of the armed forces and the symbolic chief of state. The traditional moral values held by Hispanics and featured prominently in the 2004 campaign by the Republican Party, such as those regarding family, same sex marriage, and abortion, may have been especially attractive to Hispanics, particularly the growing number of evangelical, fundamentalist Hispanic Protestants. Moreover, it seems that the national Republicans were more determined, and also more effective, in reaching Hispanic voters with the most attractive messages and in organizing more effectively at the grassroots level to get Hispanics to the polls.

The Democratic leanings of Hispanics nationally have also been evident in their voting for the U.S. congressional candidates. As Table 6.4 shows, Hispanic voters have been at least as committed to Democratic candidates for the U.S. Congress as they have been to the presidential tickets. In congressional elections, especially for the House of Representatives, the party identification of voters and candidates is even more significant in affecting the vote than it is in voting for the president. Furthermore, support for Democratic congressional candidates in 2004 has been used as evidence that any Latino shift to the Republican Party may be short lived. Even in localities where Bush garnered a significant segment of the Latino vote, the Republican congressional candidates did not share the same success. Specifically, Representative Barbara Boxer in California garnered 73 percent of the Latino vote compared to Kerry's 63 percent, and Ken Salazar did much better with Latinos than did John Kerry. The congressional elections of November 2006 added strength to the observations that Hispanic support for national Republican candidates might have been only a "blip" since early estimates had congressional Democrats receiving 61 or 70 percent of the Hispanic vote.

Table 6.4

HISPANIC TURNOUT, REGISTRATION RATE, AND PARTY CHOICE IN CONGRESSIONAL (U.S. HOUSE OF REPRESENTATIVES) ELECTIONS, 1980–2004

Year	Democrat Vote (%)	Registration Rate (%)	Turnout Among VAP (%)
1980	72	36.3	29.9
1982	75	35.3	25.3
1984	69	40.1	32.6
1986	76	35.9	20.2
1988	76	35.5	28.8
1990	72	32.2	21
1992	72	35	28.9
1994	61	31.4	24
1996	73	35.7	26.7
1998	63	33.7	20
2000	64	57.3	45.1
2002	61	32.6	18.9
2004	55	34.3	28

VAP, voting age population.

Sources: All turnout and registration data are taken from U.S. Census CPS Reports. Turnout and registration data from 1974 to 1998 are taken from CPS Report "Voting and Registration in the Election of November 1998." Turnout and registration data for 2000 to 2002 are taken from CPS Report "Voting and Registration in the Election of November 2002," and 2004 from CPS Detailed Reports "Voting and Registration in the Election of 2004." % Democratic vote for years 1980 to 2000 are taken from the *Almanac of Latino Politics* (2004), published by the U.S. Hispanic Leadership Institute. % Democratic for 2002 is taken from "Table 3-10 Congressional Vote in General Elections, by Groups, 1994 to 2004 (percent)." CQ Electronic Library, CQ's Vital Statistics on American Politics Online Edition.

Again there are exceptions, with considerable variations from state to state, the most notable being Florida, where Cuban Americans and their attendant strong Republicanism have been most evident. However, as the Cuban American population has spent an increasingly long period of time in the United States, and as other Hispanics have come into Florida in numbers almost equal to that of the Cuban Americans, Latinos in Florida are voting increasingly less Republican. Particularly in regard to Cubans, although in 1990 more than two-thirds of Cubans identified themselves as Republicans, by 1999 this number fell to 40 percent, while the proportion of Democrats and independents increased (McClain and Stewart 2006).

The greatest impact of Latinos in the electorate is experienced at the *local* level. It is in the elections for city halls, county courthouses, and school districts where Hispanics are most likely to be effective as an electorate. In many localities and municipalities, Hispanics are a majority or a near majority and are constantly increasing their numbers. Here, we should remember that Hispanics are the most urban people in the United States, with about 94 percent of the population living in urban areas. So, it is in elections for mayor, city council, county commission, school boards, and other local races where Hispanics can, and indeed do, have their greatest impact. Increasingly, Hispanic mayors are being elected to govern our cities, and the number of Hispanics on city councils, county commissions, and boards of education has also increased dramatically. Several major cities in the Southwest and West such as San Antonio, San Jose, and Los Angeles have had Hispanic mayors, and the number of Hispanic mayors throughout the country is likely to increase. At the *state* level, as of 2004, Hispanics are still a minority both in the population and in the electorate. In fact, as of 2004, Hispanics were not a majority in any state, although they are increasingly becoming a large plurality. New Mexico, for example, has a 44 percent Hispanic population. In California and Texas, about one-third of the population is Hispanic and growing rapidly. Hispanics comprise about one-fourth of the population in Arizona and Colorado. These population trends have translated into political success, as Latinos have seen sizable gains in several state legislatures and New Mexico elected Latino Bill Richardson to the Governor's Mansion in 2002 and 2006.

Underlying this voting discussion is the political resource of *numbers*. It is the amazing increase in the number of Latinos in the United States that is the foundation for building an effective and powerful Latino electorate. As the number of potential voters continues to rise, politicians will increasingly pay attention to this growing portion of their constituency. Noncitizens are generally not eligible to vote, and new residents are not likely to vote, so increasingly there will be efforts to naturalize more Hispanics so they can become citizens and perform their civic duty of casting a vote (if and when this will be to the advantage of certain politicians). Whatever the case, the *potential* is obvious.

As this great potential is increasingly recognized, Latinos as voters will most likely be courted and wooed more so than they have been in the past. The 2004 presidential elections were notable for the attention paid to Latinos as a key "target" or "battleground" group. For example, both Democratic and Republican parties spent record amounts of money trying to secure the Latino vote during the campaign (Segal 2004). One clear message from and for Hispanics in that election is that they can be won over by a combination of the right candidate, message, outreach, and mobilization. The Democratic Party cannot take them for granted, and the Republicans can move the Hispanic vote toward them significantly.

Indeed, as Hispanics' votes are sought, their vote and their rate of participation will undoubtedly increase because campaigns and campaigners' outreach efforts serve as a catalyst to mobilize Latinos into registering and voting. When politicians and candidates for office make their appeals to Latinos, promising to include the interests of Latinos on their policy agendas if Latinos support them, the likelihood of Latinos voting will increase. In turn, this will increase Latinos' leverage and influence in the political process. However, it is also true that when politicians have gone strongly against Latino interests, as occurred in California in the 1990s, this can result in an unusually large mobilization of Latino voters voting against a ballot referendum or against a candidate who has proposed or supported what are seen as anti-Latino measures. An example of potential balloting actions against potentially harmful legislation was evident in the rhetoric of Hispanics following the congressional debates and proposed legislation on immigration in late 2005 and early 2006. One proclaimed theme of the massive protest marches carried out in the spring of 2006 was "Today We March. Tomorrow We Vote!" This purported promise of an increase in electoral participation was detected in the Pew Hispanic Center (2006) survey on immigration. In the summer of that year, a large majority—three-fourths of Latinos—believed that "as a result of the debate over immigration policy in Washington, many more Hispanics will vote in the November [2006] elections..." The immigration issue appeared to have electoral consequences because national exit polls indicated that Latino support for the Republicans had dropped to approximately 30 percent compared to the widely cited figure of 40 percent who voted for Bush in 2004 (Gaoutte 2006).

In any case, given the continued growth in the number of Latinos in the United States, an increased awareness and recognition of Latinos' potential for electoral influence, and the rising proportion of the electorate that is Hispanic, the future of Latinos in the electoral process looks promising.

DIRECTION OF THE VOTE—PARTISAN AND CANDIDATE CHOICE

The Latino electorate is sometimes referred to as a bloc vote, although some experts disagree on such a designation. A *bloc* is a group of individuals, in this case voters, who vote in the same direction so often that they can accurately be viewed as a fairly cohesive unit of voters. Certainly, if a distinctive group of voters votes at a 90 percent similarity rate (e.g., African Americans), they would deserve the designation of a bloc. Latinos do typically vote together (i.e., in the same direction or for the same candidate) at about the 60 to 70 percent level. Surely at the upper limits of this range, the Latino vote could be considered bloc voting; at the lower level, the term "Hispanic vote" becomes less appropriate.

By looking at Latino voting patterns (Table 6.3) for the presidential candidates since 1960, one can observe why it is at least reasonable to speak of a Latino voting bloc. Although the data for the 1960s are a bit shaky, one can see from Table 6.3 that Latino votes from 1984 to 2004 have been between 50 and 75 percent Democratic, and in the 1960s to the 1970s, Latino votes may have been at an even much higher level of cohesion.

Only in 1980, when Latinos were notably supportive of Ronald Reagan, and in 2004, when Hispanics voted about 40 percent for George W. Bush, has support for the Democratic presidential candidate dipped to less than 60 percent. The average voter percentage that Democratic presidential candidates have received from Latino voters over the seven presidential elections prior to 2004 is 67 to 68 percent. For Republican candidates, it was 28 percent. When one compares Hispanic preference for the Democratic presidential candidates with that of white and black voters, one can see that Hispanic choices lie between those of the other two groups—a typical pattern for Hispanic political activities. The African American vote is definitely a bloc vote, being from 80 to 92 percent Democratic over the past several general elections. In our presidential elections, white voters have actually preferred the Republican candidate over the Democratic candidate in every election since 1976. When Democrats have won the race for the White House, it has more often than not been attributed to the large majorities given to them by Hispanics and, to an even greater extent, by African Americans.

This historical pattern continued into the presidential election of 2000 (Table 6.5). In 2000, Hispanics gave Democratic candidate Al Gore 62 percent of their vote and Republican candidate George W. Bush 35 percent. This compares with the white vote (81 percent of the total electorate) of which a majority, 54 percent, went to George W. Bush. Al Gore received 42 percent. African Americans were again very strongly in the Democratic camp—90 percent voted for the Democratic candidate. In this controversial election, Al Gore did win a majority of the national popular vote by a margin of 583,000 votes more than George W. Bush, but on an electoral vote basis, including an extremely controversial situation in Florida, Bush prevailed, thus gaining the presidency.

In the 2000 election, there was a variation along national origin lines within the Latino electorate. With the exception of Cuban Americans, most Hispanics voted for Gore by a large margin—Mexican Americans, 69 percent; Puerto Ricans, 71 percent; Central Americans, 74 percent; and South Americans, 69 percent. In contrast, the Cuban American vote went to George W. Bush by 79 percent (All-Politics 2000). There was also considerable variation by Hispanics within the various states. Eighty percent of New York Hispanics gave their vote to Al Gore, as did 68 percent of the Hispanics in California, 66 percent in New Mexico, 65 percent in Arizona, and 54 percent in Texas. The Florida Hispanic vote was split, 49 percent for Bush and 48 percent for Gore. (Note that these are only estimates based on exit poll data that may vary by a few percentage points.)

It is also most likely that the Hispanic vote varied by those same socioeconomic indicators that affect the non-Hispanic vote. For example, Hispanics who are in the upper class or the upper middle class most likely

Table 6.5
PRESIDENTIAL ELECTION RESULTS (CANDIDATE CHOICE) BY RACE AND ETHNICITY, 1996, 2000, AND 2004

	1996			2000			2004		
	Clinton	Dole	Perot	Gore	Bush	Nader	Kerry	Bush	Nader
Total vote (%)	49	41	8	48	48	2	48	51	1
Whites	43	46	9	42	54	3	41	58	0
Blacks	84	12	4	91	8	1	88	11	0
Latinos	72	21	6	67	31	2	53	44[a]	2
Asians	43	48	8	54	41	4	56	44	*

Sources: Voter News Service exit polling, 1996 and 2000, *New York Times*. Edison/Mitofsky exit polling, 2004, CNN.

[a]This figure generated by exit polls following the 2004 election has been widely debated. It is generally accepted that Bush garnered 40 percent of the Latino vote in 2004.

voted for the Republican candidate in greater proportions than did those Latinos in the working and lower socioeconomic classes.

A great amount of money and attention were paid to the courting of Hispanic voters in the 2000 election, at least in the early stages. Republicans were adamant that Latinos were "natural Republicans" and that in this presidential election they had a candidate who was particularly attractive to Latino voters (de la Garza and DeSipio 2004). George W. Bush had received the support of 33 to 45 percent of the Hispanic vote in Texas during his successful run for the governorship. He spoke Spanish and had Mexican Americans in his extended family. It was said that Mexican Americans in Texas liked George Bush, and all indications are that indeed that was the case. The Republicans also spent an estimated $10 million especially designated for outreach to the Hispanic electorate, buying ads in Spanish language media in key electoral states. Candidate Bush made several visits to states with significant proportions of Latinos in their electorates.

After Election Day, when George W. Bush received approximately 35 percent of the Hispanic vote, commentators differed over whether this was a victory for the Republicans. Most agreed that it was a triumph for Latinos, who had unprecedented attention focused on them as voters and who turned out in record numbers; approximately 7 million Latinos voted in 2000. Republicans proclaimed that George W. Bush had received more Hispanic votes than any other Republican presidential candidate in history and the second highest percentage of votes overall, second only to the widely popular Ronald Reagan in 1980. They saw this as a good start at overcoming the stigma that Republicans had attached to them among many Latinos. Although Democrats conceded these numbers, they also pointed out that the Latino vote for Al Gore was in an almost two-to-one proportion over that for Bush and that 35 percent was a small percentage for a candidate to garner in an election. Latino spokespersons touted this election as certainly being the one in which the "sleeping giant indeed had awakened" and predicted that from now on Hispanics would become a major force in American electoral politics (Andrade 2003).

The 2004 general election was in many ways a replay of the election four years earlier. With regard to the Hispanic electorate, many of the activities noted in 2000 were not only continued but also intensified. Both parties renewed and intensified their campaigns to attract Latino voters. This is reflected in both the Democratic and Republican parties spending record amounts of money attempting to court the Latino vote during the campaign for the 2004 presidential election (Segal 2004). In regard to voter turnout, Latino participation was estimated to have increased from 5.9 million in 2000 to at least 7 million in 2004 (Leal et al. 2005). Similarly to 2000, most of the discussion regarding Latinos and the 2004 election centered on the possible partisan realignment of Latinos, with some exit polls suggesting that as much as 44 percent of Latinos supported Republican George W. Bush. Although this figure has been highly debated, it is widely accepted that Bush garnered around 40 percent of the Latino vote, which still represents an increase from 2000 (Kamasaki, Martinez, and Munoz 2004). So, overall, the general trends identified in 2000 of increased turnout and support for the Republican candidate were heightened in 2004. However, it very well might be, as some recent scholarship has suggested, that the apparent shift of Latinos to the Republican Party will be short lived because non-Cuban Latinos are becoming more Democratic (Bowler, Nicholson, and Segura 2006).

The other interesting issue associated with Latinos and the 2004 election was the role of religion. Adam Segal, Director of the Hispanic Voter Project housed at The Johns Hopkins University, indicated that, "The Bush campaign used moral values, and especially the national discussion over gay marriage and abortion rights, as wedge issues within the Hispanic community to try to break off a conservative religious segment" (Johnson 2004, 1). This strategy appeared to work for the Republican Party because Bush did well with evangelical or born-again Christians (Lee and Pachon 2007). Latino evangelicals favored Bush 58 percent to 33 percent, and Bush also garnered 49 percent of the vote among other Christians. However, Kerry garnered strong support from Latino Catholics (68 percent to 24 percent) and non-Christians or seculars (62 percent to 29 percent) (Leal et al. 2005). These data suggest that there was a religion gap among the Latino electorate in 2004 because despite representing only 18 percent of the Latino electorate, Latino non-Catholic Christians helped Bush secure reelection. Factors beyond religion also significantly impacted Latino voter choice in 2004. For example, generational status and military experience motivated support for John Kerry, as third-generation and beyond Mexican Americans were more likely to support John Kerry (DeSipio and Uhlaner 2007), as were Latinos with military experience (Barreto and Leal 2007).

Although Latinos had in fact turned out in record numbers and continued to increase their proportion of the electorate, unlike any other distinctive group in the electorate, these increases were driven almost entirely by the unprecedented burgeoning numbers of Latinos residing in the United States. Although registration *numbers* had increased significantly, due in large part to massive registration drives by Latino organizations and the political parties, the *proportion* of Latinos in the voting age population who actually voted did not increase, but remained relatively constant, as it had since the 1970s. This meant that the gap between the general Latino population and the Latino electorate grew even wider (Figure 6.1).

Politicians readily exulted in these elevated numbers; however, students of Latino politics and political scientists still wondered why the

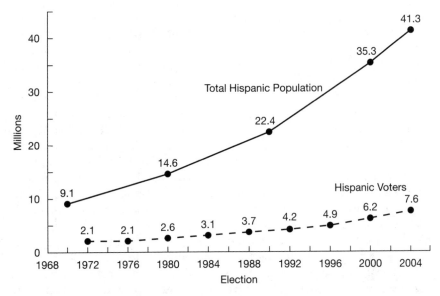

Figure 6.1   Growing divergence between total Hispanic population and number of Hispanic voters, 1968-2004. (From: *Hispanic Americans: A Statistical Sourcebook*, Pew Hispanic Center tabulations of 2004 November CPS, and decennial censuses for 1970-2000.)

Latino voting rate remains relatively low. Of course, when 40 to 45 percent of the possible electorate is disqualified because they are not citizens, this lowers the rate tremendously. But even when only citizens are counted, Latinos still have the lowest voter turnout rate of any distinctive grouping. Why is it that the rate remains so low, and what can be done to increase the relative size of the Latino electorate?

Several theories have been offered as to why Latinos vote in proportionately small numbers. The primary explanations, as noted previously, have been rooted in the socioeconomic characteristics of Hispanics, primarily their lower levels of education, income, occupation, and ages. As discussed in previous chapters, Latinos have a greater share of those socioeconomic characteristics that ordinarily depress voter turnout in populations, including the white population. For example, Latinos are nine to ten years younger than non-Hispanics in the United States, and it is well known that it is the younger age cohorts that are less likely to vote. Hispanics also have lower incomes and lower levels of education than non-Hispanic whites, and these are also correlated with lower voter participation. Being less likely to have a material stake in the society, such as owning a home, is also correlated with a lower voter turnout, and again Hispanics have a lower home ownership rate than non-Hispanics. Length of residence in one area also increases voter turnout. Because Hispanics are mobile and are comprised of a significant portion of new foreign-born citizens, they are often shorter-term residents than non-Hispanic whites. There is little doubt that these and other sociodemographic variables have a major depressing effect on Latino participation.

There are also many other cultural or attitudinal possibilities, none of which have been conclusively supported by hard evidence but that have enough credence to remain viable. Some researchers believe that Latino culture just does not manifest much interest in public affairs. In fact, studies do show that the actual political knowledge of Hispanics is actually lower than that of non-Hispanics (de la Garza et al. 1992; Delli Carpini and Keeter 1996; Verba et al. 1995), and knowledge of public affairs is highly correlated with interest and participation. Furthermore, it is often alleged, but seldom demonstrated, that alleged cultural traits such as *envidia* and fatalism mean that Latinos are not going to make any extra effort to actively participate in shaping their own political destiny through political participation in elections. However, some measurements of psychological attitudes that usually correlate highly with voter participation, such as sense of civic duty, belief in political efficacy, and feelings of patriotism, reveal high levels of these among Latinos (de la Garza et al. 1996). These measurements should be correlated with correspondingly high participation, but they are not.

Others believe that Hispanics are still so close to their home countries both physically and emotionally that they are divided in their attention to matters in the United States and their homeland and thus are not as interested in what happens in the United States. Another explanation, one that is grounded in the history of the United States, is that Latinos continue to feel the effects of decades or generations, if not centuries, of neglect and outright exclusion from the U.S. political process, and thus having been marginalized, continue to feel that way. This legacy of historical neglect is then passed on from generation to generation. Some researchers believe that it will take a special effort of those concerned with maximizing the Latino vote to overcome any or all of these attitudes. Others believe that traditional methods of building support for candidates and for participation in elections, such as campaign ads in the media, flyers and brochures, direct mail, and e-mail, do not work well with Latinos; instead, they need personal face-to-face contact by an individual, preferably another Latino, urging them to support a particular candidate or to go to the polls (Michelson 2003b, 2006; Shaw et al. 2000). This personal contact is seen as being by far the most effective means of voter mobilization among Latinos. More Latino candidates running for office was seen as another way to attract Latino voters to participate in voting. In several instances, notably the March 2002 Democratic primary in Texas in which the top two candidates were Hispanics and a historic debate was conducted in Spanish,

Texas Hispanic Democrats turned out in record numbers.[2] National survey research also indicates that Latinos are more likely to vote when co-ethnics (other Latinos) are candidates (Barreto, Espino, Pantoja, and Ramirez 2003; de la Garza et al. 1992).

In addition to the presence of Latino candidates on the ballot, statewide propositions or referenda can also be mobilization factors for the Latino community. As stated in Chapter 4, state propositions are usually placed on the ballot by the legislature or by citizens directly; then voters have a choice of approving these referenda and making them official policy in the form of a law or constitutional amendment. Several initiatives introduced to voters in California in recent years have generated great interest among Latinos. A major mobilization of Latino voters in California occurred with the debate surrounding passage of Proposition 187, an initiative supported by the Republican Party that sought to restrict public benefits to illegal immigrants. Viewed by Latinos in California as being aimed primarily at Mexicans and other Latinos, this proposition catalyzed a heightened political involvement by Latinos and Latino organizations. Mass demonstrations, large voter registration drives, and the creation of organizations in opposition to Proposition 187 were all responses to this state referendum.

After Proposition 187 was passed, other propositions were introduced in California that threatened to eliminate bilingual education in public schools and raised issues about affirmative action. In Arizona, following the model of Proposition 187, Proposition 200, which also denied public benefits to illegal aliens and required state employees to verify the legality of public contacts, was passed by voters in 2004. To this point, it has not been implemented due to challenges in court. Not only did these initiatives mobilize Latinos and spark a heightened sense of political awareness among the Hispanic community in these states, but there is also some evidence that state initiatives such as these can have a long-term impact on the participation levels and partisanship of Latinos. For example, scholars have found that the racially charged propositions in California presented previously generated a major partisan shift toward the Democratic Party, reversing a steady movement of Latino voters toward the Republican Party (Bowler, Nicholson, and Segura 2006).

Earlier in U.S. history, there were several institutional and structural features that explicitly kept Latinos from the polls. For example, monolingual English ballots were often discouraging to predominantly Spanish-speaking Latinos. In some states, most notably Texas, registration procedures were particularly onerous, requiring long periods of residence at one address, thus discriminating against more mobile occupations, such as migrant farm laborers. Moreover, registration hours were set at times that made it very difficult for working people to register in only one designated place, such as the county courthouse, thus again imposing a particular burden on working class or migrant Latinos. In many respects, the Civil Rights Act of 1964 and VRA of 1965 were policy attempts to remedy institutional practices that impeded participation by minority popula- tions. The practices of literacy tests, limited registration periods and loca- tions, poll taxes, and economic and physical intimidation were prohibited, and voting activities were monitored by federal officials. Although most literature on political participation focuses on voting, there are many other ways that one can become involved in the political process in the United States. These other forms or modes of participation include run- ning for office, working or volunteering for a campaign or organization, donating money to a campaign or organization, directly contacting an elected official, being involved with a political party, and protesting or demonstrating. As you can see, there are substantial opportunities for get- ting involved in politics in the United States, and thus many people do be- come politically engaged. The research on the participation of Latinos across these other modes of participation is rather limited in comparison to that on voting. However, there are some data to draw from here that will allow for a comparison between the participation rates of Latinos and non- Latinos in some of these areas (de la Garza et al. 1992; Verba et al. 1995). Data from the Latino National Political Survey (LNPS) allow for the as- sessment of variation within the Latino population's dominant subgroups.

These data provide the opportunity to compare the participation rates of Latinos to both Anglos and African Americans and also allow for dis- tinctions to be made within the Latino population. We refer often to Table 6.6 and Table 6.7, which include the participation rates of those groups for

Table 6.6
POLITICAL PARTICIPATION IN NONVOTING ACTIVITIES, BY RACE/ETHNICITY (PERCENTAGE)

Activity	Anglos	African Americans	Latinos	Latino Citizens
Campaign work	8	12	7	8
Campaign contributions	26	22	11	12
Contact officials	37	24	14	17
Informal community activity	17	19	12	14
Board membership	4	2	4	5
Affiliated with an organization	52	38	24	27
Protest activity	5	9	4	4
Mean no. of activities	2.2	1.9	1.2	1.4

Source: S. Verba, K. Schlozman, and H. Brady, Voice and Equality: Civic Volunteerism in America (Cambridge: Harvard University Press, 1995).

several political activities beyond voting. Verba et al. (1995) computed the overall mean number of activities in which each racial/ethnic group was involved. A comparison of these scores—2.2 for Anglos, 1.9 for African Americans, 1.2 for Latinos, and 1.4 for Latino citizens—reveals the overall pattern of lower levels of participation for Latinos. However, an understanding of Latino participation needs to move beyond a summary of activities and explore specific political participation arenas.

As reflected in Table 6.6, both Anglos and Latinos trail African Americans in campaign involvement, and interestingly, there is no difference between Anglo and Latino involvement in campaigns, with only a slight (1 percent) advantage for Latino citizens compared to Latinos generally. Data from the LNPS adds to this discussion by indicating that all three Latino subgroups trail slightly behind Anglos in propensity to wear a campaign button.

An important finding, given the great importance of money to modern campaigns, is that Latinos have traditionally contributed to political campaigns at significantly lower levels than the other two groups. Regardless of citizenship status, less than half as many Latinos contribute to political campaigns when compared to Anglos (Verba et al. 1995). Interestingly, as highlighted in Table 6.7, the gap between Anglos and Latinos in political contributions is much smaller in the LNPS data. Among Latino subgroups, Mexicans were most likely to contribute (9 percent), with Puerto Ricans being the least likely (6.47 percent). However, Hispanics' use of monetary resources seems to be increasing significantly.

During the 2000 election campaign period, Hispanic individuals contributed some $47 million to candidates, parties, or political action committees (PACs). Slightly more than half of those contributions went

Table 6.7
POLITICAL PARTICIPATION IN NONVOTING ACTIVITIES BY NATIONAL ORIGIN (PERCENTAGE)

Activity	Mexican	Puerto Rican	Cuban	Anglo
Wore a campaign button	17.9	17.8	18.1	21.7
Made a political contribution	9	6.4	7	12.6
Wrote to the press	12.1	9.1	14.4	20.2
Signed a petition	39.9	20.7	23.8	49.4
Attended a public meeting	17.7	16.6	12.4	21.1
Volunteer for a political party	7	4.4	4.5	4.6
Went to rallies	9.1	7.9	8.9	9.2

Source: R. de la Garza, L. DeSipio, F. Garcia, J. Garcia, and Angelo Falcón, *Latino Voices: Mexican, Puerto Rican, and Cuban Perspectives on American Politics* (Boulder, CO: Westview Press, 1992).

to Democrats. The Federal Election Committee reported that in the 2003/2004 election cycle, Hispanic PACs contributed more than $1.8 million to candidates. This was an increase of nearly three times the amount given in the 2000 election. The rapid rise and development of PACs among Latinos seems to be an especially significant development given the critical importance of money as a political resource in U.S. politics. It also demonstrates the movement of Latinos toward organized political inputs. Most of the Hispanic PACs were affiliated with political parties, and their money was fairly evenly divided between Republicans and Democrats. This marks another significant development as Latinos take another step toward moving into the political mainstream as major players.

Analysis of non-electoral participation also reveals a trend of lesser participation, as Latinos tend to have lower participation rates in this area as well. One of the most efficient means of expressing one's views to government is to directly contact public officials. However, as indicated in Table 6.6, Latinos use this political activity at much lower rates than either Anglos (37 percent) or African Americans (24 percent), with not much difference between Latinos generally (14 percent) and Latino citizens (17 percent; Verba et al. 1995). Contacting a public official requires a certain level of knowledge and communication skills, resources that are probably possessed less among Spanish-dominant Latinos. Overall, the presence of proportionately fewer Latino elected officials may also depress this mode of participation because only 23 percent of Latinos reported that the official they contacted was Latino. This is much lower than the 49 percent of African Americans who reported that the person they contacted was African American and drastically lower than the 94 percent for Anglos. Latinos may be less likely to believe that their concerns will be responded to when they are expressing them to someone from another racial or ethnic group. This suggests that Latinos of all national origins are also less likely to write the press for political reasons than Anglos, with Puerto Ricans being the least likely to do so. However, although still trailing Anglos by a significant margin, a much greater percentage of Latinos, particularly Mexican Americans, sign petitions (de la Garza et al. 1992).

Latinos again lag behind both African Americans and Anglos in informal community activity, although the difference between Latinos generally (12 percent)/Latino citizens (14 percent) and Anglos (17 percent) is relatively minor (Verba et al. 1995). Informal community activity usually involves being involved in neighborhood or local issues, including the schools. As Table 6.7 reflects, the difference between Anglos and Latinos in regard to attending a public meeting is also slim, with the exception of Cubans, who are five percentage points less likely to attend a meeting than Mexicans.

The mode of participation beyond voting that has the greatest level of involvement across all three racial/ethnic groups is affiliation with a political organization. More than half of Anglo respondents (52 percent), 38 percent of African American respondents, and 24 percent of Latino respondents indicate that they have some affiliation with a political organization. This trend from the Verba et al. (1995) data is reinforced by other literature that finds lower levels of organizational involvement for Latinos (de la Garza et al. 1992; Marquez 1993b). However, there is only a marginal difference between Anglos (4.6 percent) and Latinos of Puerto Rican (4.4 percent) or Cuban (4.5 percent) origin in regard to volunteering for a political party, and Mexicans (7 percent) participate in this activity more than Anglos.

As we discuss in other contexts in this book, the Latino community has used protests and demonstrations to express their political views in the past, most notably during the Chicano movement. Analysis of the Verba et al. (1995) data suggests that Latinos engage in protest activity at nearly the same rates as Anglos, but trail African Americans in this mode of participation. Furthermore, when looking specifically at attending rallies, the difference between Latinos and Anglos is virtually nonexistent for Mexicans and Cubans, and slim for Puerto Ricans (de la Garza et al. 1992). This tendency to use protest activity as a vehicle for political expression has been reflected in the political debate regarding national immigration policy that has generated mass protests, walkouts, and demonstrations among large numbers of Latinos. These mass mobilizations suggest that this form of participation is not just a thing of the past, a historical marker, for the Hispanic population. The tremendous scale of these activities and the impact they have generated strongly suggests that we must approach the study of political participation much more broadly than just looking at voting, or other forms of electoral participation for that matter, especially when analyzing the Latino population.

Although there had been some speculation about the potential of the immigration policy to mobilize primarily Latino immigrants similar to the impact of Proposition 187 in California during the 1990s, no one could have predicted the huge scale of the national protests during the "national day of action" on Monday, April 10, 2006. There were an estimated 500,000 protestors dressed in white to symbolize peace and solidarity in both Dallas and Los Angeles; 200,000 in Washington, DC; 50,000 in Denver; and more than 100,000 in Phoenix, which represented the largest protest in the history of the state of Arizona (McFadden 2006). In addition to the huge turnouts in these major Latino strongholds, there were large turnouts in other places not traditionally associated with the Latino population. Tens of thousands of largely Latino protestors emerged in Atlanta, Georgia and Madison, Wisconsin, and an estimated 4,000 each in Boise, Idaho and Birmingham, Alabama. It was estimated that the total for all late April/early

May marches may have reached 3 million participants in some fifty cities. This massive turnout has been recognized as the largest collective political effort of the U.S. immigrant population in American history.

Verba et al. (1995) examined the role of resources in political participation. It is clear that all forms of political participation require some resources. For example, donating money to candidates obviously requires the resource of money, and voting requires time, information, and citizenship. From this standpoint, it is understandable why the Latino immigrant population, which lacks the financial resources and citizenship requirements necessary to effectively communicate their needs and concerns to government, has used less conventional means of interest communication. Stated simply, protest politics is the most efficient mode of participation for the thousands of demonstrators in cities such as Dallas, Los Angeles, and Chicago, whose most abundant resource is their numbers. It will be interesting to see if the population that marched today will actually vote tomorrow as they consistently stated ("Today We March, Tomorrow We Vote").

SUMMARY AND CONCLUSION

Electoral participation, including voting in elections, is a necessary, if not sufficient, condition for exerting political influence. Although voting in and of itself does not guarantee that public officials will enact policies that are in line with their electoral supporters' preferences, *not* voting almost definitely ensures that those interests will be ignored. In a democracy, voting is the most common act of holding elected officials accountable. If an individual or group does not vote, or votes at very low rates, their input into the behavior of public officials will be minimized.

Hispanics have a history of relatively low participation in elections, and more particularly in voting. One major reason for this has been a history of discouragement and even outright exclusion by the majority society. Even though such legislation as VRA has greatly advanced the participation and effectiveness of Hispanics at the polls, the effects of this discriminatory legacy live on. This includes not only a lower level of a tradition of participating in elections but also socioeconomic and attitudinal factors that are correlated with a lower level of political participation among all groups. Although these negative features and nonparticipant socialization are passed on through the generations, a large proportion of Latinos are new to the U.S. political system. At the start of the twenty-first century, nearly half of Latinos were not citizens. It takes years for many immigrants to become citizens and even longer before attaining a stake in this society makes it more likely that they will participate. The number of Hispanic Americans certainly calls attention to the potential for Latinos to become a much sought after and influential bloc of voters. However, to this point, there has been more potential than actuality, as Hispanic voting rates have remained notably low compared to other groups. The continued low rate of voting remains incompletely explained, with historical, socioeconomic, psychological, and cultural explanations all being used to partially account for this. However, candidates and elected officials are well aware of the astounding increase in the raw numbers of Latinos, and they ignore this demographic fact at their own peril. The 2004 elections, with their heightened focus on the Hispanic population, most likely indicate that the once "forgotten Americans" will henceforth be significant players in the electoral dramas of this nation. The size and importance of the Latino electorate continues to grow, and its impact is increasingly being felt at national, state, and local levels. At least with regard to voting, Hispanics are slowly moving into the electoral mainstream. Will their steadily increasing numbers move the mainstream of campaigns and elections? It already seems to have made the flow wider and altered the course of the conduct of campaigns. But will Hispanics' becoming an increasing factor in election inputs in and of itself make any significant change in the direction of government policy making? That remains to be seen.

Notes

[1] For a discussion of these disputed percentages, see Kamasaki et al. (2004) and Leal et al. (2005).

[2] See William C. Velasquez Institute (2002).

7

Political Participation—Collective Action: Interest Groups, Organizations, Coalitions, and Leadership

In examining the voting behavior of Hispanics, we have seen that the proportion of the U.S. electorate comprised of Hispanics continues to grow. The American electoral mainstream is widening. Even though the rate of Hispanic electoral participation, or more precisely, voting, continues to lag behind that of other groups, Latinos are still seen as a *potentially* more influential electorate because the numbers that participate in elections continue to increase. Yet, we know that there is much more to effective political activity than the act of voting. Although voting does not guarantee that a group's interest will be transformed or converted into public policy, if a group does *not* vote, it is almost certain that that group *will be* ignored.

Voting is essentially a solitary, individualistic act, and as individuals, there are very few Hispanics who can exert significant influence on the political system. Much more effective in influencing political decision makers to support their interests are activities that are undertaken by collectivities of people, or groups. In fact, the pluralist model holds that groups are the most important actors in democratic politics, and it is through the interplay of group activity that virtually all interests are represented, reconciled, and reflected in public policy. In this chapter, we look at various forms of group activity exhibited by Latinos and examine their manifestations and effectiveness.

There are at least a few ways in which individuals may multiply the political resources of numbers, time, and money. Those methods generally involve attachments with others in groups. The first way is to associate with other individuals with similar interests and become a distinct, recognizable group, or an *interest group*. Sometimes these groups are very large, and sometimes they are very small. Sometimes they are loosely organized, and sometimes they are structured. In any case, when relatively under-resourced individuals, such as Hispanics, affiliate with other group members, that is, when they are involved in *coalitions* or *alliances*, their resources are greatly multiplied. The few economic resources that an individual may have, when multiplied by tens or hundreds, can turn into a substantial amount that can be used to influence politics. A large group of like-minded individuals is much more likely to be paid attention to than is one solitary person seeking redress of grievances or attention to his or her particular interests. Even though Hispanics work more hours than non-Hispanics and are more likely to have time-consuming jobs with inflexible hours, and thus have less free time than non-Hispanics, if each group member can contribute a little time, that accumulated time can be substantial and well spent.

People must come together on the basis of shared interests or characteristics; that is, there must be enough commonality between members of a group to provide some cohesiveness to the group and to give them a well-identified interest, direction, or goal (Garcia 2003, 21–24). This is particularly true for political groups, as compared to say social or fraternal organizations. Although groups that are relatively weakly organized, such as protest movements, can have an impact on the political system, it is also true that increased *organization* can be a major multiplier of individual and group resources. A well-organized, highly disciplined, highly cohesive, and well-led group maximizes its chances for success. *Leadership* is particularly important because skilled and effective group leaders can not only mold and hold the organization, but they can also be most effective in presenting an organization's interest to the outside society and the political system. Thus, effective leadership is an extremely important resource for any group that wants to make its mark on the political system.

The conventional wisdom or mythology with regard to Hispanic organizations has been that Hispanics are either difficult to organize or have lacked organizations throughout their history. As with many such stereotypical myths, this too is distorted and exaggerated, and is basically due to a misunderstanding of the nature of Hispanic community organizations (Tirado 1970).

Anglo historians and social scientists interested in looking for the organizational bases of Hispanic communities have sought the typical Germanic, Weberian model of a bureaucratic organization. These features include well-defined roles for individual members, with a strict division and specialization of labor, hierarchical structures of leadership roles, elected officers, dues paying memberships, written policies and procedures, and clearly formulated purposes or objectives laid out in a written constitution or bylaws. Using these criteria, they inferred that Hispanics do not have the kinds of organizations they were looking for, or at least very few of them, and certainly not many that were specifically political in nature. What many do not know and what other more culturally sensitive researchers have found out, is that Hispanics have a long history of community organizational life, but they do not fit the classic Weberian model. Instead, they are often multifunctional and multipurpose rather than unifunctional.

Good examples of these throughout history have been the *mutualistas* or mutual assistance, self-help groups that have existed in many Mexican American communities. These are multipurpose organizations, rather free form in nature, that would provide assistance to Latinos as they interacted with the new Anglo American society. They could provide such things as liaison with various agencies of the U.S. political system, such as schools, law enforcement agencies, social service agencies, and other local government bureaucracies. Legal assistance, for example, could be provided, as well as assistance with language translation and pointers as to where individuals could contact the system in order to have their needs addressed, or perhaps how housing could be obtained, familiarity with zoning requirements, requirements for establishing small business, licensing, and so on.

In addition to these organizations, many other organizations have existed, or do exist, in Latino communities in the past and in the present, that were and are, in essence, Hispanic organizations, but that are not recognized as such. In a typical Hispanic community, for example, there could be several organizations associated with the local churches, usually a Catholic Church. There are often athletic associations or sports clubs as well as recreational organizations of various sorts. Several businesses, often small businesses, associate with each other to seek support or assistance for their endeavors from various public agencies. Young Latinos often belong to various youth organizations in the community. Veterans' organizations with virtually 100 percent Hispanic membership also existed but were not considered ethnic organizations. These community-based organizations (CBOs) are often comprised of a large percentage of Hispanics, perhaps 80 or 90 percent Hispanics, and have provided some Hispanic-specific services such as translations, yet they often were not considered to be ethnic organizations. In addition, even though these organizations may be involved in the resolution of conflict or the solving of problems involving the government, they were not designated as "political" agencies or organizations.

In fact, when the Latino National Political Survey (LNPS) asked its nationally representative samples of Mexican Americans, Cubans, and Puerto Ricans about their knowledge of any *ethnic* organizations that were specifically designed to help their particular ethnic group, few, if any, organizations were mentioned. The only organization mentioned at any significant level was the League of United Latin American Citizens (LULAC). However, for every LULAC member, there are dozens of other Hispanic individuals who belong to many other organizations performing many of the same functions, yet these groups do not bear a title that designates them as an ethnic organization or even, more particularly, as a Latino political organization.

This is reinforced by the data that we have from such sources as the LNPS and the works by Verba et al. (1995), which indicate that Hispanics' memberships in organizations are very comparable, if not somewhat lower than that of non-Hispanics. We have seen that one way to multiply the relatively scarce resources that Hispanic individuals have is to form groups or organizations. One form of such organization that has not gone unnoticed by the public has been those kinds of groups that can best be classified as part of a social movement. Most notable in this respect are the various groups that were part of the Chicano movement and that were discussed earlier in this book—groups such as the United Farm Workers (UFW) led by César Chávez and Dolores Huerta, or even more militant radical groups, such as the Brown Berets or the Black Berets. Perhaps as important, but much less noticed by the general public, are CBOs such as the community service organizations and interfaith organizations based on the Saul Alinsky model that have led to much community education and organization around local issues and interests in Hispanic communities. Many of these are connected with religious institutions as part of the interfaith organizational structure led by such distinguished and competent leaders as Ernesto "Ernie" Cortez. This reliance on congregations of faith generally affirms meaningful goals in life and serves as institutions built on personal networks of family and neighborhood (Cortes 1996). Interfaith groups such as the Community Organized for Public Services (COPS) active in San Antonio in the 1960s and 1970s focused on issues such as inadequate drainage infrastructure and rising utility rates on the heavily Mexican west side of town (Marquez 1993a). These organizations have made great strides in educating the people in Latino communities, developing indigenous community-based leadership, and organizing around issues that are of immediate and material interest to the communities, such as the improvement of municipal facilities or services. They identify natural community leaders and provide training in communications and organization. The community members themselves identify those issues most important to them; these are typically the lack of public services, neglect, or discrimination. Much practical, hands-on experience in discourse, debate, presentation, and organization is provided to the communities and their leaders to prepare them for direct confrontation with the establishment powers, such as school boards, city councils, and county commissions.

Even prior to the Chicano movement, there were many explicitly political organizations devoted to forming an organized political base to promote Hispanic interests. Included among these was the Political Association of Spanish-Speaking Organizations, which was a group of organizations such as the Teamsters Union that helped empower previously disfranchised citizens in largely Chicano towns such as Crystal City, Texas. Predecessors to more modern organizations included others primarily based on college campuses, such as the Mexican American Youth Organization (MAYO); United Mexican American Students, which was very active in California; and El Movimiento Estudiantil Chicano de Aztlán, which is still active on many university campuses. Functioning as electoral organizations were groups such as the Mexican American Political Association in the 1950s and the "Viva Kennedy" clubs in the early 1960s. Both were among the most visible political organizations that were active and visible in the electoral politics of those respective eras. Another study has shown that Latino barrios and communities have a rich organizational life, even though it is not often structured in a form that is readily recognized by outside researchers. Such organizations and associations have been very useful to the development and utilization of resources found in Latino organizations that can be used to exert influence on public authorities and decision makers (Pachon, Segura, and Woods 2001).

COALITIONS AND ALLIANCES

In addition to joining other individuals in forming organizations, the other major way to multiply the resources of individuals is for a group to join other groups in a *coalition* or in an *alliance*. The same principles that apply to individuals also apply to groups, in the sense that increasing their numbers also increases their resources and hence the potential political clout available to them. Particularly when a group is a minority group, it may often be of great benefit to the minority to approach other minorities or even a majority group to reinforce and fortify their numbers and other political resources. Throughout the modern era of Latino political history, that is, since World War II and, more particularly, since the period of the Chicano movement, there has been much talk about Latinos entering into coalitions with other groups in order to maximize each member group's influence. The idea is appealing and can be theoretically sound, philosophically logical, and morally appealing; however, in practicality, it has not proved to be so readily accomplished. In fact, there have been at least as much opposition and contention between Latino groups and others as there have been instances of successful cooperation (Vaca 2004). The major reason for this is that each group has its own interests or objectives, and any time there is a coalition, some of the group's objectives must be compromised in order to advance those objectives that are held in common by the coalition's member groups.

Obviously, no two groups would have completely identical interests; therefore, the cost of coalition politics is sometimes quite high because a group must compromise a substantial number of its objectives in order to push forth others in conjunction with its coalition partners. Although the benefits of combined group efforts in advancing interests that are held in common can be quite powerful and accomplish a great deal, if the costs of compromise are much greater than the benefits that would come from coalition, a coalition will not form or will not last. In addition, each group must have its own power base and be resourceful enough to be needed as a coalition member that brings additional resources to the group endeavors.

Many of the coalitions that have been successful in the past have been coalitions that have been rather *ad hoc* or temporary in nature and have been focused on one particular occurrence event or issue (e.g., an election). After that event or issue has been successfully addressed, coalitions have often disintegrated (Carmichael and Hamilton 1967).

Whenever coalitions and alliances are discussed, the question often arises as to with what groups Latinos share enough interests to coalesce? (Or perhaps one should first address the question of whether there is a community of interests among Latinos themselves. This is an extremely important and unresolved question that must also be addressed and to which our attention is later turned.) Do Latino interests overlap considerably with other groups to the extent that they can form coalitions or perhaps even relatively permanent alliances? Obviously, the major requisite is some basic commonality of interest, although there will always be some differences. Most often, the presumed answer to this question is that the most likely allies of Hispanics will be other ethnic or racial minority groups, other "peoples of color" (Rich 1996). Several common interests come to mind when one speaks of coalitions between Hispanics and African Americans or Native Americans, so-called "people of color." These groups have suffered injustices throughout history to one degree or another and certainly have been subject to discrimination by the majority of white society. There has been considerable prejudice levied against these groups, including negative stereotyping and *de facto* and, in some cases, *de jure* discrimination. Even in twenty-first-century America, these groups still find themselves excluded or at best ignored in many situations and are still too often subject to prejudice and discrimination. These groups and others also share in common that they have been recognized by the federal government as deserving of special treatment as "protected groups." In addition, largely because of their treatment by the majority society, they are commonly found at the lower levels of the socioeconomic ladder, having higher levels of unemployment, less prestigious jobs, less educational attainment, and other lower socioeconomic indicators, as presented in Chapter 3. Although these commonalties would seem to make for natural alliances, and there have been some successful examples of electoral coalitions (Cordova 1999), unfortunately there are several considerations that often work against and sometimes cancel out what would seem to be a natural coalition (Jennings 1994; Rodriguez 2002; Vaca 2004).

One is that these groups actually have quite different histories in the United States and are perceived differently by the host society and, disappointing as it may be, often harbor prejudices and negative stereotypes against each other (National Conference of Christians and Jews 1992). This latter point has been documented in more than one survey.[1] In addition, and probably just as important, these groups have been forced throughout history to compete for the scraps that have been left over, for the lowest-paying positions and jobs, and for minimal government services and benefits. This competition not only for the limited material benefits but also for recognition has often caused some jealousy and animosity between the groups (Falcon 1988; McClain 1996; Mindiola, Niemann, and Rodriguez 2002). A 2003 study of the perceptions of Latinos, blacks, and whites in Durham, North Carolina, found that the mostly immigrant Latinos in that area of the south harbored negative stereotypical views about African Americans—more negative than whites held toward blacks. A majority of Latinos believed that they had more in common with whites than with blacks (McClain et al. 2006). Obviously, the results of this study, although limited in scope, if duplicated elsewhere, do not bode well for future coalitions between African Americans and the increasing number of foreign-born Latinos.

In August 2005, in part as a reaction to the tensions often manifested in behavior in schools and on the streets, such as in Los Angeles, some Latino and African American leaders announced the formation of a new alliance to help resolve these stresses. Christina Chávez of the UFW and the Reverend Al Sharpton led the initiation of a coalition called "The Latino and African American Leadership Alliance." Despite these efforts, tensions between Latinos and African Americans have escalated in the Harbor Gateway area of Los Angeles, causing many to predict more significant racial conflict in that area between the two minority groups (Maddox 2007).

One might surmise that Native Americans and Hispanics would be natural allies because they are both "territorial minorities" largely concentrated in the Southwest, both conquered by the U.S. military forces, and both having a treaty relationship with the United States, in addition to the similarities mentioned previously (de la Garza, Kruszewski, and Arciniega 1973). Selective reminders of historical occurrences, such as the conquest of the Southwest and its native people by the Spanish conquistadors, have often opened old wounds and rubbed salt in them, thus driving Native Americans and Hispanic Americans further apart.

Nevertheless, despite these differences, there have been several occasions where coalitions between two or more of these groups have been successful in combined political activities, such as securing benefits from government or preventing legislation that is seen as destructive, injurious, or insulting to their communities from being passed, or for bringing redress of grievances before governmental councils and having them successfully addressed. Another example has been some electoral coalitions that have managed to put together an *ad hoc* coalition of voters and that have managed to install in office members of minority groups or at least representatives who are sympathetic and supportive of minority groups' interests. As the Hispanic population continues to burgeon in the United States and the Native American population increases slowly, in addition to the rapidly increasing Asian American population, there should be, particularly in the nation's cities, more opportunities for urban and community interethnic coalitions.

As groups approach each other in relative size and power, it is much easier to form a coalition. One of the conditions for a successful coalition is for the component members to be of relatively equal strength so as this condition is approached, more successful coalitions may be formed (Carmichael and Hamilton 1967). Most of these coalitions will be "coalitions of immediate interest," that is, coalitions that come together to serve a specific purpose at a particular time. Once that is accomplished, they may or may not continue. Most important is the kind of mutual realization of a common situation and a determination to work together to solve local problems at a community grassroots level. When such coalitions and alliances are successful at the neighborhood and community level, they may then be leveraged and grown into larger-scale organizations to operate at a municipal, county, or even state level.

As the news-making results of the 2000 U.S. Census increasingly were made known, and the phenomenal growth and dispersion of the Hispanic population was being reported, more talk was heard among African American community representatives that a coalition between blacks and Hispanics would make a lot of sense and that leaders of both groups should work together to advance common interests and to put differences behind them for the greater good of both groups. This discussion was based on the fact that combined Latinos and African Americans represented more than one-fourth of the U.S. population and a plurality in several cities.

There have been several examples of successful interethnic coalitions. There are coalitions that occur during election times as campaigners target various segments of the population and try to create a winning majority or plurality by forming a coalition of recognizable demographic groupings. For example, the 2005 electoral coalition forged by Antonio Villaraigosa comprised of both Latinos and African Americans helped make Villaraigosa the first Latino in more than a century to win the mayoralty of Los Angeles. These coalitions are usually not formally negotiated and arranged, nor are they permanent alliances; instead they are really the result of particular campaigns. Often they are not realized until *after* the elections are over, when analysts look back and see that indeed there were certain combinations of various demographic groups that formed the winning coalition. So, these are often "after the fact" coalitions in which the grassroots members are not involved in active negotiation, bargaining, and discussion with each other. After such coalition victories, the various elements of the coalition often place their somewhat divergent claims on the victorious candidate. They may claim that each was the reason for the victory and should be rewarded with such perquisites as appointments, jobs, contracts, and the enactment of policies on that group's political agenda. Inevitably, at least some of these claims are sometimes conflicting with one another.

Much more permanent and constructive coalitions are those in which the members of the community are actually in discussions with one another, and in the give and take of the discussion of mutual problems and ways to solve this problem, a more solid and permanent basis is laid for a more harmonious, peaceful, and politically effective coalition for future endeavors. There are also coalitions that occur primarily among elites, which are usually found again on a temporary basis around particular issues, often in a defensive posture. These are sometimes found in legislatures, such as the Congressional Black Caucus and the Congressional Hispanic Caucus, forming alliances for or against a particular piece of legislation. For example, in 2005, these legislative groups were allies in supporting the renewal of the Voting Rights Act (VRA) of 1965. Similar coalitions can be found in the state legislatures and local legislatures, that is, city councils, county commissioners, or school boards throughout the United States.

Other bases for coalitions can also be found besides those of people of color. Although class differences are seldom the basis for serious and public discussions in the United States, economic lines of cleavage could certainly form the basis for a coalition. For example, Hispanics, being mainly working class and at the lower income levels of society, could form economic-based coalitions with other people similarly situated economically, including the much larger group of white people who are in the same economic class. There have been coalitions along economic lines throughout history that have existed at the local level, sometimes briefly at the national and state levels, and often at community levels. These often have not endured for long but instead are often directed at a particular problem of an economic nature. One of the major obstacles to such coalitions is the fact that social and political relationships between the white majority and people of color, irrespective of socioeconomic level, have not always been overly positive. In fact, several studies have shown that it is the lower economic, least educated group of white citizens who tend to be the most resistant to many kinds of social acceptance or contact with various people of color (Hood et al. 1997). Moreover, prevailing American ideology has looked down on any kind of attempt to organize politically along economic or class lines. Often, even the mere mention of class interest is dismissed with warning cries of fomenting eminent "class warfare."

There are other possible bases for coalition, such as *ideology*, for example. In fact, history has shown that persons who have very liberal or radical ideologies will coalesce regardless of ethnicity or economic status

(Gilliam 1996; Sonenshein 1993). During the Chicano movement, for example, many upper economic class white liberals were drawn into the civil rights movement to assist blacks, Hispanics, Native Americans, and Asians to gain full constitutional rights and privileges. In the 2005 mayoral election in Los Angeles, one basis for the victory of Antonio Villaraigosa was an electoral coalition of white liberals and Latinos (Sonenshein and Pinkus, 2005).

COALITIONS: INTRA-HISPANIC AND LATINO COALITIONS

We previously discussed possible coalitions of Latino groups with other non-Latino groups such as other racial and ethnic minority groups, economic groups, and ideological allies. However, this assumes that Hispanics themselves are perhaps a more cohesive and unified group than is actually the case. There is considerable discussion about the extent to which various Latino groupings have affinity for one another (Padilla 1985; Shorris 1993). Certainly, we have some data that show that there may have to be some coalition building done *within the Latino grouping* as well as between Latinos and other groups. That is, it is not at all clear that there is a psychological atmosphere among Latinos that is conducive to forming a pan-Latino coalition of unified Latino interests (Garcia 2003). It is often the case that the interests of national origin groups of Latinos can be quite distinct. This was brought forth dramatically in 1999 with the furor over the refugee child, Elián Gonzalez, who had escaped from Cuba to Florida and was being kept by distant Cuban American relatives from returning to his father and his closer relatives in Cuba. Although the Cuban American community was strongly unified in their opposition to returning the boy, surveys of other Latinos, including Mexican Americans, showed that their opinions were to the contrary, and much more in line with the general U.S. population, which was favoring the boy's return to his father and to the island of Cuba. Mexican Americans had a hard time appreciating the tremendous publicity and time, effort, and money spent on the case of this one little boy when Mexican American children are forcibly returned to Mexico almost daily after trying to enter the United States to join their families.

The LNPS has provided some attitudinal evidence that demonstrates that the psychological basis for an intra- or pan-Latino coalition is not readily apparent (Table 7.1). In Table 7.1, one can see that by and large each of the three Latino groups did not perceive that it had much in common politically with the other two major Latino national origin groups. When they were asked whether they shared *cultural* concerns with the other Latino groups, the answers were generally quite positive, but in this instance when they were asked about common *political* concerns, their answers were mostly negative in that they did not see that they had common

Table 7.1
PERCEPTIONS OF CULTURAL AND POLITICAL COMMONALITIES AMONG LATINOS

	Mexicans	Puerto Ricans	Cubans
Extent of cultural similarities			
Very similar	304 (19.7%)	118 (20.1%)	122 (18.0%)
Somewhat similar	842 (54.6%)	318 (54.3%)	366 (56.9%)
Not very similar	395 (25.6%)	150 (25.6%)	187 (27.5%)
Extent of political similarities between Mexicans and Cubans			
Very similar	116 (7.8%)	46 (8.3%)	32 (4.8%)
Somewhat similar	556 (37.3%)	209 (37.7%)	160 (24.2%)
Not very similar	820 (55.0%)	300 (54.1%)	469 (71.0%)
Extent of political similarities between Mexicans and Puerto Ricans			
Very similar	191 (12.7%)	46 (8.2%)	47 (7.2%)
Somewhat similar	607 (40.5%)	235 (42.0%)	196 (30.2%)
Not very similar	700 (46.7%)	279 (49.8%)	406 (62.6%)
Extent of similarities between Puerto Ricans and Cubans			
Very similar	191 (12.7%)	46 (8.2%)	47 (7.2%)
Somewhat similar	607 (40.5%)	235 (42.0%)	196 (30.2%)
Not very similar	700 (46.7%)	279 (49.8%)	406 (62.6%)

Source: R. de la Garza, L. DeSipio; F. Garcia, J. Garcia, and Angelo Falcón, *Latino Voices: Mexican, Puerto Rican, and Cuban Perspectives on American Politics* (Boulder, CO: Westview, Press, 1992).

political concerns with the other Latino groups. When the three largest Latino national origin groups were asked about the politically common concerns between Mexicans and Puerto Ricans in the United States, the opinions were evenly split between Mexicans and Puerto Ricans, while two-thirds of Cubans said that those two groups, Mexicans and Puerto Ricans, did not have any common concerns. When these groups were asked about the political commonality of Mexicans and Cubans, the majority of all three groups said that they did not have a common political agenda, and almost three-fourths of Cubans were of this opinion. When they were asked about the common political similarities between Puerto Ricans and Cubans, Puerto Ricans and Cubans themselves said that they did not have common political agendas. Only a majority of Mexican Americans said that they did perceive some common political concerns between Puerto Ricans and Cubans. Thus, at that time, the average Latino did not see that Latinos had much in common politically, at least at this abstract level.

However, it should be noted that these data are abstract, hypothetical, and more than fifteen years old. It is likely that since the 1990s there has been increasing interchanges and communications between the various Latino groups. As Mexicans, and to a lesser extent Puerto Ricans and Cubans, spread out across the country, they are more likely to encounter other Latinos and become more acquainted with each other's concerns, commonalities, and common interests while previously they have been rather isolated and concentrated in different parts of the country. However, a look at the *Washington Post* (1999) National Survey of Latinos indicated that nearly half of Latino respondents (48.9 percent) still agreed with the statement that Latinos in the United States share few political interests and goals (*Washington Post* 1999). However, following the mass marches on immigration in the spring of 2006, a majority (58 percent) of Latinos believed that Hispanics/Latinos from different countries today [were] working together to achieve common political goals (Pew Hispanic Center 2006). Therefore, at least in terms of perceived political common interests, it is not certain whether Latino perceptions on this matter have changed much since the 1990s. The postmarch feelings may have been a temporary positive "blip" of Latino opinion, or it might mark the beginning of permanently altered feelings about unity.

Yet, the media, government agencies, campaigners, and public officials keep referring to Latinos and Hispanics and talking about them as implicitly having common features, problems, and interests. This has undoubtedly led to an increasing emphasis on being a member of this Latino group and less emphasis on being a distinctive member of a national origin group. Most important, in several cases, Latinos of different national origins have rather easily entered into coalitions to advance common Latino interests, whether they are to preserve affirmative action and equal opportunity in the city of Chicago or to elect public officials in New York or Los Angeles. When Latinos face a common problem in a concrete situation with which they can deal most effectively in a coalition, they have often entered into these panethnic coalitions and been quite successful in their efforts.

It is also noteworthy that the massive immigration demonstrations of spring 2006 seem to have acted as a catalyst toward feelings of commonality and political community among Latinos. A 2002 National Survey of Latinos showed that a plurality of Hispanics (49 percent) believed that they were not working together to achieve common political goals (Pew Hispanic Center 2002). However, in a National Survey of Latinos taken in June and July of 2006, a majority of Hispanics (58 percent) believed that Hispanics from different countries were working together politically

(Pew Hispanic Center 2006). This finding was quite different from those of the previous fifteen years. Is this a discovery of a new attitudinal basis for a Latino political community, or is it only a "blip" in the more typical perception of differences resulting from the wide publicity, the excitement generated, and the significant effect on the national government's actions resulting from the mass mobilization? Only time will tell.

One effort to institutionalize the diversity of Latinos into an organizational base, at least among the leadership cadre, is the inception of the National Hispanic Leadership Agenda (NHLA). NHLA was founded in 1991 to foster the spirit of unity among Hispanic leaders and organizations. It seeks to promote consensus among Hispanic organizational leaders to the point of producing a policy agenda reflecting the diversity of viewpoints on public issues. Its board of directors includes prominent persons from across major Latino national origins and several organizational types—professional, advocacy, labor, and so on.

So, although there are still some disparities and problems in overcoming national origin distinctions, intra-Latino coalitions and alliances will increasingly be major players in the politics of this nation, particularly in its urban areas—towns and cities.

Although this discussion about coalitions and alliances includes coalitions of Hispanics or portions of the Hispanic communities with other groups, some observers would say that the first and most important coalition that needs to take place to enhance Latino political power is among Hispanics themselves. As we know, Hispanics are an extremely diverse and heterogeneous ethnic grouping, divided along lines of national origin, immigration, generation, geographical region, and economic status. Many students of politics would say that Latinos must first have a coalition among themselves, that is, an intra-Hispanic, transnational origin coalition united in a close enough alliance that they would take a similar position on any particular issue. Survey data have not been encouraging with regard to a national Latino coalition in the abstract. However, in several cases, particularly at the community level, various national origin groups have come together under the rubric of a "Latino coalition" to act effectively in either promoting or preventing various policies and pieces of legislation. For example, Latinos of Mexican and Puerto Rican origin in Chicago due to shared cultural and structural similarities, most prominently the experience of economic inequality, formed coalitions to advance the specific policy areas of affirmative action and employment (Padilla 1985).

It is likely that since the 1990s Latinos have become a more cohesive group as the media report more about this generalized grouping of Hispanics or Latinos. We do know that people of Spanish-related ancestry have increasingly been becoming accepting of the panethnic terms of Latino and Hispanic, as opposed to terms that indicate national origin as an accepted term of identification. Also, as more Hispanics come in from different Latin American countries, the divisions become so multiplied that they actually begin to lose their sharpness. However, one can see that there are some issues that greatly activate one national origin group but that are of little significance or are even opposed by others. Yet, there are some issues that tend to unify and unite Hispanics. Usually these involve attacks on Hispanic culture, such as legislation that calls for "English as the official language" or otherwise prohibits or disrespects the Hispanic language.

Overall, although group politics is much more effective than individual politics in almost every case, there is a cost to be paid for either organization or coalitions and alliances, particularly for the latter. Organization is pretty much a necessity for successful political activities, and Hispanic coalitions are not only desirable but will also increasingly be important to Hispanic politics in particular and ethnic politics in general as the country becomes more ethnically and racially diverse.

COALITIONS WITH LABOR UNIONS

It has been advocated that some Latinos enter into alliances with labor unions in order to multiply their resources and political influence. Because a significant proportion of Latinos are in the lower occupational ranks that include laborers, skilled craftsmen, operators, fabricators, and other working class positions, it might seem logical that participation with labor unions would be a major alliance strategy. Indeed it might be so in the future, and there are signs that a closer affiliation between Latinos and labor unions is occurring. However, in the past, there has been considerable tension between trade organizations, labor unions, and Latino workers as well as considerable discrimination within the trade union movement against Latinos. The controlling authorities have often kept Latinos at the lowest levels and have not allowed them to climb the hierarchy to become foremen, supervisors, or managers, or to become officers within the trade union organizations.

Although discriminatory practices within trade unions have been rampant, there seems to be a turn in attitude among the more enlightened unions in the late twentieth and early twenty-first century. For example, several unions have been historically in opposition to a more liberal immigration policy, as they see additional workers coming into the United States who are not unionized and who would provide competition for unionized labor, more particularly competition that will work for much lower, non-union scale wages. However, labor unions over the past few decades have been decreasing in membership and have been losing some political clout and influence partly due to this decreasing membership. Thus, to preserve the organization and to become more influential, some of the more enlightened union leaders have chosen to drop their opposition to bringing in or allowing workers from Latin America or Asia into the United States, and in fact have begun to welcome these immigrants into the ranks of organized labor. Some unions were actively involved in publicizing and organizing the immigration mass protests of spring 2006. In addition, labor unions have been providing resources such as an organized labor pool, financial recourses, physical facilities, and other resources and skills in order to help Latino candidates be elected to office. A recent example of this occurred in the 2005 mayoral race in Los Angeles when the significant public employees union backed the successful candidacy of Antonio Villaraigosa. It would seem that labor organizations could be a promising basis for the primarily working class Latinos to welcome as allies and as organizational bases for their political and economic activities. This kind of alliance is certainly one that bears tremendous possibilities and could very well be nurtured in the future.

ORGANIZATIONS: INTEREST GROUPS

In addition to coalitions among groups, the other major way of multiplying resources is for individuals to enter into coalitions with other individuals to advance their common interests, that is, to form what can be loosely termed as an "interest group." At the broadest level, these are simply groups of individuals who associate with one another because they are interested in a central purpose or have something important in common. They work together by regularly associating with one another, perhaps even through meetings and by having some division of labor within the organization, which often includes the establishment of leaders, or in a more formal sense, the election of officers. They often have some norms that govern the behavior of people who want to belong to the group. Sometimes they take the form of a written constitution or bylaws. Other times, they are simply behaviorally enforced norms of what is proper and what is not. So, the term "interest group" can cover a large number of diverse associations or organizations.

In a pluralistic system, it is held that the primary players in politics are groups, and mostly these are considered to be "interest groups," which are the most effective means of influencing decision makers and obtaining political power. Organized group activities are the main agents of political action in a democratic pluralistic system.

Throughout history, Latinos have not been known for having a high level of interest or participation in organizations specifically designed to act as pressure groups and influence the political decision makers. In the United States, there has been a relatively low awareness of ethnic interest groups and relatively low membership in these. However, this should not be seen as unique to Hispanics because it is common that individuals of low socioeconomic status in the United States are the least likely to be active in political and civic organizations.

In fact, when the history of Latino communities is accurately studied, one finds that Latino communities have had many organizations. In fact, there may have been too many organizations that are fragmented and have diverse bases. Having low levels of resources requires organizing to multiply those resources, but they also act against the formation of such organizations. This lack of organizations has been most evident at the national level. In local communities, however, there have been many more interest groups functioning to articulate Latino interests and to bring influence to bear on governmental and political processes. Since the mid-1950s, Hispanic organizations have been major players in defining Latino interests, marshaling resources and mobilizing constituencies in order to present their interests to public officials in both public and private sectors. In fact, the late twentieth century found a tremendous proliferation of Latino interest groups organized for action along several dimensions. For example, there are many civil rights organizations. Moreover, there has been an explosion of professional and business associations unique to Latinos, such as the National Hispanic National Bar Association, the National Hispanic Medical Association, the U.S. Hispanic Chamber of Commerce, the Society of Hispanic Professional Engineers, the National Association of Hispanic Journalists, and various labor unions, such as UFW. It is this trend of increased salience of Latino interest groups and organizations that motivates our discussion of the role of several Latino organizations in American politics. This discussion includes the various ways organizations have evolved to meet the needs and interests of an evolving Latino community.

The development of panethnicity across all Latino subgroups since the 1960s has placed different organizational pressures and expectations on existing Latino organizations, as well as motivated the creation of new ones. In an attempt to represent the wider spectrum of all Latinos in the national arena, well-established Latino organizations have altered their focus, activities, office headquarters, and even their names. Through this process to become representative of a growing and more diverse Latino population, some organizations have risen to national prominence. These include LULAC, which is the nation's oldest and largest Hispanic member organization. Founded in 1929, LULAC is estimated to have a membership of about 160,000 members, with more than 600 local councils in every state and Puerto Rico (Marquez 1993a, 1993b). LULAC was formed in Texas and had a membership base that was restricted to Mexican-origin citizens, although many of the groups' social service activities were not limited to citizens (Marquez 1988). Politically, education has consistently been a primary focus of LULAC. In the 1940s and 1950s, this effort was focused on using litigation to combat segregated education for Mexican students in Texas and California. More recently, LULAC has been working to increase Latino access to higher education and school financing. This includes the ongoing LULAC scholarship program. In contrast to the early history of the organization, LULAC has broadened its membership base to include both non-citizens and all Latinos, not only those of Mexican origin, and become more involved at the national level. The policy scope has also become broader as LULAC has begun to deal with issues such as immigration, civil rights, affirmative action, and language policies (Kaplowitz 2005). Finally, LULAC chapters have been formed in regions outside the Southwest and in Puerto Rico.

Another example of the impact of panethnicity is the National Council of La Raza (NCLR). Similar to LULAC, NCLR, founded in 1968 as the Southwest Council of La Raza, had a primary membership base of Mexican Americans or Chicanos. Although the goals of reducing poverty and discrimination and improving economic opportunities for Mexican Americans have not changed, its activities are now aimed at all Latinos or Hispanics. Furthermore, NCLR has initiated chapters in the Midwest, Northeast, and South, with a clear central presence in Washington, DC. In fact, NCLR has now taken on a major role as the primary pan-Hispanic national lobbying organization in Washington, DC. NCLR is an alliance, an affiliation of more than 200 community-based Latino organizations across the United States. It attempts to present its positions directly to decision makers, to compile information and data that can be used to influence decisions, and to produce press releases on current public policies of interest to Latinos. Some of the areas in which NCLR is active include immigration reform, social welfare reform, and affirmative action policies.

Similarly, the National Institute of Latino Policy (NILP) was originally founded in New York City as the Institute for Puerto Rican Policy in 1982. NILP is a private nonpartisan policy center that is action oriented and focuses on issues salient to the Latino population. Although NILP has changed its name and mission to be more inclusive of all Latino subgroups, the organization continues to focus primarily on the Puerto Rican population and the East Coast more generally. For example, in 2004, NILP published the *Atlas of Stateside Puerto Ricans*, which promoted a new discussion of the relationship between Puerto Ricans in Puerto Rico and those in the United States. NILP also serves as a major clearinghouse of data related to the Puerto Rican community and Latinos generally.

LATINO ORGANIZATIONS AND LITIGATION

The Mexican American Legal Defense and Education Fund (MALDEF) and the Puerto Rican Legal Defense and Education Fund (PRLDEF) are the most prominent legal organizations that have represented Hispanic interests largely through litigation on a number of issues, including affirmative action, immigration, redistricting, minority group vote dilution, and racial profiling. Although the primary focus of both organizations founded in the 1970s has been the protection under law and civil rights for the Puerto Rican and Mexican American communities, their scope has been expanded to be more inclusive of all Latinos. The primary difference between these two organizations and the others discussed in this chapter is that the membership base of both MALDEF and PRLDEF is largely comprised of attorneys. Furthermore, both organizations have a board of directors and a general counsel to lead them. Due to not having an independent Latino constituency, both organizations have established links to other Latino leaders and/or organizations to determine which policy issues and plaintiffs to work with.

The areas of focus for both legal organizations include equality for the Latino population in education, employment, housing, and voting rights. In addition, MALDEF has included the policy area of immigration and immigrant rights as part of its core mission. Voting rights have been a major focus for both organizations for some time because PRLDEF and MALDEF have challenged the election structure of at-large districts in favor of districted elections since then. Currently, the focus of both groups in this area has been on redistricting plans to increase Latino descriptive representation, primarily through the creation of majority-minority districts.

Two cases exemplify the work of these organizations in the policy area of education. In *Plyler v. Doe* (1982), MALDEF took on the issue of free educational access by undocumented school children. The local school district required that children show proof of legal status to receive a free public education. MALDEF was successful in convincing the court that access to education is a basic right that is accorded to all persons residing in the jurisdiction of the school district. PRLDEF similarly chose the policy area of education for their first lawsuit, where they took on the issue of language rights and access to bilingual education services in *Aspira v. New York City Board of Education* (1974). This decision resulted in the Aspira Consent Decree, which forced the school system to implement bilingual education programs for non–English-speaking students and hire Spanish-speaking teachers. MALDEF's interest in education has motivated the creation of the Community Education and Leadership Development Program, established in 1975. A major focus of this program is to provide parents with the skills necessary to ensure that legal decisions are implemented by policy makers.

LATINO "INSIDER" ORGANIZATIONS

Through both the dramatic demographic changes discussed thus far and the institutional changes in the electoral process, there has been a steady rise in Latino elected officials at all levels of government. This increased descriptive representation for the Hispanic community has motivated the expansion of organizations that work within government institutions. One major organization in this realm is the National Association of Latino Elected and Appointed Officials (NALEO), which is primarily interested in increasing the number and effectiveness of Latinos in public office. NALEO not only collects data on Latino public officials but also holds training sessions to improve the performance of its constituents in their public offices. The annual NALEO conference is the nation's largest gathering of Latino elected and appointed officials. It provides dynamic professional development activities for Latino officials and serves as a focal point for establishing policy priorities for the Hispanic community. Recognizing that increasing the turnout rates of the Hispanic community will help create greater representation for Latinos, NALEO has been actively engaged in a campaign to promote naturalization among the Latino immigrant community. Another effort of NALEO intended to expand the voting base of the Hispanic community has been to become involved with the U.S. Census planning process. Specifically, NALEO has promoted the full count of all Latinos, supported complete confidentiality for respondents, translated forms and information into Spanish, and hired Latino enumerators.

Other highly visible organizations throughout the 1960s and 1970s have been the Southwest Voter Registration and Education Project (SVREP), the Midwest Voter Registration and Education Project, and the Northeast Voter Registration and Education Project. The latter two combined with other organizations to produce a larger effective group, the U.S. Hispanic Leadership Institute. These groups have been instrumental in registering hundreds of thousands of Latinos for elections since the 1970s. Their voter registration drives have been extremely successful. They have also done a lot of research, surveying Latinos primarily on electoral-related matters, and have joined groups such as MALDEF in advocating Hispanic interests in the redistricting process.

Finally, founded in 1976, the Congressional Hispanic Caucus (CHC) is a legislative organization within U.S. Congress. The primary goals of this organization are to foster a collective policy agenda for the Latino community, and to examine both executive and judicial policies that are salient to Latinos. One specific strategy of CHC has been to promote the names of several Latino federal judges to fill Supreme Court vacancies. Interestingly, not all members of Congress who are of Latino origin are members of CHC. The three Latino Republican Congress persons are not CHC members, largely as a result of the Democratic dominance of CHC and policy differences regarding Cuba. There is also a Congressional Hispanic Caucus Institute (CHCI), which is a nonpartisan organization whose mission is to develop the next generation of Latino leaders. CHCI seeks to accomplish this mission by offering educational and leadership development programs, services, and activities that promote the growth of participants as effective professionals and strong leaders. CHCI has both a fellowship and internship program, as well as an alumni association that intends to establish a network of young Hispanic leaders in government-related areas. In addition to CHCI, the Congressional Hispanic Leadership Institute (CHLI) seeks to conduct research that focuses on the Hispanic community, and provide educational and training programs. CHLI was initiated as a Republican alternative to CHCI.

These are just a few of the plethora of interest groups and organizations that have sprung up and flourished since the 1970s. Across the United States, virtually every sector of American life has produced Hispanic interest groups. Regardless of whether they are in education, employment, the professions, the arts, or avocational interests, there has been a corresponding number of interest groups organized to advance Hispanic aspects. In the early twenty-first century, Hispanics are organized as never before to effectively mobilize their members and resources to function as pressure groups in affecting the decision making of both public and private sector authorities.

There are still some obvious difficulties with Hispanic political interest groups. One is their relative youth—much of their effort must be put into protecting and strengthening the organizations themselves. Another is that many definitely have a middle class bias and need to extend their membership to the lower socioeconomic groups. This is a challenge for all organizations because of the previously mentioned barriers to participation that exist for people of lower socioeconomic status. More important for the future, Hispanics have a particular challenge in adapting their organizations so they can more easily draw the large and growing number of immigrants into their activities. These immigrants can bring not only numbers, but also new energy, motivation, desires, and skills to revitalize and strengthen the various groups. Yet, because of their newness to this society, they also need particular attention paid to their own interests and needs. In addition, many of the more well-publicized, national-level interest groups depend on much of their support from sources outside the Hispanic community, particularly from philanthropical foundations such as the Ford Foundation or government grants. There is also a large dependence on economic corporations that are largely controlled by non-Hispanics of the upper socioeconomic class. Until Latinos can develop their own strong leadership cadre and financial resources that are more independent of these non-Hispanic resources, their activities and operations must necessarily be circumscribed by their dependence on and ties to their outside supporters.

LATINO GRASSROOTS ORGANIZATIONS

Some organizations that have been most successful in working with people least accustomed to organizational activities, particularly political organizational activities, have been the offshoots of the Industrial Areas

Foundation (IAF), which was established by Saul Alinsky. Most noticeable has been the work of Ernesto Cortez, who has been successful in developing political interests and activism in low-income *barrios* and *colonias* (Marquez 1993b). Using the IAF approach, Cortez and others go into a community and help the neighborhood identify its own problems, bring forth and develop its own natural community leaders, take its own form of identification, and train these people in the skills they will need to confront the decision-making elites who have the power to deal with these community problems. Workshops are held to teach people the skills of communication, negotiation, bargaining, presentation, and organization. The style developed by most of these organizations, often operating under the interfaith banner, has largely been one of direct personal confrontation of decision makers. The typical tactic would be to attend a meeting of a decision-making board, such as a school board or city council, with a large number of community residents and activists and forcefully present the needs and demands, not allowing the decision makers off the hook until some action is taken.

The interfaith organizations so successful in Texas—COPS, Valley Interfaith in the lower Rio Grande Valley, El Paso Interreligious Sponsoring Organization; in California—United Neighborhood Organization; and in New Mexico—Albuquerque Inter-Faith have relied heavily on church affiliations, particularly affiliations with the Catholic Church, to garner the additional stable organizational leadership and resources of the religious organizations on behalf of the communities' causes. Because of their often confrontational, in-your-face style, these interfaith groups have been perceived as radical in nature. However, as visible as their tactics have been, these groups and their leaders, such as Ernie Cortez, have also been criticized as being conservative and thus doing a disservice to the Latino community. The approach taken by Alinsky-style organizations has been to teach skills necessary to succeed in politics within the system to favorably affect decisions by the system to provide benefits that other groups have been receiving, in other words, to get what they want and need. These often are mundane objectives such as sewage and sanitation systems, improved lighting, parks and recreational facilities, and better police relations. Because these organizations are only seeking a reallocation of some of the existing resources, more radical critics have often criticized them as actually strengthening the status quo of inequality between Hispanics and non-Hispanics. IAF Inter-Faith does not challenge the distribution of power in the society directly. It does not seek radical changes in the structure of U.S. institutions, nor does it seek to overturn those who currently have power, but rather it seeks to wring concessions from them. So, this conventional approach to American politics is then branded as token "reformist" politics, which is really not going to change the basic situation for Hispanics in the United States. It is accused of simply perpetuating the status quo with a few minor victories that will buy off larger attempts to make more radical, important, and basic changes in American society and the distribution of power in this society.

Although this is a legitimate criticism from a more radical perspective, for community residents who have been powerless, who have not had their voices heard, and who have been relatively ignored by the system, small victories that improve their everyday lives, as well as experiences that give them a higher sense of self-esteem and empowerment as citizens, are also important advances in Hispanic politics.

Certainly, interest and pressure group politics in the United States is the main political game that is played. Even though it is within conventional bounds, mastering this level of politics has at least provided for some short-term victories, and in the long term, because of its emphasis on community empowerment and improvement of the political skills of community leaders, it may even lead to more major changes in society, especially over a period of time, because incremental changes add up to rather substantial changes.

INTEREST GROUPS AND SOCIAL MOVEMENTS

When politics is not pluralistic interest group politics but instead is politics that involves more large-scale activities, at least some of which are more radical in their objectives, these can be more readily identified as social or political *movement* politics (Torres and Katsiaficas 1999). We have already discussed the Chicano movement, which is the prime example of Hispanic political movements in the twentieth century. Such movements not only seek a larger slice of the American pie, but also often challenge the basic values and objectives of life in the United States and seek the redistribution of power in the system. As such, they are often seen as more radical and extraordinary types of collective political action, and indeed they occur much less often and are much more notable and noticeable. However, social and political movements such as the Chicano movement and the civil rights movement take a great deal of energy, commitment, and time. Although these movements often accomplish great things and move the society in a substantial way, they often expire because of the burnout factor of people engaging in such intensive activities, and because eventually either significant reform is made by the system or the system grows tired of such disruptive and confrontational activities and squelches or ignores such social movements as well as it can. It is interesting that a survey by the Pew Hispanic Center in summer 2006 found that a large majority of Latinos felt that "the immigrant marches [of spring 2006] are the beginning of a new (Hispanic/Latino) social movement that will go on for a long time" (Suro and Escobar 2006, 8). At the least, this showed a spirit of excitement and perhaps optimistic hope among Latinos, a feeling that can lead to more interest and activity in politics. However, unlike the tumultuous era of the Chicano movement, the political and social environment of the mid-2000s was not one of general civil unrest and activism on the domestic front.

LATINA ORGANIZATIONS

Although women have played, and continue to play, significant roles in the many organizations described to this point, there is a need to discuss some of the organizations that have a specific focus on Latina issues and concerns. In some instances, these organizations were formed as counterparts to the larger Latino/Hispanic organizations. In particular, LULAC's Mujeres en Acción had the largest membership of any of the women's organizations during the Chicano movement era (Gomez-Quinones 1994). The Mexican American Women's National Association (MAWNA) was formed in 1974 as a Chicana/Latina counterpart to the National Organization of Women (Navarro 2005). A major focus of MAWNA was to develop leadership skills among its members in order to establish leadership parity. Similar to other organizations discussed in this chapter, in an effort to broaden its Latino ethnic base, MAWNA established a national headquarters in the eastern United States and in 1998 changed its name to "MANA: A National Latina Organization" (Meier and Gutiérrez 2000, 138–139). There are also women's political pressure or interest groups, such as Hispanas Organized for Political Equality (HOPE). HOPE is a nonprofit, nonpartisan organization that strives to ensure political and economic parity of Latinas through leadership, advocacy, and education. Based on these principles in 1999, HOPE created the HOPE Leadership Institute, an eight-month leadership training program that is dedicated to the empowerment of Latinas to create social change in the policy areas of health, education, and economics (Navarro 2005, 535). Latina organizations have also been successful at the grassroots level. For example, in response to state and local government initiatives to locate a prison facility and waste management site in east Los Angeles, the concerned mothers and other women in this area formed the Mothers of East Los Angeles (MELA) in 1986 (Pardo 1998). After nearly seven years of continuous mobilization that included large rallies of citizens, lobbying, and support from powerful allies such as Archbishop Roger Mahony, MELA was successful in defeating the two projects in 1992. This success sparked similar grassroots efforts in other Latino communities across the United States (Cruz 1998; Falcon and Santiago 1993).

CUBAN-SPECIFIC ORGANIZATIONS

The final group of organizations that we discuss here are those that are directly tied to the Cuban community. Some of the earliest organizational efforts among the Cuban American community were exile oriented. As a result of the history of the Cuban community discussed in Chapter 2, most of the Cuban populations' attention has focused on U.S. foreign policy toward Cuba and Castro's regime. Some of the goals of Cuban interest groups have included the creation of Radio-TV Martí, trade embargoes, the continued admission of Cuban immigrants as political refugees, and overthrowing the Cuban revolutionary government (Navarro 2004).

The most prominent of these exile-oriented organizations is the Cuban American National Foundation (CANF). CANF was founded in 1981, with an emphasis on replacing Castro's communist regime with a market-based democracy in Cuba. To this end, CANF lobbies in Washington, DC, to maintain international political and economic pressure and the isolation of the Castro regime. CANF has also been very successful in influencing the U.S. government to pass legislation to allow continued Cuban immigration. For example, one of CANF's exodus support programs initiated in 1988 has allowed more than 10,000 Cuban refugees residing in other countries with family in the United States to come to the United States. CANF also has attempted to provide a window to the outside world for Cubans on the island who are deprived of objective information and ideas from abroad. In addition to their own radio station, La Voz de la Fundación, CANF has led the effort to establish the U.S. Information Agency's Radio Martí in 1985 and TV Martí in 1990, the official U.S. broadcasting operations of uncensored and unbiased news and programming for the Cuban people.

Although the size and success of the CANF has led to the reinforcement of the image of Cuban organizations as exile oriented, there have and continue to be Cuban organizational efforts that assist the assimilation of Cubans into the political and economic spheres of the United States. Organizations such as the Spanish American League Against Discrimination and the Cuban American National Council (CNC) direct their efforts toward issues that impact Cubans and other Latinos once they reside in the United States. CNC has been especially active in the areas of education, housing, and economic development services. CNC has helped more than 3,500 at-risk students remain in school, has provided more than eighty internships to low-income students, and has made 36,800 direct job placements. CNC has also become one of the largest Hispanic nonprofit developers of section 202 housing serving low-income elderly persons in the United States and has built new housing units for 1,700 persons of low and moderate income. Therefore, although exile-oriented activities remain a critical element of Cuban organizational activities, it is clear that domestic issues are also pertinent to the Cuban American community and the organizations that represent them.

LEADERSHIP

One of the most important aspects of political organization and subsequent political success, particularly in a pluralistic democracy where groups are the primary political players, is the quality of group *leadership*. Leadership is sometimes difficult to define concisely. It is known that virtually every group or organization has a few "key people" who tend to be the most active and involved and who are instrumental in setting the direction and in providing the operations of any organization. Whether it is a club, interest group, or political party, these key people in organizations somehow manage to either have the qualities that impel them toward leadership or have developed the skills that allow them to play this essential role. There is no doubt that often the most effective political groups and organizations are those that have the most effective leadership. These leaders are key people who can and are willing to devote considerable time, energy and effort to the maintenance and goal-oriented behavior of their organizations. They can serve as spokespersons for these organizations and are often seen as being among the influential members of any society.

Hispanic leadership has gone through several stages in the United States. Although these are not clearly neat and distinctive phases, they are generally recognized as sequences in the development of leadership and leader types in the Hispanic community. From the earliest times, whenever there was a Hispanic community, natural leaders emerged. These people were often businessmen, educators, or religious leaders to whom others deferred and from whom others sought guidance and assistance. With the coming of Anglo America in 1848, a new type of leadership developed among Hispanics. Another culture's economic, political, and religious system was being imposed on the conquered Mexican American people. Many of the persons who had previously been leaders in the Hispanic community were nullified or replaced by the Anglo Americans. The Hispanic community now needed persons who could serve as *liaisons* or go-betweens for the Anglo and Hispanic communities. At the minimum, these people had to be bilingual and often bicultural. They also had to have, if not the respect, at least the acceptance, of both the Hispanic community and the now superordinate Anglo ruling hierarchy. In other words, new leaders were "intermediaries" who had to have the acceptance, if not the support, of each of the two distinct sides of the new society.

To play an intermediate role of communication and mutual understanding between the two societies, they had to engage in what is called "dual validation." This meant that the leaders of this now dichotomized society would have to be acceptable to both Anglo and Hispanic societies. Such intermediaries would have to be helpful in interpreting the needs and wants of the Hispanic communities to the Anglo Americans now in newly created positions of power in government, education, economics, and religion. The Hispanic community needed to have faith that these Hispanic intermediary leaders would present the community's needs and interests effectively and clearly to the decision makers and that the power holders would in turn have enough faith in this intermediate representative that the representatives would be paid attention to and would be able to intercede successfully on behalf of the Hispanic people. However, from their perspective, the Anglo Americans wanted these intermediaries to not only have the confidence of the native communities but also to be trustworthy and to not subvert the external power holders. But, instead, they would be cooperative with them for the mutual benefit of the Hispanic community and the Anglo power holders.

This dual validation requirement for Hispanic leaders was clearly the case in the past. Some even contend that this same type of leader is necessary today, if perhaps in a much modified and subdued form. That is, there are still Hispanic leaders or spokespersons who claim to represent the interests and values of the Hispanic people or communities and to speak for them. They must have some standing in, or acceptance by, the Hispanic community, at least to the extent that they are not disowned or repudiated by them, and yet must also be acknowledged as spokespersons or leaders by the dominant power holders in society—its media, governments, and businesses. This is a tight and precarious line to walk. If the intermediary leader becomes too close to the Anglo side and he or she can be seen as abandoning the Hispanic community and no longer speaking for it, that person consequently will be disowned by the community and will no longer have any legitimacy to speak for a sector of the Hispanic population. In fact, such a person may be accused of just being out for his or her own self-interest or will be accused of being a sell-out, a *vendido*, who is from the community but certainly is not for or of the community. Usually, in these cases, new spokespersons or leaders will arise from the community who are in much closer touch with its sentiments and interests.

Still another challenge comes from the other side. The intermediary Hispanic leader must be able to deal well with powerful decision makers in the Anglo community. Because most of the power holders in our community today, whether in corporations, educational or economic institutions, or governments are still Anglo and still mainly male, these people can reject Hispanic leaders who seem to be *too* Hispanic. They have the capacity to reject those who are not Anglicized enough either in their style of presenting themselves or in their communications, that is, those who are perceived as being too Latin in their accents or behavior. In this situation, these people could be seen as stepping out of their place and being overly ambitious. If such people are too Hispanic, then they may be perceived as troublemakers; thus, the Anglo power holders will be likely to dismiss those persons as illegitimate or inappropriate.

There was a period during which the historically typical type of leadership took a new form to meet the challenges of these times. During the Chicano movement (roughly 1964–1974), the recognized leaders displayed some attributes that were a break from the past, and to some extent, from the current qualities of leadership. The era was one of protest, activism, and militancy in which direct challenges to the mainstream establishment were presented. Moreover, there was a great emphasis on separation and self-empowerment; rejection of many mainstream organizations and institutions; and a call for self-determination, community control, and pride in ethnic culture. Leaders of that era were consequently much less concerned about their acceptance by the power structure than they were in posing effective challenges to it. In this countercultural milieu, those leaders had to have deep roots in the shared experiences of their people, a strong sense of injustice, and the will and determination to push hard for the causes of the Latino communities regardless of possible consequences or retributions. They had to be eloquent in their communications, brave and forceful in their actions, committed to the cause, and able to maintain a high level of activity and energy for themselves and among those whom they mobilized. They had to be able to rally masses of people who had been largely excluded from the system and who possessed few political resources, and motivate them to confront major centers of established power. In short, these leaders needed charisma. They also needed to have the other qualities that effective political leaders always need, such as an extensive and intensive knowledge of the U.S. political system—how it worked and how to influence it. These and additional qualities were possessed by the "big four" of the Chicano movement—César Chávez, Rodolfo "Corky" Gonzales, José Ángel Gutiérrez, and Reies López Tijerina—and many other less well-known leaders. As the civil rights era and the Chicano movement cooled down, leaders with characteristics more suited to less confrontational, more moderate political times again came to the fore. Yet, the lessons learned and the admired leadership qualities of the more turbulent era became part of the new political paradigms.

Not that there had not been effective leadership before and during the Chicano movement. There have always been key persons among Hispanics who have served the people and their communities well. Most have been known only in the localities and the national origin groups so well served by them, but several have transcended these limits and have had a significant impact across regions and national origin groupings. Fewer have received the recognition they deserved outside their communities.

Due to space limitations in this book, only a few attaining national prominence are listed here, with the caveat that there are many more who have contributed much and are equally deserving.

Dennis Chávez—Mr. Chávez was a longtime U.S. senator (1935–1962) from New Mexico, who before being elected Senator had served two terms in the U.S. House of Representatives. He championed civil rights legislation in the 1940s, helping obtain social services, employment, and educational opportunities for Hispanics. He never forgot his roots and continued to bring the plight of Hispanics and other disadvantaged minorities into the national congressional political arena.

Henry G. Cisneros—Mr. Cisneros is most widely recognized as being the first Hispanic to be elected mayor of a major U.S. city. In 1981, he was elected to the first of four terms as mayor of San Antonio, Texas. After serving successfully in that position, for which he received much recognition by the media nationally, he served as secretary of the Department of Housing and Urban Development (HUD) from 1993 to 1997, under President William (Bill) J. Clinton. Widely praised for policy and organizational successes while heading HUD, he also became president of the National League of Cities and chairman of the National Civic League.

Bert Corona—Mr. Corona was an activist who, beginning in the 1930s, was a key in union activities, coalition building, and community mobilization, primarily in Southern California. In the 1960s, he was active in Democratic Party political activities and in the UFW movement. He was a major advocate for immigrant rights and founded *Hermandad Mexicana Nacional*, the nation's largest Latino immigrant's organization, with more than 30,000 member families across the country.

Dr. Hector P. Garcia—Dr. Garcia grew up in the hostile, strongly segregated environment of south Texas in the 1920s. After leaving Texas to earn a medical doctorate and serve in World War II, he resided in Corpus Christi, where he founded the American GI Forum and was also active in LULAC, fighting rampant discrimination on several civil rights fronts—legal, educational, economic, health, and immigration— for several decades more. He was awarded the Presidential Medal of Freedom in 1984 and continued to lead the fight against poverty and injustice until his death in 1996.

Edward Roybal—Mr. Roybal was born in Albuquerque to a family that traced its roots back some 400 years to the founding of Santa Fe. He graduated from Roosevelt High School in Boyle Heights, California, and attended the University of California at Los Angeles. Roybal took office in 1963, joining Henry B. Gonzalez (D-Texas) and Joseph Montoya (D-NM) as the only Hispanics serving in the U.S. House of

Representatives; he retired in January 1993. While in Congress, he championed the rights of immigrants, although he did oppose the landmark 1986 amnesty law, which led to the legalization of more than 1.5 million Latinos. Roybal's opposition to this law was based on his belief that the employer-sanctioned provisions would lead to discrimination against all Hispanic workers. In 1967, he introduced and won approval for the first federal bilingual education law, which established English classes for migrant children and others. He was also instrumental in getting Congress to approve funds to provide medical, welfare, and educational services to eligible immigrants. As late as 1990, he voted to maintain flexibility and avoid hard restrictions in immigration measures. Roybal's strong leadership and advocacy on behalf of the rights of Hispanics paved the way for passage of the Civil Rights Act of 1964, the VRA, and other similar legislation; expanded support for community health centers; and helped improve how the U.S. Bureau of the Census collected social, economic, and health data for Hispanics. He was a co-founder of the Congressional Hispanic Caucus and the National Association of Latino Elected and Appointed Officials.

Vicente Ximénez—Mr. Ximénez lived his boyhood in the 1930s in segregated Floresville, Texas. One of the few Mexican American high school graduates, he worked to attend the University of Texas, where he became friends with Hector Garcia. After serving in World War II, he moved his family to Albuquerque, where he earned a master's degree at the University of New Mexico and became active in the GI Forum and Democratic Party politics. Ximénez was appointed by President Lyndon B. Johnson as U.S. commissioner of the Equal Employment Opportunity Commission in Washington, DC, where he served for five years. In 1967, he was chosen as the chairman of President Johnson's new Cabinet Committee on Mexican American Affairs. He later became the vice president for field operations of the National Urban Coalition.

William Velasquez—Mr. Velasquez founded SVREP and was an influential participant in other leading Latino rights and justice groups, including MAYO and the Mexican American Unity Council. From the late 1960s until his untimely death in 1988, he helped Mexican Americans and other Hispanics become electoral participants in American politics. Velasquez's dedication to voter rights and registration resulted in an unprecedented and massive mobilization of Latino voters in many areas of the United States, especially in the pivotal electoral states of California, Illinois, and Texas (Sepulveda 2003).

Raúl Yzaguirre—Mr. Yzaguirre was the longtime leader of NCLR, retiring from the organization in 2004 after 30 years. Under his guidance, NCLR developed from the Southwest Council of La Raza to a

Washington, DC-headquartered association of more than 300 affiliated community-based group members, most likely the single most
powerful Latino advocacy group in the United States.

These are but a few examples of the many Hispanic leaders who managed
to push hard against injustices and for the rights of their people, working
within the system, although often being discriminated against themselves
by that same system. There have been many others.

The major reason for the often perilous position that Hispanic leaders
have had to try to maintain for so long is the basic imbalance between
the Hispanic and the non-Hispanic white population in the United States.
As long as there is a considerable discrepancy between the two, as long
as white Americans are generally in superordinate, dominant positions
and Hispanics are largely in subordinate positions, this precarious
situation for such intermediary leaders will persist. This means that at a
national or state level of public office; in major cities; or in large corporate, educational, or religious organizations, Hispanic leadership will
most likely continue to be problematic and precarious. In those cases
when Hispanic leaders need only to be responsive and responsible to
their own smaller community at a local or community level, that leadership will continue to be natural and unaffected as it has been through the
centuries.

Too often major organizations in the United States have recognized
one or a few upcoming or potential leaders in the Hispanic community
and have decided to allow them into their circles, at least at a superficial
level. If these persons are willing to adopt the values and interests and to
try to emulate the lifestyles of the power holders, then they can become
marginal or "token" members of the leadership cadres of organizations.
These token members who are taken in and lose their roots in the community and their contacts with the Hispanic people are said to have been
"coopted" by the powerful and are simply often "window dressing," having no real basis for their power or decision making capacity themselves.
They are often just showpieces that are trotted out by the executives in
various organizations to show that their organizations are nondiscrimina-
tory, diverse, and inclusive, which is demonstrated by their exhibition of
one or a few "token" Hispanics. These token Hispanics almost always
have little or no real authority because they have no power base other than
that which can be meted out or withheld by the power holders. Because
they have no independent power base, they are at the beck and call of the
leaders of the dominant society. These tokens are often granted special
organizational positions that have little line authority and are often given
such positions as Associate Vice President for Hispanic Affairs or Deputy
Director for Hispanic Outreach or some similar title that is often just a
public relations move on the part of the power holders.

Although the situation described previously may still exist to some extent, it is disappearing as Hispanics increase in number and themselves become more powerful and influential in their own right. The basis for the intermediary or token leader is the fact that U.S. society has had great gaps or differentials in status or power between the Hispanic and the non-Hispanic community. As this gap diminishes and continues to grow smaller, the leaders of the Hispanic communities can and will have their own power bases from which to operate. They need no longer depend on the arbitrary support from above but instead can rely on their own independent power base in the Hispanic community. As Hispanics increasingly build their own population and economic power bases and form their own businesses and other organizations, as they reach higher levels of educational attainment and higher levels of wealth and home and business ownership, they are increasingly able to make it on their own. Being more independent, they can retain whatever aspects of the Hispanic culture they want to retain and still function well in American society.

HISPANIC WOMEN AS LEADERS

One of the positive features of these transitional forms of leadership is the changing role of women as leaders in Hispanic politics. Although the conventional wisdom holds that Latinas (and, to a lesser extent, Anglo women) have no role in politics because their role is in the home and the domestic sphere, this is certainly no longer true, if it ever was. Some recent studies showed that Hispanic women have long been very actively engaged in politics (Hardy-Fanta 1993; Niemann 2002; Pardo 1997). However, instead of being out front and visible, the ones running for office, and in the process seeking personal aggrandizement or feeding their personal ego needs through publicity, women, on the contrary, have been satisfied to work behind the scenes to solve and resolve the problems that their families or communities faced. Using traditional networks of communication such as they have in their neighborhoods and employing the skills of negotiation and compromise developed in the family and in the raising of children, they have often carried out much of the essential and important, if less glamorous, work of political campaigns, movements, and organizations. They have been the ones sending out press releases; preparing mailings; making phone calls; managing offices; and preparing the barbecues, *tamaladas,* or other food or fun events that are part of campaign politics. They have also been the ones that have kept the minutes of meetings, as secretaries, and often kept the financial records straight.

During the Chicano movement, several women became more visible in their leadership roles, most notably Dolores Huerta who was very much a coorganizer of the National Farm Workers Union (later the UFW), along with César Chávez. As the concurrent women's liberation and feminist movements of the 1960s and 1970s tended to help liberate women from their more traditional roles and give them more options, women, including Latinas, had the increased option of coming more into the forefront in Hispanic politics. Indeed, it may surprise some to find that Hispanic women vote in greater proportions than Hispanic men. Moreover, a greater percentage of Hispanic public officeholders are women (some 30 percent in 2000) than are Anglo officeholders (about 22 percent in 2000). Increasingly, many of the Hispanic women are becoming more visible political leaders at the grassroots, neighborhood, and community levels, often heading neighborhood associations as well as political and other community-based organizations. They have also increasingly run for political office. This heightened activity has been evident in national Hispanic organizations as well. For example, in 2005, MALDEF and NCLR were headed by Latinas. Ann Marie Tallman was the president and general counsel for MALDEF, and Janet Muriaga served as the president and chief executive officer of NCLR. In 2006, Rosa Rosales was elected national president of LULAC.

It seems that modern Hispanic leaders, whether male or female, need to have many of the same characteristics and qualifications as do non-Hispanic white leaders. For example, the National Community for Latino Leadership took a survey of more than 3,000 Latinos across the United States and asked them what qualities they most sought in Latino leaders (National Community for Latino Leadership 2001). Far and above, the first requisite characteristic was "honesty and integrity," garnering some 50 percent of the responses; all other characteristics received significantly less than 10 percent each. This requirement for their leaders to be honest and trustworthy has been found repeatedly not only in surveys of Anglo Americans but also in surveys of populations in other countries.

Some generic qualifications and skills of leadership do seem to exist, regardless of culture or gender. However, given the U.S. political and societal situation faced by racial and ethnic groups, minority, and especially Hispanic, leaders also need to have those special characteristics mentioned previously. Surveys of the Hispanic population have indicated that in addition to the more universal characteristics, they want to have their leaders exhibit more concern for the community, be of more service to collective groups of Hispanics, and not be so preoccupied with serving themselves or serving individuals. In addition to this community-serving orientation, Hispanic leaders must be able to communicate effectively in a bicultural mode, understand and share the values of both Hispanic and Anglo mainstream cultures, and bridge the two effectively.

Thus, the burden placed on Hispanic leadership is still considerable, even more so than it is for leadership in the general society. Hispanic organizations such as the Hispanic Leadership Institute, CHCI, and NALEO have recognized the critical importance of effective leadership. Many seminars, institutes, and conventions are now dedicated to leadership training and development.

As the differences and gaps between the Anglo and Hispanic peoples in the United States diminish, and the American populations become more acculturated to one another, it is likely that Anglo American leaders will also become more adept at communicating with, reaching out to, and working with Hispanic communities. There will be less need for Hispanic leaders to be coopted or token leaders. Instead, they can have a more solid power base in the Hispanic community and operate from a position of strength. Or, at a more advanced stage, both Hispanic and non-Hispanic leaders can concentrate on the tasks at hand without being overly concerned about cultural disparities and differences between the two groups adversely affecting their important roles and responsibilities in American politics and society in general.

SUMMARY AND CONCLUSION

The elements that increase the effectiveness of Hispanics in U.S. politics are dynamic, and much change has occurred since the late 1960s. Hispanics are increasingly becoming more significant allies in various situations that call for coalitions. There has been an unprecedented explosion of Hispanic organizations—in all sectors of society and at all levels of government and politics. Hispanic leadership continues to evolve, develop, and become increasingly effective.

In the U.S. political system, groups are putatively the most influential political actors. Groups generally and consistently have much larger impacts on public policies than individuals have. This is particularly true for individuals from historically disadvantaged social groupings such as Latinos. There are several ways for underresourced individuals to increase their potential for exerting influence. These include organizing themselves, having effective leadership, and entering into alliances with other groups. In any case, good organization, which usually includes effective leadership, is always a requisite for multiplying potential political influence and power. Entering into coalitions or alliances with other groups can also be an effective strategy, but it is often risky and costly because some compromise is always necessary, and intergroup dynamics are often delicate and fragile. Finding the right allies under the right circumstances is also difficult. Fortunately for Hispanics seeking increased influence, the past several years have seen an explosion in the number and types of Latino organizations extending beyond the traditional boundaries of the communities. A new, well-educated, and skillful cadre of Latino leaders has been emerging—leaders who can play key roles in bridging the Hispanic and the mainstream cultural, social, and political worlds. In fact, it was quite telling that Antonio Villaraigosa, elected mayor of Los Angeles and recognized as one of the most influential Hispanic leaders in the United States, was quoted as saying, "It's not about Latino power. It's about building a coalition" (*Time Magazine* 2005, 46). New coalitions, organizations, and leadership might infuse the political mainstream with new perspectives, modes of behavior, and eventually also policies. It is certain that Hispanics are increasingly entering mainstream politics and government.

Notes

[1] For example, results from the 1999 National Survey of Latinos (*Washington Post* 1999) indicated that Latinos do not have greater feelings of commonality with African Americans relative to their feelings toward whites. Several other studies have discovered similar attitudes.

8

Participation—Political Parties and Political Ideology

There are two major ways to increase the influence of individual Latinos on the decision makers of the political system. The first way is to organize. This can take the form of anything from social movements, such as protest movements and their various manifestations, to formal interest groups. The second way is to coalesce or ally with other groups, whether organized or unorganized. One particular and common way of coalescing or allying is to participate in what some political scientists have termed the "grand coalitions" of American politics—political parties (Campbell, Converse, Miller, and Stokes 1960; Sorauf and Beck 1988). More so than in most other countries, particularly those having parliamentary systems with proportional representation and coalition governments, the major political parties in the United States are themselves huge coalitions of various and often quite diverse elements.

Throughout the history of the United States, the party system has been dominated by two major parties, with only a few periods of realignment in which there have been, for a brief period of time, more than two national parties. However, the system has always quickly reverted back to the domination of two parties. That is not to say that there are not political parties other than the Democrats, the Republicans, and their predecessors. Over the years, many parties have existed at both the local and the national levels. However, with regard to capturing the major offices within national government and even within state governments, those victories have by and large been won by one of the two political parties that now take the form of the Democrats and the Republicans.

Each party is a coalition in itself; that is, each is comprised of many distinctive elements with various demographic characteristics. It is probably true that for most of the twentieth century the Republican Party has been the somewhat more homogeneous party, and the Democratic Party has been made up of more diverse elements. But that is just a matter of degree. To become a major party in a society such as the United States, a party has to be comprised of a coalition of demographic groupings. Although homogeneous and much less diverse political parties are able to remain more uniform in their composition and purer in their ideology, the usual price they pay for this uniformity is to remain a minor party.

Remaining a minor party means that they do not capture many, if any, national or state offices and are usually confined to winning just a few local offices at best. Without the rewards of victory, these parties have a difficult time sustaining themselves. In addition, U.S. institutions and legal structures greatly favor the continuation of the two major parties (whose members are responsible for writing the political rules, including those concerning political parties and elections). As a result, it is challenging for minor or "third" parties to be successful in the United States.

LATINOS AND POLITICAL PARTIES

By becoming part of a majority party coalition, Latinos can maximize their chances for putting persons or candidates they favor into office and having the policies they favor become public policy (as they are adopted by one or the other of the major parties). So, Latinos must determine to which party they want to ally or align themselves. An alternative route is to become a separate political party; in fact, historically, this is the route that Latinos have taken on more than one occasion. It has not been uncommon for Mexican Americans to form their own political parties throughout history. However, the most well-known and certainly most successful of the independent political parties formed by Chicanos or Mexican Americans is that which was established during the Chicano movement with the initiation or inception of the Raza Unida Party (*El Partido de la Raza Unida*). This was a party that probably had its most successful early growth in south Texas, as José Ángel Gutiérrez and other students at the University of Texas who had been active in a college student organization, the Mexican American Youth Organization, decided that more than an interest group was needed. A political party that can run its own candidates for government offices would be the only way to break the domination of what they saw as Anglo-controlled major parties. Because they wanted to run candidates for themselves under their own banner, they decided to form their own political party. The idea spread quickly, and chapters soon sprang up throughout the Southwest, most noticeably among college youth. The development and growth, as well as the success and eventual demise, of the party have been documented in several books (Garcia 1989; Muñoz 1989; Santillan 1973).

The impetus behind the formation of the party was that Chicano activists believed that the two major political parties were not only unresponsive to Chicanos but also pretty much indistinguishable. They were viewed as one and the same, with little meaningful policy differences, and they were certainly not perceived as being responsive to the needs and interests of Chicanos. Moreover, both parties were "establishment oriented" and were controlled by middle and upper middle class Anglos.

The harshest critics called the major political parties "one two-headed monster feeding from the same trough." Moreover, these party founding activists knew that if they could, or even desired to, join a major political party, they would be just a small, relatively powerless part of a large coalition. The strong principles they held regarding Chicano pride, nationalism, self-determination, and community control would most likely not be acceptable to these establishment parties, and the compromises necessary to become part of the major political parties would be unacceptable to the activists. Moreover, Chicanos wanted institutions and organizations of their own. The Democrats and Republicans had had many decades to be responsive to the needs and interests of the Chicano community, and the activists believed that they had failed to do so. For these and other reasons, the separate, "third" political party, the Raza Unida Party, was formed and organized. The *partido* ran candidates in several elections throughout the Southwest, primarily in small towns throughout Texas and California. It had its greatest electoral successes in locales with large but previously excluded majorities, such as Crystal City, Texas, and Parlier, California. Many Latino or Chicano candidates were elected to public office in towns that, although 80 or 90 percent Hispanic, seldom, if ever, had public officials from their group.

As the party continued to grow in the early 1970s, it became more diverse ideologically, and some major questions arose about the future of the party, such as the direction it should take, its organizational structure, and the scope of its activities. A major conference of *partido* members from across the United States convened in El Paso, Texas, in 1972. In this first national party convention, there was much discussion and debate about the party's approach, primarily regarding whether it should seek electoral victories in smaller communities or whether it should expand and run campaigns statewide. There were also some ideological differences between those who were more pragmatic and electorally oriented and those who were more radical and more ideologic in their approach. Several factions were evident, each with its own leader, including most noticeably Reies López Tijerina from New Mexico, José Ángel Gutiérrez from Texas, and Rodolfo "Corky" Gonzales from Colorado. These differences proved to be insurmountable at the convention, which probably marked the high point, but also the beginning of the decline, of the Raza Unida Party as a major Chicano political force. The Texas Raza Unida Party did run a statewide candidate in the early 1970s, when it nominated Ramsey Muñiz, a former Baylor University football star and attorney, to be its candidate for the governorship. There were also candidates for statewide office on the ballots in New Mexico, California, and other states. However, the Muñiz campaign was by far the most visible. He garnered 6 percent of the statewide vote in Texas. To some, this was a symbolic victory, particularly in Texas—a state that had never elected any Chicanos to statewide office. To others, it demonstrated that the strategy of a separate and independent ethnic-based political party was not a viable alternative at a level above the local one. Continued personal differences between leaders and among ideologies led to the continued deterioration of the party until, by the late 1970s, it was in existence more as an interest group than as a political party.

The experience of the Raza Unida Party and other third parties in the United States seems to indicate that it is a problematic strategy to pursue the path of a successful political party independent from one of the two major parties. At best, these parties have sometimes been able to wring concessions and compromises from the major parties, or have some of their policies taken into and incorporated by the major parties. These third parties have also been able to increase the leverage of their members by acting as swing bloc votes between the two major parties. However, given the domination of the two-party system in the United States, the successful electorally oriented, exclusively Latino party does not seem to be a viable strategy.

How then are Latinos best able to relate to what are arguably the most important political organizations in the U.S. political system—political parties? How can and should Latinos approach the two major parties? How do they become members? How do they exert influence in the parties? How have they affected each party, if at all? In the United States, it is extremely easy to become a "member" of a political party. A person can join simply by indicating a party affiliation when he or she registers to vote. Parties are not exclusive organizations. Once a person is a registered member, he or she never has to attend a single meeting, pay dues, participate in any of its activities, or even vote for its candidates. Perhaps the most important facet of being a member, albeit an inactive member of a major political party, is that a person is allowed to participate in the selection of that party's candidates when he or she resides in a state that has a "closed primary" system. In a closed primary or nominating election, only registered members of that party may participate in the voting. Beyond that, being a member of one or the other of these grand coalitions usually means being contacted during campaigns and on election day by candidates of that party as they run for office, and not too much more. As we have seen, Latinos, in general, with the notable exception of the Cubans, have been predominately Democratic for many years. More specifically, since the 1930s, Latinos have always voted in fairly large majorities for Democratic candidates, including Democratic candidates for the presidency. However, until the late twentieth century, Latinos' vote as a significant national voting bloc was not sought by national candidates for office, although in some state and local races the Latino vote had been very important prior to the 1980s.

Political scientists have determined that the most important factor influencing the way that most voters choose their candidates is based on the partisanship of the voter (Bartels 2000; Campbell et al. 1960). It has been found that it is not the way the voter has been registered, but the psychological affiliation that the voter has with the party, that is a strong determinant of the voter's preference of party candidates. Therefore, political scientists have made a considerable effort to determine the partisanship of various groups of voters in the United States, primarily by asking them to which party they are most closely attached or affiliated. The usual question asked in voter surveys goes something like this: "In general, in politics today do you feel closer to the Democratic Party or the Republican Party, or are you independent or something else?" The answers to this item, which is a measure of partisan self-identification, have been found to be closely correlated with party candidate preference in the voting booth. We have seen that Latinos vote primarily Democratic (again with the exception of the Cubans), so we would expect that their self-identified partisanship is very Democratic, and that indeed is the case. The Latino National Political Survey (LNPS) of 1990 produced results shown in Table 8.1 with regard to

Table 8.1
LATINO POLITICAL PARTY SELF-IDENTIFICATION, BY NATIONAL ORIGIN

	Mexican	Puerto Rican	Cuban	Central/South American	Anglo
		1989-1990[1]			
Democrat	67%	71%	26%	NA	53%
Independent	12%	12%	8%	NA	7%
Republican	22%	18%	48%	NA	4%
		1999[2]			
Democrat	37%	52%	29%	39%	23%
Independent	33%	17%	27%	35%	35%
Republican	16%	17%	34%	12%	31%
		2004[3]			
Democrat	47%	50%	17%	NA	NA
Independent	22%	15%	9%	NA	NA
Republican	18%	17%	52%	NA	NA
Other/Don't Know	12%	17%	15%	NA	NA

NA, not applicable.

[1] *Latino National Political Survey.*

[2] WP/KFF/HU Project, *National Survey on Latinos in America.*

[3] Pew Hispanic Center/Kaiser Family Foundation, *National Survey on Latinos: Politics and Civic Engagement,* July 2004, Registered Voters.

Latino partisanship. The results indicate that the partisanship of the Latino groups, with the exception of the Cubans, is very Democratic, more so than the Anglo Americans in the survey. The most Democratic group is the Puerto Ricans. They are followed closely by the Mexican Americans. The case is almost the reverse for Cubans, who are strongly Republican.

Subsequent surveys have shown little change in the general pattern uncovered nationwide by the LNPS. For example, the National Latino Voter Poll of 2000 (Knight Ridder News Organization 2000) revealed that 59 percent of Hispanic voters favored or identified with the Democratic Party, 28 percent considered themselves independent, and only 20 percent identified with the Republican Party.[1] The *Washington Post* (1999) National Survey provided some analysis by national origin groups in comparison with non-Latino blacks and whites. Although the numbers are different from the other results because of the different wording of the questions, the general pattern remains the same. The largest plurality of Latinos (37 percent) identified themselves with the Democratic Party, followed by 33 percent who considered themselves independent. The Republicans were only favored by 16 percent of Latinos.

This is a different pattern than that exhibited by non-Latino whites in 1999, as the largest group of whites considered themselves independent, followed by Republicans (31 percent), and the smallest group (23 percent) of non-Latino whites identified with the Democrats. Non-Latino blacks showed yet another pattern—a more strongly Democratic one—as 61 percent identified with the Democrats, 25 percent with independents, and only 4 percent with the Republicans (Table 8.2). Within the Republican Party, the differences along national origin lines in 1999 showed basically the same pattern as did the LNPS, with a new element—the inclusion of data on South Americans. The most Democratic group is the Puerto Rican group at 52 percent; the next most Democratic group is comprised of Central and South Americans (39 percent Democratic and 35 percent independent), followed closely by Mexican Americans, with the largest proportion of them (37 percent) being independent, 33 percent Democratic, and 15 percent Republican. Again, the notable exception was the Cuban

Table 8.2
PARTY SELF-IDENTIFICATION BY ETHNICITY/RACE (%)

	Democrat	Republican	Independent	Other/Don't Know
Latinos	37	16	33	15
White's	23	31	35	11
Blacks	61	4	25	10

Source: Washington Post/Kaiser Family/Harvard University Survey Project, *National Survey on Latinos in America*, 1999.

Americans, with the largest proportion of them (37 percent) favoring the Republican Party, followed by independents at 34 percent; they were the least Democratic-oriented Latinos at 29 percent. These statistics not only reinforce the general trends found in earlier survey data but also highlight the tendency of many Latinos, particularly the most recent residents, to be politically independent. There has been a growing interest in political independence and a movement away from partisanship among the general American electorate, as nearly 40 percent of Americans labeled themselves as independents in the 2000 American National Election Study (Hajnal 2004). This makes independents the largest political category in America, larger than self-identified Republicans or Democrats. This concern with the citizenry's lacking a strong tie to either political party is particularly salient among ethnic groups, with many scholars noting that a large segment of the Latino community does not identify with either the Republican Party or the Democratic Party (Alvarez and Garcia-Bedolla 2003; Hajnal 2004; Hero, Garcia, Garcia, and Pachon 2000; Pachon and DeSipio 1994).

This trend is the result of several factors, including the lack of knowledge and experience with the Democratic or Republican parties among foreign-born Americans (Hajnal 2004). With nearly 40 percent of Latinos being born outside the United States, political socialization is critical to Latino party acquisition. This is evident by the fact that in addition to being more likely to choose independence, the foreign born and those who are politically unassimilated are more likely to refrain from choosing any partisanship option, including that of independent, on surveys (Alvarez and Brehm 2002). For example, 70 percent of nonnaturalized Mexican and Dominican immigrants, 40 percent of Cuban immigrants, and 55 percent of other Latino immigrants reported that they were not attached to either party (Pachon and DeSipio 1994). However, Latinos who have made the decision to remain in the United States and become citizens exhibit stronger party attachments (Cain, Kiewiet, and Uhlaner 1991).

In the 2000 general election, the Republicans made a notable attempt to bring in what they consider to be a swing bloc vote—the Latinos (de la Garza and DeSipio 2004; Leal et al. 2005). A *swing bloc* of voters is an identifiable and fairly cohesive group that is perceived as movable or switchable in its voting support—swinging from one party to another. The Republican Party spent some $10 million in Latino outreach. Their rhetorical message was that Latinos were "natural Republicans" who had just not realized it yet. The Republicans rationalized this rhetoric by placing an emphasis on traditional social values, such as emphasis on the family, anti-abortion issues, and no special concern with gay rights, as well as emphasizing the hard work ethic of Latinos and claiming that the Republicans' support of a tax cut would particularly help small businesses, in which Latinos are particularly concentrated. Their approach was very much one of values as they claimed close affiliation in shared value positions. The Democrats, who for many years have been charged with taking the Latino vote for granted, also made a concerted outreach to solidify their Latino vote. Their message was that the Democrats have been longtime friends and supporters of the Latino community and that their record on policy positions is what mattered. They reminded Latinos that it was the Democratic Party that had been in the forefront of enacting civil rights and voting rights legislation that in general protected the rights and liberties of minority groups; that favored a more active, helpful government; and that provided the kinds of opportunities and services that Latinos needed, such as unemployment compensation, minimum wage legislation, provision of public health services, support for public housing and job training, and similar measures. So, if as some political scientists claim, voters make their decisions largely on what conclusions they come to when they keep a "running tally" over what the parties have done or not done for them, the Democrats would come out way ahead of the Republicans.[2]

In fact, another strong "push" factor for Latinos toward the Democratic Party is that the Republicans have taken positions on various public policies that the Latino community has seen as quite inimical to their interests. Such policies include supporting English-only or official English legislation, voting against funding of bilingual education, voting against many of the social welfare services that the Democrats had supported, taking a harder line against immigration, opposing affirmative action, and opposing the provision of services to immigrants and their children. This was most noticeable in California in the late 1990s, when Governor Pete Wilson and other members of the Republican Party took strong positions against these kinds of measures—that is, against the provision of education and health services to undocumented workers (the famous, or infamous, Proposition 187) and for the abolition of bilingual education in the public schools and anti-affirmative action in colleges and universities. To many Latinos in California and across the United States, it seemed that the Republican Party was hostile toward the Latino culture and interests. Even if Latinos outside California were not immediately affected, the elections in which these issues were major concerns drew a record number of Latinos to the ballot box, and Republican candidates and their proposed policy referenda were smashed. Republicans were forced to admit that they had probably made an egregious error and that they had probably set back their cause of winning over Latinos for many years. In fact, some Republicans claim that unless their party changed their position on several policy issues, they would probably lose the rapidly growing number of Latinos for an entire generation. In contrast, the Democrats were quite gleeful in their agreement that the Republicans were their own worst enemy and had probably made life much easier for Democrats for the foreseeable future. In 2006 and 2007, it was the congressional Republicans who took the hardest line on immigration, a policy position that again antagonized much of the Latino community and that concerned Republican strategists who worried about the effect this was having on their long-term hope for increased rapport with the Hispanic electorate.

Despite this, Latino politicians and activists have tried to emphasize that they are not in the hip pocket of the Democratic Party. If Republicans will compete with the Democrats in seeing which party can best serve the interests of Latinos, Latinos will follow the winner. They are not permanently wedded to the Democratic Party, as was indicated by the movement in the 2004 presidential election. This kind of strategy is essential for maximum political influence. A major member of a coalition must always have the option of exiting that alliance and joining another if its interests are not served. They cannot be taken for granted. In the meantime, as increasing numbers of immigrants are naturalized and become citizens, they are registering as Democrats by a two- and three-to-one margin. Latino immigrants tend to take up residence in areas of heavy Latino density, so they are socialized to the values and affiliations of their neighbors, and this includes learning that the Democratic Party should be their party affiliation. Moreover, the off-year election of 2006 was a step back for the Republicans. The party lost majority control of both houses of Congress. The major national issue in this election was the war in Iraq, and Latinos were even more opposed to the war than was the general public (Pew 2003). In addition, six years of Republican control of both the executive and the legislative branches had revealed the party's proclivity to cut back on government and social service programs. As we have seen, both positions are antithetical to the general values and policy preferences of most Hispanics. So, if Republicans are to regain their ascendancy in national politics, in the state houses across the country, and in governorships among the states, they will eventually have to pay more attention to the material and tangible interests of Latinos and not just employ general rhetoric, however accurate, about the similarity of some values between Republicans and Latinos.

The Republicans' hopes seem to be based on the idea that as more Latinos remain in the United States and advance socioeconomically, they will move into the middle class and become more Republican in their economic and political orientations. They also hope that as more Latinos become business owners, they will be much more sympathetic with the political party that has been concerned with business interests over others. This might indeed be the case—over a long period of time, probably several generations.

Analysis conducted by political scientists to discover the roots of the party identification of Latinos has found a different pattern for them than is found for Anglos. That is, for Anglos, income is the socioeconomic variable that is most highly and directly correlated with party identification. The higher the income, the greater will be the identification with the Republican Party. However, in contrast, income by itself is not significantly correlated with partisanship among Cubans and Mexicans, and is only slightly so for Puerto Ricans (Uhlaner and Garcia 1998). For Anglos, higher levels of education were also associated with greater Republicanism, but it is much less significant for all Latino groups. Actually, religious affiliation has been one of the variables with significant correlations with partisan attachment for all four groups. Non-Catholicism is associated with Republicanism for both Anglos and Mexicans, and most strongly for Puerto Ricans. The role of religion in partisanship for Latinos was highlighted in the 2004 election, as there appeared to be a religion gap in 2004 among Latino voters. According to the National Election Pool exit poll, Bush garnered higher support from Latino Protestants (59/40), born-again Christians (78/21), and churchgoers (61/39) (Leal et al. 2005). Age is an important demographic correlate, mainly for Mexican Americans. In fact, age is the single variable that is most highly correlated with attachment to the major parties, with the older Mexican Americans being strongly Democratic and the younger Mexican Americans being the least Democratic. So, again, income is not as strongly related to Latino partisanship, and with Mexican Americans, more education goes along with the greater likelihood of Democratic Party affiliation.

One of the most powerful demographic predictors of partisanship among all three Latino groups is their experience with U.S. politics. People of all three of the largest Latino national origins are more likely to identify as Democrats if they are older, if they were born in the United States, or if they have been in the United States longer as immigrants (Cain et al. 1991; Uhlaner and Garcia 2002). This ties in with the point made previously about knowledge of the parties and the positions they have taken on Latino interests. Apparently, Latinos learn about which party has best served their interests overall.

Recently, political scientists believe that they have discerned a new shift in voting patterns among the groups that have traditionally comprised the Republican and Democratic parties, respectively. At least among white voters, positions on moral values are having a greater effect, to some extent replacing the long-standing correlation between socioeconomic status or income and partisan voting patterns. For example, longtime working class white Democrats have been voting increasingly Republican since the 1970s, as issues such as busing and affirmative action have pushed these voters into the Republican camp (Teixeira and Rogers 2001).

Other cultural issues, such as abortion rights, have built Democratic allegiance among higher-income white professionals. Since the 1990s, this rate of change has seemed to accelerate. In the 2004 elections, moral values, including positions on same sex marriages, abortion, and stem cell research, seemed to be the major issue in presidential voting preferences (Johnson 2004; Leal et al. 2005). This brought the more conservative Christians, including Catholics and evangelical Protestants, to the Republican side. The position of the Republicans on these issues was seen as being a significant factor in attracting Latinos to support George W. Bush in record proportions.

However, these changes have not produced a full-scale reversal of the two parties' traditional constituencies. In the lower half of the income levels, the Democratic Party remains strong among African Americans, Hispanics, and white union members. Republican support has grown among nonunion whites. In the top half of the income distribution, there has been a realignment of well-educated whites who have now become one of the most reliable Democratic voting constituencies, but Republican loyalties have strengthened among small businessmen, small business owners, managers, and corporate executives.

There are implications of this for the Hispanic voter because several studies have shown that Hispanic voters are typically closer to the Republican Party with regard to many of the "hot button" moral value positions, such as gay rights, abortion, capital punishment, patriotism, and school vouchers. This could mean that Hispanics may likely follow the white pattern of increasingly voting Republican, despite the fact that Hispanic voters largely remain in the lower levels of the socioeconomic scale. Whether the 2004 vote was an indication of this trend or just a one-time "blip" remains to be seen. In addition, as Hispanics become more middle class, buy homes, move into the suburbs, and establish and operate successful small businesses—all trends that have been occurring since the 1970s and 1980s—this would also seem to impel a move toward Republican support, at least if Hispanics follow the pattern exhibited by white voters since the 1970s.

The hot debate over immigration in 2006 and the roles played by politicians of the two major parties in this policy discussion brought a new element of Latino partisanship into consideration. The punitive and exclusionary position taken by House Republicans, as well as some Republican opposition in the senate to the Senate's more inclusive bills, elicited expressions of concern by Republican Party officials and politicians. They feared that the inroads made by the Republicans in the 2004 election could be lost by the Republican legislators' positions on immigration reform. (President Bush continued to speak out on behalf of the more moderate Senate bills.) Republican opposition nationally might cause the same kind of backlash and oppositional mobilization that occurred in California's immigration debates and referenda. Post-immigration debate survey evidence must have dashed the hopes of Republican Party stalwarts who had perceived some chance of Hispanics swinging toward self-identification with the Republicans. In early summer of 2006, the party affiliation of

Latinos looked much as it has for decades. Only 22 percent of registered Hispanics identified with the Republican Party; the affiliation of Latinos with Democrats was 42 percent, and 20 percent were "something else." Although one fourth of Latinos believed that neither party had "the best position on immigration issues," twice as many favored the Democrats' position (35 percent) over that of the Republicans (16 percent). Most discouraging to the Republican Party was that when asked which party had the most "concern for Hispanics/Latinos," registered Latinos favored the Democrats over the Republicans by 37 percent to 9 percent, respectively. Thirty-seven percent believed that there was no difference (Pew Hispanic Center 2006).

POLITICAL IDEOLOGY

The political ideology of Americans is a much studied political factor, and yet one that in many ways still remains a mystery in the way it functions to affect political behavior and political participation. What is true about the role of political ideology for most Americans also seems to apply in most part to Latinos. Most Americans know political ideology as that which is laid out along a political spectrum from liberal or left wing to conservative or right wing. The terms "liberal" and "conservative" are commonly used in political discourse in the United States, and media commentators, politicians, public officials, and even the general public seem to have a feel for, or a common-sense understanding of, what these terms mean, enough so that they are used somewhat meaningfully in common political dialog. Yet, when political scientists look closely at this, it is difficult to determine what exactly political ideology stands for and whether the average person really understands what is meant by these terms. In fact, several studies show that the average person cannot clearly identify these political ideologies, and only a small, more activistic, more elite group of people can use them correctly and meaningfully (Converse 1964; Jacoby 1991).

Moreover, there are few individuals who are pure ideologues—that is, that are 100 percent liberal or conservative in their views on all political issues. Most people are a mixture of conservative and liberal positions; in fact, many, if not most, are in-between at the so-called "moderate" or "middle of the road" position. When political scientists have attempted to analyze the political ideology of the public, or more particularly of Latinos, as many questions as answers have been produced. It is not clear how people's self-perceived and self-labeled ideologies actually affect the positions they take on candidates or policy issues. Much contradictory and often unclear thinking is evidenced in the relationship between such things as political ideology and political parties. Nevertheless, because

Table 8.3
POLITICAL IDEOLOGY OF LATINOS BY NATIONAL ORIGIN (SELF-LABELED)

	Mexican	Puerto Rican	Cuban	Central/South American	Anglo
1989-1990[1]					
Liberal	29%	28%	23%	NA	26%
Moderate	36%	25%	23%	NA	35%
Conservative	35%	47%	55%	NA	39%
1999[2]					
Liberal	24%	52%	29%	39%	23%
Moderate	36%	31%	37%	49%	46%
Conservative	35%	37%	24%	30%	35%

NA, not applicable.
[1]*Latino National Political Survey.*
[2]WP/KFF/HU Project, *National Survey on Latinos in America.*

these terms are so common in political discourse and seemingly so well understood by the average person (if not by social scientists), and because little is known about political ideology over the past several years, attention has been turned to the political ideology of Latinos.

The first national reading obtained on the self-labeled political ideology of Latinos comes from the LNPS. In 1990, when the LNPS was completed, the self-proclaimed ideologies of the four ethnic groupings in the survey were as shown in Table 8.3. At that time, the largest proportion of Anglos considered themselves to be conservative (39 percent), followed by moderates (35 percent), and then self-proclaimed liberals (26 percent). Surprisingly to many, the political ideology of Mexican Americans was almost exactly the same as Anglo Americans, with 36 percent of Mexicans being conservative, 36 percent moderate, and 29 percent liberal. Cubans were distinctive by their more conservative ideology, with the majority (55 percent) seeing or labeling themselves as conservative, 23 percent as liberal, and 23 percent as moderate. Puerto Ricans' self-classification of ideology was puzzling; the largest plurality (47 percent) called themselves conservative, 28 percent liberal, and 25 percent moderate.

Again, it is not clear what these measures of mass ideology are measuring. They should relate to something else of interest, such as party identification or issue positions. Although there does seem to be a connection, it is weak and inconsistent. The ideology of Latinos appears to be an even weaker predictor of party preference than it is for Anglos (Uhlaner and Garcia 2002). This is not to say that ideology does not matter for Latinos, as

Table 8.4
SELF-LABELED POLITICAL IDEOLOGY BY RACE (%)

	Liberal	Moderate	Conservative	Dont Know
Latinos	26	34	34	6
Whites	23	39	35	3
Blacks	23	45	30	2

Source: WP/Kaiser/Harvard Project, National Survey Latinos in America, 1999.

Latino conservatives are more likely to be Republican (Uhlaner et al. 2000). It is true that in all cases liberals are more likely to be Democrats and conservatives are more likely to be Republicans, but compared to Anglos there have been more conservative Democrats among Mexican Americans and Puerto Ricans and many more liberal Republicans among Cuban Americans. It seems that ideology operates somehow differently for Latinos than it does for Anglos. One possibility is that Latinos interpret ideology differently than Anglos, particularly in the case of Puerto Ricans. However, when we look at the correlation between Latino ideologic positions and preferences on policies, they relate much the same way as they do for the rest of the public.

The 1999 National Survey of Latinos in America (*Washington Post* 1999) produced some interesting and relevant results on this topic (Table 8.4). Among non-Latino whites, the largest group was self-identified as moderate (39 percent), followed closely by conservative, and the smallest group (as in the LNPS) was liberal. The Latino pattern was similar, with 34 percent of Latinos classifying themselves as conservative, 34 percent as moderate, and 26 percent as liberals. Non-Latino blacks were more prone to identify themselves as moderate (45 percent), followed by conservative (30 percent), and liberal (23 percent). The National Latino Voter Poll of 2000 (Knight Ridder News Organization 2000) of "likely Hispanic voters" again found that the conservative bloc was the largest among both Hispanics and all voters—Hispanics were 37 percent conservative, as were 39 percent of all voters. Moderates were the next largest group—31 percent of Latinos and 32 percent of all voters. Again, the smallest group was liberals, with 20 percent Hispanics and 26 percent of all voters claiming that ideology.

We can see that the political ideology of Latinos has not changed much since the 1990s and the patterns are consistent. This surprises many observers of Latino politics, who had inferred that Latinos would be much more liberal in their political ideology than Anglos. This was probably due to the positions taken by those Latinos having greatest access to the media, such as Latino politicians, leaders of advocacy groups, academics, and other "spokespersons," who tend to be more liberal than the people in their philosophies and positions. However interesting it is that the self-classified political ideologies of Latinos are similar to those of Anglos, it is not clear what effect this has on Latinos' political behavior and political participation. Further investigation is required to understand this relationship, if indeed any relationship does exist.

SUMMARY AND CONCLUSION

The study of Latino public opinion is a relatively new endeavor. Large public opinion surveys of the Latino community have been a recent phenomenon. They have come about in response to population growth among Latinos and an increase in the number of scholars of Latino origin. This chapter provides a comprehensive discussion of the role that both partisanship and ideology have in American politics, as well as trends among Latinos in these two areas. It is clear that partisanship continues to have a huge impact on the way Americans decide who to vote for and which policy issues they support. Latinos, in particular, have had an interesting history with respect to partisanship. As a result of a lack of responsiveness from either dominant political party, leaders of the Chicano movement were motivated to create an alternative political party that had chapters throughout the Southwest. Currently, driven by significant increases in Latino population and concentration in key electoral states, both Democratic and Republican parties have exerted considerable effort to court the perceived swing bloc Latino population. In fact, due to a strategic effort by the Republican Party to use social issues and family values to mobilize Latino voters, and their more Latino-friendly presidential candidate, the Republican Party garnered a greater share of the Latino vote in the 2000 and 2004 elections. Despite this recent trend, there is little or no convincing evidence to support the claims that a close relationship between the Republican Party and the Latino community will continue to grow in the near future unless Republicans change their stances on several policy areas vital to Latinos.

Nonetheless, as long as Latino elites continue to emphasize that the Latino community is not a permanent component of the Democratic Party's coalition, attention from both parties should continue. This should provide positive outcomes for the Latino community, particularly the foreign-born population, which is more likely to be politically independent and to benefit tremendously from mobilization of the two dominant parties. Interestingly, the self-expressed ideology of the Hispanic general public is similar to the Anglo population; that is, it is already in the mainstream. However, it appears that political ideology may not have as much relevance for Latinos as it does for Anglos because ideology has a weak impact on Latino party preference and voter choice. Due to limited analyses on the relationship of Latino ideology, further research is needed to determine whether Latinos interpret ideology the same way that Anglos do before we can conclude that Latinos are a non-ideological population regarding politics.

Notes

[1] Percentages listed in this section are based on survey respondents who chose to answer partisanship questions. Because individuals may choose not to answer questions on surveys, the percentages listed in this section may not equal 100 percent.

[2] For a discussion of the running tally theory of partisanship, see Fiorina (1981).

CONVERSION AND DECISION MAKING

9

Representation—Representatives, Reapportionment, and Redistricting

CONVERSION IN THE POLITICAL SYSTEM

So far in this book, we have presented and examined the contextual factors that condition Hispanic politics, as well as the various types and forms of inputs that shape, form, and affect governments. Much of the research on Latino politics and politics in general has focused on these important aspects of the political system. However, it could easily be argued that the crux of politics is located in the conversion element of the system—that is, how, when, and why people's preferences are converted from interests and inputs to public policies. This occurs in those "black boxes" known as governments, broadly defined. This central part of any political system is where people who are public authorities make decisions as to "who gets what, when, and how." That is, how are decisions made that result in the allocation of valued resources to some groups and individuals and not to others? How, when, and why do some interests and communities become winners and others losers in the game of politics? More specifically, what happens to Latino interests once they have been aggregated and articulated through various forms of politics to those public officials who have the authority bestowed on governments to make binding choices in the form of laws, rules, and regulations, favoring some interests and not others?

In the U.S. political system, virtually all governmental decisions are made not by the people themselves but by their representatives. The American system is not a direct democracy, but a modern, representative democracy—a *republic*. With the exception of some town hall meetings and some referenda, the public's role in governmental decision making is not to make any decisions directly but to select those persons who will make decisions for them, and to attempt to influence those persons and their decisions. An important measure of success in Latino politics would be to have Latinos' participation in these activities produce results that would reflect Latinos' preferences.

To more fully understand Hispanic politics in the United States, we must better comprehend what goes on in the conversion process—that is, how governments and public officials make decisions that result in the policies that affect the population. Unfortunately, there is less research and knowledge about this crucial part of the policy-making process than there is about the other components of the political process. This is particularly true regarding the role of Hispanics in this arena. We have already examined the all-important contextual and input factor. Now, in this unit, we turn our attention to the critical activities involving the representation of Hispanics in government, and to those persons who may represent Hispanics and who make decisions that are important to Hispanics as a distinctive political constituency.

Representation is a key concept in the study of democratic politics, and consequently, it is of critical importance when discussing the status of Latinos in the American pluralist democracy. In the United States, the basis for representation is population in geographic areas. Because one of the basic tenets of the American democracy is one of equality, it is logical that people have sought to have equal representation and an equal chance of having a representative of their choice. In accordance with democratic philosophy, this drive for equality has lead to a great deal of political activity to root out processes that produce inequality and unfairness in the selection of representatives. The key question dealing with this topic with regard to Latinos is as follows: Are Latinos equally and equitably represented in the American political system? Related questions include the following: How can one determine whether Latinos are well represented in the U.S. polity? Are there various ways in which Latinos may be represented? Is one kind of representation better than another for Latinos?

After examining the issue of representation, we must look at those who (appear to) represent Latinos. We have already discussed Latino leaders in general. So, in this unit, we address the status of some of the "official" leaders of Latinos, particularly elected and appointed public officials who supposedly represent Latinos as their elected or appointed representatives. Related to the question of representatives and representation is that of decision making, and more particularly, the decision making of representatives, and how that all-important process (decision making) must be understood in order to truly evaluate the extent to which Latinos are represented by their nominal representatives.

There is a large body of literature that has examined the various aspects of the concept of representation, particularly in democratic governments (Pitkin 1972; Plotke 1997). What does it mean for an individual or group to be represented in governmental decision making? How does one determine the quantity and quality of representation? The latter question may be answered partially by looking at the various theories of representation and the ways in which representation is determined. We cannot go into these in great detail here; instead, we simply present a few typologies, explain them, and relate them to Latino representation.

TYPES OF REPRESENTATION

Representation can be divided into two major categories or typologies. One is based on the relationship of the individual representative to those whom he or she represents, and especially to what extent the representative embodies or reflects the views of those whom he or she purportedly represents. The second category deals primarily with the criteria that are used to measure the degree of representativeness of one's constituency; that is, how does one best measure representation, or what should be the criteria by which representation is measured?

TRUSTEES AND DELEGATES

With regard to the first category, the classic continuum of representation is that which places the "trustee" representative at one end of the spectrum and the "delegate" representative at the other end of the spectrum (e.g., Pitkin 1972). The representatives who are *trustees* are embodiments of the values, ideals, principles, and opinions of their constituents. However these representatives have arrived at being the pure and accurate embodiment of the values of their constituents, they are entrusted to represent these views because they are a sum of the views of those they represent. They share the attitudes, beliefs, values, and feelings of their constituents. Perhaps this is because they grew up in the same communities as their constituents and have shared living experiences, and consequently, they were socialized to the same norms, ideas, and goals, or were able to absorb the values of the community in some other way. Whatever the case, these trustees speak for their constituents rather automatically; they do not need to actively communicate with them or seek out their opinions because they are perceived as being essentially one and the same. Therefore, a trustee often acts quite independently from his or her constituency because he or she does not need to be in continuous communication with them. Trustee representatives are more likely to act without the need for external guidance, using their own best judgment.

On the opposite end of the spectrum are the so-called *delegates*. The delegates are relatively blank slates. These representatives do not necessarily incorporate the policy goals or values of their constituents into their own being. Moreover, their personal characteristics are much less important than those of the trustees because they are instructed or directed by their constituents; that is, they are given a mandate by their constituents as to the constituents' policy positions. A delegate must therefore have open and accurate communications with their constituents so they can "mirror" their interests. In the abstract and at the extreme, delegate representatives are not allowed to express their own values; instead, they are representatives who will be constantly checking with their constituents and voting in the manner in which their constituents instruct them.

Of course, in reality, there are very few pure trustees or delegates, although representatives may lean more toward one model or the other. Most of them fall in-between and are a combination of the two extremes. In fact, those who both vote for their own values, which in fact are a reflection of their communities' values, and vote for the mandates of their constituents in a combination manner have been given a classification of "politico." (This is not to be confused with the Spanish word that is a designation for politicians, which is also the word *politico*.)

These considerations are important when discussing Latino representation and representatives. They bring up the issue of whether a representative from a Latino district would be more likely to represent Latinos if he or she is a Latino him- or herself. The assumption is that a Latino representative would automatically share most, if not all, values and policy preferences of Latinos because he or she grew up as a Latino, absorbed the experiences of other Latinos, and consequently, would vote as Latinos should vote. However, it may not be that important for a delegate to be Latino him- or herself as long as that person keeps in touch with the Latinos in his or her constituency. That is, he or she would be constantly receiving instructions from the Latino constituents and would be told how to vote to advance Latino interests. This all relates to a question which is often debated about Latino representation and representatives: "Do representatives of the Latino people need to be Latinos?" An affirmative answer would indicate a large degree of trusteeship.

DESCRIPTIVE AND SUBSTANTIVE

A second group of categories or types of representation also relate to important questions in Latino politics. These deal primarily with the criteria or the standards by which representation should be measured. Different authors have devised different categories. Here, we present a few common typologies.

DESCRIPTIVE REPRESENTATION   One very common type of measurement that determines representation is based on a simple counting or enumeration of the number of representatives who are of Hispanic heritage. This is based on the concept of *descriptive representation,* or when a constituency elects a representative who shares particular traits but not necessarily policy views (Pitkin 1967). Indeed, this is the most common way of determining Hispanic representation. Although it is the easiest to determine, it is still not without problems. It is fairly simplistic and crude. Some observers have stated that "the most widely used indicator of a group's position in a political system is the presence of members of that group in elective offices" (Browning, Marshall, and Tabb 1984, 19). This is again an example of descriptive or passive representation. It is based on the demographic characteristics of the members of a representative body and the relationship of those demographic characteristics (or a comparison of those characteristics) to a particular constituency. For example, it is often said that a constituency has x percentage of Latinos. Therefore, if there is less than x percentage of Latinos in, for example, a legislature, they are underrepresented. If there are x, they have equal representation or parity, and if there are x plus representatives, they are overrepresented. Although simplistic, this is a very commonly used method of determining representation. In fact, for some Latinos, placing a proportionate number of Latinos in decision-making positions seems to be the main objective of their politics. Often, it seems to be the end goal of their political activities, and not much thought seems to be given to any consideration past obtaining an equal number, or a proportionately fair number, of Latinos in office. This numerical equality is sometimes termed *parity.*

The group that has been most often associated with keeping track of the number and proportions of Latinos in public office is the National Association of Latino Elected Officials (NALEO). Over the years, NALEO has issued annual reports indicating the number of Latinos who are elected as well as the appointed officials throughout the United States at all levels of government—national, state, and local.[1] When descriptive or passive demographic representation is studied, there is one clear and indisputable conclusion: Hispanics are severely underrepresented in the United States. That is, Hispanics have lower proportions in virtually every representative body in the United States than is their proportion in their communities. This is most dramatically and clearly demonstrated at the national level. For example, Hispanics are severely underrepresented proportionate to their population (estimated at 14 percent of the nation in 2005) in all three branches of the national government—the executive branch (i.e., the presidency), the cabinet and the federal bureaucracy, the legislative branch (i.e., U.S. Congress), and the judicial branch (i.e., the federal court system). We look at these findings in greater detail later in this chapter; however, at this point, note that the United States has not yet seriously considered a Hispanic president or even nominated a Hispanic vice president. There have been relatively few Latinos in the president's cabinet or other high-level executive agencies, just as Latinos are also underrepresented in the lower levels of the national bureaucracy. In the national legislature (the U.S. Congress) in 2002, there were no Latinos in the U.S. Senate, and there had only been three Latinos in the U.S. Senate in its entire history, all of them coming from the state of New Mexico— Octaviano Larrazolo, Dennis Chávez, and Joseph Montoya. In the U.S. House of Representatives in the year 2000, there were only 19 Latino members of the 435, or about 4 percent. This number has been climbing slowly over the past few decades but is still far below parity.

The 2004 elections demonstrated this incremental progress. Three additional Hispanics were elected to the U.S. House of Representatives, raising the number to twenty-three voting members. Perhaps the biggest breakthrough for Latino representation in the national legislature came with the election of two U.S. senators. Ken Salazar, a former state attorney general, was elected from Colorado, and Mel Martinez, a former cabinet member in the Bush administration, became the first Cuban American senator elected from the state of Florida. The representation levels of Cuban Americans in U.S. Congress was recently increased with the nomination of Robert Menendez to serve out the remaining year in Governorelect Jon Corzine's Senate term, giving New Jersey its first minority senator. Menendez was sworn into office on January 18, 2006, and was immediately faced with the important task of voting on the U.S. Supreme Court nomination of Samuel Alito.

With all Latino incumbents winning reelection, the only change in Latino congressional representation in 2006 was the addition of Albio Sires (D-NJ), who gained the seat formerly held by Robert Menendez before he was appointed to the U.S. Senate. Therefore, the total number of Latinos in the House of Representatives (23) and the Senate (3) remained the same after the 2006 election. With Democratic control of the house following the 2006 elections, Speaker-designate Nancy Pelosi has appointed several Latino U.S. Representatives to lead committees and subcommittees in the 110th Congress. For example, U.S. Representative Nydia Velázquez (D-NY), who has been ranking member of the House Small Business Committee since 1998, has been officially appointed to chair this full congressional committee, making her the first Latina in the history of the House to chair a full committee. In addition, U.S. Representative Silvestre Reyes (D-TX) has also been appointed to chair the House Intelligence Committee.

The national court system has a very low percentage of its judges who are of Hispanic backgrounds (Solberg, Spill, and Bratton 2005). Reynaldo G. Garza became the first Hispanic federal judge when he was appointed by President John F. Kennedy to the U.S. District Court for the Southern District of Texas in 1961. Garza also became the first Hispanic judge on a U.S. Court of Appeals when he was appointed by President James "Jimmy" Carter to the Fifth Circuit Court of Appeals in 1979. Currently, there are twelve Latinos judges seated on the appellate division of the federal courts.

In examining the "lower" levels of government (i.e., state and local), the numbers look relatively better, but typically they are still under parity. At the state level, Latinos are below their proportion in every state legislature but that of New Mexico, and even there they are somewhat lower than their proportion in the population generally.

Table 9.1 demonstrates the number and proportion of Latinos in the various state legislatures in states that have the largest numbers of Latinos. Again, as at the national level, these numbers have been rising slowly and steadily, particularly since the 1970s.

In state-level executive agencies, Latinos have been very scarce; in modern history, there have only been three states that have had Hispanic governors: Arizona (Raul H. Castro, 1975–1977), Florida (Robert "Bob" Martinez, 1987–1991), and New Mexico. The latter state has had five Hispanic governors, including three in modern times—Jerry Apodaca (1975–1978), Toney Anaya (1983–1986), and Bill Richardson (2002–). Early in its statehood, while Hispanos were still a majority in New Mexico, Ezequiel C. de Baca (1917) and Octaviano A. Larrazolo (1919–1920) were governors. There are also very few other Latino statewide elected executives in positions such as lieutenant governor, attorney general, secretary of state, treasurer, and auditor. Again, New Mexico is the exception, often having a proportionate number of Hispanics in these positions; in fact, five of the six statewide executive offices are currently held by Hispanics, including two Latinas. Texas did not elect its first statewide Latino executive until the 1990 election, when it elected Dan Morales as state treasurer, and California did not do so until the late 1990s, when it elected its first Latino to a statewide elected office. In the fifty state court systems, there is a very low proportion of Latinos in the judiciaries of every state, always below the number of Latinos in each state's population. More is said about these state positions, as well as local offices, in Chapters 10 and 11.

It is at the local level, scattered among the nearly 88,000 local governments (U.S. Bureau of the Census 2002c), where one is most likely to find a proportionate number of Latino elected and appointed officials in proportions roughly equal to the number of Latinos in local communities such as counties, cities, towns, and school districts. The greatest numbers are found in school districts, and this is generally a good sign because education is of such high priority to Hispanics. These numbers are increasing dramatically in the twenty-first century, as Latinos are increasing their numbers in local communities and dispersing throughout the United States. This increase in Latino representation on school boards is critical to Latinos in education overall because Latino school board membership has been shown to have a positive effect on the number of Latino administrators and teachers (Leal, Meier, and Martinez-Ebers 2004). In fact, there has been a major revolution in the number of Hispanics who have taken seats on county commissions, city councils, and school boards since the 1980s in

Table 9.1
HISPANIC ELECTED OFFICIALS, 2005

United States

Total HEOs at Federal and State Level: 266

Level of Office	Total HEOs: 5041			DEM		GOP		*		IND		N/P	
	M	F	Total	M	F	M	F	M	F	M	F	M	F
U.S. senators[a]	2	—	2	1	—	1	—	—	—	—	—	—	—
U.S. representatives	16	7	23	13	6	3	1	—	—	—	—	—	—
State officials	6	3	9	4	3	2	—	—	—	—	—	—	—
State senators	40	20	60	32	19	8	1	—	—	1	—	—	—
State representatives	122	50	172	101	43	20	7	—	—	—	—	—	—
County officials	319	179	498	191	108	8	7	108	62	—	—	12	2
Municipal officials	1,221	430	1,651	262	72	24	7	364	148	4	1	567	202
Judicial/law enforcement	519	159	678	247	81	13	6	198	52	—	1	61	19
Education/school board	1,128	632	1,760	119	58	8	2	482	260	2	2	517	310
Special district officials	142	46	188	19	2	2	—	73	24	1	—	47	20
Subtotals	3,515	1,526	5,041	989	392	89	31	1,225	546	8	4	1,204	553
Totals		5,041			1,381		120		1,771		12		1,824

DEM, Democratic office; GOP, Republican office; *, no party stated; IND, Independent office; N/P, nonpartisan office; M, male; F, female.

Source: NALEO Educational Fund, 2005 National Directory of Latino Elected Officials.

Note: This information was compiled by NALEO before the late 2006 appointment of Robert Melendez (D-NJ) to the U.S. Senate.

[a]Third U.S. Senator took office in 2006.

particular, and this trend is likely to continue as Latino communities increase in size across the United States. Most notably in the large metropolitan areas, Hispanics have not been as well represented as they have been in smaller towns and villages, where they have recently taken majority control of largely Hispanic communities.

Of interest in the past few years has been the candidacy of Latinos for mayoral positions in the large metropolitan areas. In 2001, the candidacy of two Latinos in the mayoral elections of New York City generated considerable notice. Among the most notable of these large city mayoral elections was the bid of Antonio Villaraigosa to become mayor of Los Angeles in 2001. Mr. Villaraigosa lost a hard-fought race to his opponent, James Hahn. This Southern California metropolitan area is now about 47 percent Latino. In 2005, Villaraigosa, who had won a seat on the Los Angeles City Council, was one of two candidates competing in the mayoral run-off election against the incumbent mayor, Hahn. Villaraigosa did win the contest, becoming the first Latino mayor in Los Angeles since 1872. Over the past few decades, Latinos have become mayors of such cities as Los Angeles and San Jose, California; San Antonio and El Paso, Texas; Miami, Florida; Denver, Colorado; and Albuquerque and Santa Fe, New Mexico, as well as in 225 or so villages, towns, and smaller cities as of 2004.

The overall trend in the number of Hispanic elected and appointed officials is one of an increasing number of these kinds of representatives. Progress has been slow, but it has been steady and seemed to be accelerating in the early 2000s. Yet, in the year 2005, of the 500,000 or so elected public official positions in the United States, still only about 5,000 positions, or roughly 1 percent, were held by Latinos. Obviously, when this 1 percent is compared with the 14 percent of the population of the United States that Latinos comprise, one can see that this group is still heavily underrepresented in elected governmental positions in the United States.

SYMBOLIC REPRESENTATION   Another type of representation that is important in Hispanic politics is that of the *symbolic* nature. This usually refers to representation that has a psychological or emotional effect rather than a tangible or material one. When some Latinos see persons from their group, "one of their own," in high positions such as public office, they may be filled with pride. Such representation can show Latinos that they are as good as anyone else and that they can achieve their goals. Knowing that one of their own is in a position of influence or power may make Latinos believe that things will be better or that they are in fact being represented, simply because there are some brown faces in office. Latino representatives who are symbolic representatives may serve as role models for others, particularly for persons who are striving for high places in many types of institutions—whether educational, religious, corporate, or political. Latinos may thus be encouraged by the presence of such representatives to strive for positions of political influence or power. In any case, symbolic representation provides *recognition*, a psychological satisfaction or an emotional payoff to Latinos without necessarily providing any kind of tangible or material reward. This is the result of individuals looking for symbolic representatives outside their districts.

SUBSTANTIVE REPRESENTATION   Finally, there is what many consider to be the most important type of representation—a type that is sometimes called *substantive* or *active representation.* This kind of representation involves representatives being actively engaged in articulating Latino (or other) group interests in the group policy-making arena. Such representation would mean that Latino representatives are not only aware of Latino preferences, needs, and wants but would also work actively to promote those policy goals. Their emphasis would be on tangible and material payoffs. Theoretically, such representation could be provided to the Latino community by either a non-Latino or a Latino. The important thing would be that the representatives would be effective, or at least try to be effective, in representing Latino interests to or among decision makers, to promote or encourage those interests, and to work to have favorable policies passed and implemented on behalf of the Latino community. Welch and Hibbing (1984) were the first to empirically study the substantive representation of Latinos in the U.S. House of Representatives. They defined representation of this sort to exist when a group can be represented without having its own members in representative roles, but rather by having its representatives act and vote in accordance with its policy preferences (Welch and Hibbing 1984, 329).

Thus, to speak of Latino representation and representatives is more complex than it seems to be initially. There are varying types of representation, and any person claiming to be a Latino representative should be involved in at least one of these types of representational activities. The Latino communities themselves vary in what they expect of their representatives. Some Latinos seem to be satisfied with simply increasing the number of Latinos in policy-making positions, whereas others are rewarded emotionally by seeing Latinos in role model positions. Still others are most concerned with how successful their representatives are in providing them with the resources and opportunities that they are seeking and that they see other non-Latino members of the community already possessing.

The approximate number of Hispanic elected officials in the year 2005 was as follows[2]

U.S. senatorial: 3
U.S. congressional: 23
State executives: 9

State legislators: 232
City and county officials: 2,149
Judicial officials: 678
School board officials: 1,760
Special district and other miscellaneous: 188
Total: 5,041
(NALEO 2005)

It is likely that the continuous increase nationwide in the number of Latino officials will both accelerate in numbers and will have various favorable impacts on the Latino communities throughout the nation. There is considerable room for optimism in the steady increase of elected and public officials. The number and location of Latino public officials seems to be on the upswing since the turn of the twenty-first century. This is driven by the overall increase in the Latino population, the rising socioeconomic levels among them, and their dispersion and growth in many new areas. As long as Hispanics continue to be actively engaged in politics, putting quality candidates up for office and supporting these candidates at the ballot box, Latino representation will most likely continue to improve in both quantity and quality.

REAPPORTIONMENT AND REDISTRICTING

Every ten years, there is a major political squabble that results from a demographic adjustment—the decennial census. Historically, this count of residents in the United States mandated by the U.S. Constitution has been a major point of political contention and seems to have become even more contentious in recent decades. Certainly, the 2000 U.S. Census caused a tremendous amount of political conflict and competition both before and after it was conducted, and this included considerable involvement by Latinos. The census is more than just a determination of how many people live in the United States. The results of the count taken by the U.S. Census Bureau provide the official numbers that are used by policy makers in several ways, all of which have great impact on the public. For example, population counts are used to help determine the allocation of federal funding for various government-sponsored programs. The primary constitutional reason for the census count is to determine representation in the U.S. House of Representatives. The total membership number of the lower chamber is fixed at 435, and as the population of the United States increases and shifts from one area of the country to another, the number of representatives from each state, which is based on population, must be adjusted. States that lose population may eventually lose representatives, whereas states that gain population gain representatives, and therefore additional political power, in the House of Representatives. This realloca-tion of the number of U.S. representatives from each state is termed *reap-portionment*. Because the Hispanic population has been growing in leaps and bounds over the past few decades, their numbers have significantly affected the reapportionment of the 435 seats among states.

In addition, after the numbers for the U.S. Congress are determined, the state legislatures for each state decide where the boundaries for each U.S. congressional district ought to be within their states. So, it is the *state* legislatures that draw the lines that determine which people will be in-cluded in which U.S. congressional district. This process is known as *re-districting*. Not only are the state legislatures responsible for drawing the lines for the U.S. House of Representatives districts, they are also respon-sible for drawing the district boundaries for other governments within each of their respective states. This usually includes the state legislative districts and other statewide offices that are elected in districted elections—perhaps a state board of education, or a public utilities or public regulatory commission. After the census numbers are provided to localities, cities, counties, boards of education, and other governments that are elected on a districted basis, the lines of those districts must also be redrawn so the pop-ulations in each district are roughly equal. The rule for an equal number of people being in each district is in line with the requirement laid down by the U.S. Supreme Court during the "reapportionment revolution" of the 1960s, when it held that, in order to assure "one person, one vote" (i.e., that each person's vote be equal to that of every other person's), districts must contain roughly the same amount of people.[3] Otherwise, the voters living in areas with fewer residents who elect one representative would have pro-portionately greater power than those living in highly populated areas with only one representative. So, one of the requirements in redistricting that the courts oversee is that the populations of electoral districts be roughly equal.

In the past, there have been many incidents of state legislatures and local governments drawing district lines to put some groups at a tremen-dous advantage and others at a disadvantage. The number one rule in drawing districts always has been, and continues to be, the protection of incumbents. Those persons who are in office and are charged with re-cre-ating the districts have almost always made certain that the district lines are drawn so they themselves will continue to be elected. Because most of the legislatures are divided along party or other lines, it is usually the ma-jority party or majority faction that has the final say about how the lines are drawn. Thus, there is also a heavy bias toward preserving the domi-nance of one political party, the majority party, or one major faction in nonpartisan legislatures. The courts have held that protecting the incum-bent and drawing lines to protect partisan advantage is within constitu-tional boundaries.

When district lines are drawn so that they appear to discriminate against a particular group (by favoring another group), this is termed *gerrymandering.* Throughout U.S. history, one major form of gerrymandering has been the drawing of district lines to exclude, or work to the disadvantage of, racial or ethnic groups, such as Hispanics. Particularly in some of the states in the Southwest, legislative districts have been drawn to include incumbent Anglo or non-Hispanic politicians; this puts Hispanics and/or other minorities at a great disadvantage. Latinos have sued state and local governments over this "dilution" of their voting power. In several instances, and often based on either the U.S. Constitution or the Voting Rights Act of 1965 and its amendments, Latinos have been able to win some legal victories in these matters. Latinos who have sued state and local governments have demonstrated convincingly that the way the districts were drawn discriminated against their having an equal opportunity to elect one of their own in the districts in which they reside.[4] They have convinced the courts that race and ethnicity are major considerations in the voting decision of voters. Latinos tend to vote for other Latinos (everything else being equal), and whites or Anglos tend to vote for other whites or Anglos. Therefore, legislatures have historically drawn districts so Latino communities are split into several districts; this way, in any one district, their percentage is very small, and they are unable to muster the necessary numbers of voters for their candidates. This is known as "cracking" the Hispanic vote. For example, in Los Angeles County in 1984, the Mexican American Legal Defense and Education Fund (MALDEF) challenged the division of Latinos into several different supervisory districts, arguing that this division had prevented the election of a Mexican American to the county board of supervisors since the 1850s (Geron 2005). This was eventually resolved by the U.S. district case *Garza v. County of Los Angeles* (1990), in which the court decided that the county supervisors had violated the Voting Rights Act of 1965 by intentionally denying the Latino community from electing a candidate of its choosing to the board of supervisors.

Another tactic that has been used when there is a considerable, but scattered, number of Hispanics in a large area has been to create an oddly shaped district that roams about the countryside picking up clusters of Latinos and "packing" them into one overwhelmingly Latino district. In this case, therefore, Latinos are assured one, but only one, representative from a district that is 80 or 90 percent Hispanic; however, there are no Hispanics left in other areas in which they could conceivably pick up another representative or two. These practices, and others that had a similar effect, have been judged to produce "minority vote dilution" and are deemed illegal by the courts.

Since the 1960s, the courts have monitored redistricting throughout the United States, and when legislatures and other redistricting bodies have failed to meet the constitutional requirements of fairness, the federal courts have generally not hesitated to draw up districting plans that are fair to minorities. Throughout the 1970s and 1980s, the courts, including the U.S. Supreme Court, generally upheld districts that had been drawn to counteract the long history of discrimination against minorities and their exclusion from the possibility of electing some of their own. These were now districts that had a significantly large majority of Hispanics and that had elected Hispanic candidates. The progress made as a result of these districts is clear when looking at the sizable gains made in overall Latino representation. In 1973, there were only 1,280 Hispanic elected officials in the six states with the highest Latino populations (Lemus 1973). By 2004, however, there were 4,583 Latino elected officials, with nearly 30 percent of them being Latina (National Association of Latino Elected Officials 2004). However, in the late 1980s and 1990s, the Court began to waver on district maps that were drawn to maximize the opportunity for Latinos and other minorities to elect some of their own. In some cases, there are no clear guidelines as to what the court will and will not accept with regard to so-called "ethnic gerrymandering". Although the Court has struck down a few congressional districts that were drawn to favor African Americans in the South because of their unusual shape, the Supreme Court and lower courts up until 2000 have upheld redistricting, which has promoted the election of Hispanic representatives, such as that of Luis Gutiérrez, U.S. Congressman from the Chicago area (4th District) of Illinois. In a 1998 ruling, the U.S. Supreme Court upheld the districting of the Illinois 4th District that had been challenged in *King v. Illinois Board of Elections* (1996). Realizing that the way the lines are drawn had a great impact on the potential for electing Latino representatives to office, various Latino groups such as MALDEF, the Puerto Rican Legal Defense and Education Fund, the Southwest Voter Registration and Education Project, and NALEO have lobbied governments and government agencies, including the U.S. Census Bureau, trying to exert pressure to ensure that Latinos will have an adequate and fair opportunity to elect Latinos to office. The lobbying continues even after the U.S. Census Bureau issues its population reports. This time the pressures are put on the district line-drawing bodies, particularly the state legislatures themselves, and there is a great deal of controversy and conflict in determining where exactly lines are going to go and who will be included and excluded from these various districts.

With the increase in the number of Hispanics throughout the United States, it has been very important to make sure that this increase in population is proportionately reflected in an increase in the number of districts that are likely to elect Latino representatives at all levels—national, state, and local. Because the census is only done every ten years and the population dynamics are continuous, this meeting between demographics and politics reaches an almost frantic pace in the year or two after the census data are given out. Latinos are very active at all levels, particularly at the local levels of county commissions, city councils, and school boards, trying to ensure that the lines are drawn so the increase in Latino populations will be reflected in an increase in Latino representation. It is hoped that from those adjustments, an increase in Latino political influence and power will also ensue.

In 1975, a great legal boost was given to Latinos striving for fair and equal representation when the Voting Rights Act of 1965 was amended to extend the constitutional protections that had been given previously to African Americans to Latinos and other "language minorities" (de la Garza and DeSipio 1997). Since then, Latinos have had a solid statutory basis on which to present their case for representation.

AT-LARGE AND SINGLE-MEMBER DISTRICTS

Another feature dealing with a characteristic of legislative districts in the United States that was challenged in the courts by Hispanic organizations was the existence of multimember districts.[4] In some electoral arenas, such as school and city councils and county commissions, several candidates were elected from one electoral district to fill all seats of the policy-making body. For example, the seven-member school board might have voters going to the polls to select them from a large district, such as the entire school district. These multi-member elections usually encompassed rather large areas, and often had non-Hispanic whites as a majority and Hispanics as a minority. The results would often be that non-Hispanic whites, based on their bloc voting, would elect all members of the board or the legislature who were non-Hispanic. So, in this case, the majority could rule entirely, and the minority, however substantial, would not have an opportunity to elect even a minority of Hispanic representatives. These multimember electoral districts were challenged in the courts, and in many cases, city councils, county commissions, and school boards were ordered to carve up the large community electoral area into several districts and to elect one representative from each geographic district. Because Hispanics tend to be more concentrated in some parts of the town or school district than others, this would give them an opportunity to elect at least one member, or a few members, from those areas of town in which they resided. There has been considerable change in the number of at-large versus districted elections across the United States. For example, following the landmark U.S. Supreme Court case, *White v. Regester* (1973), extensive changes were made to electoral districts in Texas. In 1970, approximately half of the state legislature and nearly all city council members and school board trustees were elected from at-large districts. By 1976, all legislators were elected from single-member districts, with significant changes to city council and school board election systems as well (Davidson and Korbel 1981). To some extent, the increase in Latinos in local political offices has been due to the establishment of these districted rather than at-large elections. In fact, this dividing of large multi-member districts into several smaller districts has resulted in a tremendous number of Hispanics and other minorities being able to elect city councilors, county commissioners, and school board members in areas that had historically been without Latino representation.

The combination of judicial decisions in favor of reapportionment and redistricting, which enhanced the opportunity of Latinos and other minorities to elect members of their own group, as well as the abolition of multi-member elections in large areas, the establishment of smaller multi-member district areas, and a few other reforms has made a tremendous difference in the number of Hispanic elected officials throughout the United States. It has also allowed Latinos as members of the voting electorate to be more influential players in politics. Particularly as their numbers increase, these reforms have allowed Latinos to choose representatives who are more desirable and who are more likely to represent their interests. It is through Latinos unaffected by minority vote dilution that they will enhance their political power in the electoral process. In several places in this book, we point out how the number of Latino elected officials has increased and consider the significance of this increase in the number of Hispanic elected and appointed officials.

Moreover, the courts have also ruled that, in addition to the other requirements for fair redistricting, the districts must be fairly "compact" and "contiguous," and as much as possible should represent "natural communities of interest."[5] Hispanics and other minorities have used these criteria to further their appeal for redistricting, which creates districts that include most or all of a Hispanic community rather than breaking it into several districts. This has produced a significant number of so-called "majority-minority" districts in which Latinos comprise a large majority of the residents, usually at least 65 percent. In turn, this has resulted in a significant increase in the number of Latinos being elected to governmental office.

One unanticipated consequence of the fairer redistricting that has enhanced the election of Latino representatives has been that, in many cases, the Latino incumbent earns a safe seat on a governing board. If a community is 80 or 90 percent Hispanic, it is very likely to elect a Latino representative. Once the Latino representative becomes an office holder, he or she will accrue the many strong advantages of incumbency. This usually leads to continuation of the incumbent in office and may result in little or no competition for the office holder. A consequence of low levels of competition for political office is often an extremely low voter turnout due to the lack of choices and lack of mobilization from viable opposition. This has led some scholars to propose that rather than have "Latino-dominant" districts in which 80 or 90 percent of the voters are Hispanic, it might be preferable to have some "Latino-influence" districts where Latinos number perhaps 40 to 50 percent of the voters (de la Garza and DeSipio 1997). Thus, competition would be assured in the district, and yet the support of Latinos would be almost essential to win an election. Certainly, candidates would have to seek out the Latino vote and pay attention to the needs and wants of Latino voters in order to strengthen the possibility of their being elected. This is reinforced by research that has attempted to determine the threshold, or the critical percentage of minority population, that is needed to elect a minority candidate (Cameron, Epstein, and O'Halloran 1996; Lublin 1997). In short, the average district with a simple Latino majority has a 57 percent chance of sending a Latino to Congress, and increasing the Latino percentage to 55 percent raised this probability to 84 percent (Cameron et al. 1996). Therefore, it is clear that Latinos can have a significant impact on the outcome of elections even without the use of Latino-dominant districts.

REPRESENTATIVE DECISION MAKING

Suppose that reapportionment and redistricting were done in accordance with the guidelines laid down by the U.S. Supreme Court and other courts; that the burgeoning Hispanic population has been reflected in a significant number of Latino-dominant or Latino-influence districts; and that, consequently, Latinos have elected some of their own (i.e., Latino representatives), whether those persons are U.S. Congress members, city councilors, county commissioners, or school board members. Now, how can those representatives, those elected officials, best go about representing their constituencies, that is, the people who reside in the districts from which they were elected, or if construed more narrowly, those people who supported them in their successful candidacies? Public officials in a representative democracy have a great responsibility. It is up to these persons to act in a way that promotes the interests of those they represent. We already discussed various theories of representation, and in practice, some public officials tend to pay either more or less attention to what their constituents say, and some may be more self-directed than constituent-directed when it comes to deciding what they do. Public officials are decision makers. They have to decide which of the multitude of competing interests and pressures on them will be preferred, favored, and chosen as that one that the representative will choose and support in the making of law. In fact, some political scientists define decision making as "the essence of politics," holding that politics features the competition and conflict of ideas, interests, and groups, all presenting various ideas of what government and representatives ought to do. It is up to the representative to resolve that conflict by making a decision, by choosing one course of action that he or she will work toward making into law or public policy. This is politics as the resolution of conflict or competition through decision making which authoritatively allocates values and resources (Easton 1965).

Hispanic public officials are faced with the hundreds of various interests, whether from individuals or groups, that converge around any one significant policy issue. They will be pressured by interest groups that are taking various positions on an issue, by individuals who have access to that representative, and by members of that representative's political party (and political parties are important to that member's career and success in office). Within any legislative body, there will be officers and other influential long-term members who will do some internal lobbying on a representative, trying to push his or her vote in one direction or another. Often, these decision makers also pay attention to public opinion polls of their constituents, which are increasingly affecting the decision making of public officials. They are subject to the media reports, particularly television and newspapers, which often scrutinize a public official's actions. In addition, representatives are subject to the wishes of their friends and family members. These are just some of the external influences coming to bear on a representative's decision making. Of course, there are also internal, personal pressures. An individual is not a blank slate. Each representative will also have his or her own preferences and values. It is hoped that he or she will have a personal value system or ideology, or at least a conscience, that will affect his or her choices and preferences.

So, there is a plethora of pressures that come to bear on any public official. However, for a Latino public official, there is almost always an additional factor or consideration—the ethnic or, more particularly, the Hispanic factor. If a representative is chosen by a majority of Hispanic voters, there is a presumption that that public official will represent Hispanic interests. Putting aside for the moment the definition of a Hispanic interest, there is still an additional major consideration that most Hispanic public officials must pay attention to, that is, their membership in a distinctive ethnic group. Does their being Hispanic mean that they have to take into special consideration Hispanic interests over those of other interest groups? If the representative is Hispanic, will he or she automatically have a slightly different set of needs, values, or interests than a non-Hispanic person? Perhaps, most importantly, must an Hispanic representative or a representative from an Hispanic constituency pay special attention to the Hispanic voice coming from his or her constituents? Do Hispanic representatives have an additional obligation over and above those held by all public officials to represent a distinctive ethnic group that has been excluded and discriminated against and has fought long and hard to obtain some level of political success, as marked, for example, by those representatives being elected to a public policy-making body? This goes back to the question we asked previously. Does it make any difference whether an elected official is Hispanic? The assumption is often that if a representative is Hispanic, then he or she will inevitably be more likely to represent Hispanic interests.

Surprisingly little research has been done on this issue of Hispanic representation. There have been a few studies of Hispanic legislators' voting behavior in state legislatures (Bratton 2006; Mindiola and Gutiérrez 1988) and a few studies of the voting behavior of members of the U.S. House of Representatives (Hero and Tolbert 1995; Segura and Bowler 2005; Santos and Herto 2002; Vigil 1996; Welch and Hibbing 1984). The research is minimal, and the answers are far from being complete. However, an interesting debate emerges because there is conflicting evidence on whether Latino representatives vote differently than non-Latinos. There have been scholars who provide evidence supporting the notion that Latino representatives vote more liberally than non-Latinos (Kerr and Miller 1997; Welch and Hibbing 1984). For example, Welch and Hibbing (1984) found that Latino representatives, as well as representatives with more Latinos in their districts, had lower Conservative Coalition support scores from 1972 to 1980. However, Hero and Tolbert (1995) found no statistical difference between the voting scores of Latinos and non-Latinos for the years 1987 and 1988. Santos and Huerta (2001) also found that such "Latino representation matters only modestly in explaining the substantive representation of Latinos" (p. 73). Although further research in this area is needed to clarify this debate, it does seem that there is an overall difference in the way that representatives from Hispanic constituencies or districts vote. They do tend to vote less conservatively and more in line with the issue positions of major Hispanic organizations. There also seems to be some effect on the behavior of authorities caused simply by having the presence of Hispanic members within a decision-making body and on how the other members of the body will act on matters affecting Hispanics.

Scholars have also been interested in whether the presence of Latinos in congressional districts impacts the voting behavior of members of Congress. Again, the results of these studies are decidedly mixed. Much of the early work in this area concluded that there was no meaningful relationship between Hispanic populations and the ideology of members of Congress measured by interest group ratings (Hero and Tolbert 1995; Kerr and Miller 1997). However, Lublin (1997) found that the presence of Latinos in a district correlates with more liberal ideology scores among Democratic members of Congress and more conservative scores for Republican members. Lublin contends that this is a result of Democratic members representing districts with Latinos of Puerto Rican and Mexican origin who are overwhelmingly Democrat, compared to Republican members representing Cubans, who also tend to be Republican.

A recent comparative study of Latino legislators in seven states with the highest proportion of Latino population provided some strong evidence that having Latinos in state legislatures (descriptive representation) does produce significant policy effects on the legislative process (substantive representation) on certain kinds of issues (Bratton 2006). This link between descriptive and substantive representation is most often found in "uncrystallized issues"—issues that are relatively new and on which the parties have not taken clear positions. Latino legislators were much more likely to introduce legislation that was related to "ethnic interests," such as bilingual education, discrimination, and immigration, than were non-Latino legislators. So, the policy agenda of state legislatures that included Latino legislators was significantly affected by their presence in at least this manner. An electoral district that was significantly Latino was more likely to be correlated with the introduction of education, health, and welfare policy measures than was the presence of Latino legislators. Committee memberships were not significantly affected by Latino legislators. The effect of Latino legislators on the successful passage of bills was mixed. Their success in passing bills compared to their non-Latino colleagues varied by state and by chamber of the legislature. Florida was an exception to the general findings of this study.

One revealing study involved the interviewing of elected and appointed Latino officials at all levels across the United States, both in and out of Washington (de la Garza and Vaughan 1984). These individuals were asked whether they felt a special obligation to represent Hispanics in their functioning as public officials. At the time of the study, the members of Congress would not say whether they felt obligated to articulate Hispanic concerns. Public officials who were more likely to feel a special obligation to act on behalf of Hispanics include the appointed officials more so than the elected officials. Simply being Hispanic did not seem to make a difference. Those characteristics that did seem to correlate with an elected official being more aware of, and supportive of, Hispanic needs were that he or she was from the civil rights generation, had been active during that period, had experienced discrimination personally, and was of a lower socioeconomic background.

There is also a body of research that suggests that there are benefits to having more Latino representatives in office beyond the relationship with substantive representation. Most notably, there has been some debate regarding the impact of descriptive representation on political participation for minority groups. Some scholars suggest that descriptive representation increases mobilization for the Latino electorate, and strengthens both internal and external efficacy for this group, all of which increases political participation for Latinos (Barreto et al. 2004; Brischetto 1998; Gay 2001). Of course, as discussed previously in this chapter, de la Garza and DeSipio (1997) argued that the advances in descriptive representation through the creation of majority-minority districts may have unintentionally weakened the link between Latino voters and electoral institutions by emphasizing who gets elected over who votes. The most recent research in this area by Barreto et al. (2004) indicates that residing in majority Latino districts ultimately has a positive and enduring effect on the propensity of Latino voters to turn out. However, the probability that non-Hispanic voters turn out decreases as they are subject to increasing layers of majority Latino districting. Furthermore, scholars have suggested that descriptive representation improves the relationship minority communities have with political institutions, and can increase trust in government for racial and ethnic groups (Gay 2002; Phillips 1998). Therefore, descriptive representation may be valuable and necessary to the American political system, even if Latinos are able to be adequately represented by non-Latino elected officials.

SUMMARY AND CONCLUSION

In this chapter, we introduce the concept of representation and how the Latino community is represented in American government. This discussion includes definitions of the various forms of representation and information on how well Latinos are represented across these various forms. It is clear that Hispanics are increasingly entering the mainstream of elected and appointed public officialdom. With the noticeable increase in the number of appointed and elected officials across the United States being in line with the burgeoning Latino population, much more research is needed. A careful examination should be made of who Latino representatives feel obligated to represent and whether they have a special obligation to the Hispanic electorate. This sense of obligation may extend well beyond their own electoral constituencies to the larger Hispanic "community," regardless of where they are located geographically. Alternatively, if they experience the same influences as non-Hispanic representatives once they are elected, then that information would have great significance for Hispanic elections in particular and Hispanic politics in general. However, much more research is needed on the subject before we can even approach conclusions on the many questions raised about Hispanic representatives' decision making.

Chapters 10 and 11 advance this discussion by investigating the role of the Latino community in national, state, and local governments.

Notes

[1] Formerly published as the *National Roster of Hispanic Elected Officials*, *The Directory of Latino Elected Officials* is now in its twentieth year of publication.

[2] These figures do not include the Chicago local school council members or New York City's thirty-two community education councils, which were included in some earlier NALEO reports.

[3] See cases such as *Baker v. Carr* (1962), *Gray v. Sanders* (1963), and *Wesberry v. Sanders* (1964).

[4] The following cases dealt with multi-member districts: *White v. Regester* (1973) and *City of Mobile v. Bolden* (1980).

[5] The courts established requirements for fair redistricting in *Bush v. Vera* (1996), *Shaw v. Reno* (1993), *Miller v. Johnson* (1995), and *Thornburg v. Gingles* (1986).

10

The National Government and Latinos

Regardless of whatever biases the U.S. pluralistic political system may contain, Latinos have multiple opportunities to affect public policy. The U.S. Constitution, with its concerns for plural factions and the danger of tyranny, diffused and fragmented power along several lines. Although this dispersion of power may lead to a significant amount of inefficiency and difficulty in coordination, it has also protected Hispanics from any coordinated or centralized tyranny and continues to offer Hispanics multiple points of access into the political mainstream.

There are two major ways in which governmental power is constitutionally divided in the United States. The first is what is called the "*division* of power," which is the separation of the national, state, and local "levels" of government. The other is the "*separation* of powers," which spreads the policy-making process at any of the previous levels among the executive, legislative, and judicial branches.

In this chapter, we look at the constitutionally supreme level of government, the national level (often referred to as the federal level), and at the three major branches of government within that level: (1) the U.S. presidency and the executive branch; (2) the U.S. Congress; and (3) the national or federal court system, headed by the U.S. Supreme Court. The supremacy of the national government over the sovereignty of states and localities has evolved through practice, custom, and perhaps, most important, the Civil War. Today, most people pay more attention to the national government and its politics and policies than they do to those of their own state and local governments. The authority and power of the national government is supreme, and the U.S. Constitution is the law of the land. Any individual or group that is seeking governmental power and subsequent effects on the fundamental policies, rules, laws, and regulations of the United States must necessarily be concerned with, and involved in, politics at the national level. Therefore, if Latinos want to be major players in the formulation of U.S. policies, then they must spend a significant amount of their time and resources on the politics, processes, and policies of the U.S. government. We first examine the status of Latinos in national politics in each of the three branches. Then, in Chapter 11, we look at Latino political involvement at the state and local levels.

Exercising or achieving proportionate power for Latinos at the national level may be the most difficult political challenge that Latinos face. Throughout the history of the United States and, to some extent, even today, Latinos have not been recognized as a national minority; that is, they have been perceived as regional or localized in location and significance. Much of this has been due to the fact that for much of their history Latinos actually have been concentrated in certain geographic areas. Mexican Americans have resided largely in the Southwest; Puerto Ricans in the large cities of the Northeast, particularly in New York; and Cubans in the Miami-Dade County area of Florida. Thus, although they could not possibly be overlooked in these areas of the country, the decision makers in Washington, DC, largely avoided recognition of their existence; they were marginal at best. To compound this matter, until recently Latinos were a relatively small proportion of the nation's population, less than 10 percent until the 1990 U.S. Census. There is little doubt that not being the nation's largest distinctive racial ethnic minority and being concentrated primarily in areas far from the corridors of power in Washington, DC, were major factors in Latinos being the "invisible minority" to national decision makers. However, there is also no doubt that since the 1980s and 1990s, changes are occurring that are significantly altering the situation and that have made Latinos, in many people's judgment, a *national minority* to which the U.S. government must pay attention.

The first and most dramatic of these changes has been the burgeoning growth of the Latino population—the demographic factor. As discussed in previous chapters, the fact that Latinos became the nation's largest distinctive ethnic racial minority in the early twenty-first century made a huge impact on the nation's institutions, including the national political institutions and officials of our national government. This milestone has already had major political ramifications, and it promises to have even greater impacts in the future. The other major factor that has opened the eyes of many federal public officials to the status of Latinos is the dispersion of Latinos across the country. Although still fairly concentrated, there has been a noticeable movement of Hispanics into areas in which they were formerly absent or were in small numbers. This geographic dispersion has taken two forms. At one point, Latinos were the most urban of all distinctive ethnic groups; in the 1980s, more than 90 percent resided in urban areas. However, since the 1980s, there has been a significant movement into the suburbs.

Second, and arguably even more important in the long run, is the movement into states and regions that until the 1990s had little or no experience with Latinos. The two major areas of in-migration for Latinos have been the southeastern United States, primarily the states of the Old Confederacy, and many small towns and rural areas of the Midwest. The "Old South" has had a well-known history of conflictual race relations between blacks and whites, but now they are experiencing significant increases in a group that is neither primarily black nor white. The social, cultural, and political adjustments that will come from this will present many challenges and opportunities. In the Midwest, Latinos have primarily resided in large urban areas such as Chicago, but attracted by jobs in poultry, meatpacking, and factory work, as in the South, Latinos are moving into many of the small towns throughout the midwestern United States.

These demographic and geographic changes have been instrumental in pushing Latinos' recognition as a national minority that is a significant player in national politics. In addition, Latinos have found themselves strategically located to affect the elections to the highest national office, that of the U.S. presidency. Somewhat in 1996, but most notably in the 2000 and 2004 presidential elections, those involved with national elections—whether candidates, campaigners, consultants, or media pundits—were caught up in "discovering" and courting this new, potentially powerful national voting bloc in presidential elections.

This is discussed further as we examine the presidency and the rest of the national executive branch. These are followed by an examination of the relationship of Latinos to the U.S. Congress and to the federal judiciary.

THE PRESIDENCY AND LATINOS

The U.S. president is the most powerful person in the nation and arguably the most powerful person in the world. For Latinos to win the presidency, or more realistically to have considerable influence with the president or to have a considerable number of Latino decision makers within the presidency and the executive branch, would be a tremendous advantage to Latinos in pursuing the Latino political agenda. The U.S. Constitution describes a limited president, primarily a commander-in-chief of the nation's armed forces and an administrator who would "faithfully execute" the laws of the new national government. However, due to the necessity of having a powerful, single chief executive and a highly visible symbol of the nation, as well as some favorable interpretations of the president's constitutional powers and congressional delegations of power to the president, the president and the larger office, the presidency, has grown tremendously in power since the 1800s, particularly during the twentieth century.

To meet the expectations and demands placed on this position, the presidential role has expanded to become "the presidency," which comprises all offices that report directly to the president. These include the vice president; the president's cabinet, which consists of heads of executive departments and other agencies and close advisors; and the Executive Office of the President, which includes several important agencies, consisting primarily of the president's closest and most influential advisors, such as those in the White House staff, the National Security Council, the Office of Management and Budget, and the Council of Economic Advisors. Moreover, because of his role as the chief administrative officer of the United States, in theory, the entire federal bureaucracy, including every civil service agency (unless it has been specifically established otherwise), reports to the president of the United States. The George W. Bush administration made two important additions to the Executive Office of the President: the Office of Strategic Initiatives led by Karl Rove and the Office of Faith-Based and Community Initiatives. The president's primary constitutional responsibilities include being the chief executive in charge of managing the bureaucracy; commander and chief of our armed forces; the nation's chief diplomat and ambassador; the chief legislator, the source of most congressional initiatives and agenda; the nation's leader in crisis situations such as 9/11; the moral leader of the nation; and the unofficial leader of his or her political party.[1] In addition, the president is the ceremonial and symbolic head of state, representing the nation, much as the crowned monarchs do in other countries. This, along with his other powers, allows him to be the foremost public opinion leader in the United States, and as such, he has a lot to do with setting the nation's agenda.

Until the beginning of the twenty-first century, no Latino had been a serious contender for the U.S. presidency. In fact, there have been virtually no Latinos who have even declared themselves as candidates of the major parties in seeking the nomination for their party's presidential candidacy. The only exception before 2007 was in the 1980 presidential election when Mr. Benjamin Fernandez, a conservative millionaire Republican businessman from California, was briefly involved in the run for the Republican Party presidential nomination. The highest office of the land has always been occupied by white Anglo males, all of northern and western European heritage, and there has been only one Catholic elected to the presidency (John F. Kennedy). This top position will be a difficult post for any minority to achieve, but it is not unlikely that either a woman or an ethnic male will be a serious contender for the presidency in the first two or three decades of the twenty-first century, and perhaps will even become the president before midcentury. A Gallup Poll conducted in September 2006 revealed that 61 percent of Americans believed that they were ready to elect a woman as president and 58 percent would accept an African American, but less than a majority (41 percent) believed that America was ready for an Hispanic president (Jones, 2006). It may be more likely that, prior to election as president, the U.S. vice presidency will be occupied by a woman or an Hispanic American. Through presidential election year 2004, this had not yet been the case, although the Democrats did have a female vice presidential candidate, Geraldine Ferraro, on their slate with Walter Mondale in 1984. No Hispanic has been nominated as vice president, although Bill Richardson, former congressman from New Mexico, was believed to have the inside track for a vice presidential nomination, running with Al Gore as presidential candidate in the year 2000, before he encountered some unexpected public relations difficulties. However, after being elected twice as governor of New Mexico, in early 2007, Richardson declared himself to be a candidate for the presidential nomination of the Democratic Party. With his foreign policy and executive experience, Richardson may be the most viable individual to become the first major Latino presidential or vice presidential candidate.

Even though it will probably be at least a few decades before there is a Latino president, Latinos are continuing to urge the president to forcefully support the Latino agenda; to place as many Latinos as possible in high-ranking executive positions in the larger presidential office, such as the cabinet and the office of the presidency; and to achieve a proportionate number of persons in the civil service and the executive branch of government, particularly in the higher, more policy-making levels of the national government. As Latinos increasingly become recognized as a national minority, they will undoubtedly have increasing influence on the president.

This also holds true with regard to presidential elections because Latinos are strategically positioned to affect the election of the president due to their high levels of concentration in those states having the largest blocs of Electoral College votes. Throughout the 1980s and 1990s, and most notably in the years 2000 and 2004, it was noted that Latinos were a critical bloc of voters for presidential candidates to woo and win if they were to be successful. Latino activists and spokespersons themselves proclaimed for several elections in the 1980s and 1990s that Latinos would be the critical "swing vote" in determining either the nominees of each of the major parties or in winning the presidential election itself. Again, the reason for this is that Latinos have been situated primarily in the states with large populations and consequently with large numbers of electoral votes, such as California, Texas, New York, Florida, and Illinois.

This strategic scenario of the "critical Latino swing vote" first came to a head prior to the 2000 election, when not only the usual cadre of Latino activists, but also the mainstream press and political pundits, pointed at Latinos as being absolutely essential to presidential victories in both the primaries and the general elections. This was repeated less confidently in the 2004 election because Latinos had not made a critical difference in the extremely close 2000 election (de la Garza and DeSipio 2004). There are several conditions necessary for Latinos to become a critical swing vote in presidential elections. Perhaps the most important one is that the election must be close in each of the big electoral vote, "swing" states, or across the nation. The other necessary condition is that Latinos must indeed be a *swing* vote; that is, they must have a history, or at least the possibility, of swinging back and forth in support of one party's presidential candidate or another. Neither of these latter two conditions has been met in recent presidential elections. For example, in the year 2000, Latino activists and political pundits proclaimed early in the campaign that the Latino vote was absolutely essential for Al Gore or George W. Bush to win the presidency. The presidential candidates visited areas of Latino residents and appealed directly for the Latino vote, saying they would support Latinos' highest priorities, making several references to Latino values, and sprinkling their speeches with Spanish. However, when polls taken in the various states revealed that either the votes in most of these large states were not going to be close or Latinos were not changing their traditional voting patterns, much less attention was paid to Latinos by the presidential candidates and their campaigns. Yet, both Al Gore and George W. Bush did continue to talk more about Hispanics and their interests than had been the case in previous campaigns. So, up to that point, the year 2000 probably marked the presidential year in which Latinos were most widely and officially recognized as being potentially major players in presidential elections.

The Latino vote was again listed among the "battleground" or critical swing voting groups in 2004. Although the efforts of both parties were greater than in 2000, more modest expectations were posed. Latinos were considered significant (especially for the future), and each party went after a targeted proportion of the Latino electorate. It can be said that Latinos have "arrived" as an important target group in presidential elections, and this will likely continue to be so. However, it is notable that in 2000 and 2004, the largest states (e.g., California, Texas, New York) each demonstrated lopsided majorities of Latinos for one candidate and were judged noncompetitive states by the campaigners. Nevertheless, Latinos will continue to be an important voting constituency in the twenty-first century, will be courted by the presidential campaigners, and will continue to be on the radar screen of the elected presidents, particularly if Latinos continue to exert pressure on presidents once they are in office.

One way Latinos do this is by continuing to put pressure on presidents to appoint Latinos to high and influential positions within the president's cabinet, the Executive Office of the President, or the federal judiciary. Various Latino groups keep a close watch on presidential appointments and are quick to point out how many (or how few) Latino appointments have been made by each president because presidents over the last several elections have promised to make their high appointments much more diverse than they have been in the past. Second, various Latino group organizations, such as the National Association of Latino Elected and Appointed Officials (NALEO), the National Association of Latino Appointed and Elected Officials, and the National Council of La Raza, closely watch the president's policy agenda, particularly the proposals including proposed legislation that the White House sends to Congress in the president's role as chief legislator. The Latino groups then often score or grade, and certainly comment on and publicize, the president's being either attentive or inattentive or contrary to Latino concerns and positions on various policy issues.

Particularly beginning with George H. W. Bush (Sr.) in the early 1990s, NALEO pointed out in a press release that President Bush had appointed only fifteen Hispanics among the 1,312 employees in the Executive Office of the President in 1990, just 1.1 percent. Some Democratic senators later joined in on the attack on George H. W. Bush's record, giving him only an "average" grade on his appointing Hispanics to government posts. But Republican U.S. senators rebutted this, saying that Bush had the best record toward Hispanics of any president in recent memory, noting that the president had appointed 280 Hispanics to "top-level government posts" since elected in 1989, more so, the Republicans claimed, than any previous U.S. president. These appointments included Hispanic physician, Antonia Novello as U.S. surgeon general, and two cabinet appointments, Interior Secretary Manuel Lujan, Jr., and Education Secretary Lauro Cavazos. Republicans compared this to the absence of any Hispanic appointments to the cabinet during the previous Democratic administration. The congressional Democrats also attacked the senior President Bush's record on issues affecting Hispanics directly, giving Bush's performance two Fs, two Ds, and one C. On his policy advocacy for Hispanics, the senatorial Democrats gave George H. W. Bush an F for his education record, an F for his record on employment, a D for his stance on civil and voting rights (he originally opposed the 1991 Civil Rights Act and had promised to veto the "motor voter" bill), a D for his record on health care, and a C for his appointment of Hispanics, as previously mentioned.

President William "Bill" J. Clinton, first elected in 1992, promised to have a presidential cabinet that "looked like America" and proceeded to make some high-level appointments of Latinos to office. Clinton's cabinet appointments included Bill Richardson and Federico Peña in the Department of Energy and Henry Cisneros as head of the Department of Housing and Urban Development.

George W. Bush, first elected in 2000 and re-elected in 2004, continued the accelerated pace of making Latino appointments. Most notably, President Bush placed Latinos in very important positions; he appointed Alberto R. Gonzales as Chief White House Counsel and Carlos Gutiérrez as secretary of the U.S. Department of Commerce. In 2005, President Bush made Alberto R. Gonzales the first Hispanic attorney general of the United States. Gonzales had been appointed to high levels by Bush when he had been governor of Texas and was also widely rumored to be one of the president's top choices for the U.S. Supreme Court when there was a vacancy. President Bush also named some California Latinos to key posts, including Hector V. Barreto to run the Small Business Administration and Ruben Barrales to the White House as Bush's Deputy Assistant for Inter-governmental Affairs. He also named the former California city mayor, Rosario Marin, to the largely ceremonial post of Treasurer of the United States.

Interestingly, this latter appointment followed a pattern of Republican presidents nominating Latinas to be U.S. Treasurer, the person whose signature appears on the nation's currency. The first had been the appointment of Romana Acosta Banuelos, who was appointed by Richard Nixon in 1971. Ronald Reagan's Treasurer was Katherine Davalos Ortega, and the elder George Bush named Catalina Vasquez Villalpando to the post. Ms. Marin was the fourth. Anna Escobedo Cabral, a Mexican American, was appointed U.S. Treasurer by President George W. Bush in December 2004. Even though the particular appointment is not one that has a tremendous amount of substantive policy-making influence, it does illustrate how appointments of Hispanics to visible national positions can provide recognition or symbolic representation for Latinos, serving as role models for Latinos, and giving Latinos a certain amount of pride in seeing one of their own being visible at high levels of the national government.

George W. Bush also wanted to appoint an Hispanic woman, Linda Chávez, to a cabinet appointment. Ms. Chávez previously served in governmental positions and headed some conservative organizations in the private sector. She was also a media journalist who wrote largely conservative position papers and columns on various issues. The nomination brought a tremendous uproar and reaction against her appointment from the largely Democratic and liberal Latino constituencies around the nation. Apparently, the negative reaction by Latinos was influential enough to result in Ms. Chávez offering her withdrawal from the nomination. Many suspected that the president had suggested, or at least hoped, that this controversial nomination would not proceed any further. Following the "surprise" congressional victories in the 2006 elections, with the GOP falling back to about 30 percent of the Hispanic vote, President Bush named Sara Martinez Tucker as Under Secretary of Education. Republicans claim that President Bush has appointed more minorities, including Hispanics, to federal positions than any other president in history.

In any case, because of these precedents and the increasing political significance of Latinos nationally, presidential candidates and the president from now on will be attuned to the needs and wants of Latinos in the nation as never before. More Latinos will be considered for appointments to high positions in the executive branch, and their policy preferences will increasingly be considered as the president introduces legislation to Congress or simply brings various policy matters before the American public. The president has that unique vantage point or "bully pulpit" as no other person does, to demand the attention of the body politic and the media.

THE FEDERAL BUREAUCRACY

The execution and administration of the many programs of the federal government as they are implemented throughout the nation requires a large number of administrators of all varieties. These people who work for the government in various departments, offices, agencies, and bureaus of the national government are often termed the "federal bureaucracy," or less flatteringly, "bureaucrats." Although the decisions that are made at the highest levels of the national government, such as within the presidency, are extremely important, particularly because they set the agenda and decide which issues ought to be brought forth for consideration and shape those issues in major ways, it is at the level of actually carrying out those policies that is often the most important and has the greatest impact on people. Few people, and most certainly even fewer Latinos, have direct contact with the president or any high-ranking national public officials. However, all citizens, sometimes on an almost daily basis, are affected by or have contact with those people who are charged with actually applying the laws to the public. In fact, it is likely that Latinos have less contact with high-level decision makers and more contact with what has been called the "street-level bureaucracy" than do non-Hispanic whites. Because Latinos are still relatively less powerful and lower on the socioeconomic level, they are much more likely to come into contact with the lowest level of the federal bureaucracy than to have contact with high-level executives or to have friends in high places in the federal bureaucracy. So, it is with the clerical staff and public administrators who are interacting directly with Latinos with whom contact is most likely to be made and whose decisions most directly and immediately have an effect on Latinos lives.

There has probably been too little attention paid to having the federal bureaucracy either staffed by a proportionate number of Latinos or to being particularly responsive to Latinos. In fact, many who have looked at this situation have found that the federal bureaucrats often tend to be either unfamiliar with Latino wants, needs, and values, or are even particularly dismissive of, or rude to, Latinos in their dealing with them. Many of the bureaucracies have been slow in coming around to having people who can translate Spanish for Latinos who are most comfortable in that language. Furthermore, Latinos have been, and continue to be, underrepresented within the federal bureaucracy, which has been suggested to have an impact on the level of responsiveness directed toward the Latino community by the bureaucracy (Pachon 1988). For example, a report by the Office of Personnel Management in 2001 to President Bush reported

6.6 percent Hispanic federal employees and called for more affirmative action on this matter.

The little attention that has been paid to the federal bureaucracy and its relationship to Latinos has been primarily leveled in two directions—one is the appointment of a fair number of Latinos to the managerial and supervisory high-level positions within the civil service; the second has been at the number or proportion of Latinos throughout the federal bureaucracy. Although the number of Hispanics in the civilian federal workforce has been increasing since the 1980s, Hispanic representation is still fairly low. The underrepresentation of Hispanics in the federal workforce has been partly due to past employment practices, which until the 1960s included overt discrimination. More recently, however, many of the discriminatory barriers have been reduced. Yet, the government has been slow to address Hispanic underrepresentation. For example, between 1984 and 1990, the number of Hispanics in the civilian workforce advanced 21 percent, but Hispanic representation in the government workforce rose only 13 percent. Of course, hiring practices and promotion practices vary widely throughout the government, from department to department. The general situation is that Latinos are most conspicuously absent at the senior-level, higher-paying jobs, representing only 1.5 percent of these in the general schedule system. In 1990, Hispanic federal employees overall were also at a lower grade level than were non-Hispanics. As of 1998, Hispanics constituted 6.4 percent of the permanent federal workforce compared to 10.8 percent of the civilian labor force. Hispanics had comprised 5.2 percent of the federal workforce ten years earlier (U.S. Office of Personnel Management 1999). On October 12, 2000, President Clinton issued Executive Order 13171, recommending policies that would improve the representation of Hispanics in federal employment, within merit system principles. Despite this order, Hispanics were still underrepresented in 2004, as they comprised 7.46 percent of the federal civilian workforce (U.S Equal Employment Opportunity Commission 2005). As of June 2006, Hispanic representation in this area has remained nearly the same, increasing to only 7.5 percent. Furthermore, the most recent figures indicate that Hispanics are hired into the lowest-paying federal positions (Gruber 2007). Although progress has undoubtedly continued to be made since the 1990s, Hispanics are still underrepresented both in the highest levels of the appointed ranks of the bureaucracy and throughout all levels of governmental employment. This remains so even as the national government has had a policy of affirmative action and several agency initiatives that theoretically would significantly boost the number of minority employees, including Latinos.

Again, it should be stressed that it is extremely important to have Latinos or Latino-responsive people in our public agencies to fairly represent and serve the Latino population that has long been unfairly excluded, underserved, and underrepresented. The fair representation of Latino needs within the executive branch headed by a responsive president will continue to be high on the political agenda of Latinos.

THE NATIONAL LEGISLATIVE BRANCH: THE U.S. CONGRESS

At the national level of government, we have at least the three well-known branches of government—the presidency, the legislature, and the judiciary. The U.S. Congress has sometimes been called the "first branch" of government, as it is the first branch included in the U.S. Constitution, and a long list of powers to be exercised by the national government are actually assigned to Congress. The chief responsibility of the national legislature is to create and pass legislation, which includes the rules, regulations, and public policies of the United States. In doing this, they are to represent directly or indirectly the wants and needs, desires and preferences of the American people. Congress itself is divided into two houses, again offering more access points to Latinos and others who want to influence the public policy-making process. The so-called upper house is the U.S. Senate, which is comprised of 100 members, 2 from each state, regardless of population. The so-called lower house, the U.S. House of Representatives, is actually the most democratically created of the two because its members reflect the number of people in the United States, and it is the only constitutional body that has always been directly elected by the people. Members of the House must frequently (every two years) go back to their constituents and ask that they be re-elected. Senators serve much longer (six-year) terms. Under the original Constitution, senators were selected by state legislatures rather than by the people and were to be the more elite, knowledgeable, "refined" chamber, constituted to exert control on the directly elected House of Representatives and to represent each state as a political unit rather than the people directly (until the passage of the Seventeenth Amendment in 1913, which mandated the direct popular election of all senators, the election of U.S. senators was constitutionally assigned to the state legislatures).

Because members of Congress are elected from fairly large electoral districts—in the case of the senators, the entire state, and in the case of U.S. representatives, electoral districts of about 660,000 people each—it is not easy for a minority population to elect one of their own to Congress. Certainly, this has been true historically for Latinos, and it has only been fairly recently that Latinos have been represented in Congress in any noticeable numbers.

The U.S. Senate has had few Latinos included among its 100 members because senators must win running on a statewide, at-large basis. Until 2004, there had only been three Hispanics who have ever served in the

U.S. Senate—all from the state of New Mexico. The first senator was Octaviano Larrazolo, a Republican and former governor, who was elected to fill an unexpired term vacancy from December 1928 to March 1929. Next, and the most prominent, was Dennis Chávez, Democrat, who served in the Senate from 1935 to 1962. He had previously been elected congressman from New Mexico in 1930, and served two terms in the House before being appointed to the Senate in 1935 and thereafter being elected four times. Senator Chávez was influential in passing bills of benefit to the Hispanic community, including civil rights legislation. He sponsored a bill that would create a federal Fair Employment Practices Commission and was a major supporter of the Civil Rights Act of 1957 and 1960. The most recent Hispanic U.S. senator from New Mexico was Joseph M. Montoya, also a Democrat, who served two terms (1964–1976). When these Hispanic senators were elected from New Mexico, the Hispanic population of the state was either in a majority, as in the case of Senator Chávez, or in a near majority, as in the case of Senator Montoya. As the Hispanic population approaches majority proportions in a few other states, such as Texas and California, the opportunities for the election of more Hispanic U.S. senators will undoubtedly increase.

It was a bit of a surprise when two Latino senators—Colorado's Ken Salazar and Florida's Mel Martinez—were elected in 2004 because they came from states with a lesser proportion of Hispanics. Ken Salazar was elected to the U.S. Senate after serving six years as the attorney general for the state of Colorado. Ken Salazar currently serves on the Senate Committees on Agriculture, Nutrition and Forestry, Energy and Natural Resources, and Veterans Affairs. Interestingly, Ken's older brother John Salazar was elected to the U.S. Congress in November 2004 from Colorado's 3rd Congressional District. Mel Martinez, the first Cuban American to serve in the U.S. Senate, reflects the partisanship trend associated with the Cuban population in Florida, by being elected as a Republican in 2004. Prior to serving Florida in the U.S. Senate, Martinez most recently served as U.S. Secretary of Housing and Urban Development under President George W. Bush. Senator Martinez has been nominated by President Bush to serve as the next general chairman for the Republican National Committee, making Martinez the face of the Republican Party. The representation levels of Cuban Americans in the U.S. Congress was recently increased with the nomination of Robert Menendez to serve out the remaining year in Governor-elect Jon Corzine's Senate term, giving New Jersey its first minority senator. With the swearing in of Menendez on January 18, 2006, there were three U.S. senators of Latino origin.

The first Hispanic elected to the U.S. Congress (House of Representatives) was Joseph Hernandez, who was elected to represent the Territory of Florida in 1822. This, however, was a nonvoting position. The only Hispanic to serve as a full-fledged member in the U.S. Congress during the nineteenth century was Romualdo Pacheco, a Republican from California. Although Mexican born, Pacheco had an English stepfather and an English education. After California was taken from Mexico in 1848 and given statehood in 1850, Pacheco held a succession of political offices up to the governorship of California in 1875. He ran for Congress in 1876 and took his seat in the House of Representatives in early 1877. However, the election was contested, and the House decided that his opponent was the rightful victor and unseated Pacheco. He returned home and ran again successfully twice more. After serving those terms, he became an ambassador to Honduras and later Guatemala.

No other Hispanic was elected to Congress again until 1912. From that year on, Congress has included at least some Hispanic representation, with the exception of the periods of 1927 to 1931 and 1941 to 1943. The 1960s were important years for Hispanics in Congress. Prior to this, Hispanic representation was limited mainly to congressmen from New Mexico and a few isolated cases from Florida, California, and Louisiana. But with the reapportionment and redistricting revolution of the 1960s, the number of congressmen began to increase, and the localities they represented became more diverse. Henry B. Gonzalez was elected in 1961 and Eligio "Kika" de la Garza was elected in 1964, both of whom were from Texas. Edward Roybal was elected from Southern California in 1962. The first Puerto Rican elected was Herman Badillo, elected to Congress in 1970 from the south Bronx. The first Cuban and Latina elected to the U.S. Congress was Ileana Ros-Lehtinen. As the twenty-first century began, there were five females among the Hispanic representatives in the House.

By 1999, there were eighteen Hispanic members in the U.S. Congress—all in the House. Texas had the largest number of representatives at six, followed by California with five; New York and Florida were represented by two Hispanics each; and the states of Arizona, Illinois, and New Jersey each had one Latino member of the U.S. House of Representatives. Of the eighteen Latino members, fifteen were Democrats and three were Republicans. One more was elected in 1998 to bring the number of full-fledged members of Congress to nineteen in 2000 (there have also been nonvoting representatives in the House from Puerto Rico and Guam). This number has increased slowly over the years, with a noticeable increase of six members, from eleven to seventeen, occurring with the 1992 elections (and following the 1990 U.S. Census and subsequent redistricting).

By 2001, there were twenty-one Latinos in the House, and after the 2004 election, there were twenty-three. The greatest number was from California with seven (all Democrats), followed by Texas with six—five Democrats and one Republican. Florida had three (all Republicans, including two brothers); Arizona and New York had two (Democrats); and Colorado, Illinois, and New Jersey each had a single Latino Congressman (all Democrats). Of the twenty-three, nineteen were Democrats, and four were Republicans. Sixteen were men, and seven were women. The only change in Latino congressional representation following the 2006 elections was the addition of Albio Sires (D-NJ), who gained the seat formerly held by Robert Menendez before he was appointed to the U.S. Senate. Therefore, the total number of Latinos in the House of Representatives (23) and the Senate (3) remained the same after the 2006 election. With the greatly increasing Hispanic population, the numbers should continue to increase significantly.

It is interesting to note that if Hispanic representation in the U.S. House of Representatives was in proportion to their numbers in the U.S. population in the year 2000, there would have been three times the number of Hispanic representatives. If Hispanics participated in voting to the extent that reflected their numbers in the population and voted overwhelmingly for Latinos, there would be approximately fifty-four members in the House. After the 2000 U.S. Census, there were twenty-four congressional districts with Latino populations greater than 50 percent (Geron 2005, 113). For the rate of Latino members of the House of Representatives to continue to rise, Latinos will need to win in electoral districts where Latinos are not the majority of the population.

The U.S. Congress is organized along political party lines, and the party in the majority traditionally controls the House. This party will contain the positions of leadership, such as the Speaker of the House and the all-important committee chairpersons. Over the years, the party having control has fluctuated. It has been predominantly Democratic since World War II, and because Latino representatives have been largely Democratic in their party affiliation, this has increased the influence of Hispanic congresspersons. When Republicans have had control of the House, the influence of all Democrats, including the great majority of Latinos, has diminished. When the U.S. House of Representatives was taken over by the Republicans in 1994, the Republican house leadership announced that it would no longer fund with public monies what they called "special interest" caucuses or working groups within Congress. This meant that the Congressional Hispanic Caucus (CHC) and the Black Congressional Caucus would have to depend entirely on private funds for their support, such as staff, office supplies and equipment, and mailings.

Until 1999, all members of the U.S. House of Representatives who were Hispanic or Latino were members of CHC. This was an organization that was started by Latino members as a kind of mutual support group, and one that would hopefully be more influential in congressional activities. CHC has become an important institution for Latino politics. It is able to take positions on issues and publicize them widely. As a group, it is also able to command not only media attention but also the attention of the president, legislative leaders, and other governmental and nongovernmental influentials, including the media. In addition, CHC has formed an institute that is open to all who want to become members and that has sponsored various programs, including leadership training programs for Latino youth, and awarded various forms of scholarships. Within Congress, the influence of CHC has waxed and waned, depending on the particular members of the caucus, the issues with which they were dealing, and the larger political environment, including the nature of the leadership of Congress. In the 1970s and 1980s, when the CHC membership ranged from six to eleven, there was a significant amount of disunity and even dissension within the caucus. The members' partisanship, national origins, and constituency interests pulled them in different directions. These disagreements were often ideological or partisan, and of course, the first obligation of the representatives was to represent their constituencies back home in the states. If the constituencies took strongly varying positions on an issue, this would often be reflected in the division within CHC. Therefore, the caucus was often unable to speak with a unified voice to represent Latinos.

In the 106th Congress (1999–2001), the three Republican Hispanic representatives decided not to become members of CHC because their positions on issues varied so much from the stance taken by the Democratic-dominated caucus. The two Republican representatives from Florida, who were Cuban Americans, and a conservative Republican from Texas, Representative Henry Bonilla, did not participate in caucus activities. They were joined by a fourth Republican, Mario Diaz-Balart from Florida, whose brother Lincoln was an incumbent in 2004. In 2005, six members of the (now all-Democratic) CHC are female, and it seems likely that an increasing number of Latinas will be elected to Congress because their proportion of elected officials across the nation is generally higher than that for non-Hispanics, and because Latinas are increasingly visibly active in politics. In 2007, there was once again dissension within the CHC, as several female congresswomen raised concerns regarding the lack of respect afforded to female members. This issue became public when Representative Loretta Sanchez resigned from the CHC after allegedly being called a derogatory name by CHC Chairman Joe Baca. Sanchez also raised concerns about whether Baca was properly elected CHC chairman in November 2006 and about his general attitude toward female lawmakers. This internal division has once again raised questions about the ability of the CHC to represent the interests of all Latinos.

The Republicans in Congress elected Resident Commissioner Luis G. Fortuno of Puerto Rico to lead the CHC. This group was established in 2003 and is composed of Republican members of Congress who are of Hispanic or Portuguese ancestry, as well as congressional members whose constituencies have a substantial Latino population.

In addition to being a member of the majority party, it is also important to have a long tenure in Congress because seniority (continuous service) is still a significant factor in representatives being selected for committee and subcommittee chairmanships. Much of the significant work of Congress is done in the various and numerous committees of the House of Representatives. Because the 435 members constitute a large body, much of the fact finding, information gathering, and legislation formulating are done at the committee and subcommittee levels. The committees' recommendations carry a lot of weight when they are reported to the full House, so having Latinos placed on committees that deal with the subjects most important to Latinos is a high priority. When the Democrats won majority control of the House in the 2006 elections, several Hispanic representatives were awarded important positions on committees and subcommittees. Speaker of the House Nancy Pelosi named Representative Xavier Becerra of California to be assistant to the speaker. Sylvestre Reyes of El Paso became chairman of the House Intelligence Committee and Nydia Velazquez from New York became House Small Business Committee chairman. In addition, Speaker Pelosi selected Representative Hilda Solis of California to serve as vice-chair of the Democratic Steering Committee.

Notable Hispanics who had long congressional careers included E. "Kika" de la Garza, a Democrat from Texas who was a former chairman and ranking member of the House agricultural committee. He had served thirty-two years in the House. Another was Henry B. Gonzalez, who was a thirty-seven-year veteran of the House and was a former chairman and ranking member of the banking committee. Also very influential was Representative Manuel Lujan, Jr., a Republican from New Mexico, who served twenty years in the House before becoming President George H. W. Bush's Secretary of the Interior in 1989. In addition, another member was Bill Richardson, a Democrat from New Mexico, who left the House in 1993 to become U.S. Ambassador to the United Nations and then Energy Secretary in the administration of President Bill Clinton. In 2002, he was elected governor of New Mexico.

Perhaps most influential in the early years of Latino representation in the House was Representative Edward Roybal, a Democrat from California. Originally from New Mexico, Representative Roybal began his service in 1963 and was chairman of the Select Committee on Aging, Health, and Long Term Care subcommittee, and the chairman of the Treasury, Postal Service and General Government subcommittee. He also founded NALEO and CHC. He retired after thirty years of service, at the age of seventy-six. He was succeeded in office by his daughter, Lucille Roybal-Allard, who was elected from a congressional district adjacent to the downtown, East Los Angeles district her father represented since he was elected in 1962. He had previously become the first Mexican American member of the Los Angeles City Council in sixty-six years, and he served thirteen years on the council, devoting much of his time to developing community health and child care programs. In the U.S. Congress, he continued to push social and economic reforms. Shortly after his election in 1962, he was instrumental in winning approval for the first federal bilingual act, and he introduced a successful bill to create a cabinet-level Committee for Spanish-Speaking People.

In the upper house, the Senate, the longtime senator from New Mexico, Dionisio (Dennis) Chávez, was especially notable. Following two terms in the House, Chávez served in the Senate from 1935 until his death in 1962. He served as chairman of several Senate subcommittees and committees, including the powerful Public Works committee. In this position, he was instrumental in improving this country's infrastructure, including the interstate highway system. He was a strong supporter of the New Deal and an advocate of civil rights as far back as the 1940s. In 1944, he introduced a bill for the establishment of a Fair Employment Practices Commission "to prohibit discrimination in employment because of race, creed, national origin, or ancestry" (Vigil and Lujan 1986, 7). Although he campaigned for years to pass such civil rights legislation, Southern Senators would filibuster it. Although others avoided the subject or denied the existence of discrimination against Hispanics, Senator Chávez never hesitated to point out the issues of discrimination against Hispanics, blacks, and others at a time when it was either ignored or denied. Not only did he impact policy and serve as a role model for Hispanics, but he also provided much-needed assistance for Hispanic youth to attend higher education, including law schools, in Washington, DC.

There has been a slow and fairly steady increase in the number of Hispanic legislators in the U.S. Congress over the years, and it is likely that this will continue. Even though the numbers are greatly below the level of being proportionate, most Latinos would agree that in general this has been a positive development. Latino representatives can serve as role models and can bring Latino interests into the congressional legislative process in several ways; and by simply being there can affect the behavior of non-Hispanic legislators, who thereby will probably be more sensitive and positive about matters affecting Hispanics.

But one of the key questions remains. Does the pure presence of Latinos in the national legislature (i.e., descriptive representation) improve the representation of Latino *substantive* interests? In the production of legislative policy at the national level, are Latino members of Congress only symbolic representatives, or are they effective policy representatives, reflecting Latino interests and affecting the outcome of legislation in ways that make life better for Latinos? This question cannot be satisfactorily answered at this time because of the small amount of research that has been done on the matter. For example, two studies of the same voting record of Hispanic House members in the 100th Congress (1987–1988) arrived at diametrically opposed conclusions. One study concluded that the role call voting behavior of Latino members of the House was not distinctive from that of non-Hispanic legislators and that there was no evidence of direct substantive representation of Latinos (Hero and Tolbert 1995). A later analysis of the same situation claimed faulty interpretations and understandings in the original study, and asserted that Hispanic House members did behave distinctively on direct roll call votes and that indeed there was direct substantive representation of Latinos on votes on issues of importance to Hispanics (Kerr and Miller 1997).

The earliest study, by Welch and Hibbing (1984), concluded that Hispanic representation in Congress and the proportion of Hispanics in congressional constituencies did correlate with liberal policy representation. Looking at an nine-year period and 1,740 votes (1972–1980), there was a positive correlation found between a larger population of Hispanic voters and more liberal voting records of non-Hispanic representatives from those districts. Moreover, the Hispanic representatives themselves voted less conservatively than did non-Hispanic representatives.

In the Hero and Tolbert (1995) study, although little direct substantive representation was found, Latino representatives did have somewhat distinctive voting records. However, they were not statistically correlated with the number of Latinos in their electoral districts. Although there was not a direct match between Latinos in the electoral districts and their particular Latino representatives, overall the record of Latinos seemed to be consistent with Latino preferences—a kind of "collective" or "indirect" representation. The Democratic Party affiliation of the Latino representatives seemed to be the main reason for correlated voting. The authors called this "indirect" substantive representation.

There has also been some discussion regarding other positive benefits of descriptive representation or of having members of racial/ethnic groups in government institutions such as Congress. Most notably, there has been some debate regarding the impact of descriptive representation on political participation for minority groups. Some scholars suggest that descriptive representation increases mobilization for the Latino electorate, and strengthens both internal and external efficacy for this group, all of which increases political participation for Latinos (Brischetto 1998; Gay 2001). However, de la Garza and DeSipio (1997) argued that the advances in descriptive representation through the creation of majority-minority districts may have unintentionally weakened the link between Latino voters and electoral institutions by emphasizing who gets elected over who votes. They argued that the highly partisan and uncompetitive nature of these "safe" districts essentially create uncontested general elections with little mobilization that in turn decrease Latino political participation. Given the lack of clarity regarding the impact of descriptive representation on either Latino political participation or substantive representation, it is clear that more work needs to be done in this area.

Before leaving this brief discussion of Latinos and the U.S. Congress, we might ask an important if broad, and perhaps unanswerable, question. Have Hispanic interests been favorably treated by the U.S. Congress, regardless of the quantity or quality of Hispanic representatives in the national legislature? This is almost as difficult to answer, as is the question of whether the U.S. public is adequately represented by its elected officials in the U.S. Congress. First, one would have to clearly define and measure the "interests" of the represented group and then use some kind of a measurement to compare those interests to the decisions (or votes) of the legislators. This is a difficult task, whether it is attempted for Hispanics, any other distinct group, or the general public. At this point, we can only venture some tentative generalizations. Until the 1960s, Congress did not seem concerned with the interests of Hispanics, the "invisible minority," per se. It did pass some legislation regulating the immigration and employment conditions of Mexicans, primarily agricultural workers, in the United States in the 1930s and in the 1950s. Most of this legislation furthered the interests of U.S. employers benefiting from the relatively inexpensive flow of labor, but it has had a great impact on Mexican and Mexican Americans in the United States. Sometimes Congress passed legislation that has worked to the benefit of Latinos even when not specifically focused on them, such as various social welfare and social service programs—unemployment compensation, minimum wage laws, the right to unionize and bargain collectively, antipoverty programs, health benefits, the Head Start program, subsidies for higher education, urban development, and many other similar programs. These have benefited Latinos because of their focus toward people of generally lower socioeconomic status. Congress has also passed legislation that has helped prevent discrimination against Latinos and secure their constitutional rights as distinctive, "cognizable" minorities, such as the Civil Rights Acts of 1957, 1960, 1964, and 1968 and the Voting Rights Act of 1965 and its many extensions and amendments. In more recent years, the national legislature has enacted legislation that is directed to Hispanics, such as the Hispanic Education Act of 1998. In 1998, Title V was added to the Higher Education Act of 1965. Title V was designed to encourage greater numbers of Hispanics, particularly those with low incomes, to enroll in graduate schools. To qualify as "Hispanic serving," at least 25 percent of the student population must be Hispanic, 50 percent of which must be low income. Various other laws and policies supporting bilingual education and Hispanic-serving institutions of higher education have also been passed. Even though Congress has historically been biased in favor of the mainstream culture, and more particularly the wealthier and otherwise privileged segments of Anglo America, particularly since the 1930s, it has enacted a considerable amount of legislation that has been supportive of Hispanics in one way or another.

The National Hispanic Leadership Agenda (NHLA) has scrutinized the voting records of the U.S. Congress and has produced some "congressional scorecards." In these, the votes of senators and representatives on key issues identified as being especially important to Latinos in the areas of economic mobility, the workforce, education, civil rights, immigration, and health. These are votes on bills for which NHLA has communicated its consensus position to the individual representatives. Each member's votes are recorded and reported on each bill as being a percentage of times that each took the pro-NHLA position. Although additional actions of members of Congress need to be considered when evaluating their support of Hispanic public policy issues, this scorecard certainly is one way to influence the representatives while providing important information to their constituents (NHLA 2005).

It is likely that with the continued growth, and particularly because of an increase in participation by Latinos in politics across the United States, one result will be an increasing number of Hispanic members of Congress, and sometime in the future, additional U.S. senators. This will certainly increase the representation—symbolic and substantive—of Latinos in the "first branch" of government at the national level. An interesting sidelight is that around the turn of the twentieth century, several members of Congress, including both Democrats and Republicans, began taking Spanish language lessons. It is reasonable to assume that these continuing developments will make the U.S. Congress increasingly aware of, more representative of, and more responsive to Latino needs and interests.

THE FEDERAL JUDICIARY

The United States has a dual court structure. One is comprised of the courts in the states and territories. The other is the national or federal court system, which consists constitutionally of the U.S. Supreme Court as the highest interpreter of the laws of the land and an entire system of lower federal courts devised by Congress. The lower courts are comprised primarily of three levels. The first level of courts in which criminal trials occur and lawsuits are litigated is the U.S. district courts; these courts entertain questions dealing with our national laws and the U.S. Constitution, as well as issues among states. The intermediate level comprises the U.S. Court of Appeals. There are twelve U.S. appellate court "circuits" in the nation. Each of them is overseen by the court of appeals for that circuit. These are not courts of original instance, or trials, but rather they hear appeals from the lower district courts. If cases are appealed from this level, they may go to the U.S. Supreme Court for another hearing, although only a small percentage (usually fewer than one percent) of such cases are actually accepted and heard.

It is not generally well known, but it would be hard to overestimate the importance of the federal judiciary to the status of Latinos (Falcon 2002). The national courts, including the U.S. Supreme Court, by and large have made decisions that have been favorable in guaranteeing equal opportunity to Latinos as well as eliminating discriminatory practices against them. All judges and justices in the federal court system are appointed by the president with the advice and consent of the Senate to lifetime positions (officially "during good behavior"). As such, because they have much longer tenure than elected officials do, and because ultimately they decide what the federal laws, including the U.S. Constitution, mean and how they are applied, federal courts are extremely important to the advancement of Latino political causes. Considering the fact that there have been and continue to be few Hispanics in the federal judiciary, over-all the courts have been quite staunch allies, particularly since the 1950s, in defending the rights of ethnic and racial minorities, including Latinos.

For the past several years, Latinos have made it well known that they want additional representation in the national court system, particularly at the highest level, the U.S. Supreme Court. Having a Latino Supreme Court justice would be the highest kind of symbolic Latino representation, as well as a perfect role model signifying to the nation that Latinos can and should be at the highest levels of government. Until 2005, there had not been an Hispanic appointed as one of the nine Supreme Court judges. However, when Supreme Court justice positions are open, there is increasing pressure to appoint an Hispanic. In fact, there had been much speculation about whether President George W. Bush, who had made it a point to become a presidential "amigo" to Hispanics, would appoint an Hispanic to the highest court of the land if and when a Supreme Court justice retired or died. Hispanic hopes were dashed in late 2005, when two vacancies came open and President Bush did not nominate an Hispanic for either open position, including that of chief justice of the U.S. Supreme Court.

As important as such a high recognition would be, it is probably at least as important substantively to have a fair number of Latinos in the lesser courts of the federal judiciary—the U.S. Court of Appeals and the U.S. district courts. In 2005, there was a small percentage of Latino members in the federal judiciary. For example, there are currently only twelve Latino judges seated on the appellate division of the federal courts. As Table 10.1 indicates, Hispanics have had proportionately far fewer appointees to both federal district and appellate courts than both Anglos and African Americans under most recent presidents. Hispanics represented only 1.1 percent of district court appointments under President Richard M. Nixon and have reached a high on district court appointments under George W. Bush with 10.7 percent. No Latino was appointed to the federal appellate courts until 3.6 percent of all appointments under President

Table 10.1
ETHNIC-RACIAL APPOINTMENTS TO FEDERAL DISTRICT AND APPELLATE COURTS, BY PRESIDENTS L. JOHNSON TO G.W. BUSH

	L. Johnson	Nixon	Ford	Carter	Reagan	G. Bush	Clinton	G.W. Bush
	District Courts (Percent)							
Race/Ethnicity								
White	93.4	95.5	88.5	78.2	92.4	89.2	75.1	82.1
Black	4.1	3.4	5.8	13.9	2.1	6.8	17.4	6.5
Hispanic	2.5	1.1	1.9	6.9	4.8	4.0	5.9	10.7
Asian American	0	0	3.9	0.5	0.7	0	1.3	0.6

	L. Johnson	Nixon	Ford	Carter	Reagan	G. Bush	Clinton	G.W. Bush
	Appellate Courts (Percent)							
Race/Ethnicity								
White	95.0	97.8	100	78.6	97.4	89.2	73.8	79.4
Black	5.0	0	0	16.1	1.3	5.4	13.1	11.8
Hispanic	0	0	0	3.6	1.3	5.4	11.5	8.8
Asian American	0	2.2	0	1.8	0	0	1.6	0

Source: Vital Statistics on American Politics (2005–2006), Table 7-5 Characteristics of Federal District and Appellate Court Appointees, Presidents L. Johnson to G.W. Bush (percent).

Carter. President Clinton appointed the greatest percentage of Hispanics with 11.5 percent.

Latino advocates consider it extremely important to have Latinos in the federal judiciary because many relevant issues are before the federal courts, such as those involving voting rights, redistricting, school funding formulas, mandatory sentencing, English-only situations, racial profiling, immigrant rights and policy, and other similar issues. Latino advocacy organizations, such as the Mexican American Legal Defense and Education Fund and NALEO, have been active in bringing cases involving the dilution of Latino voting rights and discriminatory practices into the U.S. court system. The assumption is that the presence of Latino justices would mean that these cases would receive an even more favorable hearing. Because the president makes these appointments, there is considerable pressure exerted on the president to appoint an Hispanic justice each time a vacancy occurs. President Clinton was particularly active in following his promise to make the federal judiciary "look more like America." He appointed twenty-four Latino judges, or 6.3 percent of his total appointments to the federal judiciary. Although some critics believe that the consideration of race, ethnicity, or even gender in the appointment of federal justices is not a proper consideration, surely the vast underrepresentation of Latinos in the ranks of the federal judiciary represents the past legacy of minimal opportunity, including outright discrimination, which should not be perpetuated in those bodies that determine the meaning of our federal statutes and policies.

The fact that the federal courts have often been in the vanguard of protecting minorities, including Latinos, has been an outstanding example of how in a system of both majority rule and minority rights, the rights of minorities must somehow be protected against domination by the majority. The federal courts are not elected and are not politically responsible to the majority. They are able to make their decisions on the bases of legal arguments and philosophical considerations. Also, the courts have been valuable allies because fewer political resources are needed to advance Latinos' interests in court than are those political resources, for example, to run a successful campaign in the legislative or executive branches. A good example of this protection of minority rights in the face of majority opinion and political power to the contrary, was the famous case of *Brown v. Board of Education* (1954), when the U.S. Supreme Court ruled that separate segregated schools were inherently unequal and thus were unconstitutional. For Latinos, the area of school finance has been a major focus of Latino legal attention. They have also focused on issues of school desegregation and bilingual education. For example, the 1973 *Keyes v. Denver* (1973) decision made by the U.S. Supreme Court included Mexican Americans as an identifiable minority group and thus Hispanics were constitutionally entitled to recognition for desegregation purposes. Latino groups seem to have been more interested in bilingual education than in desegregation, and in a landmark case, *Lau v. Nichols* (1974), the court decided that non–English-speaking students were denied equal education unless they were provided with appropriate educational services.

Another major issue for Latinos has been voting rights. The national Voting Rights Act of 1965 and its 1975 and 1982 amendments have been challenged by some states, but the courts have upheld the voting rights of "language minorities," largely Hispanics and Native Americans, against the biased electoral practices of local and state governments. They have protected minorities against "vote dilution" by such devices as at-large elections and the drawing of district boundaries to minimize the effects of Latino voter mobilization.

The area of affirmative action has also been one in which the courts have been very much involved. Most of these cases have involved African Americans, but some of them have also had direct implications for Latinos. Although in the 1970s and 1980s many case decisions have upheld various practices of affirmative action, in the 1990s the U.S. Supreme Court, in several close decisions, seemed to require much stricter standards for affirmative action programs.

SUMMARY AND CONCLUSION

In conclusion, representation of Latinos at the national level is limited. With regard to descriptive representation in all three branches of the federal government, the number of Latinos in elected and appointed federal offices is well below their proportion in the population or even in their voting population. Key to enhanced opportunities for Latinos in the executive branch is a president who is supportive of Latino interests. Latinos are strategically placed to affect the presidential elections; they have recently been recognized as such and strongly courted by presidential candidates. However, due to the nature of recent presidential elections, Latinos have not played the critical role that has sometimes been expected of them. This has been due to both the nature of the specific elections and the relatively low percentage of Hispanics voting in these elections.

Although the evidence is mixed with regard to the representation of Latino interests in the U.S. Congress, it is clear that descriptively the numbers of Latinos are well below where they ought to be, with only three Latinos serving in the U.S. Senate and being very much below proportion in the House of Representatives. Due to the Voting Rights Act and census counts involving fair redistricting in increasingly Latino populated areas, the number of Latino members in the House has slowly increased over the years. The Latino congressional delegation has recently been much more visible and often more unified than in the past, and there is reason to believe that their influence will continue and will increase over the years, although progress is slow and sometimes unsure.

The federal judiciary by and large has been an ally of Latino political interests, rendering several decisions that have advanced the interests of Latinos. However, some of the decisions have been contrary to those interests. These depend largely on the particular membership of the Supreme Court at any one time. Equally, if not more, important are favorable judgments made daily in the U.S. district courts and the U.S. Court of Appeals. Currently, Latinos are vastly underrepresented in these institutions. However, as the number of Latinos with legal training and experience in the law and in lower and state judiciaries increases, there are likely to be more presidential appointments and congressional approvals of Latinos in the federal judiciary.

Although it is not certain that increased descriptive representation will result in an increase in tangible, substantive representation of Latino interests, it is likely. As Latinos increasingly become a national minority, they will be paid more attention to by the national government and its institutions, and it is likely that the national public officials, in turn, will pay more attention to the interests, needs, and wants of the Latino people in the United States.

Notes

[1] For a complete discussion of the president's primary constitutional responsibilities, see Berman and Murphy (2005).

11

Latinos in State and Local Governments

As mentioned previously, one of the major characteristics of the U.S. Constitution, indeed one of the original inventions of the American Republic, is that of *federalism.* Federalism refers to the division of powers—that is, the division of governmental powers between the national government and the governments of the states. The concept of such a differential allocation of governmental powers among the nation and its states is a result of America's unique history. The states (as colonies) existed long before the national government—some of them for more than a century before the national government—and these states had fully viable governments performing the conflict resolution functions that are standard to governments around the world.

After the successful revolution against England (1775–1783) and the winning of national independence, the newly independent country moved cautiously toward a national government, first attempting a "weak league of friendship" among the states, with a very weak central government, under the Articles of Confederation (1781–1787). However, the sovereignty and continued independence of the states caused many problems for the newly conceived nation, and a constitutional convention that met in Philadelphia in 1787 devised a new system of government. This was to be somewhere between the traditional, age-old forms of governments that revolved around an all-powerful central government and that of a weak "firm league of friendship" among states, each of which maintained a great deal of sovereignty. This "great compromise" resulted in the *federal* system, which attempted to strike a balance between the powers of the national or "central" government and that of the member states, which themselves retained some sovereignty. Although the U.S. Constitution was written to have strong state governments and a relatively weak national government, over the 200-plus years of U.S. constitutional history, the national government has grown in power by accepting more responsibilities at the demand of the people, responsibilities that were not adequately met by individual states.

Although most of the publicity and the media spotlight are on the national government, it is probably the case that individual citizens are affected more so in their day-to-day lives by state and local governments than they are by the national government. The U.S. Constitution, written in 1787, assigned specific duties to the national government and left all others to the states. Therefore, it is the states that maintain primary responsibilities for the health, safety, and welfare of the people.

Because states retain such an important role in our federal system, Latinos who seek to use politics to advance their causes must be highly engaged in politics at all levels—state, local, and national. When we examined Latinos' roles in the national government, we saw that their roles were complicated by the fact that the U.S. government has a *separation of powers* between the legislative, executive, and judicial branches. Furthermore, each of the fifty American states also has a separation of powers within themselves; that is, each state has a separation of responsibilities for primary functions of government—the executive or administrative, the legislative, and the judicial functions. So, even though the national government is extremely complex, these complexities are additionally mirrored in each of the fifty state (plus the District of Columbia) governments. Therefore, given the scope of this book, it is impossible to go into great detail about the politics of fifty states and Latinos' involvement in those states. An examination of each state's government is impossible because there is significant variation among states. Each state has its own modifications of government, its own history, and its own socioeconomic context. Just as it is extremely difficult to generalize about all fifty states, Latinos' situations in each state differ significantly. Within our constraints and limitations, the best we can do is mention a few major facts about Latinos in state governments and politics, generalizing when we can and pointing out some of the more interesting specifics occurring in certain states when possible.

It is probably safe to say that the situation of Hispanics in every one of the fifty states varies significantly. Latinos have individual histories in each (Abalos 1986; Novas 2003). Often, the settlement patterns of Latinos vary from state to state, and each national origin group has many different historical roots and experiences (Estrada et al. 1981). For example, the Hispanos of New Mexico had viable communities and governments existing as far back as the early 1600s, while the Southwestern part of the United States in which they settled was still the northern frontier of New Spain two centuries before there was an independent nation of Mexico. Consequently, the Hispanos of New Mexico have been interacting with the governments of their colony, their territory, and later their state for about 400 years. In contrast, in some of our states, the Latino presence is quite recent, at least in any significant numbers. In the most heavily populated Latino states, such as Texas and California, the preponderance of the

Latino population has migrated into those states primarily during the twentieth century, although there were a few thousand Mexicans living in some areas of Texas for about 250 years and in California for about 200 years. The same, to a lesser extent, is true in Arizona and most of Colorado. New York has a significant Latino population, primarily Puerto Rican until the past few decades or so, and there have been Puerto Ricans in New York for most of the twentieth century. However, it was not until the mid-twentieth century that a large number of Puerto Ricans took up residence in New York City, since then, they have spread mainly throughout the urban Northeast.

The large Latino population in Florida is the most recent of the three largest national origin Hispanic groups.[1] Most of the Cuban Americans migrated to that state, and particularly to the Miami-Dade County area, after the takeover by communist revolutionary Fidel Castro in 1959. Previously, there had been a smaller number of Cubans working primarily in tobacco plants on the west coast of Florida in the 1800s, and they were also present in the New York area (de los Angeles Torres 1999; Masud-Pilato 1996). One could go on to recount the in-migration of various Latino national origin groups into each state (because every state in the United States now has Latinos residing in it), and in each state the situation would be different. Each governmental, social, political, economic, and historical context is different, and the history of each Latino's residence in that state, as well as his or her history of interactions with other residents, will vary from one state to another.

Much of the activity that will be of great importance to Latinos now and in the future will occur at the state and local levels. Although advancements at the national level are extremely important, the fact that Latinos are still a fairly small *national* minority (12.5 percent) according to the 2000 U.S. Census (and an estimated 14.1 percent in 2005) means that it will be much more difficult for them to exert significant influence at that level than in the states, whereas in some states they comprise 20, 30, or even more than 40 percent of the population. Even though Latinos are located in all states, they are fairly concentrated in just a few—Arizona, California, New Mexico, and Texas. Table 11.1 gives the population of Latinos in each of the fifty states.

Because the large influx of Latinos into the United States is continuing, areas that already have relatively large proportions of Latinos will continue to grow their Latino populations at a rapid rate. Also, important to remember is that Latinos are also dispersing throughout the United States. In percentage terms, there are extremely large increases in some of the states since the 1980s and 1990s. For example, the five states in which the Latino population grew the fastest were North Carolina, whose Hispanic population increased by 394 percent; Arkansas, 337 percent; Georgia, 300 percent; Tennessee, 278 percent; and Nevada, 217 percent. As significant as it is that Latinos are increasing, sometimes dramatically, in their state populations, it is also important to note that as of 2005, Latinos are still a

Table 11.1
HISPANIC POPULATION IN THE AMERICAN STATES, 2000

	Total Population 2000	Hispanic Population 2000	Percent Hispanic 2000	Rank by Number of Hispanics 2000
United States	281,421,906	35,305,818	12.5	N/A
Alabama	4,447,100	75,830	1.7	38
Alaska	626,932	25,852	4.1	44
Arizona	5,130,632	1,295,617	25.3	6
Arkansas	2,673,400	86,866	3.2	36
California	33,871,648	10,966,556	32.4	1
Colorado	4,301,261	735,601	17.1	9
Connecticut	3,405,565	320,323	9.4	18
Delaware	783,600	37,277	4.8	42
District of Colombia	572,059	44,953	7.9	40
Florida	15,982,378	2,682,715	16.8	4
Georgia	8,186,453	435,227	5.3	11
Hawaii	1,211,537	87,699	7.2	35
Idaho	1,293,953	101,690	7.9	31
Illlinois	12,419,293	1,530,262	12.3	5
Indiana	6,080,485	214,536	3.5	22
Iowa	2,926,324	82,473	2.8	37
Kansas	2,688,418	188,252	7.0	25
Kentucky	4,041,769	59,939	1.5	39
Louisiana	4,468,976	107,738	2.4	30
Maine	1,274,923	9,360	0.7	49
Maryland	5,296,486	227,916	4.3	20
Massachusetts	6,349,097	428,729	6.8	12
Michigan	9,938,444	323,877	3.3	17
Minnesota	4,919,479	143,382	2.9	27
Mississippi	2,844,658	39,569	1.4	41
Missouri	5,595,211	118,592	2.1	29
Montana	902,195	18,081	2.0	46
Nebraska	1,711,263	94,425	5.5	33
Nevada	1,998,257	393,970	19.7	14
New Hampshire	1,235,786	20,489	1.7	45
New Jersey	8,414,350	1,117,191	13.3	7
New Mexico	1,819,046	765,386	42.1	8
New York	18,976,457	2,867,583	15.1	3
North Carolina	8,049,313	378,963	4.7	15
North Dakota	642,200	7,786	1.2	50

(Continues)

Table 11.1
HISPANIC POPULATION IN THE AMERICAN STATES, 2000 (*continued*)

	Total Population 2000	Hispanic Population 2000	Percent Hispanic 2000	Rank by Number of Hispanics 2000
Ohio	11,353,140	217,123	1.9	21
Oklahoma	3,450,654	179,304	5.2	26
Oregon	3,421,399	275,314	8.0	19
Pennsylvania	12,281,054	394,088	3.2	13
Rhode Island	1,048,319	90,820	8.7	34
South Carolina	4,012,012	95,076	2.4	32
South Dakota	754,844	10,903	1.4	48
Tennessee	5,689,283	123,838	2.2	28
Texas	20,851,820	6,669,666	32.0	2
Utah	2,233,169	201,559	9.0	23
Vermont	608,827	5,504	0.9	51
Virginia	7.078,515	329,540	4.7	16
Washington	5,894,121	441,509	7.5	10
West Virginia	1,808,344	12,279	0.7	47
Wisconsin	5,363,675	192,921	3.6	24
Wyoming	493,782	31,669	6.4	43

N/A, not applicable.

Source: Population Reference Bureau, analysis of data from http://www2.census.gov/census_2000/datasets/demographic_profile/ (various files, June 2001).

numeric minority in every state. Their being a minority has significant implications for the strategies that they can pursue in these states. Latinos cannot count on the strength of being a majority as a resource for political success. Any and every statewide election is of such a large scope that any Latino candidate must be successful in forming coalitions with other groups in order to be elected to office.

Indeed, when one looks at the numbers of Latino elected officials in each state, the general pattern that becomes clear is that in every state, with the possible exception of New Mexico (about 40 percent of New Mexico's state legislators were Latino in 2007), Latinos are proportionately underrepresented in every branch of government. Although the numbers of Latinos in statewide elected offices have been increasing over the past few years, as Table 11.2 indicates, underrepresentation remains a problem. Very visibly for decades, if not centuries, Latinos have been severely underrepresented in state governments. This trend is reflected by a recent report that indicates that despite making up 42 percent of the U.S. population in 2000, only 16 percent of key appointed policy positions in

Table 11.2
LATINO REPRESENTATION IN STATE GOVERNMENTS, 2005

Totals	
Latino state officials	9
Latino state senators	60
Latino state representatives	172

Latino Representation in State Legislatures by State

	Officials	Senators	Representatives	State Population
Arizona	0	5 (17%)	11 (18.3%)	28.0%
California	1	10 (25%)	19 (24 %)	35.0%
Colorado	0	2 (10%)	5 (7.6%)	19.2%
Illinois	0	4 (6.7%)	7 (6%)	14.0%
Florida	0	3 (7.5%)	14 (11.6%)	19.1%
New Jersey	0	0 (0%)	5 (6.25%)	15.0%
Texas	1	7 (22.5%)	29 (19.3%)	34.9%
New Mexico	5	14 (33.3%)	30 (42.8%)	43.4%
Connecticut	0	0 (0%)	4 (7.2%)	10.6%
Delaware	0	0 (0%)	1 (2.4%)	5.9%
Georgia	0	1 (1.7%)	2 (1.1%)	6.7%
Hawaii	0	1 (4%)	0 (0%)	7.9%
Idaho	0	0 (0%)	1 (2.8%)	8.9%
Indiana	0	0 (0%)	1 (1%)	4.4%
Kansas	0	0 (0%)	4 (3.2%)	6.1%
Maryland	0	2 (4.2%)	2 (1.4%)	5.4%
Massachusetts	0	1 (2.5%)	3 (1.8%)	7.7%
Michigan	0	1 (2.6%)	1 (.9%)	3.6%
Minnesota	0	0 (0%)	1 (1.5%)	3.5%
Nebraska	0	1 (2%)	0 (0%)	7.0%
Nevada	1	1 (4.7%)	1 (2.3%)	22.9%
New Hampshire	0	0 (0%)	2 (.5%)	2.1%
North Carolina	0	1 (2%)	1 (.8%)	6.1%
Oregon	1	0 (0%)	2 (3.3%)	9.6%
Pennsylvania	0	0 (0%)	1 (.5%)	3.7%
Rhode Island	0	1 (2.6%)	3 (4%)	10.5%
South Carolina	0	0 (0%)	1 (.8%)	3.0%
Tennessee	0	0 (0%)	1 (1%)	2.9%
Utah	0	0 (0%)	2 (2.6%)	10.6%
Washington	0	1 (2%)	2 (2%)	8.5%
Wisconsin	0	0 (0%)	1 (1%)	4.4%
Wyoming	0	0 (0%)	1 (1.6%)	6.7%

Source: State Population Data Comes from U.S. Census 2004; American Community Survey Representation Data Comes from 2005 National Directory of Elected Officials.

state governments in 2004 were held by racial and ethnic minorities. More important, Hispanics held the lowest share of executive positions at 4 percent (Center for Women in Government and Civil Society 2005).

When the executive branches of the American states are examined for the presence of Latinos in the year 2005, few can be found. For example, there is only one Latino governor in the American states—Bill Richardson in New Mexico. In fact, in recent history, there have been very few. Arizona elected an Hispanic governor, conservative Democrat Raúl Castro, in 1974. At the same time, New Mexico was electing its first Hispanic governor of the modern era, Jerry Apodaca. Many states have a "plural executive"; that is, there is more than one executive public official elected statewide. When Apodaca was elected governor, five of the other eight statewide executive positions—attorney general, secretary of state, auditor, commissioner of public lands, and corporation commissioner—were also held by Hispanics (New Mexico did have two Hispanic governors early in the century—Ezequiel C. de Baca in 1917 and Octaviano Larrazola from 1919 to 1920). Since then, the only other Hispanic governors of states were Toney Anaya, who was elected governor in 1982 in New Mexico, and Bob Martinez, a Cuban American and native of Tampa, Florida, who in 1986 became Florida's first Hispanic governor and the first Republican governor since Reconstruction. Although in some states the governor is a relatively strong executive with substantial constitutional and political powers, and in other states, this position is relatively weak with relatively limited powers, the governor is always the most visible elected official of a state and the single person who represents a state as its chief and its symbolic leader. Therefore, it is a highly prized position, and one to which Latinos certainly should aspire. Given the increasing numbers of Latinos in several states as they approach 30 to 40 percent of the electorate, and as a whole new cadre of Latinos are elected to other offices and gain experience in other positions, it is likely that there will be additional Hispanic governors during the first half of the twenty-first century.

Unlike the national government, states also have other statewide elected executive positions; that is, the executive officers who are charged with a particular area of public policy and who are elected directly by the voters as a statewide constituency. These include such offices as lieutenant governor, attorney general, secretary of state, state treasurer, state auditor, superintendent of education, agricultural commissioner, state controller, and various other offices. As with governors, because the electoral districts for these offices actually comprise entire states in which Latinos have always been a minority, there have been very few of these statewide executives elected who are Hispanic. For example, the state of Texas elected its first statewide Latino executive in 1990 when Dan Morales was elected attorney general. California came along several years after that, when it elected its first statewide Latino elected official in 120 years—Lieutenant Governor Cruz Bustamante—in 1998. The 2002 election cycle brought forth some additional progress, as five Latinos were elected to statewide offices in New Mexico (positions ranged from attorney general to state auditor), Colorado and Nevada elected Latino attorney generals, and Oregon elected a Latino superintendent of public instruction. Given the recency of these successes, it will probably be awhile before Lations occupy the premier spot of governor in many of the states. But when this does happen, it will be a great accomplishment both tangibly and symbolically.

THE STATE LEGISLATIVE BRANCHES

As with the national government, states also have legislatures, and all of them are bicameral (with the exception of the state of Nebraska); that is, they are composed of two houses, as with the national government. In fact (apart from the tribal governments of Native Americans), the oldest U.S. constitutional governments are the state legislatures of some of the original thirteen colonies. All bicameral state legislatures have an upper house, the Senate, and a lower house, which is either called the House of Representatives or the State Assembly. State Senates are typically smaller than the lower houses; consequently, their electoral districts are larger. That is, a state senator represents more people, and as a result there are generally smaller proportions of Latinos in the states' upper houses than there are in the lower houses. In 2003, there were only sixty-one Latino state senators representing seventeen states, compared to 160 Latino state house representatives from twenty-five states (Geron 2005, 114). Lower house districts are usually smaller geographically with smaller constituencies, and thus offer Latinos a better chance of being elected, especially when those districts are heavily populated with Latinos.

Again, a generality with regard to Latinos in state legislatures (with the exception of New Mexico) is that they are underrepresented compared to their proportion in the population of each state. In 2004, the total number of Latino state House representatives was only 2.8 percent of the total number of 7,280 seats nationally, compared to 8.2 percent for African Americans (Center for Voting and Democracy 2003). However, there has been significant progress with regard to Hispanic representation in the state legislatures, and this is one area in which Latino public officials seem to definitely be on a steady pattern of increase. Table 11.2 shows the number of legislators in those states that do have Latinos in their legislatures and some of the change that has occurred over time. Overall, Latinos held elected offices in thirty-nine states in 2003, indicating Latino representation in 80 percent of state legislatures. In 2003, there were 211 Latino state legislators across the nation (160 representatives, 51 senators), up from 163 state legislators in 1995, and 114 in 1985 (Geron 2005, 114). In regard to partisanship, in 2000, 86 percent of state legislators identified themselves as Democrats and 14 percent as Republicans (Menifield 2001). It is clear that the creation of Latino majority districts through coverage of the Voting Rights Act of 1965 has been pivotal in increased rates of Latino representatives at the state level. For example, in 2001, twenty-seven of the twenty-eight Latino state representatives in Texas were elected from majority-Latino population districts (Geron 2005, 115). However, California offers some optimism that Latinos can gain access to state offices in non-majority Latino districts. In 2001, six of the nineteen Latino members of the California State Assembly were elected from non-majority Latino districts, including all four Latino Republican assembly members (Table 11.2).

In a few of these legislatures, such as that of New Mexico, Texas, and California, Latinos have assumed positions of leadership, such as speaker of the House or Senate president pro tempore, and they have assumed the chairmanships of some committees of importance to their constituencies.

This increase in the descriptive representation of Hispanics in the legislatures of the states is also likely to result in more substantive representation for this group. More of the issues of interest and importance to Hispanics, particularly policies dealing with cultural matters such as language, will increasingly become part of the legislative agendas of the American states (Bratton 2006).

COURTS AND LATINO JUDGES IN THE STATES

As with the national government, each state has its own separate system of state courts as well as other elements of the criminal justice system. Typically following the national pattern, the state court systems are headed by a state supreme court with a lower level of appellate courts or courts of appeals and then a whole variety of trial courts at the lowest level. Often, there are two levels of trial courts: one level that deals with more serious criminal and civil cases, and another level of many minor courts that deal with less serious cases, such as traffic violations. These can take the forms of municipal courts, such as traffic courts, domestic relations courts, small claims courts, probate courts, or police courts. In a few states, the justice of the peace or magistrate system still survives. Unlike the federal judiciary, whose justices are all appointed by the president for terms of "good behavior," which are generally lifetime terms, state courts are chosen in several different ways. Some courts may be appointed by the governor with confirmation by the state Senate or another body. Some of them are elected by the legislature. The two most popular methods are (1) by popular election through the vote, and (2) by a modified appointment plan in which a relatively long list of nominees is compiled by a blue ribbon commission of some type, which then makes its recommendations to the governor, who then appoints the judges. Particularly after the initial appointment, the voters are then asked whether the judges will be maintained in office or whether the office will be vacated, known as a vote for retention, after which the nominating commission then again makes recommendations to the governor for appointment.

There seems to be little difference in the quality of justice dispensed by elected verses appointed judges. State courts seem to be much more deeply involved in the lives of most citizens and in the other branches of government than are the federal courts. Some of the courts issue advisory opinions about the activities and jurisdictions of other parts of the governments, and virtually all interactions that citizens have with the courts are with the state-level court system, not with the national or federal courts. Because state and local courts are so actively involved in both governmental actions and the lives of citizens, the state courts are critically important arenas for the making and carrying out of public policy. Thus, Latinos are and should be concerned about the courts and the criminal justice system. This is particularly true because minorities, including Latinos, are disproportionately affected by the criminal justice system. Latinos are more often arrested and prosecuted than are non-Hispanic whites. For example, in a study consisting of ten states, Latino men were found to be incarcerated at rates between five and nine times greater than those of white men (Human Rights Watch 2000). However, it is critical to look beyond incarceration rates to determine if this trend is due to a discriminatory criminal justice system or simply higher rates of criminal activity among Latinos. A recent study conducted by National Council of La Raza provides detailed analysis of Latinos and the criminal justice system, and finds that Latinos face specific challenges at each stage of the system. Specifically, concerns related to racial profiling, problems in prosecution and detention, disparities in legal representation, and problems with sentencing all contribute to greater rates of incarceration among Hispanics (Walker et al. 2004).

Although data on the number of Latinos in state courts are limited, they do provide us with a general assessment of the status of Latinos in state judiciaries. However, whether appointed or elected, the general pattern seems to be once again that Latinos are underrepresented, probably even more so than in the legislative branch, in comparison to their population in each of the states or in each of their judicial districts. Reflecting this overall trend of underrepresentation of Latinos in the courts, Latinos comprised only 2.2 percent of about 60,000 sitting federal and state judges in 1997. This was a decline from 1990, when Latinos made up 3.39 percent of the 32,394 sitting federal and state judges (Méndez and Martínez 2002). A more recent report by the Lawyers' Committee for Civil Rights Under

Law reported that Hispanic judges comprised 2.8 percent of all state judges in the United States (Lawyers' Committee for Civil Rights Under Law 2005). This general trend is confirmed by a recent Puerto Rican Legal Defense and Education Fund (PRLDEF) report that found that Latinos hold only 998, or 3.7 percent, of the nation's 26,196 state court judgeships (Falcón 2002). This lack of representation is reflected in the fact that twenty-one states do not have any Latinos on their courts. The PRLDEF report also analyzed the role of the Latino population at the state level and representation within the state courts, and found that New York had the worst level of Latino judicial representation among the ten states with the greatest Latino populations (Falcón 2002). This suggests that gains in Latino population alone will not necessarily lead to increased representation within the state courts because state leaders will need to commit to the diversification of the court system.

THE LOCAL GOVERNMENTS—COUNTIES, MUNICIPALITIES, AND SCHOOL BOARDS

If gathering information about Latinos in the fifty states and generalizing about Latino politics in those states is difficult, it pales in comparison to the challenges of presenting the status of Latino politics in local governments across the United States. This is unfortunate because it is in these localities—counties, cities, towns, and school boards—where the most dramatic and perhaps most important political activities by Latinos are occurring. It is the local governments, acting within a delegation of sovereignty by the states, that actually provide most of the direct services to the citizens of this country—services such as public safety; police and fire protection; law enforcement; education; the provision of utilities, such as power, water, and sewer; and the maintenance of the infrastructure, such as streets, bridges, lighting, public buildings, recreational facilities, and activities. These public policy areas, and many more, are directly provided by local governments, and it is in the localities in which Latinos, particularly since after World War II, and most dramatically in the Chicano movement period of the late 1960s and early 1970s, and certainly in the 1990s and early twentieth century, have been the most active and have made the most visible and perhaps most significant changes in their political status.

In this chapter, we can only hope to make a few generalities about Latinos' political activities at the local level and present a few case studies of Latino politics at this level. Generalization is particularly difficult because although there is only one national government and fifty state governments, there are approximately 88,000 local governments (including almost 10,000 school districts) in the United States (U.S. Bureau of the Census 2002c). These have been increasing in number—about 3,000 or 4,000 every year. These include about 3,000 county governments; 19,000 municipal governments; 16,000 township governments; 14,000 school districts; and 33,000 special districts, or governmental units, which have the power to tax, pass laws, and implement them for particular purposes, such as fire protection, housing and urban renewal, insect control, conservation, drainage and flood control, air quality control, and water usage.

One type of special purpose district that is so universal and numerous that it might not be considered a special district are those districts that are charged with providing for the education of the citizenry, that is, public school districts. These are usually headed by elected local officials and have been the subject of much political activity. Recall that Latinos most often cite education as number one in the area of public affairs priorities, and it is an issue Latinos ranked as their highest priority in determining their choice for president in 2004.[2] Local governments are not sovereign entities, as are state and national governments. Their powers are not derived directly from the people through constitutions. Instead, they are "creatures" of the state; that is, each state creates or originates local governments at its will and assigns limited powers of government to local governments. Much like they can be created, local governments can also be abolished by state governments, although certainly in the case of cities, towns, and villages, this would not likely be done. However, most states reserve the right to determine what powers can be properly executed by towns, cities, and school districts, and retain the right to change the charters and rules and regulations under which counties and towns operate.

Local governments often also feature some separations of power—three branches of government—although they take so many forms that they are much less distinctive than they are at the state and certainly at the national level. Sometimes local governments have chief executives, such as mayors in cities, but some cities do not have a mayor in their form of government but are instead run by a plural group, sometimes called a city council or a city commission, that is not only charged with the usual powers of a small legislature, that is, making laws, but is also responsible for administering or executing those laws. This they often do by hiring a public administrator, such as a city manager. This form of government with a plural combined legislature and executive branch is most often found in counties. Counties are often governed by a county commission or board of supervisors, which exercises both legislative (i.e., law making) and executive (i.e., administrative) powers. Most large city urban areas have the mayoral-council forms of government, and mayors often equal or even surpass state governors in the recognition and publicity given to them by the public and the media. Counties often have elected officers, such as sheriffs, district attorneys, county clerks and assessors, and other officials who are also involved in the administration of county public responsibilities.

Most people who participate in politics do so at the local level, even when it is not recognized as such. Because the day-to-day activities of schools, police, park and street maintenance, and noise and pollution control often affect people in their local neighborhood settings, it is at this level that people most often organize and present their opinions to local governments. It is not uncommon for people individually or in groups to attend school board, county commissions, or city council meetings to let their views be known to these public officials, and it is precisely at this level of local activity where most activity is found among Latinos and where Latinos have made their greatest gains since the 1960s and 1970s.

Latinos have long been urban people. In fact, during the 1990s, Latinos were the most urban of all "cognizable" ethnic groups, being about 95 percent residents of urban areas. Therefore, they are greatly affected by local governments, particularly governments of the large metropolitan areas. Large metropolitan areas have complex governmental organizations, often embodying several overlapping layers of governments, including county, city, and special district governments, including educational school districts. Large metropolitan areas, particularly the densely populated central city, are the homes of most Latinos. Because Latinos live in these areas, and because they are directly impacted by so many of the services that local governments provide, it is in this arena that Latino political activity has been most common, and indeed, most intense.

In the 1960s and 1970s, many of the successes in Latinos' electing their representatives to school boards, county commissions, city governments, and judgeships occurred in small towns and cities in which Latinos had overwhelming population majorities and yet had little or no representation in city, county, or school governments. The prime example of this is Crystal City, Texas. This little town in south-central Texas had Mexican Americans as 90 percent of its population, yet its city council and school board were comprised entirely of Anglos. The Texas Latinos in Crystal City, as in other small cities in Texas and other states, were subjugated by the Anglo minority, who not only held political positions of power but also controlled the economic infrastructure of the cities. Hispanics were excluded and precluded from challenging the power system. However, due to the "radical" activities of some Chicanos, primarily young people who were college educated and participating in the Chicano movement, they formed political coalitions, political parties, and interest groups. They were able to mobilize the majority Mexican American population and win electoral victories, taking over the city council, the county commission, and the school board.

These victories in the 1960s have been widely publicized and studied, and have stood as a symbol of what can be done when Latinos organize, mobilize, and employ effective strategies and smart tactics in situations in which they are the majority population (Navarro 1998; Shockley 1974).

Similar victories occurred in other towns throughout the Southwest, most notably in California, where in several small towns such as Parlier, Latinos elected members to the city council, elected their own mayors, and often took over the school boards. The Raza Unida Party, mentioned previously, was very involved in the takeover in Crystal City and other small towns in both Texas and California, in addition to other organizations, such as the Mexican American Youth Organization and the United Mexican American Students. Such mobilizations, then and now, serve as great sources of pride for Latinos and are examples of Latino political success. However, these successes became much more difficult to achieve when the arena of political conflict became much larger, such as expanding to the state level or even to a large metropolitan area. In fact, it was not until the 1980s that Latinos were elected to mayorships of midsize cities, and to this date, there are few mayors of large cities. Most notably, as of 2005, Denver, Colorado; San Antonio, Dallas, and Austin, Texas; and Los Angeles and San Jose, California, have had Hispanic mayors.

There was a great deal of publicity and hope cast on the Latino run for the mayorship of the city of Los Angeles in the year 2001. The city had a 47 percent Latino population and about a 22 percent Latino electorate. This is an example of an increasingly common situation in large metropolitan areas. Even though our largest cities, such as Los Angeles, New York, Chicago, and Houston, have relatively large percentages of Latinos, a successful mayoral candidate still needs to generally engage in the politics of coalition in order to win a majority of the votes. In Los Angeles in the year 2001, former speaker of the California State Assembly (the lower house of the state legislature), a native Californian Latino, Antonio Villaraigosa, survived as one of the top two candidates in the mayoral run-off election. In the "primary" election, another well-known Latino candidate, Xavier Becerra, who had run a campaign directed almost exclusively at Latinos had placed low in the standings. Mr. Villaraigosa disclaimed being a strictly ethnic candidate and emphasized that he was running to represent all of the city's people whom he wanted to bring together. He went on to run against a public official, James Hahn, with a name well known in the city and especially respected in the African American community. For months, there was a lot of speculation as to whether the nation's second largest city could and would elect a Latino mayor. The "city of angels," founded by Hispanics, had not had a Latino mayor since the 1870s. This, of course, would be of great symbolic importance not only to Latinos in Los Angeles and in California but also across the nation. Villaraigosa was not elected, although he did run a good race and attracted votes from a diverse electorate. His loss was attributed by some to a negative attack advertisement portraying him as an unsavory, drug-related character from the barrio who would be soft on criminals. Latinos voted overwhelmingly for Villaraigosa, but not in sufficient numbers to make their coalition electorally successful. Nonetheless, in that same election in June 2001, Los Angelenos did elect two Latinos to high-ranking positions as city attorney and president of the city council.

As presented previously, four years later, Villaraigosa ran for mayor again, repeating his theme that he would be a mayor for all Los Angelenos and would work to bring them all together. This time he won, defeating incumbent mayor James Hahn with the support of a multiethnic coalition (Sonenshein and Pinkus 2005). So, the mobilization that occurred around this election in Los Angeles showed that Latinos are increasingly going to be a force to be reckoned with, especially in elections in populous counties and cities, and more particularly, in large metropolitan areas. After all, this is where many new immigrants are taking up residence because there is already an infrastructure, jobs, and a social environment in place that are somewhat attractive to them.

In New York, Mr. Fernando Ferrer, of Puerto Rican heritage, ran for mayor of the nation's largest city in the year 2001. He was a former Bronx Borough president and member of the city council of New York City. In a hotly contested Democratic primary, he placed second to Mark Green. Latinos and African Americans strongly supported Ferrer and were upset that the media was saturated with negative advertisements portraying Ferrer as a distinctive outsider who would be "divisive" as a mayor. Ferrer's supporters were so angry at what they contended was his opponents playing the "race card" that they did not work to support the winning Democratic candidate in the general run-off election. Influential Latino and black leaders sat on their hands and did not work to support the party's candidate. Latinos in New York City typically support Democratic candidates with 70 to 80 percent voting levels, and New York City's black electorate is typically at least as supportive. However, in this election, the Latino vote split almost evenly between the Democrat Green and the Republican Michael Bloomberg. The white vote was strongly for Bloomberg, who spent more than $50 million of his own money on the campaign and who was endorsed by the highly popular incumbent mayor, Rudy Giuliani. Ferrer again ran for mayor in 2005, and again came up short, this time losing to Republican Michael Bloomberg. Interestingly, Bloomberg was able to secure a sizable segment of both the black and Latino vote, and even secured the endorsement of the mayor of San Juan, Puerto Rico.

Also memorable is the well-publicized victory of Federico Peña, who was elected mayor of Denver in the 1980s. His campaigns, directed at building coalitions across ethnic lines, have been harbingers of the election strategies that Latinos are using in mayoral elections across the United States (Hero 1992b, 116–130). Peña went on to be appointed to two successive cabinet positions in the Clinton administration. The election of Peña was an example of the kind of strategies Latinos must use to win electoral victories in municipalities such as Denver, where Latinos are a sizable voting bloc but where sizable numbers of other ethnic and racial groups also exist.

These elections indicate that the Latino electorates are key players in urban elections. Successful candidates cannot win without substantial Latino support. Yet, Latino candidates cannot run on exclusive Latino platforms but must put together coalitions of voters that cross ethnic and racial lines. Ethnicity and race will continue to be important considerations in elections, and it is always tempting for non-Latino candidates to use an opposing candidate's ethnicity to scare off potential supporters of different backgrounds.

Miami-Dade County, Florida, has long had Latino mayors. This is due to the high concentration of Cuban Americans in that area and to their high voting turnout rates (Grenier and Perez 2003). Following the dramatic leap in state representation in 1982 (three Cubans were elected to the Florida State Senate, and eight to the House from south Florida), the growing group of Cuban legislators formed the Cuban American Caucus in the state legislature (Moreno and Warren 1992). It is an understatement to say that Cuban Americans are major players in Florida politics. In fact, despite accounting for less than one third of the state's Latino population, and about 5 percent of the state's total population, Cuban Americans maintained 3 of 25 U.S. congressional seats, 3 of 40 state Senate seats, and nearly all the state House seats in majority Latino districts, plus the Speakership of the House, Mark Rubio, as of the early 2000s. In their mayoral election of 2001, the two top vote getters were both Latinos. One, Maurice Ferre of Puerto Rican background, had been elected mayor several times previously. The other, Manny Diaz, was a Cuban American lawyer who had represented the Florida relatives of Elián Gonzales in their struggle against returning the boy to his father in Cuba. The Cuban-born Diaz won handily garnering 70 percent of the area's Hispanic vote.

Although it is likely that Cuban Americans will continue to dominate local politics in Miami-Dade County, in the adjacent Broward County, Latinos from a diverse background are exerting political influence and becoming elected to local offices. In this county, there are currently six Hispanics, ranging from judges to city commissioners in office that reflect the Puerto Rican, South American, and Cuban constituencies of the county (Geron 2005, 144).

Many smaller cities, and increasingly, several midsize cities, throughout the Southwest have also elected Mexican American mayors in the last three decades of the twentieth century. The first Hispanic to become mayor of a midsize city was Raymond Telles, who was elected mayor of El Paso, Texas, for two terms, beginning in 1957 (Garcia 1998). The large city of San Antonio has elected two Hispanic mayors, Henry Cisneros and Edward Garza, in 2001. In contrast to the campaign strategy of Cisneros, Garza's electoral strategy was to actively campaign for Anglo voters while expecting to use ethnic ties to secure the Latino vote even though he did not specifically campaign to them (Austin, Wright, and Middleton 2004). New Mexico's largest cities, Albuquerque and Santa Fe, have also elected Hispanic mayors. Finally, Latinos have shown the ability to win elections for mayor in cities where they are not the dominant population. For example, in 2001, Gus Garcia was elected mayor in Austin, Texas, and Eddie Perez won election as major of Hartford, Connecticut. Furthermore, the city of San Jose, California, elected Ron Gonzalez to mayor in 1998.

In the East, some of the midsize cities, such as Passaic, New Jersey, have recently elected a Latino mayor, and increasingly there are victories for mayorships across the United States in areas where Latinos reside and are increasing in the population. The presence of Latino candidates from subgroups other than the big three of Mexican, Cuban, or Puerto Rican are also becoming more prevalent. The politics of *coalition* seem to be essential in these cities, as was the case in Hartford. Latinos must draw votes and support from non-Latinos to become mayor and must govern on behalf of all city residents if they are to be judged successful.

The victory of Hispanic mayors throughout the United States, primarily those in the 1980s and 1990s, have demonstrated that it is possible for Latinos to gain the most visible and sometimes the most powerful governmental position in urban areas, and that they can do so by appealing to a broad coalition of voters. Although they usually draw large percentages of the Latino vote, usually 50 or 60 percent, they must also appeal to non-Latinos. The strategy to appeal to non-Latinos often involves the process of *deracialization*, or making race or ethnicity a nonfactor in the election. Several Latino mayoral elections are frequently cited as examples of successful deracialization campaigns, including Peña in Denver (Hero 1992b), Cisneros and Garza in San Antonio (Austin et al. 2004), and Villaraigosa in Los Angeles (Sonenshein and Pinkus 2002, 2005). Sometimes Hispanic coalition politics have involved African Americans, whereas other times they have involved a coalition of various Latino groups. The latter has been particularly true in the cities of the Northeast, where there is more likely to be significant proportions of more than one Latino group. This has also been the situation in Chicago.

In addition to increased attempts since the 1980s to win the top executive position, (the mayorships of several cities including the largest ones), Latinos have been very active in seeking to win office in the legislative bodies of municipalities, namely, county commissions and city councils (Rosales 2000). There has been a surprising lack of representation, particularly outside New Mexico, in these legislative representative bodies of cities and towns for Latinos. For example, as of 2007, the city council of Phoenix, Arizona, did not have a Latino member. In many localities, these multimember bodies are the most important government agency in that they often decide what issues go on the agenda to be entertained by decision makers. They are subject to various interests, which help them formulate these policies and push them toward making a decision in one group's favor or another's. They are the primary law- or policy-making bodies in cities, counties, and school districts, and thus their membership and the politics that occur in their elections and governing are of utmost importance to Latinos. There have been relatively few studies of these local legislatures, although they are increasing with the increase in the number of scholars studying Latino politics and with the growing activity of Latinos toward participating in these bodies.

One of the most famous pioneering studies is that by Browning et al. (1984), who studied ten city governments in California and the representation of Latinos and their coalition allies in these bodies. They looked at the extent of "incorporation" of Latinos into the majority or dominant ruling group within each city governing board and found that this did not make much difference as to the policies that were passed that benefited Latinos. However, there were other beneficial results such as the appointment and hiring of more Latinos and other minorities, as well as the improvement of relations between police and the community. Hero (1986) also studied the cities of Denver and Pueblo in Colorado with regard to political incorporation into city governments. He found that although Pueblo had a much larger proportion of Latino residents, it was in the more actively mobilized Latino communities in Denver that Latinos were more involved. He attributed this to the fact that the government structure of Denver was more important in promoting political mobilization. Some policy responsiveness to the Latino communities was found in Denver. However, in Pueblo and in the California cities that had a different governmental structure, Latino political influence remained relatively minor.

Hero (1986) explained that the major differences between the two types of city governments are those between "reformed" and "unreformed" city governments. Throughout most of U.S. history, until the late nineteenth and early twentieth centuries, city governments were often partisan in nature and run by powerful, sometimes ethnic-based, small groups of people, including a group leader sometimes called the city "boss." Particularly in the big cities of the Northeast and the Midwest, these bosses headed what are called "urban political machines." These machines were quite powerful in running the city, deciding who got the benefits from city government and who did not, and who got jobs, city contracts, and city services, and who did not. If individuals or ethnic groups wanted to be looked on favorably by the boss and his cohorts, the city machine, they had to go along with the mayor, who controlled all city departments, including the police, the fire fighters, the social service-welfare agencies, and often the local judges. The machine would provide jobs in the form of patronage appointments to public jobs as well as intervention on behalf of jobs in the private sector. It would make sure that law enforcement was benevolent, and it would provide welfare services to those who needed them, such as fuel during the cold winter months and even foodstuffs for people who were impoverished. There was an all-important exchange relationship here. In turn for protection, patronage, and favors, the local urban political machines expected total allegiance to and support for it. It was highly organized at succeeding levels from ward captains to precinct captains and even into neighborhoods, with machine representatives heading units at each level. It was these people's responsibility to make sure that the machine was kept in office, primarily by mobilizing voters and getting out the vote to re-elect the boss/mayor and his cohorts.

It has been said that the political machine was essential in incorporating new immigrant ethnic groups as they arrived in America having no or few resources, including jobs; often being quite impoverished; and having no or few connections. The people in the ranks of the machine would take these immigrants in hand and help them become established in their new residence, providing them with the resources needed to begin their new life. In turn, the machines expected complete support and loyalty from these ethnic groups, most particularly in the form of votes. This reciprocal relationship between the boss and the ethnic masses is a prime example of the "exchange" view of politics. The machines were reportedly instrumental in incorporating groups such as the Irish, the Greeks, the Italians, and the Polish into both the political life and the social and economic lives of the cities. Also, throughout the years, members of these ethnic immigrant groups would reportedly work their way up the ranks in the machine hierarchy, the party organization, and thus win some semblance of political power. Although some contend that this type of operation of the urban political machine is really part of a "rainbow myth," there is also compelling evidence that it was instrumental in incorporating ethnic groups into the political, economic, and social lives of the urban areas. If so, there would at least be a possibility that a group such as Latinos, who arrived in the late nineteenth and early twentieth century, could take advantage of this same machine operation.

However, at the turn of the twentieth century, there began a major reform movement that was fueled by a revulsion and rejection of the corruption and domination of the city bosses and their political machines. Good government reformers managed to change the way cities were governed so these "unreformed cities" were reformed along good government lines, including doing away with partisan city elections and making them nonpartisan; changing the election of city councilmen from neighborhood districts throughout the city, or from "wards," to at-large city-wide elections; and initiating merit-based civil service–type employment instead of widespread patronage appointments, thereby cutting back on the number of political patronage jobs that could be appointed. Other important actions included reducing the mayor's powers to transform strong mayors into relatively weak mayors by giving them fewer powers of appointment, fewer powers over the budget, and less involvement in the policy-making process. As a substitute, plural bodies of government, such as city commissions or city councils, were formed that had at least equal and sometimes superior powers to the mayor.

Over the next few decades, the newer cities, particularly in the West and Southwest, almost all became "reformed" cities rather than the old-style unreformed cities. Consequently, immigrants arriving in the newly structured reformed cities did not have the opportunities afforded to them by the old-style unreformed type of structured cities. The unreformed cities had been more likely to seek the involvement of immigrants in government. The urban machines needed the political support of the immigrant masses. They provided jobs and welfare benefits in return for support, as well as some opportunities for immigrants to advance upward through the ranks of the machine in the public sector. Therefore, Latinos are not benefiting from the aspects of machine politics in the same way as immigrants from other backgrounds did in the past. During this same progressive era, reforms at the state and national levels—such as the introduction of civil service "merit" systems—pretty much destroyed most vestiges of political machines throughout the United States. Scholars continue to study reformed versus unreformed municipal governments to determine what effects these government structures have on policy making and normal with regard to their effect on the kinds of policies they produce and the incorporation of various groups of people. For example, scholars have found that unreformed cities tend to be more responsive to disadvantaged groups, whereas cities with reformed structures tend to spend less money for social services (Hero 1986; Stein 1989). This seems to be another example of how Latinos' concentration in reformed cities works against their political interests. Research to this point therefore seems to indicate that, although it is difficult for Latinos to penetrate the largely non-Hispanic white power structure in unreformed city situations, it is even more difficult to do so in modern-day reformed cities.

However, as Latinos increase in number in localities, particularly in large cities, the sheer power of numbers seems to be having an impact on the influence, if not immediately the power, that Latinos are having. This is true not only for cities but also for other local units of government such as counties and school districts. There is no doubt that, increasingly, Latinos are being elected to decision-making positions in these governments. In fact, out of the approximately 5,000 or so Latino elected officials, more than 4,000 are public officials operating at these local levels, and the numbers have been increasing steadily over the years with a noticeable upswing expected by many students of Latino politics. This has implications for potential coalitions between Latinos and other racial/ethnic groups. Many note that local politics is a zero-sum game, where gains made by one group necessarily mean losses for another. This perspective would suggest that increases in the number of Latino elected officials at the local level have come at the expense of other groups, most notably, African Americans.

It was mentioned previously that Latinos had won mayorships and taken over city governments in some small cities with majority Latino populations, particularly in the Southwest. This also occurred at the county level in Miami-Dade County, Florida, and was largely due to the mobilization of overwhelmingly Latino populations. Latino populations are increasing rapidly in localities throughout the United States. Although it is not exactly known when this occurs, other than at some point below a majority, the number of Latinos cannot be ignored. Any person running for local office has to pay attention to the Latino population and include in his or her campaign some provisions for attracting the Latino vote. In addition, more Latinos will continue to be elected to office. This trend became even more noticeable in the early twenty-first century, as Latinos have become mayors of several midsize cities and a few large cities, made good runs at the mayorships of large metropolitan areas such as New York, and succeeded at winning the mayorship in Los Angeles.

It is not immediately evident that winning office in counties and cities makes any kind of major change in the social and economic lives of Latinos. There certainly is a high level of symbolic gain achieved by Latinos as they recognize one of their own being elected to high office, such as a mayorship or city council. However, how much these important symbolic victories do for the socioeconomic standing of Latinos remains questionable (Regalado 1997). It may be equally important that Latinos participate to a degree in voting and lobbying. Even though they are not the majority or did not elect a Latino to office, they are politically influential enough that campaigners and office holders of any ethnicity cannot ignore the needs and wants of Latinos.

So far, with the exception of Miami-Dade County and some cities in New Mexico, plus some small towns, primarily in the Southwest, Latinos have not had any major successes in making city government particularly responsive to them and their needs. It does seem, however, that as Latino numbers increase, as they become more middle class, and as they are in the United States for a second or third generation, Latinos will at least be proportionately represented in city, county, and school district governments. This is not to say that being elected to office will be sufficient to provide Latinos with equal opportunity and equal influence because the social, and particularly the economic, factors underlying the political institutions and processes of the cities may not change. Even if they do change, city governments, although the most immediate, are the least powerful of governments because they themselves are not sovereign. It will be at the national and state levels where decisions are made that will greatly constrain, control, and affect what cities and counties can and cannot do. The big decisions that set the parameters for many local decisions will be made at the higher levels of government—at the state and national levels. Therefore, Latinos must continue to try to actively exert political influence at the higher levels of government, even though it is much more difficult to do so than at the local levels.

One area in which electing Latinos to office has seemed to make a significant if somewhat indirect difference has been at the school district level. As we mentioned previously, school district governments are the most common form of special district government in the United States. Typically, there is an elected school board that is responsible for hiring and controlling the chief administrative officer and the superintendent of instruction, as well as serving as a mini-legislature, reflecting the needs of its constituents, passing legislation for the schools that provide the best education possible for the children living in those districts. This level of office has become increasingly salient for Latinos because school board officeholders have surpassed city council members as the largest cohort of Latino elected officials (National Association of Latino Elected Officials 2005).

Although Latinos have increased their overall representation on school boards, a closer look at the figures reveals that room remains for significant improvement. In 2003, there were 1,694 Latino school board members across the United States. However, nearly 83 percent of these members came from just three states: California (510), New Mexico (158), and Texas (736); (National Association of Latino Elected Officials 2003). Perhaps an even more alarming statistic is that Latinos comprise *less than one percent* of the total number of elected officials representing the 14,500 U.S. school districts. Therefore, although progress has been made, it is clear that Latinos remain underrepresented in this critical policy-making institution.

This lack of representation at the school board level is critical when one analyzes results from a few studies that show that indeed when Latinos are visible and active in school boards, this has its primary salutary effect on Latino schoolchildren and on the hiring of more Latino teachers (Meier and Stewart 1991). In addition, lowered levels of "secondary" discrimination against Latinos, such as a disproportionate amount of disciplinary actions and lower dropout rates, tend to be the result of having more teachers who are familiar with the Latino culture and Latino children's needs (Meier, Stewart, and England 1989). Yet, public schools throughout the United States continue to be underresourced and subject to considerable criticism and pressure to reform. The problems for minority children, and Latino children in particular, tend to be among the worst. Greater Latino representation on school boards and administrative positions is critical to the ability of the Latino community to overcome the many challenges in education that they currently face.

SUMMARY AND CONCLUSION

In the 2000s, Latinos are making substantial progress in state and local government and politics. It is at the "grassroots" levels that the presence of Hispanics is most prevalent. Although most citizens' attentions are focused on national and international public affairs, it is state and local politics that have the most frequent and direct effects on the public. As Latinos increase in numbers, particularly in the cities and counties, it is expected that they will progressively become significant players in local politics. This will be most noticeable in smaller and midsize jurisdictions. This is because in local areas, Latinos are becoming a greater proportion of the populations and the electorates in municipalities and counties. These gains are especially notable in areas that have had very small or even no Hispanic populations but are now electing city councilors, county commissioners, township committee members, and school board members. It is true that as the size of the population of the area governed increases, Hispanics are usually a smaller proportion of the electoral constituencies and thus are less likely to be as significant in that jurisdiction's politics. In almost every case, Hispanics must be part of electoral coalitions, usually with substantial support by non-Hispanic whites, to be successful even at these subnational levels. Yet, the increasing growth of the Hispanic electorate promises to become even more widespread and pervasive—many more smaller streams feeding into the national mainstream.

Notes

[1] See Grenier and Perez (2003) for a specific focus on the Cuban American population.

[2] This reference was drawn from analysis of the *National Survey of Latinos: Politics and Civic Participation* (Pew Hispanic Center 2004b).

OUTPUTS OF THE POLITICAL SYSTEM

12

Latinos and Public Policies

In this chapter, we deal with public policies and their relationship to Latinos. Many contend that the realm of public policies—the actual *outputs* of the political system—are the most important aspect of government and politics. Governments such as those in the United States exist to do things for their citizens, or sometimes to prevent things from being done to them. In any case, the authorities in a political system take the various inputs that we have discussed in the first two units of this book, and through the complicated and not yet well-understood policy-making process, convert or transform all of these needs, demands, and interests into public policies. Public policies most often take the form of laws that are passed, or rules or regulations that are formulated, and then promulgated and finally implemented. In system terms, these are known as the outputs of the system.

Public policies have an impact on all people, and many people have an impact on public policies, directly or indirectly. There is no doubt that Latinos do impact some public policies. Nor is there any question as to whether they are affected by them. The more difficult and interesting questions are "Do Latinos have the kind of impact on the policy-making process that they want to have—effects that increase equal opportunity and represent the preferences, interests, and concerns of Latinos?" and "Do they have access and influence comparable to that of others?" We may conclude that Latinos generally do not have inputs into the system that are as numerous or active as those of non-Hispanic whites; that is, Latinos are generally less politically influential than are some other groups. We have also seen that in the policy-making process, those public authorities who actually make the decisions on issues include a disproportionately small number of Latinos. U.S. policy makers also do not seem to be as responsive to Latinos as they are to some other groups. Latinos do not seem to have equal influence on the same (high) level of public policy makers, as do others, although their influence is increasing. Throughout this book, we see that an increase in the number of Latinos certainly increases the *potential* for Latinos to become more influential, and perhaps even powerful, in the political arena and thus to have governments at all levels be more likely to act favorably on those issues that are of concern to Latinos.

When one examines public policies and Latinos, one must deal with the issue of "the Latino agenda." This somewhat confusing and ill-defined subject has arisen many times in our discussion. The Latino agenda is basically the list of issues or policies that reflect the concerns, wants, and needs of Latinos—in short, Latino political interests. These are the areas in which Latinos hope that public officials will act on behalf of Latinos to advance their interests and preferences. It is neither simple nor easy to draw up a definitive list of public policies to comprise a Latino agenda that would be agreed on by all Latinos. This would most likely be true for any large group of people, and it is certainly the case for a group as large and heterogeneous as the Latino population of the United States. However, through opinion survey research and other means, including the issues articulated by spokespersons for the various Latino communities and organizations, we have a pretty good idea of some of the main unresolved concerns of Latinos.

One question that is often asked is "Is there an 'exclusive' Latino agenda; that is, is there a *unique* set of issues that concerns Latinos greatly—more so than it does other groups?" The answer to this is probably "no," or at least if there is such a list, it is a very short list. By and large, Latinos have many of the same concerns as other under-resourced or disadvantaged people in the American system. This has been shown repeatedly in survey research. Two things generally distinguish the Latino political agenda from that of mainstream Americans or other groups. First, Latinos sometimes have a slightly different order of priorities as to what are the major issues facing their communities or what they would most prefer governments to do for them. Second, there are a few issues that seem to be of particular importance or significance to Latinos. These issues, as one would expect, generally deal with items of concern that are related to Latinos as a distinctive, cognizable *cultural* group. Such issues include language policy, most often taking the form of bilingual education; issues of unequal treatment or discrimination against Latinos; and, increasingly, the incorporation of immigrants from Latin America. Perhaps surprisingly to some, these issues are usually not near the top of the list on the Latino public policy agenda. Some issues, such as immigration policy, are often believed to be high on the Latino agenda, and for some Latinos, it is a high priority issue; however, by and large, it has not been near the top of the list.

In this chapter, we briefly examine some of the issues that are of concern to Latinos in the early twenty-first century. It should be noted that many of them are the same issues that are on the agenda of other more mainstream groups—particularly people of lower socioeconomic status (SES) or those belonging to a cognizable ethnic or racial minority group, as are most Latinos. At this point, we have neither time nor space to explore these issues in great depth, for much could and sometimes has been written about each of them. However, it is hoped that this summary presentation provides some ideas and facts about the issues that are of significant concern to Latinos and that have a good chance of being recognized and addressed by public officials as Latino influence and power increases in the United States.

EDUCATION

On virtually any list of Latino public policy priorities, education is ranked as number one in importance. For example, Latinos ranked education as their highest priority policy area in determining their choice for president in 2004 (Pew Hispanic Center 2004a). Education is also often a top priority for the general American public. The American public school system is a tremendous enterprise, seeking to provide a low-cost education to all members of a large and diverse nation. Many of the founding fathers, such as Thomas Jefferson, realized that if a democracy were to be successful, an educated citizenry was absolutely essential. The people must either participate in government or, more commonly, at least have an interest in, or knowledge of, what the government was doing. The populace must know how to participate and how to present their interests to public officials. Therefore, they must be able to avail themselves of an education that will give them the basic skills of literacy and computation, plus teach them at least the essentials of their own history, of basic scientific principles, of the study of the society around them, of the behavior of people, and of the essentials of citizenship, or civic education. Moreover, it is commonly accepted that the more education an individual receives, the better his or her life chances for success are. Any such huge undertaking by governments, particularly by state and local governments in the United States, must be a central concern for the citizenry.

There is considerable evidence that Latinos, and, more specifically, Mexican Americans, believe that a good education is the best key to advancing in this society. Often, Latinos will state that the single best way to succeed, to become a successful person, is not through politics or any other route, but rather through education. The route to success is through getting a good education. Yet, as shown in Chapter 3, Latinos' educational achievements lag significantly behind that of white and even black Americans, and with the increase in immigration, much of which is from Latin America, the challenges to the American public education system are even greater than they were previously. Similar to other Americans, all Latinos want a "good" education and are generally critical of the education system. However, there are some special concerns that somewhat distinguish Latinos from other Americans. Historically, Hispanics in the United States have received a distinctly inferior education to that of non-Hispanics (Carter 1970). In fact, for many years, most notably in the state of Texas, and California Mexican Americans were segregated from whites in schools. The Mexican American schools had poor facilities and certainly provided unequal educational opportunities (McPartland and Braddock 1981).

After schools were officially desegregated in compliance with federal laws and court decisions [e.g., *Mendez v. Westminster* (1947), *Keyes v. School District No. 1413* (1973), *San Antonio School District v. Rodriguez* (1973), *Board of Education of Oklahoma City v. Dowell* (1991)], several aspects of differential treatment between Latinos and non-Hispanic whites remained. To distinguish the earlier stage of overt, separate school facilities for Latinos and whites, which could be termed primary or "first-generation" discrimination, another term has been coined—"second-generation discrimination" (Fraga, Meier, and England 1986; Meier and Stewart 1991; Meier et al. 1989). This term includes a kind of differential and negative treatment that Latinos experience in schools that is more a form of *institutional racism* or *discrimination*, much more subtle and difficult to detect, but still has a harmful effect.

Institutional discrimination is a process that occurs "when the rules or procedures of an organization are such that the neutral application of these rules or procedures results in a disproportionate impact on minorities" (Meier and Stewart 1991, 206). Second-generation discrimination may take a variety of forms. For example, it may involve the grouping of students into differential tracks of curriculum based on alleged ability, with a disproportionate number of Latinos being placed in special education or compensatory classes. Disciplinary practices are markedly differential in their application toward Latinos than others. For example, with the exception of Cubans, Latinos are disproportionately suspended or expelled from school than Anglo students, and do not have anywhere near adequate representation within gifted or college-track grouping programs. Latinos are also significantly overrepresented in classes for the "educable mentally retarded." Studies have shown that Hispanics in the classroom are significantly less likely to be recognized or called on by the teacher.[1] Although such differential treatment might be explained by school district resources, language differences, or recency of immigration, researchers have found that those factors did not explain second-generation discrimination. Instead, such discrimination is correlated with the lack of political representation, the social class of Latino students, and their ethnicity. Among Latino national origin groups, only Cuban American achievement has been comparable to that of Anglos. Although Puerto Ricans usually lag behind Cubans and Mexican Americans on most measures of socioeconomic advancement, it is Mexican Americans who have the lowest level of educational achievement, the highest proportion of dropouts, and the lowest graduation rates in the area of education (Schmidt 2003). The dropout rate for Mexican immigrants is a robust 61 percent, nearly twice the rate of other Latino subgroups. The high dropout rate of Mexican Americans continues even as other measures of educational success have slightly improved for Latinos.

As mentioned previously, it seems that when Hispanics are represented in some official capacity in the schools, such as having Latino school board members, principals, and teachers, much less differential treatment and more success for Hispanic students is the result.

As Latinos increase their SES and reside in the United States for successive generations, second-generation discrimination does seem to be lessening. However, the problem of dropouts in particular continues to be a major concern of Hispanics, particularly Mexican Americans and Central and South Americans. Immigration from Latin America, especially Mexico, has greatly aggravated the situation. Specifically, scholars have found that foreign-born Latinos are more likely to drop out of high school and less likely to enroll in college (Schmidt 2003, A8; Vernez and Abrahamse 1996). This has a strong impact on the overall educational attainment of the Latino population. For example, Latino males older than twenty-five years have 10.6 years of schooling. However, when immigrants are removed from the equation, the educational attainment rises to twelve years (Schmidt 2003). Undoubtedly, this is one aspect of the broader challenge of incorporating a large number of immigrants into the U.S. mainstream.

BILINGUAL EDUCATION

Although it is known that education is a top public policy concern for Latinos, it is often assumed that the reason for this is the debate over bilingual education. The topic of bilingual education continues to be a hotly debated issue, not only among educators but also among people who are concerned about education, and this includes a large number of people in the United States. When the Latino people themselves have been asked whether they favor or oppose "bilingual education," the results are quite unusual for responses to questions surveying public policy preferences. There is an extremely high percentage of Latinos (80–95 percent) who form a consensus in favor of bilingual education, and importantly, this is in marked contrast to a large percentage of non-Hispanics who are opposed to bilingual education. This has led to the conclusion that language policy is the issue area that has the highest level of consensus among Latinos and that separates Latinos from other racial/ethnic groups (Uhlaner and Garcia 2002).

If one were to stop at this level, one would think that bilingual education is perhaps the most clearly defined and important of the Latino public policy agenda issues. However, if one delves further into the issue, the picture becomes much more complex and murky. The first and perhaps greatest stumbling block in analyzing bilingual education as an important educational issue for Latinos is to carefully define what is meant by the phrase "bilingual education." There is substantial variation in people's understandings of what this means. It receives its highest uncritical support as a symbol of the protection and promotion of the Latino culture (Houvouras 2001). Certainly, language is one of the most important manifestations of a culture, and Latinos are very proud of their culture. Feeling as strongly about education as Hispanics do, and combining this with the primary symbol of their culture and with one of the most important activities in which their children can engage, bilingual education attracts huge proportions of support. Non-Hispanics often react in an entirely different manner to their perception of bilingual education. For generations, the public schools have been seen as special places where the ideals of America are instilled in the minds of the youth, and the "Americanization" process is an integral part of the curriculum. Mainstream Anglo Americans often react to the symbol of bilingual education as some kind of a foreign intrusion into the American public school system. Yet, when bilingual education is carefully defined, the distribution of support or opposition changes tremendously. In fact, Latinos themselves can be divided in their support for bilingual education, depending on the clarification of meaning.

One meaning of bilingual education, which virtually everyone supports, is that children in the public schools ought to learn more than one language. Most people agree that one mark of an educated person is the ability to be able to converse, read, or write in more than one language, and that it is desirable to have some fluency in more than one language. At this level, both Latinos and non-Latinos can usually agree that this is desirable. Bilingualism appears to be the desired goal for Latinos because more than 70 percent of each subgroup indicated that learning two languages is the primary objective of bilingual education (Schmidt 1997). In fact, many schools require, or at least recommend, courses in a non-English language. Another interpretation of bilingual education is that non–English-speaking children—in our case, Latinos who are Spanish speaking—be given their early few years of education in Spanish, but that as much English language instruction as possible be given to them as early as possible. Typically, this would mean something like three years of the use of Spanish with Spanish-speaking students, and after that, the transition would be made as quickly as possible to an all-English language curriculum. This approach encompasses educating the child in a language that is comprehensible, but only for a short while, until those children can deal with English language instruction.

Of course, there are a few "extremists" who say that the best way for Spanish speakers to learn English is to have complete and immediate English immersion and a minimal amount of (or even no) Spanish used. This is akin to the method of learning swimming by tossing a child into deep water and knowing, or hoping, that the child will usually struggle hard enough to survive and "learn" how to swim. Another variant of bilingual education (and there are many more than are mentioned here) is that Spanish-speaking students receive all their instruction in Spanish for several years, usually at least six or seven, and that they begin to take some English instruction along with this, so that at some point, usually in middle or high school, they develop some proficiency in both English and Spanish.

Another variation, and one that is supported by some Latino activists, is that Spanish-speaking students be taught in their native language and that this continues throughout their public education until graduation. This also usually includes a large dosage of not only language but also other Hispanic cultural manifestations, such as history, music, clothes, and architecture that go along with the language. This is the "Spanish language and cultural maintenance" approach that holds that because Latinos are American residents and taxpayers in support of the public schools, Spanish speakers are entitled to be taught in their native language throughout their public school career. This "maintenance and promotion" approach is opposed by many non-Hispanics, as well as by some Hispanics, who believe that such an approach helps maintain or even create a linguistically and culturally separate group of Americans, thus leading to separatism or "ethnic tribalism" after graduation. Moreover, opponents argue that an all Spanish language curriculum would be of great disservice to students because the primary language of the United States is English and as much educational effort as possible ought to go into developing the English-speaking skills of all students, including Hispanics. In fact, surveys of Hispanics show that they overwhelmingly want their children to learn English as quickly and as well as possible because they realize that this is a key to success. This is exemplified by more than 90 percent of Latinos in the Latino National Political Survey (LNPS) agreeing that all citizens and residents of the United States should learn English. Later studies have consistently found similar attitudes (Citrin et al. 2007).

These are just a few variations on the theme of bilingual education. Because this issue is so intensely symbolic, it will probably continue to be heatedly debated. However, in these debates, people often speak right past each other because they first do not agree on what they mean by bilingual education. Specialists themselves disagree on the effects of various approaches on the education of the child; that is, what approach is most successful in producing a well-educated, literate, knowledgeable graduate.

At minimum, educators must meet the children entering the school at the place where they are; that is, if the children are Spanish speaking, it would make sense that the Spanish language should be used for some period of time. However long that period of time should be—one year, three years, or more—continues to be hotly debated.

Moreover, a complicating factor has arisen. A large interest group and bureaucracy of pro-bilingual education practitioners and specialists have developed. The federal government, and, to a lesser extent, state governments, provide millions of dollars for bilingual education training. The dollar amounts provided are often based on the number of children who are classified as needing bilingual education. This has resulted in instances of non–Spanish-speaking individuals with Spanish surnames being placed in bilingual education classes, even against their wills and those of their parents. In any case, the development of a large pro-biligual education interest group and bureaucracy certainly serves as a force and a political influence to keep such programs going, aside from their strictly educational merits.

Because this issue is so highly charged emotionally, research that is done in the area is often discounted, often by "counter" research that results in contradictory results. As more Spanish-speaking immigrants come to the United States, the debate over bilingual education will undoubtedly intensify. It is hoped that continued experience with bilingual education, including well-controlled, objective, and sound educational experimentation and research, will help resolve the debate by providing the best form of bilingual education, which will help Latinos become well-functioning, well-educated, contributing citizens of the United States.

DISCRIMINATION AND AFFIRMATIVE ACTION

As a cognizable ethnic minority in the United States, one of the significant concerns of Latinos is their treatment in this society. Latinos have been subject to a long history of discriminatory practices, including being shunted into separate facilities such as schools, restaurants, theaters, swimming pools, and even cemeteries. They have been directed to separate drinking fountains, rest rooms, and seating areas in public facilities. They have been excluded through intimidation from exercising the franchise and seeking public office and directed away from college prep and professional tracks in schools, suppressions that have kept them on the lower rungs of society. They have endured economic exploitation, particularly for their labor, and social exclusion from many of the United States' societal organizations. In short, Latinos have experienced a significant amount of exclusion and discriminatory practices throughout their history in the United States. Separation, exclusion, and discrimination continue to be concerns for Latinos and items on the Latino political agenda. It must be recognized that at least the most overt forms of discrimination have been diminishing since the 1970s and 1980s, but the more subtle and difficult institutional discrimination continues. Moreover, the legacy of this history is still being felt because 56.4 percent of Latinos believe that discrimination directed toward Latinos is a big problem in the United States (Pew Hispanic Center 1999). There is also a perception by Hispanics that the great attention given to immigrants and immigration, particularly the mass marches and demonstrations in 2006, may have heightened discrimination. A Pew Hispanic Center report (2006) showed that in 2002, 44 percent of Latinos believed that "discrimination against (Hispanics/Latinos) [was] a major problem in preventing (Hispanics/Latinos) in general from succeeding in America" (4). In 2004, the proportion feeling this way was 51 percent; in 2006, after the demonstrations, that number had grown to 58 percent (Pew Hispanic Center 2006, 4). Therefore, combating discriminatory practices often appears on Latinos' lists of concerns for political action. This concern has taken various forms of public issues, policy, and activities over the years. The following are brief discussions of some of these issues.

RACIAL PROFILING

Throughout history, there have often been significant tensions between local law enforcement agencies, which are the agents of the legitimized use of force by the dominant power structure. These agencies offer many examples of treating whites, particularly more well-to-do whites, much better than people of color. During the Chicano movement of the 1960s, Latino communities even believed that they needed to establish quasimilitary forces, such as the Brown Berets and the Black Berets, to help protect the community against what they considered to be the use of force and outright oppression by the "occupation shock troops" of the white society—the police. One example of a clash between such quasimilitary forces and the police occurred in California. Several pitched battles took place in Oakland between the Black Panthers and the Oakland police force, and between various Chicano groups, including the Brown Berets in Southern California, and the Los Angeles Sheriff's Department and Los Angeles Police Department. Currently, there continue to be instances of severe harassment, if not brutality, by police forces against Latinos.

One of the latest manifestations of this differential and prejudicial treatment has been the practice of "racial profiling." This involves law enforcement agents using what they consider to be racial characteristics to automatically place a person under heightened surveillance or suspicion (Harris 2002). It often leads to stopping, searching, and citing Latinos for relatively minor violations. Strictly speaking, even though Latinos are not a racial group, but rather an ethnic group, they are often cognizable because most of them are either brown, having features of their Native American ancestors, or black, reflecting their lineage from their African American ancestors, particularly in the Caribbean region. Statistics have shown that Latinos, as well as Latin Americans, are more likely to be under suspicion by law enforcement officers and are more likely to be stopped and also questioned or searched simply because of their distinctive appearance. For example, a December 1999 report of the New York City Police Department's pedestrian "stop and frisk" practices by the state attorney general provided glaring evidence of racial profiling in the nation's largest city. Hispanics comprise 23.7 percent of the city's population, yet 33.0 percent of all "stops" were of Hispanics. In contrast, whites are 43.4 percent of the city's population but accounted for only 12.9 percent of all stops. A 2007 report by the U.S. Department of Justice stated that while "whites, blacks, and Hispanics were stopped by police at similar rates; blacks and Hispanics were searched by police at higher rates than whites" (Durose et al. 2007, 1). Law enforcement officials often either deny this differential treatment or defend themselves by stating that Latinos or African Americans commit more crimes than do European white Americans. However, careful analysis of statistics shows that the proportion of Latinos who are under surveillance and are stopped by law enforcement officers is not proportionate to the actual rate of conviction for crimes by Latinos or African Americans. Certainly, this presumption of guilt, or at least suspicion of Latinos, that takes the form of racial profiling is an activity that bothers many Latinos and is one about which they are seeking redress of grievances against law enforcement officials and a halt to such practices.

AFFIRMATIVE ACTION

Affirmative action, or the providing of a special advantage to Latinos or other minorities to compensate for past injustices or grievances against these groups, has been a practice since at least the 1970s (Garcia F.C. 1997). There also has been a long-lasting controversy over what it is exactly, what it ought to be, and whether (or how long) it ought to be continued. There is no single major federal law that mandates affirmative action for minorities, although the federal government has categorized several groups as those that are to be officially "protected" by the federal government and for which affirmative action policies seem most appropriate. These federally protected groups include women, African Americans, Hispanic Americans, Asian Americans, Native Americans, and Pacific Islanders. There are more than 160 separate laws, policies, rules, and regulations at the federal level alone that pertain to affirmative action. In addition, there are certainly thousands of similar policies at the state and local levels that bear on the status of these protected groups. In addition, much of the private sector has seen fit to institute its own policies of affirmative action, even when not mandated by the federal government, either because of a sense of justice and fair play or because they think that such actions give them an economic advantage, that is, it is good business.

Affirmative action can take many forms. The most common involve college admissions and scholarships, the hiring and promotion of individuals in public or public-supported enterprises, and the awarding of government contracts. Each of these areas has been hotly debated, and much legislation and many court decisions have been generated in each of these areas. Although it is beyond the scope of this book to detail the history of affirmative action in these areas, there are many excellent works on the topic.[2] The topic continues to be a controversial one, and frequently, a situation arises that causes the debate to flare up, if not nationally, at least on a local or state basis. For most people—even for Latinos—the topic is a difficult one to deal with because it involves the clash of so many basic values. It is also difficult because, as with bilingual education, the words that are used in the debate are often major contributors to misunderstanding rather than aids for clarification.

The awarding of a certain percentage of government contracts to minority-owned firms has been the practice since President Richard M. Nixon's "Philadelphia plan" in 1968. Although it has taken various forms over the years, in essence the plan involves giving minority firms preference when bids are received for various federal government projects. This practice has been challenged in the courts, and in some of the most recent U.S. Supreme Court decisions, such as *Adarand Constructors v. Pena* (1995), the Court has ruled some of these practices unfair and has narrowed their scope, even though such practices are still common and legal at the state and local levels. The idea behind this is to give minority- and women-owned businesses the opportunity to break into the long-established "old boy" networks of connections between contractors and those issuing the contracts. It is also meant to give emerging minority-owned business enterprises some equal opportunity compared to those that have been amassing contacts and resources over the years.

Perhaps the next most controversial are affirmative action statutes, again most noticeably at the federal level but also in some states and localities, that give extra points or advantages to members of the protected minority group when they are applying for employment or seeking promotion. There is no doubt that for most of this nation's history, racial and ethnic minorities, particularly African Americans and Native Americans, have been excluded both with the backing of the law and extralegally from being hired. It was said with a great deal of accuracy that these groups' members were often "the last to be hired and the first to be fired." There was considerable discrimination not only in hiring but also in allowing individuals from ethnic groups to advance through the ranks. They were often kept at the most menial and lowest paid job levels. Also throughout history, those organizations that were instituted primarily to help the working person—the labor unions—have also often been guilty of discriminatory practices against minorities. However, this changed considerably in the late twentieth century. Ethnic minorities, including Latinos, have become the mainstays and stalwarts of many unions.

Across the United States, affirmative action in employment and advancement can take many forms, but typically a member of a protected group is given the opportunity to be hired in a job when his or her qualifications are equal or roughly equal to those of non-minorities. The idea is that minorities such as Latinos have been excluded for so long that special actions are needed to break up the institutional bias against them and to help diversify the workforce, bringing new perspectives and new talents into the labor pool. As Latinos, for example, enter into better employment positions, they can serve as role models, and they can also work to bring other excluded and disadvantaged groups into the workforce.

Perhaps the most continuously controversial area is with regard to education, more particularly related to admission into colleges and universities. Again, throughout most of U.S. history, many colleges and universities have been largely white, middle class institutions and have operated in ways that have worked to the disadvantage, or even to the exclusion, of Latinos as well as other ethnic and racial minorities. Latinos often suffer from poor precollegiate education that does not allow them to compete for admission into better colleges and universities. In addition, many of the exams that were given to filter out students, such as the national standardized exams, were also argued to be culturally biased against Latinos and other ethnic and racial groups of largely lower economic standing. Furthermore, Latinos in the lower socioeconomic positions often could not afford to send their children to institutions of higher education but had to put them to work to contribute toward helping the family at the earliest possible time.

It is well known that education, particularly higher education, is a major route not only to better jobs but also to better general social and economic advancement. Throughout the late twentieth century, various colleges and universities, under pressure from Latinos, blacks, and civil rights organizations and encouraged by progressive governmental actions, instituted programs to bring students onto the campuses from groups that had previously been largely underrepresented. This included women, Hispanic Americans, African Americans, Native Americans, and other similar groups. Special recruiting was often done in areas of high Latino concentration, for example, and special scholarships were set up for Latino students. Moreover, admission decisions were restructured so that membership in a minority group such as Hispanic Americans would result in additional points toward qualifying for admission being awarded to the individual student applicant.

These affirmative action programs have resulted in a significant change in the composition of student bodies in colleges and universities throughout the United States and have given opportunities to Latinos that they might otherwise never have had. However, as in other areas, these policies and practices have been challenged in the courts and through other avenues of the political process. In the 1990s and early 2000s, the U.S. Supreme Court and some federal circuit courts made some decisions, such as the *Hopwood* decision in Texas and those involving admissions procedures at the University of Michigan (e.g., *Gratz v. Bollinger* [2003], *Grutter v. Bollinger* [2003]), that restricted the use of race or ethnicity as major criteria in college admission decisions. In 1996, the U.S. Supreme Court let stand an earlier decision by the U.S. Fifth Circuit Court of Appeals that ruled unconstitutional a procedure used by the University of Texas Law School. The University of Texas had employed a system that sought to meet percentage targets of ethnic and racial minority students by the use of various processes that favored minorities. Historically, the school had a low percentage of minority students matriculated in it.

In the pivotal *Grutter* case involving the University of Michigan Law School, the U.S. Supreme Court in 2003 ruled 5–4 that the university's affirmative action admissions program was needed to provide a much-needed diverse student body in the professional school. They concurred that the extra points awarded minority applicants were not part of a "quota system" and were constitutional. Justice Sandra Day O'Connor cast the deciding vote in *Grutter*, saying that affirmative action was still needed in America, but she hoped that it would not be necessary for more than another generation or so. In the University of Michigan undergraduate *Gratz* case, the Court ruled 6–3 that the awarding of points to minority applicants violated the equal protection clause of the U.S. Constitution.

In November 2006, Michigan voters passed a ballot proposal by a 58 to 42 percent margin that banned public institutions, including state and local governments and public colleges and universities, from considering gender, race, ethnicity, or national origin for education, public employment, or contracting purposes. It became law in late 2006 and was challenged in the courts; however, it was denied review by the U.S. Supreme Court in January 2007.

The most famous case, which still sets the underlying principles for affirmative action in higher education and was used as precedent by both plaintiffs and defendants in the Texas and Michigan cases, is the 1978 case of *Regents of the University of California v. Baake* (1978). Mr. Baake had sued the university, contending that his possible admission into medical school had been unfairly taken from him and was awarded to a minority applicant even though he had higher qualifying scores than did several minority applicants. On appeal by the regents, the U.S Supreme Court ruled that Mr. Baake was unfairly treated in the admission process and that "race and ethnicity could be used as one consideration in the admission process but could not be the sole criteria or even the dominant reason for admission."

That is, it is allowable for colleges to use "narrowly targeted" processes to enhance the diversity of their students. Other cases have also held that states can consider race, ethnicity, and gender in the interests of diversity or to remedy a proven history of discrimination and exclusion. Because we have few national universities and almost all institutions of higher education are either state or local institutions, or else are in the private sphere, there is no consistency across the United States with regard to affirmative action policies and practices in college admissions and the awarding of scholarships. The *Hopwood* decision applied to the University of Texas and other schools in that multistate region that were covered by the jurisdiction of that judicial court of appeal. The university has since found other ways to give opportunities to Latinos to attend the University of Texas at Austin, and similar alternative positive actions have been undertaken by other affected universities.

Perhaps the biggest continuing controversies have occurred in California. Much of the controversy has been over admission to the ten-campus system of the University of California, and more particularly, its most prestigious campuses within the system—those at Berkeley and Los Angeles. In the late 1990s, the Board of Regents at the University of California, yielding to the pressure of various groups, did pass a policy that ruled out affirmative action as an admission policy to the university. That policy has continued to be challenged by Latinos and other groups and is likely to be rescinded. However, in 1996, through its initiative and referendum process, the state of California did pass a state constitutional amendment (Proposition 209) that made it illegal for any public agency in the state to give preference to "any individual or group on the basis of race, sex, color, ethnicity, or national origin in the operation of public employment, public education, or public contracting." This included granting preferences in admission to a college or university. Of course, Latinos and others continue to challenge this law in the courts and through the political process, pressuring the state legislature, the executive branch, and the University of California Board of Regents.

Undoubtedly, Latinos have benefited tremendously from "affirmative action" practices at the national, state, and local levels, and in private institutions. Historically, the initial national legislation that was passed had been specifically aimed at African Americans, who had suffered the debilitating effects of slavery, had been segregated legally and illegally, and had been clearly oppressed for centuries in the United States. As time went on, other minority groups, such as Latinos, pressed their claims because they too experienced exclusionary treatment and a legacy of discrimination, and a continued disadvantage because of these.

In the early twenty-first century, affirmative action programs continue to be controversial, if not at the forefront, of public debate on issues. Occasionally, there is significant demand to abolish these programs. Its opponents state that they are unfair to individual whites who must pay the price for some actions in which they themselves did not participate but instead were the result of practices and policies that took place generations or even centuries ago. There is also the claim of "reverse discrimination"; that is, some whites, especially white males, believe that to be a member of the majority white group works against them in obtaining contracts, jobs, promotions, scholarships, or college admission. Moreover, opponents claim it is a violation of the American value of fairness to give preferential treatment to one group—all members of one group—based simply on that group's ethnicity or race. They claim that it causes hostility between groups and that each person's qualifications should be judged on a case-by-case basis. Opponents claim that the U.S. Constitution is and ought to be "color blind." Other opponents believe that although affirmative action was an acceptable program and was a just and fair idea instituted to overcome the devastating legacy of prejudice and discrimination, it was meant to be a temporary boost to discriminated groups, not a permanent fixture. After more than three decades of affirmative action, opponents believe that ethnic and racial minorities are now able to compete on an equal basis. Moreover, they also claim that there are so many laws on the books that protect Latinos from discriminatory practices that there is no need for an additional advantage to be given to Latinos in the form of preferences.

Yet, there are still many defenders of affirmative action. They do tend to be members of the ethnic and racial minority groups who realize that they have benefited from affirmative action policies. White women, who have also benefited greatly from affirmative action—indeed some believe that they have benefited more than any other group from affirmative action—are somewhat ambivalent about the subject, having mixed feelings about whether the programs should be continued. African Americans are by far the staunchest defenders of affirmative action programs (McClain and Stewart 2006). Latinos are somewhere in-between (Lopez and Pantoja 2004). In some cases, Latinos strongly support affirmative action; in other cases, they do not. Most of this has been discovered through survey research questions that ask Latinos how they feel about affirmative action and its various manifestations. Research shows that Latinos' responses vary a great deal along several dimensions (Garcia F.C. 1997; Lopez and Pantoja 2004; Uhlaner and Garcia 2002). One of the most important factors is the actual wording of the questions themselves. If Latinos are simply asked whether they prefer affirmative action, they overwhelmingly support it. However, when Latinos are asked whether Latinos and other minority groups need "preferential" treatment or a "special advantage," they are quite divided on the subject. Simply worded questions, usually those that include the phrase "affirmative action," seem to generate the most support among Latinos (Uhlaner and Garcia 2002). Moreover, Latinos are divided based on their particular socioeconomic characteristics.

For example, Puerto Ricans tend to be the most in favor of affirmative action, Mexican Americans a little less so, and Cubans the least of these major groups (de la Garza et al. 1992). Economic standing also makes a big difference in the opinions of Latinos because those who are well-off tend to be the most opposed to affirmative action measures compared to those at the lower rungs of the socioeconomic ladder.

Indeed, some critics of affirmative action policies have stated that instead of being race- and ethnic-based, affirmative action should be based on class, on economic standing, rather than simply on ethnicity or race. These people ask whether it is fair that an upper middle class Latino youth whose father is a successful businessman or professional be given preferential treatment in college admission because of his ethnicity over a white student applicant from a struggling working class family. With Latinos, there is also the problem of to whom these advantages ought to apply. Should these affirmative action policies apply only to Latinos whose ancestors have paid taxes, fought in this nation's wars, and worked hard in building this country, dedicating their labor to it for at least two or three generations? Is it fair that a recent immigrant from Guatemala or El Salvador be entitled to the same advantages as a third- or fourth-generation Mexican American? As anyone can see, affirmative action is a difficult public policy. There are no clear-cut answers.

Recently, academics and other defenders have turned to defending the policy by stressing that this is a multiculturally diverse country and that our institutions should reflect that multicultural *diversity*. In particular, colleges and universities, which are reportedly broadening, mind-expanding experiences, ought to have the diversity of perspectives that various cultures can bring to the campus as students learn from one another through their interactions. Another strong argument made in favor of affirmative action is that it is the best way to counter the institutional biases and discrimination that still exist, however subtle in form, in many of our institutions and organizations. In this manner, affirmative action is a *countervailing bias* that can counteract continuing institutional discrimination.

Although the courts, including the U.S. Supreme Court, have been making a few decisions in the area, they have been careful not to make any sweeping decisions at the national level. The national legislature has not been very active in dealing with the question either. In 1997, President William (Bill) J. Clinton, caught in the maelstrom of one of the periods of conflict and controversy over affirmative action, declared that his position was to "mend it, not end it." This reportedly meant that the moral idea behind it is a good one, but that its applications need to be monitored and when necessary changed so that they will be as helpful and as fair as possible to all parties. Certainly, affirmative action will continue to be one of the major issues on the Latino agenda and one over which political activity will be engaged.

THE ECONOMIC SITUATION

As we saw in Chapter 3, most Latinos are still clustered near the bottom of the economic ladder in the United States. Progress has been made and continues to be made, particularly since the 1980s. Despite discrimination and exclusion, Latinos have worked hard and persevered, and have made significant inroads into the middle class in just a few generations. Also promoting optimism in this realm, Hispanic household incomes in 1997, 1998, 1999, and 2000 did show increases of slightly more than 5 percent—a real and significant increase.

Still, Latino unemployment is always higher than that of non-Latinos, even though Latinos are in the job market, that is, actively looking for employment in higher proportions than are non-Latinos. They are also still more concentrated in lower-paying, labor-intensive, non–white collar, non-managerial jobs than are whites. This inequality holds regardless of generation, although it is most evident for recent immigrants and less pronounced for second- or third-generation Latinos. Part of this problem is related to the relatively lower educational attainment levels of Latinos, as discussed previously. Part of it is simply due to continuing bias and the historical legacy of discrimination and exclusion. For example, even in the public service (i.e., the federal bureaucracy, which ought to be the standard of being equally open to all), Latino representation is at about 80 percent of parity (Pachon 1988). Employment in the federal government is greatest in the lowest grade levels, and parity decreases in the higher-paying levels and is quite low in senior executive positions. This lack of parity or equality in public employment is also true for state and local jobs. Studies of most state and local governments have shown that Hispanics are represented far below their proportion in total employment. Other studies have shown again that in state and local occupational structures, Hispanics are concentrated in lower-level positions, such as service and maintenance positions.[3] Some of the employment in the cities of the Southwest, particularly those with a multigenerational Hispanic population, show levels of parity or even over parity, for Hispanic populations, although they tend to be in lower-paying jobs.

As Hispanics gain representation on city councils, on county commissions, and in mayoral positions, the more likely it is that Hispanics will have a fair proportion of the jobs at all levels. As the Hispanic population booms in urban and suburban areas, and its political potential and actual political power increases, it also becomes more likely that Hispanic representation in public employment will increase. However, if the immigrant population from Latin America continues to consist mostly of poorly educated, low-skilled labor, then it is most likely that newer Hispanics will continue to be concentrated in the dirtiest, hardest working, menial, lowest-paying, and often dangerous jobs. Because Hispanics must often take jobs in industries such as the livestock slaughterhouses and poultry preparation plants and jobs working with dangerous factory and farm equipment positions, they are also most likely to be exposed to the risk of the most serious injuries on the job.

HOUSING

Homeownership is the primary method of acquiring financial stability for American households and is the primary means of establishing community stability. However, Latino home ownership generally lags a great deal behind that of non-Hispanic whites. Because of factors such as the necessity to move from job to job or place to place following the job market, having low-paying jobs, and related reasons, it has been historically more difficult for Latinos to qualify for home ownership. Although some 69 percent of all Americans and 76 percent of Anglos own their own residences, only about 49 percent of Hispanics have their own domicile ownership. (The LNPS showed Mexican American home ownership at 49 percent and Anglos at 64 percent.) However, due primarily to lower interest rates and increased information dissemination to Latinos, the percentage of Latino homeowners has increased from approximately 46 percent in 2003 to the near 50 percent rate in 2005 (Becerra and Jauregui 2005). This increase reflects a larger trend over the past decade in which the homeownership rate of Hispanics has outpaced the growth of other groups, in some cases by as much as three times.

Despite the advancements made in this area, Hispanics who are interested in becoming homeowners face tremendous barriers. Studies indicate that Latinos have not proportionately benefited from the record low interest rates and strong housing and refinance booms of recent years, posing a threat to the gains made thus far (Congressional Hispanic Caucus Institute [CHCI] 2004). CHCI recently conducted a series of focus groups to identify barriers to homeownership for Hispanics. Probably the most daunting of these barriers is economic status. The focus groups indicated that there is a severe lack of affordable homes and that many Latino households do not have high enough incomes and/or savings to purchase a home in the prevailing market. In addition, many Latinos lack information regarding the home buying process and are not aware of the opportunities available to them (e.g., first-time home buyer programs). This is compounded by a lack of trust or fear of mainstream lending institutions. Unfortunately, this often leads Latinos to predatory realtors and lenders who may speak Spanish but do not have the best interests of the consumer in mind. These focus groups have prompted a series of proposed recommendations from CHCI, as well as a fellowship program through CHCI to empower Latino housing professionals and increase homeownership opportunities for Latinos nationwide.

Another point is that Latinos seem to be more residentially segregated than would be expected based solely on SES. Although Latinos are less residentially segregated than are African Americans, some studies have found that lending institutions engage in "red lining"—that is, racial and ethnic discrimination in home lending practices—and that race and ethnicity, not income, appeared to determine whether home loans were made.

Residential ownership is positively related to engaging in political activity; thus, as Latino home ownership increases, which it is doing, this will be a factor that will also tend to encourage and promote participation in the political process. Homeownership also contributes to the stability of neighborhoods and can increase the social capital of communities. Therefore, it is critical for Latinos to continue the positive trends established in this area through the efforts of groups like CHCI.

CRIME AND CRIMINAL JUSTICE

Because Hispanics are often a distinctive, cognizable ethnic group in the lower socioeconomic ranks, it is not surprising that this group also has a distinctive relationship with the criminal justice system. The justice system is one area in which Hispanics are overrepresented— unfortunately, not on the bench, in law enforcement agencies, or in the legal profession but in detention, arrests, and incarceration. A report by the National Council of La Raza stated that "Hispanics represented 13% of the U.S. population in 2000, but accounted for 31% of those incarcerated in the federal criminal justice system" (Walker, Senger, Villaruel, and Arboleda 2004). Moreover, as popularly believed, this is not due to Latinos committing more crimes but to inequitable treatment during arrest, prosecution, and sentencing (Morin 2005; Walker et al. 2004). Ethnic and racial minorities have historically had more troublesome relationships with police, the courts, and prisons than have members of the core culture, particularly those of greater economic means (Morin 2005). Much of this relationship is only found in media reports or in verbal accounts based on experiences and observations. However, the benchmark report of the U.S. Commission on Civil Rights, "Mexican Americans and the Administration of Justice in the Southwest," indicated that all levels of the criminal justice system were viewed as discriminatory Anglo institutions from which Mexican Americans do not expect fair treatment.

There are a few major studies of Latinos and the criminal justice system in the United States from which to draw (Lopez 1995; Martinez 2002; Mirande 1987; Morales 1972; Urbina 2003; U.S. Commission on Civil

Rights 1970; Walker et al. 2004). In addition to the overall relative paucity of research on Latinos, most official reports do not keep records by ethnicity; more often, such records are kept by race, and Hispanics are usually placed into the "white" category of race. Nevertheless, the relationship of Latinos to the U.S. criminal justice system is important to include as an important policy issue. Not only has it been a special concern of Hispanics throughout their history, but it is also almost always included among the "most important issues" facing the Hispanic community when surveys are taken.

Throughout U.S. history, both immigrants and racial minorities have often been suspected of criminality, stereotyped as especially prone to violence or criminal acts, and been given special attention by law enforcement agencies. This has been as true for Hispanics as it has been for the Irish and Italian immigrants, African Americans, and Native Americans. There has been a long history of tension and even conflict between law enforcement agents and Latinos (Mirande 1987; Morin 2005). The Texas Rangers were established especially to keep "Mexicans" and those perceived as *bandidos* in "their place" in 1838. The infamous "Zoot Suit riots" and the Sleepy Lagoon case involved *pachucos* and "Zoot Suiters" being attacked by servicemen and police in Los Angeles in 1942 and 1943. During the Chicano movement, this hostility was one of the major points of political protest and action, culminating in the "police riots" of 1970 and 1971 that resulted in at least one civilian fatality and hundreds of injuries (Morales 1972; U.S. Commission on Civil Rights 1970). As discussed previously, racial profiling has included "driving while being Latino," which implies that police disproportionately target Latinos. The continuing problematic situation along the Mexican border has continued to fuel some hard feelings among some Latinos, border patrols, and related law enforcement agencies.

Although there is evidence that the crime rates in concentrated Hispanic population areas such as barrios are noticeably high, much of this is due to an intense targeting of law enforcement officers in these areas. Federal health statistics show that per capita drug use rates between whites and minorities are actually very similar. Immigration law violations also account for these reportedly higher crime rates. Latinos constitute the vast majority of those arrested for immigration violations. In fact, arrests for immigration violations increased 610 percent from 1990 to 2000 (Walker et al. 2004). This is critical for Latinos because minor crimes such as shoplifting or fighting in school can result in deportation.

Latinos themselves experience a higher incidence of victimization than do non-barrio residents. The rise and expansion of gangs and organized crime, many having a base in immigrant communities, have increased the problems of interaction between law enforcement and some in the Latino community. The reasons for this are complex and not fully understood, but most likely include lower economic and social status, limited employment opportunities, and marginalization by society. The tension between the police and some Latino communities has been long-standing and continues today. Many Hispanics continue to believe that they are subject to more harassment and brutality and that police treat them with disrespect and more hostility than they do Anglos.

There is also a feeling and some evidence that the U.S. court system does not administer justice as fairly and equitably to Latinos as it does to non-Hispanic whites. Hispanics are proportionately more likely not only to be arrested but also to be brought to trial and to be sentenced to imprisonment than are Anglos. In general, the rate of sentencing for incarceration of persons accused of crimes is higher for Hispanics than for whites (Steffensmeier and Demuth 2000); however, the imposition of capital punishment is not (Urbina 2003). Latino youth are particularly affected by the current operation of the criminal justice system. They have greater interaction with the criminal justice system than Anglos, and the number of young Hispanics in the justice system has increased significantly in recent years (Walker et al. 2004).

The public policy issue of crime and criminal justice is a long-standing and highly salient one for Hispanics. Although the particular composition of the elements of most concern changes over time, this area continues to be high on the Latino political agenda. The continued challenges of immigration, also discussed in this chapter, are likely to increase the visibility of criminal justice issues for Latinos.

HEALTH

Lower SES usually leads to poorer health conditions, and this is certainly true for Latinos. Regardless of which measures of SES are used or how health is measured, there is a mountain of evidence that suggests that higher SES equals better health (Marmot 1999; Smith 1999). Higher SES levels increase access to medical care and health insurance, as well as decrease exposure to hazardous social and physical working and living conditions. Given the overall lower SES levels of Latinos in comparison to whites, there should be much attention paid to the status of Latinos in the area of health policy.

Latinos tend to have much less access to both general and top quality medical care than do non-Hispanic whites, and the gap in access to health care appears to be growing. There are severe disparities among both Latino children and adults when it comes to use of health services. For example, among children ages six to seventeen years, 16 percent of Latinos have not seen a physician in the past two years, compared to 7 percent of non-Latino whites (Brown, Ojeda, Wyn, and Levan 2000). The 2005

National Healthcare Disparities Report found that although disparities in access to health care have diminished for all other minority groups, they have widened for Hispanics. Specifically, researchers at the U.S. Department of Health and Human Services note widening disparities between Hispanics and Anglos in the following areas: diabetes care quality, higher rates of HIV/AIDS cases for Hispanics, longer and more frequent delays in illness/injury care for Hispanic patients, and less access to mental health treatment for Hispanics (National Alliance for Hispanic Health 2005).

Latinos also have significantly lower levels of health insurance. This is critical because health insurance provides an important degree of financial access to health services. The lack of health insurance among Latinos thus adversely affects their access to health care. Approximately 37 percent of Latinos in the United States are without any public or private health insurance. This is more than 2.5 times the uninsured rate of 14 percent among non-Latino whites (Brown, Wyn, and Teleki 2000). The low rate of health insurance among Latinos is due primarily to their low rates of employment-based health insurance, the primary source of health insurance for the non-elderly population. Latino access to employment-based health insurance (EBHI) is lower than among other ethnic groups and has been in a state of decline since the 1990s (Cooper and Schone 1997). Among subgroups, employees of Mexican and of Central and South American backgrounds have the lowest rates of EBHI (52.3 percent and 51 percent, respectively; Brown and Yu 2002). SES accounts for most barriers to health insurance that Latinos face. Latino employees are more likely to have lower educational attainment, to work for a small company, to work in noncoverage industries, and to work for lower wages—all characteristics associated with low levels of EBHI.

Nativity and citizenship status are also key factors in gaining access to health insurance. A recent study of Mexican Americans conducted by Stanford University indicates that Mexican-born children who immigrate to the United States are nine times more likely to grow up without health insurance than American-born white children. Generational status is clearly a major factor for access to health insurance among the Mexican-origin population; 63.9 percent of first-generation Hispanic children are uninsured, compared to 26.1 percent of second-generation and 16.4 percent of third-generation Mexican Americans (Burgos, Schetzina, Dixon, and Mendoza 2005).

Finally, some diseases seem to be particularly endemic to Latinos. At the top of this list is cardiovascular disease, which is the leading cause of death among Latinos and accounts for nearly one third of Latino deaths (Alcalay, Alvarado, Balcazar, Newman, and Huerta 1999). Cardiovascular diseases are highly correlated with many other illnesses associated with Latinos, mainly diabetes. In fact, diabetes has often been described as the

"Latino disease," and this reference is supported by research exploring the impact of the illness on Latinos. For example, the American Diabetes Association has a number of statistics specific to the Latino community listed on their Web site. These statistics include that the prevalence of type 2 diabetes is 1.5 times higher in Latinos than non-Latino whites, and that 2 million, or 8.2 percent, of all Latino Americans ages 20 years or older have diabetes. In regard to national origin, Puerto Ricans have the greatest percentage of their population (26 percent) between the ages of forty-five and seventy-four who have diabetes, followed by Mexicans at 24 percent and Cubans at 16 percent.[4] Furthermore, the Latino age-adjusted death rate of 18.8 per 100,000 population due to diabetes is nearly 64 percent higher than the non-Hispanic white rate of 11.5. In addition to diabetes, the Latino death rate due to HIV/AIDS is 16.3 per 100,000 population, more than twice the non-Hispanic white rate of 6 (Hayes-Bautista 2002). It is important to note that although the death rates associated with both of these diseases is higher for Latinos than whites, Latino death rates are lower than those for African Americans in both cases.

LANGUAGE POLICY

The language of an ethnic group is often one of the most important defining aspects of that group. Experts tell us that language is an embodiment or an encapsulation of the history, life experiences, and perceptions of a people. Undoubtedly, language is one of the most important manifestations of a culture. One of the defining characteristics of Latinos, if not the most important outward characteristic, is the language spoken, which obviously is Spanish. Although there are variations and colloquialisms in the Spanish spoken by the various Latino nationalities and subgroups, and fluency varies tremendously among individuals, language arguably may be the single most important defining characteristic of Hispanic Americans. Not that all Latinos speak Spanish fluently—to the contrary, it is estimated that, at most, 55 to 60 percent of Latinos in the United States are fluent in Spanish. With the increasing immigration, these numbers were rising at the turn of the twentieth century. Visible results of this include an increasing number of Spanish language media, such as newspapers, magazines, and other periodicals; radio stations; and television stations.

As Hispanic immigration increased in the late twentieth century and the Spanish language was increasingly heard and seen, there seemed to be a considerable renewal of the traditional American concern with language (Schmidt 2000). A concern with language can be traced back to the founding fathers because the writers of the U.S. Constitution themselves argued over whether there ought to be an official language for the country, and if so, what it ought to be. Throughout U.S. history, as different waves of immigrants entered, bringing with them their own languages, they have developed institutions to communicate with each other in that language, such as their own media and the use of their language in local schools. But there has always been a reaction by mainstream America against these minority languages and concern about them, if not outright attempts to make them illegal or otherwise eradicate them.

The last wave of major political action against non-English languages was during the last great period of immigration into the United States, around the turn of the twentieth century, and particularly following World War I. In the 1920s, along with the nativist movement, came the passage of legislation by several governmental units outlawing the use of non-English languages or making English the exclusive or official language. With the coming of more serious economic concerns in the 1930s, including the Great Depression, and with the advent of World War II, governmental attentions were directed elsewhere. Beginning in the 1960s, as immigration began to increase again, particularly from Latin America, attention was once again cast on languages. Given the more progressive nature of those times and the pressures put on government to support the language of the new minorities, several bilingual education programs were supported through governmental actions, including court decisions and administrative regulations.

In the 1970s, as immigration increased, as bilingual education programs also multiplied, (with some showing very limited success or even failure), and as the segregation of Hispanics increased, a concern about non-English languages and non-English language programs arose once again. Not only did critics increasingly attack bilingual education, but there also arose a general uneasiness with foreign-speaking residents in this country. There were several reasons given for feeling that this was not a good thing. For one, some people believed that speaking a language other than English (or its American version) was likely to lead to disunity—that keeping one's native language would result in ethnic, cultural, or tribal groupings and identities being more important than an overall feeling of national unity or patriotism. There was also a belief that it was somewhat unpatriotic or un-American not to learn the de facto official American language of English. The concern was that such separateness would undermine a national identity and would result in a tribalized or significantly weaker United States. Some believed that it was only right that people wanting to become Americans would also become Americanized in their language. Others believed that, for their own good, immigrants needed to learn the common language and learn it well, so they could succeed in this country and contribute to the well-being of themselves and their communities.

Therefore, in the 1980s, many states in the United States considered restricting the use of non-English language or making English the "official" language. It was not always clear what was meant by an official language, although legislation often mentioned that English was to be used in the legislatures, in the courts, and in official documents. But which activities were "official" and which were not, and how they were to be enforced, was always an open question.

Latinos have been extremely defensive and protective about their language and have rallied to defend it from attacks, which they see as insulting, racist, or at least unnecessary. Even Hispanics who do not themselves speak the language or use the Spanish language media are offended by attacks on the language because they are believed to be attacks on their ancestry, their culture, or on these individuals themselves. If individuals are not fluent in Spanish, some of their relatives, such as parents or grandparents, almost always use the language, and it symbolizes many close personal relationships, as well as other good things about their own existence and their culture. Hispanic opposition has been very strong and strongly consensual in opposition to official English or English-only measures. Such measures have either been passed by state legislatures or by the voters of states in referenda balloting. In the year 2001, some twenty-two or twenty-three states currently had official language policy measures on the books, usually making English the official language, and virtually every state had at least considered it. As evidence of how symbolic this issue is, many of the official English measures that existed in the 1990s were a result of policy enacted by state legislatures in the states of the Deep South. It is ironic that at that time many states in the southeastern United States had the lowest number of Hispanics of any other region in the country, yet they also had the most legislatively enacted statutes against speaking non-English languages. It is in those other states where the Hispanic population was significantly higher that, more typically, the initiative process—which placed an issue on the ballot and then was followed by a referendum in which the voters approved the issue—enacted pro-English policies. Outstanding examples are in California and Arizona, both states having significant Hispanic, mainly Mexican American, populations, and both states having passed constitutional amendments making English the official language. Although a majority of Latinos voted against these measures in both states, the larger non-Hispanic majority vote took precedence. California's constitutional amendment passed in 1986 and similar measures passed in Arizona, Colorado, and Florida in 1988. Each state's policy was different in form and substance. In Arizona and California, these measures were challenged by Latino organizations in the courts, and the courts either struck down the measures or found them to be largely symbolic and therefore limited in application or implementation, in effect rendering them inoperative. In 2005, the state legislature of West Virginia passed an official English law as well.

Yet, as immigration continues to boom, and as Latinos disperse in noticeably larger numbers throughout the United States, there is no doubt that there will be continued and even renewed efforts to limit the use of Spanish (and probably Asian) languages and require Latinos to speak and use English. During the congressional debate over immigration reform in 2006, the Senate passed two amendments on language. One asserted that English is the "national" language; the other stated that English is the "common and unifying language" of the United States. Such legislative action is unnecessary (and it is difficult to understand what it actually means and to realize its implications) because, with extremely few exceptions, Latinos are eager to learn English. In 2004, a majority of Latinos were of the opinion that "immigrants have to learn English to say they are part of American society" (Pew Hispanic Center 2004a). They realize that English is certainly the common and unofficial, if not official, language of the United States and that mastery of and fluency in English is one of the keys to succeeding in America. It is a rare Latino immigrant parent that does not want his or her child to learn English at the earliest opportunity and who has not stressed the importance of this to his or her children. In fact, 92 percent of Latinos think that "teaching English to the children of immigrant families is very important." This compared to 87 percent of non-Hispanic whites and 83 percent of blacks who felt this way (Pew Hispanic Survey 2003). In the past, there has been such pressure to succeed in using English that some generations of Hispanic Americans have lost most or all of their fluency in Spanish and, unfortunately, have become monolingual in English. Many have thus been forced to relearn or learn the language at a later age, which is much more difficult than growing up speaking the language. Surely, there is room in the United States for bilingualism or multilingualism, so although the dominance of English as the language of government, commerce, and industry and as one uniter of the American people remains, other languages such as Spanish can remain the language of friends, relatives, and the home, and even as an auxiliary or even ancillary language of the marketplace. More tolerance and understanding with regard to the use of Spanish and its relationship to English can result in a society that is much more flexible and much more able to deal with a large sector of the Western Hemisphere's population.

IMMIGRATION POLICY

In a sense, the issue of immigration underlies many other policy issues salient to both Latinos and all Americans. As well as having great implications for Latino politics, it is generally the burgeoning immigration phenomenon that has created a demographic situation that more than any other factor has called the nation's attention to Latinos. As a nation of immigrants, one might expect that the U.S. national government would have a mature and well-developed policy on immigration and immigrants.

However, perhaps because the United States is a nation of immigrants and has become what it is through successive waves of immigration, the contrary is closer to the truth.

Although there are some major pieces of national legislation and immigration once again has become a major topic for policy makers in the twenty-first century, the United States actually has an underdeveloped position on immigration. There have only been a few major pieces of legislation passed by the national government, and these have often been the result of, or reactions to, changes in immigration practices in a reactionary form. For example, the National Origins Quota Act of 1924 was passed in reaction to the large waves of immigrants escaping Europe during and after World War I. These immigrants, largely from southern and eastern Europe, were seen as extremely foreign and difficult to assimilate, were often of separate and undesirable "races," and were usually viewed as a threat to the existing order, and even to the national (Anglo) character, of the United States. Whether these immigrants were from Italy, Greece, Poland, the Balkans, or China, the majority society feared being inundated by these "foreign hordes" and thus passed legislation prescribing very small quotas for immigrants from these new areas. In contrast, quotas for "old stock" Americans from northern and western Europe were extremely generous. Asians and Latin Americans were given very small quotas for each country.

This quota system was the basic law of the land until the McCarran Act of 1965, which did away with the quota system and changed the basis for immigration to the United States. That law is still the basic governing document of the land regarding immigration, although it has been modified since then. With the change in the national laws beginning in the 1960s, and increasing numbers of political refugees from Asia and Latin America, increasing numbers of what were seen as racially different, difficult to assimilate, threatening kinds of people provided a catalyst for once again discussing immigration and immigrants.

The various Latino national origin groups are affected differentially by immigration policies. By far, the largest impact is on Mexicans. Puerto Ricans are not directly subject to immigration policies because regardless of whether they reside on the mainland or the island of Puerto Rico, they are all U.S. citizens. The vast majority of Cuban Americans came to the United States as political refugees fleeing from the takeover by the Communist, Fidel Castro, or they are the descendants of those political refugees. As such, they have not been generally subject to the same immigration laws as Mexicans or immigrants from Asian countries, and in fact, immigration from Cuba is currently restricted by law. By far, the largest number of immigrants coming to the United States in the early twenty-first century is from Mexico, followed by immigrants from Asia and Central and South America. However, many of the Central American immigrants are actually refugees from wars and other disastrous political or economic situations, and as such, some have been given a special status and are not officially considered to be immigrants (Chávez 2004). Current immigration laws tend to favor immigrants who have job skills that are needed in the United States and are also aimed at bringing families together.

As mentioned previously, the 1980s and 1990s saw unprecedented waves of immigrants coming from Latin America and Asia. In 2001, it was estimated that there were approximately 8 million Mexican-born residents in the United States. Some have become citizens through the naturalization process. Others who came legally earned permanent resident status, and others entered the country illegally. These undocumented immigrants were estimated to number anywhere between 3 and 9 million in 2001, with the actual number probably being about 6 to 7 million. By 2005, most estimates were in the 8 to 20 million range, with 11 to 12 million being the figures most commonly cited (Passel 2005). Most of these immigrants have come to the United States looking for employment opportunities and eventually a better quality of life. Many of them are young males who come to the United States, and even though they earn very low wages by American standards, are doing quite well by their home country standards. They often send most of their earnings back to their families in Mexico or in the other countries from which they have emigrated. It has been estimated that some $16 to $20 billion were being sent to Mexico in 2005. Eventually some return to their homelands, but many work to bring the rest of their family into this land of opportunity, either legally or illegally.

The chance for a better life through hard work and economic success in the United States is the major "pull" factor for immigrants. The major "push" factor tends to be the low standard of living in the "labor exporting" countries, such as Mexico, in addition to social, political, and economic situations that have in the past given little hope for improvement (DeSipio and de la Garza 1998). However, with the turn of the twenty-first century and improving relations between the United States and Mexico, it is hoped that the United States will consider policies to develop the Mexican economic system and thus reduce the need for such vast migration numbers out of that country.

The last major piece of legislation passed by the federal government with regard to immigration was the Federal Immigration Reform and Control Act (FIRCA) of 1986. This act tried to improve standards by which migration could be regulated and by which immigrants could be naturalized. It also had law enforcement provisions and stipulated sanctions against employers hiring undocumented workers. Another provision granted amnesty to the 5 or 6 million immigrants who had entered the country illegally but who could now become citizens without fear of being deported (i.e., returned to their native land) or suffering other criminal sanctions. FIRCA enforcement provisions, particularly those stipulating sanctions against employers, have been largely ignored. However, FIRCA has had a major impact on the rate and dispersion of immigration from Mexico. A recent study of immigration from Mexico argues that the combination of restrictive immigration policies initiated by FIRCA and the passage of the 1994 North American Free Trade Agreement disrupted the existing Mexican-U.S. immigration system (Massey, Durand, and Malone 2002). This disruption changed Mexican migration from seasonal to permanent and spread Latino immigrants from a few border states to locales across the country, negatively impacting U.S. labor markets and increasing income inequalities. Ironically, the authors here suggest that while the U.S. federal government sought to restrict Mexican immigration with the passage of FIRCA, their actions created exactly the opposite effect.

The number of illegal immigrants entering the United States is estimated to be about 1 million a year. The vast majority of these come across the 1,951-mile long common border between Mexico and the United States, entering into the states of California, Arizona, and New Mexico or Texas. In 1994, California Governor Republican Pete Wilson led a campaign for California's infamous Proposition 187. This proposition, to be placed before the state's voters for acceptance or rejection, was a harsh measure designed to withhold any health and social services from undocumented immigrants and also to withhold educational services to the children of such "undocumenteds." The campaigns both for and against the proposition were dramatic and controversial, and strong anti-immigrant ads for the press, radio, and television were produced and published by interest groups who were strongly antiimmigration. They played on the fears, the xenophobia (fear of outsider foreigners) and racist or prejudicial feelings that some people harbor, and they seemed to be designed to threaten or scare the voters into supporting the proposition. Although the majority of Latinos in California voted against it, the larger non-Hispanic population voted in large majorities for it, and the proposition did pass. This campaign, pushed strongly by Republicans in California, particularly the state's Governor, Pete Wilson, lead to a considerable mobilization of Latino voters. It spurred naturalization among previous permanent residents, as well as voter registration and get out the vote activities, and produced a record turnout among California Latinos. The concentrated advertising campaign run by Republicans, at a time when the state was becoming a majority-minority state, did great damage to the standing of the Republican Party in California. For example, the average Hispanic vote for Republican candidates fell from 30.7 percent between 1988 and 1994, the year of Proposition 187, down to 22.8 percent from 1996 to 2000. The most populous state in America, with the largest number of electoral votes and with one third of all the Latinos in the nation, has been a Democratic stronghold since Proposition 187 and the passage of a few other anti-minority, anti-Latino measures supported by Republicans.

One result has been that the Republican Party has suffered long-lasting, if not irreparable, damage not only in California but also across the nation. Although Proposition 187 was a state measure, it was publicized nation-wide. Latinos throughout the nation, regardless of how they felt person-ally about immigration, were offended at these attacks on members of their own ethnic group. Even third- and fourth-generation Latinos had some sympathy for people from their ancestral homelands who were try-ing to simply make their way in life through hard work and who should not be deprived of basic human welfare services. Consequently, Latinos across the nation from many, if not all, of the Latino national origin groups developed an even more negative animus toward the Republican Party than was previously held, perceiving the party as mean spirited and un-necessarily anti-Hispanic. This perception was most likely reinforced by such actions as Republican Congressman Tom Tancredo from Colorado proposing in 2005 that the constitutional right of citizenship for children born in the United States be abolished if the children were born to undoc-umented entrants.

This should not be taken to mean that Hispanics are united in their policy positions on the issue of immigration. In fact, surveys show that there is considerable variation on how Latinos feel about immigration. The native born are more likely to favor a more restrictive policy than more recently arriving Latinos (Binder et al. 1997), as are wealthier, more educated, and older Latinos (Hood et al. 1997). In addition, perceived dis-crimination is correlated with believing that more immigrants should be allowed to enter the United States because Latinos who believe that dis-crimination against Latinos/Hispanics is a big problem are more likely to support increased immigration (Sanchez 2006). But one must separate the feelings that Latinos have toward immigrants from the feelings they have toward immigration. The former is usually quite sympathetic and sup-portive; the latter is usually quite variable and uneven. For example, Lati-nos are more likely than whites, Africans Americans, or Asians to support amnesty for illegal immigrants (Cain and Kiewiet 1987). Furthermore, Mexicans in general are more likely to support policies that facilitate the political and social integration of Mexican immigrants, such as bilingual education and immigrant access to services and citizenship (de la Garza 1998).

Public spokespersons for Latinos tend to be strongly proimmigration, favoring as open a border as possible, easy naturalization, and, in some in-stances, complete amnesty for undocumented immigrants. But as with many other issues, these spokespersons and leaders of advocacy organi-zations do not completely reflect the opinions of the Latino masses as measured by survey research. When Latinos themselves are asked how they feel about immigration, there are considerable numbers who exhibit substantial ambivalence. Some believe that the borders need to be protected and immigration slowed, if not closed. Overall, the LNPS indicated that 75 percent of Mexican Americans, 79 percent of Puerto Ricans, and 70 percent of Cuban Americans agreed with the statement that there are too many immigrants coming to the United States.[5] At the other extreme, there are a few who call for completely open borders or even deny the existence of borders. In-between there is a great majority who are not quite sure what immigration policy should be but who realize that immigration is a mixed blessing.

Some surveys have found that a majority of Latinos believe that our immigration policy is a bit too liberal and want to tighten the restrictions, but opinions vary, depending on where respondents live (Polinard, Wrinkle, and de la Garza 1984). Those who live along the borders who are directly affected by the situation obviously feel much more intensely because they are more personally and directly affected by this matter than are people for whom it is an abstract issue. People who are first-generation Mexican Americans and have close relatives in Mexico would feel quite differently, for example, than those who are three, four, or even more generations removed. Again, there is substantial variation in attitudes by national origin not only among Latino groups but also among various groups in the general population. The socioeconomic position of Latinos also makes a difference in their positions on immigration, with the most highly educated often being the most in favor of a more liberal "open door" policy (Hood et al. 1997). Latinos, particularly Mexican Americans, who are at the lower socioeconomic levels and are affected directly by the competition for labor positions with immigrants, who are willing to work long hard hours for very minimal wages, are often opposed to a liberal immigration policy.

The preceding sounds as if immigration has been a major concern of Latinos, one that has been high on the Latino policy agenda. In fact this has not been the case. Surveys in the 1990s showed that immigration was a matter of secondary importance. However, as this country is increasingly impacted by immigration, particularly from Latin America, and is increasingly becoming Latinized, and as immigrants are spreading throughout the United States, immigration policy became increasingly important on the political agendas of Latinos and the nation in general. In fact, in 2001, President George W. Bush seriously considered granting amnesty to as many as 3 million illegal Mexican immigrants because his advisors recommended that the administration propose legislation that would grant legal residency to undocumented Mexican immigrants who have been working in the United States. This was not only driven by the impact of the increasing number of immigrants into the United States but also by political considerations, namely, a hope that such a move would help dispel the Republican Party's antiimmigrant image. Political pundits differed in whether such a strategy would actually bring Latinos into the Republican camp in significant numbers or would just add to the overwhelming number who would even be stronger stalwarts voting for Democratic Party candidates (DeSipio 1996).

So, at the turn of the twentieth century, immigration was becoming a major policy consideration. In January 2004, President Bush again presented some ideas on immigration, including a temporary "guest worker" program, but there was no follow-through on this by his administration. Several immigration bills were introduced in the U.S. Congress with varying provisions. Congressional leaders announced late in 2005 that they would take up the topic of immigration reform in a serious way in early 2006. In November 2005, President Bush once again put the public agenda spotlight on immigration in major speeches in the southwestern United States. His rhetoric was significantly different from what it was in his earlier speeches that had emphasized the significance of finding ways to keep immigrants working in jobs that are needed but which most Americans will not do. The emphasis changed to the illegality of undocumented immigration and measures to secure the border. He also called for a temporary guest worker plan whereby undocumented immigrants would be allowed to stay for some period of time (three or six years) but would then have to return to their country of origin for at least a year before applying for reentry into the United States. Little emphasis was put on enforcing or increasing employer sanctions for hiring undocumenteds, or on clarifying or expediting the path toward naturalization and citizenship.

Much of the renewed interest is driven by demography and politics. The other major consideration is economic because there is no doubt that the inexpensive labor that immigrants contribute, as well as the expenditures they make, are of significant economic benefit to the United States, and particularly to employers, who benefit tremendously from cheap labor. It should be noted that another effect is that the availability of the immigrant workers also lessens the need for, and consequently the wages of U.S. workers. If there were no demand for this inexpensive labor in the fields, factories, plants, and service sectors of the United States, immigration pull would be diminished greatly. Experts do not agree whether immigrants are actually a drain on the economy, costing in services provided to them much more than they contribute, or whether they are a credit, contributing positively to the U.S. economy. There may be differences as to whether these calculations are based on short- or long-term considerations. One analysis of the economic impact of immigration suggests that during periods of economic growth in the United States, immigrants tend to benefit the economy, and there was not much public sentiment against immigration. However, during periods of economic stagnation, there are rising economic problems for immigrants, a greater demand on resources by immigrants, and consequently greater anti-immigration sentiments among the public (Bean and Stevens 2003). It does seem that many of the costs of immigration are levied on the individual states that are charged by our constitutional system with providing most of the health, safety, welfare, and educational services to its residents, whereas the national government is more removed from these immediate considerations and may benefit from increased productivity and lower labor costs in the long run. In any case, because experts disagree about the hard facts of immigration, much of the debate is currently based on emotions, political strategies, and partisan considerations. Most Latino organizations and spokespersons will probably continue to be pro-immigration; and most of the American population, including Hispanics, will probably continue to be ambivalent about this matter.

In 2005, much attention was given to the immigration problem by the media when a loosely knit group calling themselves the "Minutemen" gathered along portions of the Arizona border to watch out for "undocumenteds" crossing the border. Critics charged them with vigilante tactics of taking the law into their own hands; some opponents contended they were white supremacists, xenophobic if not racist, and posed a great potential for violence because some of them were armed. Latinos formed some counter-Minutemen groups that organized to travel to the border, confront the observers, and protect the safety of the immigrants. The Minutemen countered that they were just patriotic and law-abiding citizens volunteering to help the understaffed U.S. Customs and Border Protection and the U.S. Immigration and Customs Enforcement (ICE) of the Citizenship and Immigration Service do their jobs. Although no major incidents of violence had yet occurred, the Minutemen were expanding their activities and the potential for trouble had not diminished. Although the press coverage (and perhaps also the activities and membership) of the Minutemen had diminished by 2006, they continued their patrols and attempted to expand their activities to the southeastern states as Latino populations in that region of the country increased. Their prominence was widely publicized evidence of the nation's lack of an effective immigration policy and enforcement.

Major events occurred in early 2006 that elevated immigration to a high place on both the Latino agenda and the nation's list of concerns. In December 2005, the U.S. House of Representatives passed legislation that took a hard stance on immigration. The bill—HR 4437, the Border Protection, Antiterrorism and Illegal Immigration Control Act of 2005—was sponsored by House Judiciary Committee Chairman James Sensenbrenner, a Wisconsin Republican, and was backed by the Republican leadership; it was opposed by business lobbies, labor unions, religious organizations, and many Latino groups such as the National Council of La Raza. The vote was divided strongly along partisan lines, with a large majority of Republicans supporting the measure and most Democrats opposing it. The bill focused on strengthening the border, including building a 700-mile double fence along it, and imposing major criminal sanctions on undocumented immigrants, their families, and their employers, including detention and expedited returns. It did not address any possibilities of otherwise bringing the undocumented out of the shadows and providing any paths to legality, including permanent residency or citizenship.

When the U.S. Congress reconvened in 2006, several bills on immigration were proposed in the U.S. Senate, some of them in reaction to the Sensenbrenner bill passed by the House. Many Senate Republicans believed that the House bill was flawed because it contained no guest worker program. The most discussed and debated bill was a bipartisan bill by Senators John McCain, R-Ariz, and Edward Kennedy, D-Mass, that among other things would permit 400,000 workers to enter legally each year after paying back taxes and fines. In general, the Senate bills were more comprehensive and more inclusive than the Sensenbrenner bill.

The action by the House and the debate in the Senate brought forth a major and largely unexpected manifestation of mass Latino politics in the spring of 2006, as discussed more thoroughly in Chapter 6. On May 1 and again on May 10, as many as 1 million or more immigrants and supporters in dozens of cities in the U.S. marched and demonstrated, calling for immigration reform. The widespread publicity given to these mass demonstrations by the media had major impacts. The American public could no longer remain unaware of the situation, and the public policy makers were catalyzed into action. Public opinion polls in spring and summer 2006 revealed that immigration was considered to be the second most important problem facing the nation, second only to the war in Iraq. Polls during this period indicated that most Americans favored a middle ground in reforming immigration laws, one balancing border enforcement with opportunities for undocumented residents to obtain legalized status (Connelly 2006). In light of this, policy makers began addressing the issue as never before.

The main locus of national action was in the U.S. Senate, where many debates were heard and many bills introduced. President Bush, who had earlier mainly just spoken about immigration, now addressed the issue more directly, more frequently, and in more detail. He advocated provisions that seemed to be those most favored in the Senate and urged the House, and especially the Republicans there, to work with the Senate toward a more inclusive and less punitive plan. The main points included in the most highly publicized Senate legislation, that which seemed to form the most likely basis for enacting legislation, were a tightening of border security, including increased vigilance against possible terrorists, drug control, and all forms of illegal entry; a quota—some limit to the number of immigrants legally admitted each year; enforcement of sanctions against employers who knowingly hired undocumented workers; a path to permanent residence or citizenship for the millions of illegal immigrants already here, after some sort of "restitution"—either a financial penalty or back taxes—was paid, after some length of time as a resident, and after some assimilation requirement, such as learning English or learning about and accepting American values and institutions; and a "guest worker" program that would allow immigrant workers into the country to provide labor or services for a limited period of time before having to return to their country of origin.

In election year 2006, politicians were extra cautious about their actions and most sensitive to their electoral bases. A compromise between the House and the Senate appeared unlikely, as conservative House members, mainly Republicans, dug in their heels, even as President Bush continued to encourage a compromise. In the summer of 2006, the House began holding "field hearings" in various locations across the United States, purportedly to ensure that they were in tune with their constituents on this issue, but decidedly a clever political move. Later that year, with the general elections looming, a "partial" immigration bill passed both the House and the Senate and was signed into law by the president. The law addressed the most pressing and consensual concern of most Americans—border security. It called for the building of a 700-mile fence, along with the provision of other enhanced security devices. However, funds to support this law were not fully allocated. The possibility of major comprehensive legislation on immigration by the Republican-controlled Congress faded away.

The election of November 2006 brought the Democrats into a majority in the 110th Congress. The House had a 233-201 Democratic majority, and in the Senate there were an equal number of Democrats and Republicans. In 2007, congressional Democrats promised passage of immigration reform, and many competing variations were introduced. One of the most prominent was a bipartisan bill introduced by Representatives Luis Gutierrez, D-Illinois, and Jeff Flake, R-Ariz, titled the Security Through Regularized Immigration and a Vibrant Economy (STRIVE) Act. Developed in consultation with Senators McCain and Kennedy, it also included provisions for border security, a "path to citizenship," a guestworker program, an overhaul of the visa system for legal immigrants, and a provisions for illegal immigrants otherwise eligible for citizenship to return to their country and return legally.

In April 2007, the Bush administration released a new immigration plan that was far more conservative than the one passed by the Senate in 2006. This plan would grant illegal immigrants work visas but require them to return home to apply for U.S. residency and pay a $10,000 fine. Furthermore, the plan called for a visa that would allow undocumented workers to apply for three-year work permits as "guestworkers" that would be renewable indefinitely but cost $3,500 for each renewal. The plan was met immediately by thousands of protestors in downtown Los Angeles on April 7, 2007, who argued that the cost of work permits under this plan was prohibitive for low wage earners. On May 1st May Day of 2007, as the year before, there were demonstrations and marches in the streets of many cities, but they were considerably smaller than the ones in 2006. This was attributed to the heightened fear of immigrants due to ICE raids the previous year, to the negative reaction that the previous marches had in some quarters and to the failure of any comprehensive immigration reform during the previous year. As of mid-2007, none of the several competing proposals had been passed. But at least now, due mostly to the engagement in politics by masses of Latinos, the long-avoided immigration issue was at the forefront of this nation's public issue agenda and the political party most in favor of comprehensive immigration reform was in the congressional majority.

It seems inevitable that the immigration flow will continue as long as the demand for cheap labor by U.S. employers continues; the employer sanction provisions are ignored; the opportunity for a better life for Latinos and others is easily available; and until reasonable, fair and just policies governing immigration are devised, hopefully in consultation with our neighbors to the south.

One definite consequence of increasing numbers of Latino immigrants is the growing pool of Latinos who are eligible for citizenship. The current general requirements for naturalization include being at least eighteen years of age, living as a legal permanent alien for five years in the United States, having a good moral character, being able to function in English, and demonstrating knowledge of U.S. history and government. Unfortunately for Latinos, the overall pattern has been a relatively low level of naturalization, particularly for Mexican immigrants. Previous research focused on Mexican immigrants has indicated that Mexicans who are proficient in English, who lived in the United States for a longer period of time, who have higher levels of education, and who have higher incomes are more likely to become naturalized (Pachon and DeSipio 1994). The 1990s saw a steady increase in naturalization rates among Latinos. This rise in naturalization rates was the product of many factors, including the INS Green Replacement Program, the approval of Proposition 187 in California, the enactment of the Personal Responsibility and Work Opportunity Act of 1996, and Mexico's approval of dual citizenship (Garcia 2003, 176). Rising numbers of naturalized Latinos should continue, adding a boost to the already growing Latino electorate. Especially promising are the results from recent research, which suggest that voter registration and turnout rates for naturalized citizens do not vary significantly from that of native-born Latinos (Bass and Casper 1999; Valle and Torres 2003), with participation being particularly high among naturalized cohorts who came into the electorate at a time of contentious politics for the Latino community (Barreto et al. 2005).

One of the major messages coming from the immigration activists demonstrating in the spring of 2006 was "Today we march. Tomorrow we vote." Although the long-range effects of immigration politics are not clear, it is certain that they have moved into the mainstream of Latino politics and U.S. politics in general and perhaps eventually even the mainstream itself will be moved.

LATINOS AND FOREIGN POLICY

Until the turn of the twentieth century, Latinos have played a very minor role in foreign policy and international relations (de la Garza and Pachon 2000). This has been due to several factors. One is that Latinos have been a small national minority until recently and consequently have had only minimal political representation, influence, and power at the national level. Foreign policy is strictly the prerogative of the national government. Our state and local governments do not have foreign policy-making powers. Yet, some relatively small ethnic populations in the United States have been quite involved in international relations and national foreign policy making. These have usually taken the effect of pro–home country organizations and lobbies in the United States, which have exerted considerable pressure on the executive branch and the Congress to take particular positions on issues occurring in their homelands. Perhaps the most noticeable in the United States are the pro-Israeli lobbies supported by several Jewish individuals and evangelical Christians and organizations in the United States. In addition, Irish American groups have been quite vocal and somewhat effective in lobbying the U.S. government on matters related to the long continuing struggles between Protestant Northern Ireland and Catholic Ireland. Generally, there have not been effective or even involved Latino foreign lobbies. The one notable exception is the Cuban American lobby, which has been quite successful since the 1960s in having the United States maintain pressure on Cuba and the Castro regime. This has included an embargo of goods, trade, and tourism, which has officially been held very firmly since the 1960s. Although attitudes began to loosen and the embargo restrictions began lifting somewhat in the last years of the Clinton administration, the Republican administration of George W. Bush seemingly once again tightened restrictions on trade and other relationships with Cuba—all in an attempt to expedite the end of the Castro regime. More recently, the U.S. government announced a decision to keep Cuba out of the inaugural World Baseball Classic, citing the standing embargo against the Communist island nation. This was strongly supported by south Florida Cuban Republicans who urged the administration to keep Cuba out of the games.

In general, the attitudes of most Latinos in the United States toward their home country have not included a continuing involvement with the politics or government of those homelands. In fact, many have left countries with governments that have not been supportive of the plight of the common people and have sometimes been quite corrupt. Although many Latino immigrants still hold warm feelings toward their country and the people of their former homelands, this has not generally been carried over into either a pro or con active involvement with the government and politics of these countries. Indeed, most measures of Latino public opinion show that their interest in developing foreign policy lobbies in the United States on behalf of their homelands has been virtually nonexistent. There has been some activity by some of the more activist Mexican American groups to improve relations between Mexico and Mexican Americans, but no Mexican lobby approaching the Israeli or Irish lobby has yet appeared, and it may take awhile for such internationally oriented political activism and organization to develop. Many Puerto Ricans on the mainland maintain a continuing interest in the island's politics and status.

SUMMARY AND CONCLUSION

This chapter examines some of the major issues of greater or lesser concern to Latinos. These complex concerns must be communicated to political decision makers through the political process; that is, they must be placed on the public agenda for debate, study, consideration, and resolution. Most of these issues are of equal concern to Latinos and non-Latinos, although some, particularly those relating to Hispanic culture, including language, are either of more concern to Latinos or are strongly supported by Latinos and substantially opposed by non-Latinos. What happens to these issues, how they are finally resolved, how they are shaped by public debate and exposure by the media, and how political pressures will produce related laws or policies will be greatly affected by Latino involvement in politics. The greater the involvement by Latinos, the more likely it is that these policies will be handled in ways that are most favorable to Latino needs and interests.

Until the twenty-first century, Latinos have had little effect on major legislation at the state and national levels. With the rise in demographic numbers and the notable increase in political influence, if not power, Latinos will have the opportunity to place their concerns on the public agenda and to effectively shape the policy-making process in each policy area. Most likely, issues that directly affect Latinos—that is, issues that are formulated, debated, and implemented at the urban/local and state levels—will be those in which Latinos will have the greatest role and the greatest impact. National and international levels of policy making, perhaps with the exception of such culturally related issues as immigration, will probably be much less affected by Latino politics.

Notes

[1] Information taken from a series of reports conducted by the U.S. Commission on Civil Rights (1971–1974).

[2] See, for example, Belz (1991), Conchas and Goyette (2000), and Davis (1990).

[3] See Rodney Hero's (1992a) *Latinos and the U.S. Political System: Two-Tiered Pluralism.*

[4] The statistics presented here can be found on the American Diabetes Association Web site at https://www.diabetes.org/diabetes-statistics/prevalence.jsp.

[5] The 73.8 percent of Anglos is lower than that of both Mexicans and Puerto Ricans.

13

The Mainstream—Broader, Browner, Better: Summary, Some Observations, and Conclusion

In this book, our intent is to provide a comprehensive overview of Latinos and their relationship to the U.S. political system. Research on Latino politics is still in its early stages, so there is still much room for hypothesizing and speculation. More questions are therefore raised than answered. One goal of this book is to be as objective as possible and to avoid being trapped in any ideological line of thinking other than to search for the truth, present the best available evidence, and allow readers to come to their own conclusions. The only known biases (other than favoring fact-based objectivity whenever possible) have been to avoid any "party line"; to urge the use of reason in attempting to understand the past, present, and future status of Hispanics in U.S. politics; and to support the democratic ideals of the United States, including freedom and equality. Along with the latter is the belief in the ideals of a representative government, fairness, justice, and the inclusiveness of all people who are guaranteed equal respect and treatment and to whom government should be fair and equally responsive.

It should be obvious by now that although Hispanics have been loyal, patriotic, hard working, tax paying residents of the United States for centuries, they have been discriminated against and have not been given equal opportunity. This history has, in turn, created a legacy that still interferes with true Latino inclusion into the political, social, and economic systems of this country. It should also be clear that the twenty-first century is a time of great change for the Hispanic population. Probably as much change will occur in the first two decades of this century as has occurred in the past 200 years. With regard to Hispanics' advancement and integration into all aspects of American life, including politics, it is unclear what the status of Hispanics will be in twenty or even fifty years. However, it is apparent that the trend is positive. Driven by the booming numbers of Latino immigrants, Hispanics have finally been recognized by the major private and public institutions of this country. Documented increases in numbers of Hispanics were most dramatically evidenced by the 2000 U.S. Census, which reported that they were an equal or larger ethnic group than African Americans and that their rate of growth was several times that of African Americans and the general population. Often termed a "sleeping giant," Hispanics as a group appeared to have undergone a great activation. But they were never asleep. They were just not on the radar screen of most Americans, although many suffered serious discrimination during their history that is virtually unknown to the general public. However, the publicity that has been given to the dramatic demographic increase of Hispanics has certainly brought them an increased hope of having a better chance than ever of realizing their full potential. If demography is not destiny for Hispanics, then it certainly is a major, and perhaps critical, factor in Hispanics' increased rate of political visibility and importance in U.S. politics.

We began this book by examining the context of U.S. society in which Latino politics takes place. Political activity, which includes the competition among individuals or groups for governments' attention and governments' approval of a group's agenda, can only be isolated from the rest of society in an artificial way in order to study it and understand it better, but in reality it is completely intertwined with the historical, psychological, sociological, cultural, and economic features of the United States.

Moreover, it has been difficult to generalize about Latino politics because Hispanics may arguably be the most heterogeneous or diverse of all other cognizable ethnic or racial groups in the United States. Latinos come from about two dozen different nations, each of which has its own history, economy, social, and political systems. Each group has had different patterns of migration and encountered different experiences in the United States. Furthermore, national origin and generations are major lines of diversity among the Latino community. But the process is not over. Latinos are continuing to migrate to the United States as some have ever since there was a United States and even for more than a century before that time. This continuing and increasing immigration is one major distinction between the history of Latinos and that of other ethnic groups such as Italian Americans or Jewish Americans. Indeed, there is considerable disagreement as to whether there is a single Latino "community" in the United States. However, the reality of a Latino community increases everyday, as government, the economic sector, and the media continue to refer to and take actions with regard to a group called Latino or Hispanic. Also contributing to the unity of these groups are their combined efforts and activities in politics, as well as generally increasing levels of interaction among them and a heightened awareness of each other.

We have seen that Latinos have been and still are a disadvantaged group. The history of most Latinos has been one that has been marked by exclusion, segregation, discrimination, and unequal opportunities for advancement. Overall, among the various ethnic groups, Latinos remain near the bottom of the socioeconomic ladder. Moreover, it is most likely that Hispanics in general (excluding some celebrities and some material aspects of Latin popular culture) are still viewed negatively and stereotyped in a negative way; that is, they are generally not valued by this society. Given an attitudinal and socioeconomic environment that is not particularly supportive, Hispanics remain not only socioeconomically disadvantaged but also a relatively powerless group. They are underresourced and underrepresented—a group that has less political influence and power than their historical presence, contributions, and numbers warrant.

Hispanics have been loyal to and supportive of the U.S. political system. However, their political interest inputs have been minimal compared to those of most other groups. Some of this has been due to the lack of explicitly political organizations. However, since World War II, and reenergized by the Chicano movement, there is now a plethora of groups advocating for Latino interests, particularly at the local levels, but also to some extent at the state and national levels of government. Increasingly, Latino interest groups are more effectively presenting Latino needs and concerns to governmental decision makers. At this point, Latinos' roles in political parties have not been particularly successful. Attempts at independent parties, such as the Raza Unida Party, have gained some limited local success, helping mobilize the people and serving as symbolic victories. Latinos have not been major players within the national Democratic and Republican parties because the parties have not historically paid much attention to the Latino potential electorate. Increased registration drives and legislation such as the Voting Rights Act of 1965 and its amendments, plus the increasing numbers of Latino residents, did change this situation somewhat at the turn of the twentieth century. Beginning with some efforts in 1990, but much more visibly so in the 2000 and 2004 presidential elections, both parties are making notable efforts to win the support of this ever-expanding electorate. Immigration and higher-than-average birth rates continue to focus attention on the potential for a larger Latino electorate that can significantly affect the parties' futures. Overall, with the notable exception of Cuban Americans, Latinos have been staunch supporters of the Democratic Party, and the Democratic Party has too often taken their support for granted. The other major party, the Republicans, have not been overly concerned with the Latino vote historically, at least since the New Deal era, but in the 1990s, they began to realize that one way to become and remain the majority party would be to make significant inroads into the support of a group that they had either ignored or alienated due to the policies advocated by some of the party leaders. In the early twenty-first century, Latinos find themselves courted increasingly by both major political parties, which gives them additional opportunities to influence the parties' agendas and consequently the parties' positions on various policies.

One measure of the political power of a group is the number of public officials from that group. By this measure, Latinos are relatively powerless. Of the approximately 530,000 elected officials in the United States, only about 1 percent—approximately 5,000—are Latino. Again, there is change in the wind, as this number has continued to increase steadily over the past few decades, and this trend should continue, and perhaps even increase dramatically, throughout the twenty-first century. In fact, it surprised many when research showed that although Latinas have traditionally taken a role that has been offstage, less upfront, and less visible than that of male Hispanics, they have been active players in the politics of the Latino community. They even have a higher proportion of women among Hispanic elected officials than there are proportions of women among all U.S. elected officials. Even though Hispanics have had difficulties developing "external" effective leaders outside their communities, community-based leaders have been quite successful. The dilemma of Hispanic leadership will remain as long as there is a clear demarcation between the subordinate position of Latinos in general and the superordinate or dominant position of non-Hispanic whites. One of the challenges of Latino leadership is to be able to bridge that gap successfully and to provide leadership that earns the support of both Hispanics and non-Hispanics. Similarly, non-Hispanic leaders must realize that the "browning of America" also has great implications for their own support, styles, and activities. Realizing the importance of skilled leadership, there has been a tremendous increase in the number of Hispanic leadership training institutions, seminars, and workshops offered by such groups as the Congressional Hispanic Caucus Institute and National Association of Latino Elected Officials.

One persistent and difficult problem in the area of providing input into government is that of participation. Latino participation has remained stubbornly below that of other groups for many years. This has been particularly true for electoral participation, where the number of eligible and even registered Latinos who actually turn out to vote remains a challenging problem that must be overcome if Latinos are to gain power commensurate with their numbers.

What is it that Latinos desire? What is the objective of increased recognition and representation? Spokespersons, including elected officials and leaders of advocacy organizations, have not hesitated to present their views of the Latino political agenda. However, the recent attention paid to measuring Latino public opinion has given the previously ignored voices of Latinos an alternative way of expressing their concerns and desires. Surprisingly to some, opinion surveys reveal that the Latino political agenda is not much different from that of most Americans. In fact, perhaps Latino objectives can best be expressed as wanting a "fair share" slice of the American pie. That is, they share the American dream of success through hard work, and they desire the best education possible, equal opportunities at job training and at being employed in good jobs with a good possibility of advancement, living in an environment that is free of crime, and being safe and healthy. Latinos are generally inclined to look to government to ensure fair opportunity and to provide a safety net, in an environment that is as free of discrimination and disadvantage as possible. Great strides have been made in the fight against exclusion and discrimination. The historical bias of politics and government favoring white Anglo males has diminished considerably; however, the bias in favor of those individuals and groups who belong to the privileged and wealthy class continues, even in a pluralistic political system.

What is on the "uniquely Latino" political agenda? Generally, Latinos vary only slightly from non-Hispanics of similar economic position in what they want from governmental policy making. These generally relate to cultural matters, such as the protection and promotion of the Spanish language as perhaps the most significant embodiment of the Latino culture. Antidiscrimination policies must also be continued, safeguarded, and strengthened. Institutional bias continues to be a problem working to the disadvantage of Latinos, and new approaches to affirmative action programs must be devised to provide effective countervailing biases. The greatest challenges will be generated in the areas related to immigration. The United States must place this issue high on the agenda of national policies. Immigrants, the largest number being from Latin America, are changing U.S. society in manifold ways; as a result, means must be found to accommodate and incorporate these new residents into our society and our political system in the most appropriate and beneficial ways.

Although we have generally spoken about Latinos at the national level of government, because this level of government receives the most publicity, it is actually at the state level, and even more at the local levels, that politics will have their greatest effects on the everyday lives of the Latino people. It is beyond the scope of this book to fully present the multiplicity of political activities that have occurred in the local communities, where the most significant numbers of Latinos reside, but this is where much of the action has taken place and will continue to do so. Certainly, this can be seen in the large metropolitan areas, which have large populations of Latinos, such as New York, Los Angeles, Chicago, and Houston. In fact, Latinos have already become mayors and have gained other high public positions both at the state and local levels in areas where there have never before been such successes. Latinos are also noticeably but incrementally gaining public office in towns and counties throughout the South, the Midwest, and New England. As Latinos increasingly disperse throughout the United States in significant numbers, more political activity will occur at the local level in the counties, townships, cities, villages, and school districts as Latinos press for increased representation and responsiveness to their policy needs. The resulting debates over immigration, bilingual education, and language policy continue to become more prominent. Latinos will be even more involved as influential players in the debates over these policies, and their inclusion will mean that the policies that do emerge will be more representative of the population of this country.

Perhaps Latinos, particularly Mexican Americans, will begin to play a more important role in U.S. foreign policy toward Latin America, and in particular, Mexico. Certainly, debate over issues such as immigration is healthy for the United State because this is one public policy area that has been grossly underdeveloped. Development of such a policy requires high-quality, unbiased research and expert analysis, as well as a consequent thorough rethinking and evaluation by both policy makers and the public.

What about the future of Latino politics in the United States? It is always risky to venture into forecasts about the future but difficult to resist speculation. However, speculation based on projections of the matters discussed in this book can help clarify what exists now and what outcomes are most likely forthcoming from a political system that includes Latinos as important players in the American political process. Any forecast has to be positive based on several factors. The future depends, of course, not only on what Hispanic Americans do but perhaps, more importantly, also on the actions and reactions of the rest of American society, particularly those who currently hold the powerful positions in our major institutions. Given this major condition, the direction of the political forecast looks positive but the slope appears gradually upward, and one can be fairly optimistic about Latinos' political futures for several reasons. As most political observers would agree, the American system does allow for advancement, and it is basically pluralistic. However, in general, it still remains heavily biased in favoring those of higher socioeconomic status and members of the majority non-Hispanic white culture, as well as, to a lesser extent, those who are males. It is certainly not as open as some of the pluralists have contended, but neither is it as closed to "minority" groups as some of the more radical interpretations would hold. Even though the internal colonial model of closed, elite control offers some historical insights that are useful in explaining various aspects of the political legacy of Latinos, there are too many current circumstances that do not square with this model to accept it as the most accurate analytic perspective. Persons interested in Latino politics must try to look clearly and objectively at the facts, at the reality of the situation, and remain free from prejudices and ideologic blinders. In doing so, one can reasonably conclude that, if things continue on the current track for Hispanic Americans, at some point in the future—however distant that future—Hispanics will approach parity, as well as full acceptance and integration into the political system. They are rapidly becoming part of the American mainstream culturally, socially, and, albeit less rapidly, even economically. Hispanic Americans will not only move into the mainstream of American politics, but it is also likely that they will change and move the mainstream in slightly new directions. As America becomes more Latinized, the main-stream will become more multicultural and diverse. The nation's politics should reflect this, although more slowly and to a lesser extent than other spheres of human activity due to the basic biases in the allocation of power that have persisted throughout U.S. history.

Perhaps it is appropriate here to call attention to the following univer-sal phenomenon, one that is often overlooked or ignored in discussions of Latinos in U.S. politics. With all the talk of the demographic explosion of Latinos and the "browning of America," or the Latinization of this country, only one side of a genuine process of mutual accommodation is emphasized. When cultures meet, particularly in a mostly open and free society, the manifestations of those cultures interact with one another, blending, merging, churning, and producing something new in each of the cultures involved. In more specific terms, migrants from Latin America cannot help but become acculturated in many ways to the dominant U.S. mainstream culture, including its politics, and will likely become Latinos who are quite different from Mexicans, Cubans, Puerto Ricans, Salvado-rans, and Dominicans. At the same time, the American culture, which already has become a major amalgam of many distinctive nationalities and cultures throughout its history, is itself changed as each culture inter-mixes with the elements that are already in this country. It is inevitable with this inexorable churning of different cultures that Latinos will in-creasingly look, behave, and think more like mainstream Americans, but it is important to point out that mainstream America also will be changing, literally from day to day, toward a new more multicultural society, made of a different blend. Such interaction between two cultures is definitely a two-way street leading to a brand new destination. The old "melting pot" analogy does not work because immigrant nationalities and immigrant cultures maintain some of their cultural characteristics throughout the years and even throughout generations. This will probably be even more the case for Latinos whose homeland culture is close by geographically and is constantly being replenished by immigrants from the ancestral homeland. Some manifestations of Latin American culture will undoubt-edly continue to persist in the United States. However, as Latinos remain here generation after generation, they will become increasingly like the new amalgam of Americans.

As the melting pot idea has been largely discredited, so should the old "Anglo conformity model." The core culture in the United States has long since ceased to be an English or even a northwestern European culture, if indeed it ever was one. Contact with the indigenous inhabitants, succeed-ing waves of immigration, and the forced importation of slaves have pro-duced a new American core culture. Of course, change often occurs in one direction more than another, and usually the culture that controls the major institutions—political, social, economic, and religious; the media;

and politics and government—will have a greater impact on the incoming culture than the other way around. Nevertheless, one only needs to be observant to notice, for example, how much U.S. culture is permeated and imbued with Hispanic and indigenous cultural items. The Spanish language, particularly in names, words, and phrases, is heard across the United States. Hispanic cultural foods are in restaurants from Boston to Seattle and from Atlanta to Salt Lake City. Music, art, literature, and other manifestations of Latino culture also permeate this society. We do not want to belabor the point, but it is one that seems so evident and yet is so often overlooked.

In fact, the people themselves are merging. Intermarriage rates are high, particularly between Latinos and non-Hispanic whites, and continue to increase as we enter the twenty-first century. The 2000 U.S. Census just began to document how many people are recognizing and claiming their multiracial and multiethnic heritage. It is not impossible to conceive that in future generations in the United States such distinctions as ethnicity, and perhaps even race, may become archaic if not obsolete.

But what does this have to do with politics? What effect does this mutual cultural accommodation, blending, and moving of the mainstream have to do with politics? Is American politics changing Latinos? Or are Latinos changing American politics? The answer to both questions is probably in the affirmative. However, the changes in the political system are probably fewer than in the social and cultural spheres. U.S. politics have changed Latinos because U.S. politics deals with power, and throughout history, Latinos have been largely excluded from political power and have had relatively little influence. Hispanics in the United States have mainly been cast in the role of subjects, not rulers. So, in politics, in particular, the flow of influence and power has been strongly in one direction. Previously, we briefly discussed the socialization of Latinos by such agencies as the American public schools, which are governmental agencies, and by government and politics directly. Certainly, our major political institutions are less multicultural and are more Anglo biased than are many of our other institutions and processes in the United States. Our constitutional system is basically a northern and western European construct, both philosophically and institutionally. This includes both the legal and the political systems. As Latinos have increasingly either forced their way into politics where there has been resistance or have been courted and encouraged to participate, it has been pretty much on terms and inline with existing institutions and practices. The major exception in several ways was the Chicano movement. Some aspects of *el movimiento* included drives for the establishment of separate parallel or even counterinstitutions. Yet, one could reasonably hold that its major successes were in the area of incorporation into and modifications of extant institutions rather than their replacement. For example, the two major political parties have continued to remain in control throughout history with rare periods of exception. Interest groups and pressure organizations, particularly those underwritten by abundant financial resources, continue to operate as they have for many years, although perhaps more effectively and influentially than ever before. The executive branch is cast in the form of bureaucracy that stems from European traditions, most notably as exemplified by the German philosopher Max Weber. Our legislatures' having an upper and a lower house reflect European forms of government, and theories of representation are also based on European philosophy. The Declaration of Independence is a reflection of the European "social contract" theories of eighteenth-century European philosophers, including its ideals of individual liberty and freedom and the relationship between a limited government and those liberties. The rule of law prevails, and the U.S. judicial system is based on the common law tradition of Britain rather than on European continental law or the governing norms of other regions of the world. These basic institutions and philosophies not only have remained the same in their basic natures throughout our history, but they have also been replicated in each of the fifty states and in many local governments. Indeed, even many of the Native American tribes have adopted, or had forced on them, constitutions and constitutional principals brought to them by the conquering European settlers. By and large, this system, with all its imperfections, has worked as well or better than most others throughout the world, especially when its operational realities have lived up to its ideals.

It would be difficult for Latinos to change the American political system, including its entire apparatus—its philosophies, its institutions, its operating principles, its organizations and its processes, and there is little evidence that this is desired by Hispanics. Very few Latinos leave the United States in protest, and many have come and continue to come to this country seeking inclusion and improvement of their lives. Of course, there have been and will continue to be Latino radicals who search for new political paradigms and philosophies that would be foreign, unusual, and therefore "radical" to the U.S. political system. But even these are usually in reaction not to the philosophy and ideals of a pluralistic democracy, but as a reaction to the faulty operation of the system—that is, when the reality does not live up to the American ethos. As we have seen, there is little evidence that radical changes of any sort will occur in the U.S. political system simply due to the increase in participation by Latinos, women, or any other group. At best, Latinos would bring some of their more desirable cultural values to politics, such as the Hispanic values of cooperation and communitarianism, which might somewhat soften the hard edges of Anglo competition and individualism. Perhaps the incorporation of people who are often distinctive in their appearance (and perhaps also in some subtle aspects of their behavior) will help further open the system, making it more accessible to a wider spectrum of citizens of the United States. It may become more inclusive of different cultural groups, as well as represent a greater range of other demographic characteristics, such as gender, economic class, and occupation. In addition, the public agenda will have amended some additional policy issues related to Hispanic culture and to immigration from Latin America. Even though these and other mild effects may occur, most likely the U.S. political system's basic economic and social premises, institutions, and other foundations will prevent major morphing of the U.S. political process. But even if major political institutional change is minimal, at least Hispanic Americans will continue to move much closer to being first-class citizens, enjoying the opportunities that other Americans enjoy and ensuring that their interests, concerns, and preferences are heard, represented, and given due consideration in the policy-making process. In addition, chances are that as time goes by and progress continues, Latinos will approach parity with non-Hispanic whites, even though generations may pass before this is achieved. What happens to immigration patterns and the way that the system reacts will have a major effect on these outcomes.

Regardless of the exact specifics of what happens to Latinos and their relationship to U.S. politics in the future, demographic and economic changes that are occurring not only in the United States but also globally will set other changes in motion that will not likely be halted. However, most likely, Latinos are on their way to becoming full participants, with all the good and bad that implies, in the U.S. political system. Therefore, one can conclude that Hispanics are at least moving *into* the American mainstream, and only the future will reveal how much Latinos are actually moving the American political-governmental mainstream. Given the overall achievements over the course of U.S. history, any such movement would most likely serve to make it broader, fairer, and more inclusive—in short, more democratic—rather than making any major changes in its direction.

References

Abalos, David T. 1986. *Latinos in the United States: The Sacred and the Political.* Notre Dame, IN: University of Notre Dame Press.

Acuna, Rodolfo. 2003. *Occupied America: The Chicano's Struggle toward Liberation.* 5th ed. New York: Longman Press.

Alcalay, R., M. Alvarado, H. Balcazar, E. Newman, and E. Huerta. 1999. "Salud para su Corazon: A Community-Based Latino Cardiovascular Disease Prevention and Outreach Model." *Journal of Community Health* 24(5):359–79.

All-Politics. 2000. *Exit Polls from 2000 Presidential Elections.* Atlanta: Cable News Network.

Almond, Gabriel Abraham, and Sidney Verba. 1963. *The Civic Culture: Political Attitudes and Democracy in Five Nations.* Newbury Park, CA: Sage.

Alvarez, R. Michael, and John Brehm. 2002. *Hard Choices, Easy Answers.* Princeton, NJ: Princeton University Press.

Alvarez, R. Michael, and Lisa Garcia-Bedolla. 2003. "The Foundations of Latino Voter Partisanship: Evidence from the 2000 Election." *Journal of Politics* 65:31–49.

American Diabetes Association. "Total Prevalence of Diabetes & Pre-diabetes." Available at https://www.diabetes.org/diabetes-statistics/prevalence.jsp, accessed April 22, 2007.

Andrade, Juan. 2003. "Waking the Giant." *Diversity Journal* 5(5):1–4.

Arce, Carlos H. 1979. *Mexican Origin People in the United States: The Chicano Survey.* Ann Arbor: University of Michigan, Survey Research Center, Inter-university Consortium for Political and Social Research.

Austin, Sharon, D. Wright, and Richard T. Middleton IV. 2004. "The Limitations of the Deracialization Concept in the 2001 Los Angeles Mayoral Election." *Political Research* 57:283–93.

Barabak, Mark Z. 2005, September 15. "Latinos Souring on Gov. and His Party." *Los Angeles Times* B1.

Bardes, Barbara, and Robert Oldendick. 2007. *Public Opinion: Measuring the American Mind.* 3rd ed. Belmont, CA: Thomson Wadsworth.

Barrera, Mario. 1979. *Race and Class in the Southwest.* Notre Dame, IN: University of Notre Dame Press.

Barrera, Mario, Carlos Muñoz, Jr., and Charles Órnelas. 1972. "The Barrio as an Internal Colony." In Harían Hahn (ed), *People and Politics in Urban Society* (pp. 465–98). Los Angeles: Sage.

Barreto, Matt, Rodolfo Espino, Adrian Pantoja, and Ricardo Ramirez. 2003. "Selective Recruitment or Empowered Communities? The Effects of Descriptive Representation on Latino Voter Mobilization." Paper presented at the annual meeting of the American Political Science Association, Philadelphia, August 31–September 3, 2003.

Barreto, Matt, and Jose Muñoz. 2003. "Reexamining the 'Politics of In-Between': Political Participation among Mexican Immigrants in the United States." *Hispanic Journal of Behavioral Sciences* 25(4):427–47.

Barreto, Matt, Ricardo Ramírez, and Nathan Woods. 2005. "Are Naturalized Voters Driving the California Latino Electorate? Measuring the Impact of IRCA Citizens on Latino Voting." *Social Science Quarterly* 86:792–811.

Barreto, Matt, Gary Segura, and Nathan Woods. 2004. "The Mobilizing Effect of Majority-Minority Districts on Latino Turnout." *American Political Science Review* 98(1):65–75.

Barreto, Matt, and David Leal. 2007. "Latinos, Military Service, and Support for Bush and Kerry in 2004." *American Politics Research* 35:224–51.

Bartels, Larry. 2000."Partisanship and Voting Behavior, 1952–1996." *American Journal of Political Science* 44:35–50.

Barvosa-Carter, Edwina. 1999. "Multiple Identity and Coalition Building: How Identity Differences Within Us Enable Radical Alliances among Us." *Contemporary Justice Review* 2:111–26.

Bass, Loretta, and Lynne Casper. 1999. "Are There Differences in Registration and Voting Behavior between Naturalized and Native-Born Americans?" Population Division Working Paper No. 28. Washington, DC: U.S. Bureau of the Census.

Bean, Frank, and Gillian Stevens. 2003. *America's Newcomers and the Dynamics of Diversity*. New York: Russell Sage Foundation.

Bean, Frank, Stephen Trejo, Randy Capps, and Michael Tyler. 2001, April. "The Latino Middle Class: Myth, Potential, and Reality." Tomás Rivera Policy Institute Report. Los Angeles: Tomas Rivera Policy Institute, University of Southern California, Los Angeles. Available at http://www.trpi.org/update/economics.html, accessed April 22, 2007.

Becerra, Alejandra, and Ron Jauregui. 2005. "An Assessment of Hispanic Homeownership: Trends and Opportunities." Washington, DC: Congressional Hispanic Caucus Institute. Available at www.chci.org/nhi/32655_Needs Assessment.pdf, accessed April 22, 2007.

Belz, Herman. 1991. *Equality Transformed: A Quarter Century of Affirmative Action*. New Brunswick, NJ: Transaction.

Berman, Larry, and Bruce Allen Murphy. 2005. *Approaching Democracy*. 4th ed. Upper Saddle River, NJ: Prentice Hall.

Binder, Norman E., J.L. Polinard, and Robert D. Wrinkle. 1997. "Mexican American and Anglo Attitudes toward Immigration Reform: A View from the Border." *Social Science Quarterly* 78:324–37.

Blauner, Robert. 1969. "Internal Colonialism and the Ghetto Revolt." *Social Problems* 16:393–408.

Blawis, Patricia Bell. 1971. *Tijerina and the Land Grants: Mexican Americans in Struggle for Their Heritage*. New York: International.

Board of Education of Oklahoma City v. Dowell (1991), 498 U.S. 237.

Bowler, Shaun, Stephen Nicholson, and Gary Segura. 2006. "Earthquakes and Aftershocks: Tracking Partisan Identification amid California's Changing Political Environment." *American Journal of Political Science* 50(1):146–59.

Bratton, Kathleen A. 2006. "The Behavior and Success of Latino Legislators: Evidence from the States." *Social Science Quarterly* 87:1136–58.

Brischetto, Robert R. 1998. "Latino Voters and Redistricting in the New Millennium." In David A. Bositis (ed), *Redistricting and Minority Representation:*

Learning from the Past, Preparing for the Future (pp. XXX–XXX). Washington, DC: Joint Center for Political and Economic Studies.

Brook Larmer. 1999, July 12. "Hispanics Are Hip, Hot and Making History," *Newsweek* 48.

Brown v. Board of Education of Topeka (1954), 347 U.S. 483.

Brown, Richard E., V. Ojeda, R. Wyn, and R. Levan. 2000. *Racial and Ethnic Disparities in Access to Health Insurance and Health Care*. Los Angeles: UCLA Center for Health Policy Research and Henry J. Kaiser Family Foundation.

Brown, Richard E., R. Wyn, and S. Teleki. 2000. *Disparities in Health Insurance and Access to Care for Residents across American Cities*. Los Angeles: The Commonwealth Fund and the UCLA Center for Health Policy Research.

Brown, Richard E., and Hongjian Yu. 2002. "Latino Access to Employment-Based Health Insurance." In Marcelo M. Suarez-Orozco and Mariela M. Paez (eds), *Latinos: Remaking America* (pp. 236–53). Berkeley: University of California Press.

Browning, Rufus, Dale Marshall, and David Tabb. 1984. *Protest Is Not Enough: The Struggle of Blacks and Hispanics for Equality in Urban Politics*. Berkeley: University of California Press.

Burgos, A. E., K. E. Schetzina, L. B. Dixon, and F. S. Mendoza. 2005. "Importance of Generational Status in Examining Access to and Utilization of Health Care Services by Mexican American Children." *Pediatrics* 115(3):322–30.

Buriel, Raymond. 1987. "Ethnic Labeling and Identity among Mexican Americans." In J. S. Phinney and M. J. Rotheram (eds), *Children's Ethnic Socialization: Pluralism and Development* (pp. 134–52). Newbury Park, CA: Sage.

Bush v. Vera (1996), WL 315857.

Cain, Bruce E., and D. Roderick Kiewiet. 1987. "Latinos and the 1984 Election: A Comparative Perspective." In Rodolfo de la Garza (ed), *Ignored Voices: Public Opinion Polls and the Latino Community* (pp. 47–62). Austin, TX: Center for Mexican American Studies Publications.

Cain, Bruce E., D. Roderick Kiewiet, and Carole J. Uhlaner. 1991. "The Acquisition of Partisanship by Latinos and Asian Americans." *American Journal of Political Science* 35:390–422.

Cameron, Charles, David Epstein, and Sharon O'Halloran. 1996. "Do Majority-Minority Districts Maximize Substantive Black Representation in Congress?" *American Political Science Review* 90:794–812.

Campbell, Angus, Phillip E. Converse, Warren E. Miller, and Donald E. Stokes. 1960. *The American Voter*. Chicago: University of Chicago Press.

Carmichael, Stokely, and Charles Hamilton. 1967. *Black Power: Politics of Liberation in America*. New York: Vintage.

Carrigan, William D., and Clive Webb. 2003. "The Lynching of Persons of Mexican Origin or Descent in the US, 1848–1929." *Journal of Social History* Winter:1–11.

Carter, Thomas P. 1970. *Mexican Americans in School: A History of Educational Neglect*. New York: College Entrance Examination Board.

Center for Voting and Democracy. 2003. "State Legislatures, 2003: Combined Percentages." Available at www.fairvote.org/vra/stateleg2003.htm, accessed April 22, 2007.

Center for Women in Government and Civil Society. 2005 *Democracy Unrealized: The Under-Representation of People of Color as Appointed Policy Leaders in State Governments*. Albany: State University of New York.

Chávez, Maria Luisa. 2004. "Overview." In Sharon Navarro and Armando Mejia (eds), *Latino Americans and Political Participation* (pp. 1–56). Santa Barbara, CA: ABC-CLIO.

Chávez, Tom E. 2002. *Spain and the Independence of the United States: An Intrinsic Gift*. Albuquerque: The University of New Mexico Press.

Citrin, Jack, Amy Lerman, Michael Murakami, and Karthryn Pearson. 2007. "Testing Huntington: Is Hispanic Immigration a Threat to American Identity?" *Perspectives on Politics* 5(1):31–48.

City of Mobile v. Bolden (1980), 446 US 55.

Claassen, Ryan L. "Political Opinion and Distinctiveness: The Case of Hispanic Ethnicity." *Political Research Quarterly* 57(4):609–20.

Conchas, Gilberto, and Kimberly Goyette. 2000. "The Race Is Not Even: Minority Education in a Post-Affirmative Action Era." *Harvard Journal of Hispanic Policy* 71(3):5–20.

Congressional Hispanic Caucus Institute (CHCI). 2004, June. "Focus Group Findings: Cross-Site Report." Washington, DC: CHCI. Available at www.chci.org/nhi/Focus.pdf, accessed April 22, 2007.

Connelly, Marjorie. 2006, April 14. "In Polls, Illegal Immigrants Are Called Burden." *New York Times* A16.

Converse, Philip E. 1964. "The Nature of Belief Systems in Mass Publics." In David Apter (ed), *Ideology and Discontent* (pp. 206–61). New York: Free Press.

Cooper, P., and B. Schone. 1997. "More Offers, Fewer Takers for Employment-Based Health Insurance: 1987 and 1996." *Health Affairs* 16(6):142–9.

Cordova, Teresa. 1999. "Harold Washington and the Rise of Latino Politics in Chicago, 1982–1987." In David Montejano (ed), *Chicano Politics and Society in the Late Twentieth Century* (pp. 31–57). Austin: University of Texas Press.

Corona, Bert. 1971. *MAPA and La Raza Unida Party: A Program for Chicano Political Action for the 1970's*. National City, CA: La Raza Unida Party.

Cortes, Ernesto. 1996. "What About Organizing?" *Boston Review* 21(6). Available at http://bostonreview.net/BR21.6/cortes.html, accessed April 22, 2007.

Craig, Stephen, Richard Niemi, and Glenn Silver. 1990. "Political Efficacy and Trust: A Report on the NES Pilot Study Items." *Political Behavior* 12:289–314.

Cruz, Jose. 1998. *Identity and Power: Puerto Rican Politics and Challenges of Ethnicity*. Philadelphia: Temple University Press.

Dahl, Robert. 1957. "The Concept of Power." *Behavioral Science* 2:201–5.

Davidson, Chandler, and George Korbel. 1981. "At Large Elections and Minority-Group Representation: A Re-Examination of Historical and Contemporary Evidence." *Journal of Politics* 43(4):982–1005.

Davis, Hugh. 1990. *The Civil Rights Era: Origins and Development of National Policy, 1960–1972*. New York: Oxford University Press.

Dawson, Michael C. 1994. *Behind the Mule: Race and Class in African-American Politics*. Princeton, NJ: Princeton University Press.

Dawson, Richard E., Kenneth Prewitt, and Karen S. Dawson. 1977. *Political Socialization*. 2nd ed. Boston: Little, Brown and Company.

de la Garza, Rodolfo O., ed. 1987. *Ignored Voices: Public Opinion Polls and the Latino Community in the United States*. Austin: Center for Mexican American Studies, University of Texas at Austin.

de la Garza, Rodolfo O. 1998. "Interests Not Passions: Mexican American Attitudes Toward Mexico, Immigration from Mexico, and Other Issues Shaping U.S.-Mexico Relations." *International Migration Review* 32(2):401–23.

de la Garza, Rodolfo O., and Louis DeSipio. 1997. "Save the Baby, Change the Bathwater, and Scrub the Tub: Latino Electoral Participation after Twenty Years of Voting Rights Act Coverage." In F. Chris Garcia (ed), *Pursuing Power: Latinos and the Political System* (pp. 72–126). Notre Dame, IN: University of Notre Dame Press.

de la Garza, Rodolfo, and Louis DeSipio, eds. 2004. *Muted Voices: Latinos and the 2000 Elections.* Lanham, MD: Rowman & Littlefield.

de la Garza, Rodolfo O., Louis DeSipio, F. Chris Garcia, John A. García, and Angelo Falcón. 1992. *Latino Voices: Mexican, Puerto Rican and Cuban Perspectives on American Politics.* Boulder, CO: Westview Press.

de la Garza, Rodolfo, Angelo Falcón, and F. Chris Garcia. 1996. "Will The Real Americans Please Stand Up: Anglo and Mexican American Support for Core American Political Values." *American Journal of Political Science* 40(2):335–51.

de la Garza, Rodolfo, Angelo Falcón, F. Chris Garcia, and John A. Garcia. 1990. *Latino National Political Survey 1989–1990.* Philadelphia: Temple University.

de la Garza, Rodolfo O., Z. Anthony Kruszewski, and Tomas A. Arciniega, eds. 1973. *Chicanos and Native Americans: The Territorial Minorities.* Englewood Cliffs, NJ: Prentice-Hall.

de la Garza, Rodolfo, and Harry H. Pachon. 2000. *Latinos and Foreign Policy: Representing the Homeland.* Lanham, MD: Rowman & Littlefield.

de la Garza, Rodolfo, and David Vaughan. 1984. "The Political Socialization of Chicano Elites: A Generational Approach." *Social Science Quarterly* 65(2):290–307.

de los Angeles Torres, Maria. 1999. *In the Land of Mirrors: Cuban Exile Politics in the United States.* Ann Arbor: University of Michigan Press.

Delli Carpini, Michael X., and Scott Keeter. 1993. "Measuring Political Knowledge: Putting Things First." *American Journal of Political Science* 37:1179–206.

DeSipio, Louis. 1996. *Counting on the Latino Vote: Latinos as a New Electorate.* Charlottesville: University of Virginia Press.

DeSipio, Louis, and Rodolfo O. de la Garza. 1998. *Making Americans, Remaking America: Immigration and Immigrant Policy.* Boulder, CO: Westview Press.

DeSipio, Louis, and Carole Jean Uhlaner. 2007. "Immigrant and Native Mexican American Presidential Vote Choice across Immigrant Generations." *American Politics Research* 35:176–201.

Diaz, William A. 1996. "Latino Participation in America: Associational and Political Roles." *Hispanic Journal of Behavioral Science* 18:154–74.

Durose, Matthew R., Erica L. Smith, and Patrick A. Langan. 2007. *Contacts Between the Police and the Public, 2005.* Washington, DC: U.S. Department of Justice.

Dunne, John Gregory. 1971. *Delano.* New York: Farrar, Straus and Giroux.

Dye, Thomas R. 1992. *Understanding Public Policy.* 7th ed. Englewood Cliffs, NJ: Prentice-Hall.

Easton, David. 1953. *The Political System: An Inquiry into the State of Political Science.* New York: Alfred A. Knopf.

Easton, David. 1965. *A Systems Analysis of Political Life.* New York: John Wiley & Sons.

Estrada, Leobardo, F. Chris Garcia, Reynaldo Flores Macias, and Lionel Maldonado. 1981. "Chicanos in the United States: A History of Exploitation and Resistance." *Daedalus* 110(2):103–31.

Fagen, Richard R., Richard A. Brody, and Thomas J. O'Leary. 1968. *Cubans in Exile: Dissatisfaction and the Revolution*. Stanford, CA: Stanford University Press.

Falcón, Angelo. 1988. "Black and Latino Politics in New York City: Race and Ethnicity." In F. Chris Garcia (ed), *Latinos and the Political System* (pp. 171–94). Notre Dame, IN: Notre Dame University Press.

Falcón, Angelo. 2002. *Opening the Courthouse Doors: The Need for More Hispanic Judges*. New York: Puerto Rican Legal Defense and Education Fund.

Falcón, Angelo, and J. Santiago, eds. 1993. *Race, Ethnicity, and Redistricting in New York City: The Garner Report and Its Critics*. IPR Policy Forums Proceedings. New York: Institute for Puerto Rican Policy.

Farrington, Brendan. 2001, September 16. "Non-Cuban Hispanics Making Their Mark on Miami." *Houston Chronicle* 39.

Fiorina, Morris P. 1981. *Retrospective Voting in American National Elections*. New Haven, CT: Yale University Press.

Fox, Susannah, and Gretchen Livingston. 2007, March 14. "Latinos Online." Pew Hispanic Center and Pew Internet Project. Available at http://www.pewinternet.org/pdfs/Latinos_Online_March_14_2007.pdf, accessed on April 22, 2007.

Fraga, Luis Ricardo, Kenneth J. Meier, and Robert E. England. 1986. "Hispanic Americans and Educational Policy: Limits to Equal Access." *Journal of Politics* 48:850–76.

Fritz, Sara, and Dwight Morris. 1992. *Handbook of Campaign Spending*. Washington, DC: Congressional Quarterly Press.

Fry, Richard. 2002, September 5. "Latinos in Higher Education: Many Enroll, Too Few Graduate." Pew Hispanic Center Report. Available at http://pewhispanic.org/files/reports/11.pdf, accessed April 22, 2007.

Fry, Richard. 2005, November 1. "The Higher Dropout Rate of Foreign-born Teens: The Role of Schooling Abroad." Pew Hispanic Center Report. Available at http://pewhispanic.org/files/reports/55.pdf, accessed April 22, 2007.

Gaoette, Nicole. 2006, November 23. "Still No Slam Dunk on an Immigration Bill." *Los Angeles Times* A24.

Garcia, F. Chris. 1973. *The Political Socialization of Chicano Children*. New York: Praeger.

Garcia, F. Chris. 1995, August. "Mexican American Values in the U.S. Southwest." Research Monograph No. 106. Albuquerque: University of New Mexico, Center for Regional Studies/Southwest Hispanic Research Institute.

Garcia, F. Chris. 1997. "Latinos and the Affirmative Action Debate: Wedge or Coalition Issue?" In F. Chris Garcia (ed), *Pursuing Power: Latinos and the Political System* (pp. 368–400). Notre Dame, IN: Notre Dame Press.

Garcia, F. Chris, and Christine Sierra. 2004. "New Mexico Hispanos in the 2000 General Elections." In Rodolfo O. de la Garza and Louis DeSipio (eds), *Muted Voices: Latinos and the 2000 Elections* (pp. 101–29). Lanham, MD: Rowman & Littlefield.

Garcia, John. 1995. "A Multicultural-America: Living in a Sea of Diversity." In D. Harris (ed), *Multiculturalism at the Margins: No Dominant Voices on Differences and Diversity* (pp. 29–38). Westport, CT: Bergen & Garvey.

Garcia, John. 1997. "Political Participation: Resources and Involvement among Latinos in the American Political System." In F. Chris Garcia (ed), *Pursuing Power: Latinos and the Political System* (pp. 44–71). Notre Dame, IN: University of Notre Dame Press.

Garcia, John. 2003. *Latino Politics in America: Community, Culture, and Interests*. Lanham, MD: Rowman & Littlefield.

Garcia, John, and Carlos Arce. 1988. "Political Orientations and Behavior of Chicanos." In F. Chris Garcia (ed), *Latinos and the Political System* (pp. 125–51). Notre Dame, IN: University of Notre Dame Press.

Garcia, John, and Gabriel Sanchez. 2004. "With the Spotlight on Latinos, Examining Their Political Participation in the United States." In S. Navarro and A. Mejia (eds), *Latino Political Participation in the Next Millennium* (pp. 121–72). Santa Barbara, CA: ABC-CLIO.

Garcia, Ignacio M. 1989. *United We Win: The Rise and Fall of La Raza Unida Party*. Tucson: Mexican American Study and Research Center, University of Arizona.

Garcia, Mario T. 1998. *The Making of a Mexican American Mayor: Raymond L. Telles of El Paso*. El Paso: Texas Western Press, University of Texas at El Paso.

García-Bedolla, L. 2005. *Fluid Borders: Latino Power, Identity and Politics in Los Angeles*. Berkeley: University of California Press.

Gardner, Richard. 1970. *Grito: Reies Tijerina and the New Mexico Land Grant War of 1967*. New York: Bobbs-Merrill.

Garza v. County of Los Angeles (1990), 918 F.2d 763 (9th Cir.).

Gay, Claudine. 2001. *The Effect of Minority Districts and Minority Representation on Political Participation in California*. San Francisco: Public Policy Institute of California.

Gay, Claudine. 2002. "Spirals of Trust: The Effect of Descriptive Representation on the Relationship between Citizens and Their Government." *American Journal of Political Science* 46(4):717–32.

Geron, Kim. 2005. *Latino Political Power*. Boulder, CO: Lynne Rienner.

Gilliam, Frank. 1996. "Exploring Minority Empowerment: Symbolic Politics, Governing Coalitions and Traces of Political Style in Los Angeles." *American Journal of Political Science* 40:56–81.

Gomez-Quinones, Juan. 1990. *Chicano Politics: Reality and Promise, 1940–1990*. Albuquerque: University of New Mexico Press.

Gonzales, Juan. 2000. *Harvest of Empire: A History of Latinos in America*. New York: Penguin Putnam.

Gonzales, Manuel G. 1999. *Mexicanos: A History of Mexicans in the United States*. Bloomington: University of Indiana Press.

Granados, Christine. 2000, December. "'Hispanic' vs 'Latino.'" *Hispanic Magazine*. Available at http://www.hispaniconline.com/hh/hisp_vs_lat.html, accessed April 22, 2007.

Granados, Christine. 2000, May. "Born Again Latinos." *Hispanic Magazine*. Available at http://www.hispaniconline.com/hh05/best_of/bo_bal.html, accessed April 22, 2007.

Granados, Christine. 2003, November 5. "Latino Culture Sweeps across U.S." BBC News.

Gratz v. Bollinger (2003), 539 U.S. 244.

Grebler, L., J. Moore, and R. Guzman. 1970. *The Mexican American People: The Nation's Second Largest Minority*. New York: Free Press.

Grenier, Guillermo, and Lisandro Perez. 2003. *The Legacy of Exile: Cubans in the United States*. Boston: Allyn & Bacon.

Grieco, Elizabeth M., and Rachel C. Cassidy. 2001, March. "Overview of Race and Hispanic Origin 2000." Census 2000 Brief. U.S. Census Bureau, U.S. Department of Commerce. Available at http://www.census.gov/prod/2001pubs/c2kbr01-1.pdf, accessed April 22, 2007.

Griswold del Castillo, Richard. 1995. *César Chávez: A Triumph of Spirit.* Norman: University of Oklahoma Press.

Gruber, Amelia. 2007, February 15. "Hispanic Representation in Government Rises—Barely." Daily Briefing on GOVEXEC.com. Available at http://www.govexec.com/dailyfed/0207/021507a1.htm, accessed April 22, 2007.

Grutter v. Bollinger (2003), 539 U.S. 306.

Gutiérrez, José Ángel. 1998. *The Making of a Chicano Militant: Lessons from Cristal.* Madison: University of Wisconsin Press.

Guzmán, Betsy. 2001, May. "The Hispanic Population: 2000." Census 2000 Brief. U.S. Census Bureau, U.S. Department of Commerce. Available at http://www.census.gov/prod/2001pubs/c2kbr01-3.pdf, accessed April 22, 2007.

Hardy-Fanta, Carol. 1993. *Latina Politics, Latino Politics: Gender, Culture, and Political Participation in Boston.* Philadelphia: Temple University Press.

Hajnal, Zoltan. 2004. "Latino Independents and Identity Formation under Uncertainty." The Center for Comparative Immigration Studies Working Paper. San Diego: University of California.

Hayes-Bautista, David E. 2002. "The Latino Health Research Agenda for the Twenty-first Century." In Marcelo M. Suarez-Orozco and Mariela M. Paez (eds), *Latinos: Remaking America* (pp. 215–35). Berkeley: University of California Press.

Hennessey, Bernard C. 1981. *Public Opinion.* 4th ed. Monterey, CA: Brooks/Cole.

Hero, Rodney E. 1986. "Mexican Americans and Urban Politics: A Consideration of Governmental Structure and Policy." *Aztlan* 17(1):131–47.

Hero, Rodney E. 1992a. *Latinos and the U.S. Political System: Two-Tiered Pluralism.* Philadelphia: Temple University Press.

Hero, Rodney E. 1992b. "The Elections of Federico Peña." In Rodney E. Hero (ed), *Latinos and the U.S. Political System: Two-Tiered Pluralism* (pp. 116–30). Philadelphia: Temple University Press.

Hero, Rodney. 1998. *Faces of Inequality: Social Diversity in American Politics.* New York: Oxford University Press.

Hero, Rodney, F. Chris Garcia, John Garcia, and Harry Pachon. 2000. "Latino Participation, Partisanship, and Office Holding." *PS: Political Science & Politics* 33(3):529–34.

Hero, Rodney, and Caroline Tolbert. 1995. "Latinos and Substantive Representation in the U.S. House of Representatives: Direct, Indirect, or Nonexistent?" *American Journal of Political Science* 39(3):640–52.

Hirsch, Herbert, and Armando Gutiérrez. 1977. *Learning To Be Militant: Ethnic Identity and the Development of Political Militance in a Chicano Community.* San Francisco: R&E Research Associates.

Hispanic Business Magazine. 2004, November 18. "Salsa Outselling Ketchup?: Marketing to Hispanics Is Hot." Available at http://www.hispanicbusiness.com/news/newsbyid.asp?id=19335, accessed May 17, 2007.

Hood, M. V., Irwin L. Morris, and Kurt A. Shirkey. 1997. "'!Quedate o Vente!': Uncovering the Determinants of Hispanic Public Opinion Toward Immigration." *Political Research Quarterly* 50:627–47.

Hopwood v. Texas (1996), 78 F.3d 932 (5th Cir.).

Horton, David M. 1999. *Lone Star Justice.* Austin, TX: Eakin Press.

Houvouras, Shannon. 2001. "The Effects of Demographic Variables, Ethnic Prejudice, and Attitudes toward Immigration on Opposition to Bilingual Education." *Hispanic Journal of Behavioral Sciences* 23(2):136–52.

"How America Responds (Part 2)." 2001, October 9. Available at http://www.umich. edu/~newsinfo/Releases/2001/Oct01/r100901b.html, accessed April 22, 2007.

Hudson, William. 2004. *American Democracy in Peril: Eight Challenges to America's Future*. 4th ed. New York: Chatham House.

Human Rights Watch. 2000, May. "Punishment and Prejudice: Racial Disparities in the War on Drugs." Human Rights Watch Report, Vol. 12, No. 2 (G). Available at www.hrw.org/reports/2000/usa, accessed April 22, 2007.

Jackson, Linda A. 1995, January. "Stereotypes, Emotions, Behavior, and Overall Attitudes toward Hispanics by Anglos." Research Report 10. East Lansing, MI: Julia Samora Research Institute.

Jacoby, William G. 1991. "Ideological Identification and Issue Attitudes." *American Journal of Political Science* 35:178–205.

Jenkinson, Michael. 1968. *Tijerina: Land Grant Conflict in New Mexico*. Albuquerque, NM: Paisano Press.

Jennings, James. 1977. *Puerto Rican Politics in New York City*. Washington, DC: University Press of America.

Jennings, James, ed. 1994. *Blacks, Latinos and Asians in Urban America: Status and Prospects for Politics and Activism*. Westport, CT: Praeger.

Jennings, James, and Monte Rivera. 1984. *Puerto Rican Politics in Urban America*. Westport, CT: Greenwood Press.

Jennings, Kent, and Richard Niemi. 1974. *The Political Character of Adolescence: The Influence of Families and Schools*. Princeton, NJ: Princeton University Press.

Johnson, Kirk. 2004, November 9. "Hispanic Voters Declared Their Independence." *New York Times* A26.

Jones, Jeffrey M. 2006, October 3. "Six in 10 Americans Think U.S Ready for a Female President." The Gallup Poll. Available at http://www.galluppoll.com/content/?ci=24832&pg=1, accessed April 22, 2007.

Jones-Correa, Michael. 1998. *Between Two Nations: The Political Predicament of Latinos in New York City*. Ithaca, NY: Cornell University Press.

Jones-Correa, Michael, and David L. Leal. 1996. "Becoming Hispanic: Secondary Panethnic Identification among Latin American-Origin Populations in the United States." *Hispanic Journal of Behavioral Sciences* 18:214–53.

Kamasaki, Charles, Clarissa Martinez, and Jessica Muñoz. 2004, November 16. "How Did Latinos Really Vote in 2004." National Council of La Raza Report. Washington, DC: National Council of La Raza. Available at http://www. nclr.org/content/publications/detail/28218/, accessed April 22, 2007.

Kaplowitz, Craig. 2005 *LULAC: Mexican Americans and National Policy*. College Station: Texas A&M University Press.

Kerr, Brinck, and Will Miller. 1997. "Latino Representation: It's Direct and Indirect." *American Journal of Political Science* 41:1066–71.

Keyes v. Denver School District No. 1, Denver, Colorado (1973), 413 U.S. 189.

King v. Illinois Board of Elections (1996), 117 S. Ct. 429.

Knight Ridder News Organization. 2000, June 7–13. *National Latino Voter Poll 2000*. Available at www.knightridder.com, accessed March 1, 2006.

Knowlton, Clark S. 1967, June. "Land-Grant Problems among the State's Spanish-Americans." *New Mexico Business* 343–56.

Kochhar, Rakesh. 2005, December 15. "The Occupational Status and Mobility of Hispanics." Pew Hispanic Center Report. Available at http://pewhispanic. org/files/reports/59.pdf, accessed April 22, 2007.

Kochhar, Rakesh, Roberto Suro, and Sonya Tafoya. 2005, July 26. "The New Latino South: The Context and Consequences of Rapid Population Growth." Report presented at "Immigration to New Settlement Areas," a conference held at the Pew Research Center. Available at http://pewhispanic.org/files/execsum/50.pdf, accessed April 22, 2007.

Lamare, James W. 1975. "Inter- or Intra-generational Cleavage? The Political Orientations of American Youth in 1968." *American Journal of Political Science* 19:81–9.

Larmer, Brook. 1999, July 12. "Hispanics Are Hip, Hot and Making History." *Newsweek* 48.

Laswell, Harold. 1936. *Politics: Who Gets What, When, and How?* New York: McGraw-Hill.

Lau v. Nichols (1974), 414 U.S. 563.

Lawyers Committee for Civil Rights Under Law. 2005. *Answering the Call for a More Diverse Judiciary: A Review of State Judicial Selection Models and Their Impact on Diversity.* Washington, DC: Lawyers Committee for Civil Rights Under Law.

Leal, David. 2004. "Latino Public Opinion?" Paper presented at the "Latino Politics: The State of the Discipline" conference, Texas A&M University and the University of Texas at Austin, College Station, TX, April 30–May 1.

Leal, David, Matt Barreto, Jongho Lee, and Rodolfo de la Garza. 2005. "The Latino Vote in the 2004 Election." *PS: Political Science & Politics* 38:41–9.

Leal, David, Kenneth J. Meier, and Valerie Martinez-Ebers. 2004. "The Politics of Latino Education: The Biases of At-Large Elections." *Journal of Politics* 66:1224–44.

Leftwich, Adrian. 1984. *What Is Politics?* Oxford: Basil Blackwell.

Leighley, J., and A. Vedilitz. 1999. "Race, Ethnicity, and Political Participation: Competing Models and Contrasting Explanations." *Journal of Politics* 61(4):1092–114.

Lemus, Frank. 1973. *The National Roster of Spanish Surnamed Elected Officials.* Los Angeles: Aztlan Production.

Lewin, Tamar. 1992, January 8. "Study Points to Increase in Tolerance of Ethnicity." *New York Times* A12.

Litt, Edgar. 1970. *Ethnic Politics in America.* Glenview, IL: Scott-Foresman.

Liu, Alex. 2001, December. "Political Participation and Dissatisfaction with Democracy: A Comparative Study of New and Stable Democracies." Research Methods Working Paper Series. Available at http://www. researchmethods.org/polParti-new-dem.pdf, accessed April 22, 2007.

Lopez, Antoinette Sedillo, ed. 1995. *Criminal Justice and Latino Communities.* New York: Garland.

Lopez, Linda, and Adrian Pantajo. 2004. "Beyond Black and White: General Support for Race Conscious Policies among African-Americans, Latinos, Asian Americans and Whites." *Political Research Quarterly* 57(4):633–42.

Lowell, Lindsey, and Roberto Suro. 2002, December. "The Improving Educational Attainment of Latino Immigrants." Pew Hispanic Center Report. Available at http://pewhispanic.org/files/reports/14.pdf, accessed April 22, 2007.

Lublin, David Ian. 1997. *The Paradox of Representation: Racial Gerrymandering and Minority Interests in Congress.* Princeton, NJ: Princeton University Press.

Magana, Lisa. 1994. "Mexican Americans: Are They an Ambivalent Minority?" Tomás Rivera Policy Institute Report. Claremont, CA: Tomás Rivera Institute Press.

Maddox, Kerman. 2007, March 21. "Latino Leaders' Silence Is Killing Blacks." *Los Angeles Times.* Available at http://www.latimes.com/news/opinion/la-oe-maddox21mar21,0,3806883.story, accessed April 22, 2007.

Marin, Christine. 1977. *A Spokesman of the Mexican American Movement: Rodolfo "Corky" Gonzalez and the Fight for Chicano Liberation, 1966–1972.* San Francisco: R&E Research Associates.

Marin, Gerardo. 1984. "Stereotyping Hispanics: The Differential Effect of Research Method, Label, and Degree of Contact." *International Journal of Intercultural Relations* 8:17–27.

Marquez, Benjamin. 1988. "The Politics of Real Assimilation: League of United Latin American Citizens." *Western Political Quarterly* 42:355–77.

Marquez, Benjamin. 1993a. "The Industrial Areas Foundation and the Mexican American in Texas: The Politics of Mobilization." In Paula McClain (ed), *Minority Group Influence: Agenda Setting, Formation, and Public Policy* (pp. 127–46). Westport, CT: Greenwood Press.

Marquez, Benjamin. 1993b. *LULAC: The Evolution of a Mexican American Political Organization.* Austin: Center for Mexican American Studies, University of Texas Press.

Marmot, Michael. 1999. "Multi-Level Approaches to Understanding Social Determinants." In Lisa Berkman and Ichiro Kawachi (eds), *Social Epidemiology* (pp. 350–7). Oxford: Oxford University Press.

Martinez, Ramiro. 2002. *Latino Homicide: Immigration, Violence and Community.* New York: Routledge Press.

Massey, Douglas S., Jorge Durand, and Nolan J. Malone. 2002. *Beyond Smoke and Mirrors: Mexican Immigration in an Era of Economic Integration.* New York: Russell Sage Foundation.

Masud-Piloto, Felix. 1996. *From Welcomed Exiles to Illegal Immigrants: Cuban Migration to the U.S., 1959–1995.* Lanham, MD: Rowman & Littlefield.

Matthiessen, Peter. 1969. *Sal Si Puedes: César Chávez and the New American Revolution.* New York: Dell.

McClain, Paula. 1996. "Coalition and Competition: Patterns of Black-Latino Relations in Urban Politics." In W. C. Rich (ed), *Politics of Minority Coalitions: Race, Ethnicity and Shared Uncertainties* (pp. 53–63). Westport, CT: Greenwood.

McClain, Paula D., Niambi M. Carter, Victoria M. DeFrancesco Soto, Monique L. Lyle, Jeffrey D. Grynaviski, Shayla C. Nunnally, Thomas J. Scotto, J. Alan Kendrick, Gerald F. Lackey, and Kendra Davenport Cotton. 2006. "Racial Distancing in a Southern City: Latino Immigrants' Views of Black Americans." *Journal of Politics* 68(3):571–84.

McClain, Paula D., and Joseph Stewart, Jr. 2006. *Can We All Get Along?: Racial and Ethnic Minorities in American Politics.* 4th ed. Boulder, CO: Westview Press.

McFadden, Robert M. 2006, April 10. "Across the U.S., Growing Rallies for Immigration." *New York Times.* Available at http://www.nytimes.com/2006/04/10/us/10protest.html?ex=1302321600&en=7f6da8e9c1d1b7a4&ei=5088&partner=rssnyt&emc=rss, accessed April 22, 2007.

McPartland, James M., and Jomills Henry Braddock III. 1981. "Going to College and Getting a Good Job: The Impact of Desegregation." In W. Hawley (ed), *Effective School Desegregation* (pp. 141–54). Beverly Hills, CA: Sage.

McWilliams, Carey. 1968. *North from Mexico: The Spanish-Speaking People of the United States.* New York: Greenwood Press.

Meier, Kenneth J., and Joseph Stewart, Jr. 1991. *The Politics of Hispanic Education.* New York: University of New York Press.

Meier, Kenneth J., Joseph Stewart, Jr., and Robert E. England. 1989. *Race, Class, and Education: The Politics of Second Generation Discrimination.* Madison: University of Wisconsin Press.

Meier, Matt S., and Margo Gutiérrez. 2000. *Encyclopedia of the Mexican American Civil Rights Movement*. Westport, CT: Greenwood Press.

Meier, Matt S., and Feliciano Rivera. 1972. *The Chicanos: A History of Mexican Americans*. New York: Hill and Wang.

Méndez, Miguel A., and Leo P. Martínez. 2002. "Toward a Statistical Profile of Latina/os in the Legal Profession." *La Raza Law Journal* 59.

Mendez v. Westminster (1947), 64 F. Supp. 544 (D.C. Cal. 1946), *aff'd*, 161 F.2d 774 (9th Cir. 1947).

Menifield, Charles. 2001. "Minority Representation in the Twenty-First Century: An Introduction." In Charles Menifield (ed), *Representation of Minority Groups in the U.S.: Implications for the Twenty-First Century* (pp. 1–12). Lanham, MD: Rowan & Littlefield.

Michelson, Melissa. 2003a. "The Corrosive Effect of Acculturation: How Mexican-Americans Lose Political Trust." *Social Science Quarterly* 84(4):918–33.

Michelson, Melissa. 2003b. "Getting Out the Latino Vote: How Door-to-Door Canvassing Influences Voter Turnout in Rural Central California." *Political Behavior* 25(3):247–63.

Michelson, Melissa. 2003c. "Political Efficacy among California Latinos." *Latino(a) Research Review* 5(2–3):5–15.

Michelson, Melissa. 2006. "Mobilizing the Latino Youth Vote: Some Experimental Results." *Social Science Quarterly* 87(5):1188–206.

Miller v. Johnson (1995), 515 U.S. 900.

Mindiola, Tatcho, and Armando Gutiérrez. 1988. "Chicanos and the Legislative Process: Reality and Illusion in the Politics of Change." In F. Chris Garcia (ed), *Latinos and the Political System* (pp. 349–62). Notre Dame, IN: University of Notre Dame Press.

Mindiola, Tatcho Jr., Yolanda Flores Niemann, and Nestor Rodriguez. 2002. *Black-Brown: Relations and Stereotypes*. Austin: University of Texas Press.

Mirande, Alfredo. 1987. *Gringo Justice*. Notre Dame, IN: University of Notre Dame Press.

Montalvo, Frank, and Edward Codina. 2001. "Skin Color and Latinos in the United States." *Ethnicities* 1(3):321–41.

Montejano, David. 1986. *Anglos and Mexicans in the Making of Texas, 1836–1986*. Austin: University of Texas Press.

Morales, Armando. 1972. *Ando Sangrando (I Am Bleeding): A Study of Mexican American-Police Conflict*. La Puente, CA: La Puente.

Moreno, Dario, and Christopher L. Warren. 1992. "The Conservative Enclave: Cubans in Florida." In Rodolfo O. de la Garza and Louis DeSipio (eds), *From Rhetoric to Reality: Latino Politics in the 1988 Elections*. Boulder, CO: Westview Press.

Morin, Jose Luis. 2005. *Latino/a Rights and Justice in the United States—Perspectives and Approaches*. Durham, NC: Carolina Academic Press.

Morin, Raul. 1963. *Among the Valiant: Mexican-Americans in World War II and Korea*. Alhambra, CA: Borden.

Muñoz, Carlos. 1989. *Youth, Identity, Power: The Chicano Movement*. New York: Verso.

Nabokov, Peter. 1969. *Tijerina and the Courthouse Raid*. Berkeley, CA: Ramparts Press.

National Alliance for Hispanic Health. 2005, January 9. "New Federal Report Finds Hispanics Losing Ground in Health Care: National Hispanic Leadership

Calls for New Federal Focus to Reverse Trend." National Alliance for Hispanic Health News Release. Available at http://www.hispanichealth.org/pdf/NHDR_News.pdf, accessed April 22, 2007.

National Association of Latino Elected Officials. 2003. *National Directory of Hispanic Elected Officials*. Los Angeles, CA: NALEO Educational Fund.

National Association of Latino Elected Officials. 2004. *National Directory of Hispanic Elected Officials*. Los Angeles, CA: NALEO Educational Fund.

National Association of Latino Elected Officials. 2005. *National Directory of Hispanic Elected Officials*. Los Angeles, CA: NALEO Educational Fund.

National Center for Education Statistics (NCES). 2000. *Descriptive Summary of 1995–96 Beginning Postsecondary Students: 3 Years Later*. NCES 2000-154. Washington, DC: NCES.

National Community for Latino Leadership. 2001, January. "Reflecting an American Vista: The Character and Impact of Latino Leadership." Available at http://www.latinoleadership.org/research/reports/20010110.html, accessed April 22, 2007.

National Conference of Christians and Jews. 1992. *Taking America's Pulse: A Summary Report of the National Conference Survey on Inter-Group Relations*. New York: National Conference of Christians and Jews.

National Hispanic Leadership Agenda. 2005, July. *National Hispanic Leadership Agenda Congressional Scorecard 108th Congress, First and Second Session*. Available at www.lulac.org/publications/108thcongress-1-2.pdf, accessed April 22, 2007.

Navarro, Armando. 1998. *The Cristal Experiment: A Chicano Struggle for Community Control*. Madison: University of Wisconsin Press.

Navarro, Armando. 2000. *La Raza Unida Party: A Chicano Challenge to the U.S. Two-Party Dictatorship*. Philadelphia: Temple University Press.

Navarro, Armando. 2005. *Mexicano Political Experience in Occupied Aztlan: Struggles and Change*. Lanham, MD: Rowman & Littlefield.

Navarro, Sharon. 2004. "Interest Groups and Social Movements." In Sharon A. Navarro and Armando Xavier Mejia (eds), *Latino Americans and Political Participation* (pp. 89–120). Santa Barbara, CA: ABC-CLIO.

Negron-Muntaner, Frances. 2004. *None of the Above: Contemporary Puerto Rican Culture and Politics*. New York: Palgrave Macmillan.

Nicholson, Stephen, Adrian Pantoja, and Gary Segura. 2006. "Political Knowledge and Issue Voting among the Latino Electorate." *Political Research Quarterly* 99(2):259–71.

Nicholson, Stephen, and Gary M. Segura. 2006. "Issue Agendas and the Politics of Latino Partisan Identification." In Gary M. Segura and Shaun Bowler (eds), *Diversity in Democracy: Minority Representation in the United States* (pp. 51–71). Charlottesville: University of Virginia Press.

Niemann, Yolanda Flores, ed. 2002. *Chicana Leadership: The Frontiers Reader*. Lincoln: University of Nebraska Press.

Novas, Himilce. 2003. *Everything You Need to Know About Latino History*. New York: Plume.

Pachon, Harry. 1988. "Hispanic Underrepresentation in the Federal Bureaucracy: The Missing Link in the Policy Process." In F. Chris Garcia (ed), *Latinos and the Political System* (pp. 306–13). Notre Dame, IN: University of Notre Dame Press.

Pachon, Harry, and Louis DeSipio. 1994. *New Americans by Choice: Political Perspectives of Latino Immigrants*. Boulder, CO: Westview Press.

Pachon, Harry P., Louis DeSipio, Chon A. Noriega, and Rodolfo O. de la Garza. 2000, May. "Still Missing: Latinos In and Out of Hollywood." Tomás Rivera Policy Institute Report. Available at http://www.trpi.org/PDFs/still_missing_in_action.pdf, accessed April 22, 2007.

Pachon, Harry P., Gary M. Segura, and Nathan Woods. 2001. "Hispanics, Social Capital and Civic Engagement." National Civic Review 90(1):85–96.

Padilla, Felix. 1985. Latino Ethnic Consciousness: The Case of Mexican Americans and Puerto Ricans in Chicago. Notre Dame, IN: University of Notre Dame Press.

Pardo, Mary. 1997. "Mexican American Women Grassroots Community Activists: Mothers of East Los Angeles." In F. Chris Garcia (ed), Pursuing Power: Latinos and the Political System (pp. 151–68). Notre Dame, IN: Notre Dame Press.

Pardo, Mary. 1998. Mexican American Women Activists: Identity and Resistance in Two Los Angeles Communities. Philadelphia: Temple University Press.

Passel, Jeffrey S. 2005, June 14. "Unauthorized Migrants: Numbers and Characteristics." Pew Hispanic Center Report. Available at http://pewhispanic.org/files/reports/46.pdf, accessed April 22, 2007.

Paul, Pamela. 2001. "Hispanic Heterogeneity." Forecast 218:1–3.

Pew Hispanic Center, Kaiser Family Foundation. 2002. "2002 National Survey of Latinos." Available at http://pewhispanic.org/reports/report.php?ReportID= 15, accessed April 22, 2007.

Pew Hispanic Center, Kaiser Family Foundation. 2003. "Survey of Latino Attitudes on the War with Iraq." Available at http://pewhispanic.org/reports/report. php?ReportID=18, accessed April 22, 2007.

Pew Hispanic Center, Kaiser Family Foundation. 2004a. "National Survey of Latinos: Education." Available at http://pewhispanic.org/reports/report.php?Report ID=25, accessed April 22, 2007.

Pew Hispanic Center, Kaiser Family Foundation. 2004b. "2004 National Survey of Latinos: Politics and Civic Participation." Available at http://pewhispanic.org/ reports/report.php?ReportID=33, accessed April 22, 2007.

Pew Hispanic Center. 2005, January. "Hispanics: A People in Motion." Pew Hispanic Center Report. Available at http://pewhispanic.org/files/reports/40.pdf, accessed on April 22, 2007.

Pew Hispanic Center. 2006, July 13. "2006 National Survey of Latinos: The Immigration Debate." Pew Hispanic Center Survey. Available at http://pewhispanic.org/files/reports/68.pdf, accessed April 22, 2007.

Phillips, Anne. 1998. "Democracy and Representation: Or, Why Should It Matter Who Our Representatives Are?" In Anne Phillips (ed), Feminism and Politics (pp. 224–40). Oxford: Oxford University.

Pimentel, O. Ricardo. 2002, January 10. "Hispanic Middle Class Growing Fast." Tucson Citizen.

Pitkin, Hanna F. 1967. The Concept of Representation. Berkeley: University of California Press.

Plotke, David. 1997. "Representation Is Democracy." Constellations 4:19–34.

Polinard, Jerry, Robert D. Wrinkle, and Rodolfo de la Garza. 1984. "Attitudes of Mexican Americans toward Irregular Mexican Immigration." International Migration Review 18:782–99.

Putnam, Robert. 2000. Bowling Alone: The Collapse and Revival of American Community. New York: Simon & Schuster.

Ramirez, Roberto. 2004, December. "We the People: Hispanics in the United States." Census 2000 Special Report. Washington, DC: Department of Commerce. Available at www.census.gov/prod/2004pubs/censr-18.pdf, accessed April 22, 2007.

Ramirez, Roberto, and Patricia de la Cruz. 2003, June. "The Hispanic Population in the United States: March 2002." P20–545. Current Population Reports. Washington, DC: Department of Commerce. Available at www.census.gov/prod/2003pubs/p20-545.pdf, accessed April 22, 2007.

Regalado, Jaime. 1997. "The Political Incorporation of LA's Communities of Color." In F. Chris Garcia (ed), *Pursuing Power* (pp. 169–89). Notre Dame, IN: University of Notre Dame Press.

Regents of the University of California v. Bakke (1978), 438 U.S. 265.

Ricci, David. 1971. *Community Power and Democratic Theory: The Logic of Political Analysis*. New York: Random House.

Rich, Wilbur. 1996. *The Politics of Minority Coalitions, Race, Ethnicities, and Shared Uncertainties*. Westport, CT: Praeger.

Ricourt, Milagros. 2002. *Power from the Margins: The Incorporation of Dominicans in New York City (Latino Communities: Emerging Voices—Political, Social, Cultural and Legal Issues)*. New York: Routledge Press.

Rivas-Rodriguez, Maggie. 2005. *Mexican Americans in World War II*. Austin: University of Texas Press.

Robinson, Linda. 1999, May 16. "Watch Out: The Rhythm Is Gonna Get You, Too Suddenly, Latino Culture is Everywhere." *U.S. News and World Report*. Available at http://www.usnews.com/usnews/culture/articles/990524/archive_001076.htm, accessed April 25, 2007.

Rodriguez, David. 2002. *Latino National Coalitions: Struggles and Challenges*. New York: Routledge.

Rosales, Rodolfo. 2000. *The Illusion of Inclusion: The Untold Political Story of San Antonio*. Austin: University of Texas Press.

Saad, Lydia. 2001, June 22. "Blacks Less Satisfied Than Hispanics with Their Quality of Life." The Gallup Poll. Available at http://www.galluppoll.com/content/?ci=4537, accessed April 22, 2007.

Samora, Julian, and Patricia Vandel Simon. 1993. *A History of the Mexican American People*. Rev. ed. Notre Dame, IN: Notre Dame University Press.

San Antonio School District v. Rodriguez (1973), 411 U.S. 1; 93 S. Ct. 1278.

Sanchez, Gabriel. 2006. "The Role of Group Consciousness in Latino Public Opinion." *Political Research Quarterly* 34:427–51.

Santillan, Richard. 1973. *La Raza Unida*. Los Angeles: Tlaquilo.

Santos, Adolfo, and Carlos Herta. 2001. "An Analysis of Descriptive and Substantive Latino Representation in Congress." In Charles E. Menifield (ed.) *Representation of Minority Groups in the U.S.* (pp. 57–75). Lanham, MD: Austin and Winfield.

Schattschneider, Elmar Eric. 1960. *The Semi-Sovereign People*. New York: Holt, Rinehart and Winston.

Schmidt, Peter. 2003. "Academe's Hispanic Future." *Chronicle Special Report* 50(14):A8.

Schmidt, Ron. 1997. "Latino Politics in the 1990s: A View from California." In F. Chris Garcia (ed), *Pursuing Power: Latinos in the Political System* (pp. 557–62). Notre Dame, IN: University of Notre Dame Press.

Schmidt, Ron. 2000. *Language Policy and Identity Politics in the United States*. Philadelphia: Temple University Press.

Segal, Adam J. 2004, September 28. "Bikini Politics: The 2004 Presidential Campaigns' Hispanic Media Efforts Cover Only the Essential Parts of the Body Politic: A Select Group of Voters in a Few Battleground States." Available at http://advanced.jhu.edu/academic/government/hvp/hvp_2004_Interim_Report.pdf, accessed April 22, 2007.

Segura, Gary. M., and Shaun Bowler. 2005. *Diversity in Democracy: Minority Representation in the United States.* Charlottesville: University of Virginia Press.

Sepulveda, Juan A. Jr. 2003. *The Life and Times of Willie Valasquez: Su Voto Es Su Voz.* Houston, TX: Arte Publico Press.

Shaw, Daron, Rodolfo O. de la Garza, and Jongho Lee. 2000. "Examining Latino Turnout in 1996: A Three-State, Validated Survey Approach." *American Journal of Political Science* 44:332–40.

Shaw v. Reno (1993), 509 U.S. 630.

Shiraev, Eric, and Richard Sobel. 2006. *People and Their Opinions: Thinking Critically About Public Opinion.* Upper Saddle River, NJ: Pearson Longman Press.

Shockley, John S. 1974. *Chicano Revolt in a Texas Town.* Notre Dame, IN: University of Notre Dame Press.

Shorris, Earl. 1993. *Latinos: The Biography of a People.* New York: Macmillan.

Sidlow, Edward, and Beth Henschen. 2004. *America at Odds.* 4th ed. Belmont, CA: Thomson/Wadsworth.

Skerry, Peter. 1993. *Mexican Americans: The Ambivalent Minority.* New York: The Free Press, Macmillan.

Smith v. Allwright (1944), 321 U.S. 649.

Smith, James P. 1999. "Healthy Bodies and Thick Wallets." *Journal of Economic Perspectives* 13(2):145–66.

Smith, Tom W. 1990, December. "Ethnic Images." GSS Topical Report 19. Chicago: National Opinion Research Center, University of Chicago. Available at http://cloud9.norc.uchicago.edu/dlib/t-19.htm, accessed April 22, 2007.

Solberg, Rorie, L. Spill, and Kathleen Bratton. 2005. "Diversifying the Federal Bench: Presidential Patterns." *Justice Systems Journal* 26:119–33.

Sonenshein, Raphael. 1993. *Politics in Black and White: Race and Power in Los Angeles.* Princeton, NJ: Princeton University Press.

Sonenshein, Raphael J., and Susan H. Pinkus. 2002. "The Dynamics of Latino Incorporation: The 2001 Los Angeles Mayoral Election as Seen in *Los Angeles Times* Polls." *PS: Political Science & Politics* March:67–74.

Sonenshein, Raphael J., and Susan H. Pickus. 2005. "Latino Incorporation Reaches the Urban Summit: How Antonio Villaraigosa Won the 2005 Los Angeles Mayor's Race." *PS: Political Science & Politics* October:713–21.

Sorauf, Frank J., and Paul Allen Beck. 1988. *Party Politics in America.* 6th ed. Chicago: Scott Foresman/Little, Brown.

Steffensmeier, Darrell, and Stephen Demuth. 2000. "Ethnicity and Sentencing Outcomes in U.S. Federal Courts: Who Is Punished More Harshly?" *American Sociological Review* 65:705–29.

Stein, Robert. 1989. "Market Maximization of Individual Preferences and Metropolitan Municipal Service Responsibility." *Urban Affairs Quarterly* 25(1):86–116.

Suro, Roberto, Richard Fry, and Jeffrey Passel. 2005, June 27. "Hispanics and the 2004 Election: Population, Electorate and Voters." Pew Hispanic Center Reports and Factsheets. Available at http://pewhispanic.org/reports/report.php?ReportID=48, accessed April 22, 2007.

Suro, Roberto, and Jeffrey S. Passel. 2003, October. "The Rise of the Second Generation: Changing Patterns in Hispanic Population Growth." Pew Hispanic Center Study. Available at http://www.pewtrusts.com/pdf/pew_hispanic_2nd_generation_101403.pdf, accessed April 22, 2007.

Tam-Cho, Wendy K. 1999. "Naturalization, Socialization, Participation: Immigrants and (Non-)Voting." *Journal of Politics* 61:1140–55.

Tamor, Lewin. 1992, January 8. "Study Points to Increase in Tolerance of Ethnicity." *New York Times* A10.

Tate, Katherin.1993. *From Protest to Politics: The New Black Voters in American Elections*. New York: Russell Sage Foundation.

Taylor, Ronald B. 1975. *Chávez and the Farmworkers*. Boston: Bacon.

Teixeira, Ruy, and Joel Rogers. 2000. *America's Forgotten Majority: Why the White Working Class Still Matters*. New York: Basic Books.

Thornburg v. Gingles (1986), 478 U.S. 30.

"The 25 Most Influential Hispanics in America." 2005, August 22. *Time Magazine* 46.

Tirado, Miguel. 1970. "Mexican American Community Political Organization: The Key to Chicano Political Power." *Aztlan: Chicano Journal of the Social Sciences and the Arts* 1:53–78.

Torres, Rodolfo. D., and George Katsiaficas, eds. 1999. *Latino Social Movements: Historical and Theoretical Perspectives*. New York: Routledge.

Tropp, Linda. 2007. "Perceived Discrimination and Interracial Contact: Predicting Interracial Closeness among Black and White Americans." *Social Psychology Quarterly* 70:70–81.

Truman, David B. 1951. *The Governmental Process: Political Interests and Public Opinion*. New York: Knopf.

Uhlaner, Carole. 1991. "Perceived Prejudice and Coalitional Prospects among Black, Latinos, and Asian Americans." In Byron Jackson and Michael Preston (eds), *Ethnic and Racial Politics in California* (pp. 339–71). Berkeley, CA: Institute for Governmental Studies.

Uhlaner, Carole Jean, and F. Chris Garcia. 2002. "Latino Public Opinion." In Barbera Norrander and Clyde Wilcox (eds), *Understanding Public Opinion* (pp. 77–102). Washington, DC: CQ Press.

Uhlaner, Carole, Jean, Mark Gray, and F. Chris Garcia. 2000. "Ideology, Issues, and Partisanship among Latinos." Paper presented at the annual meeting of the Western Political Science Association, San Jose, CA, August.

Uhlaner, Carole Jean, and F. Chris Garcia. 1998. "Foundations of Latino Party Identification: Learning, Ethnicity, and Demographic Factors among Mexicans, Puerto Ricans, Cubans, and Anglos in the United States." Irvine, CA: Center for the Study of Democracy Research Monograph Series.

Urbina, Martin G. 2003. *Capital Punishment and Latino Offenders: Racial and Ethnic Differences in Death Sentences*. New York: LFB Scholarly Publishing.

U.S. Bureau of the Census. 1999, December. "The Hispanic Population in the United States." Current Population Report P20–525. Washington, DC: U.S. Census Bureau, Department of Commerce. Available at http://www.census.gov/prod/2000pubs/p20–525.pdf, accessed April 22, 2007.

U.S. Bureau of the Census. 2001a, September. "Money Income in the United States: 2000." Current Population Report P60–213. Washington, DC: U.S. Census Bureau, Department of Commerce. Available at http://www.census.gov/prod/2001pubs/p60–213.pdf, accessed April 22, 2007.

U.S. Bureau of the Census. 2001b, September. "Poverty in the United States: 2000." Current Population Report P60–214. Washington, DC: U.S. Census Bureau, Department of Commerce. Available at http://www.census.gov/prod/2001pubs/p60–214.pdf, accessed April 22, 2007.

U.S. Bureau of the Census. 2002a, March. "Annual Demographic Supplement to the March 2002 Current Population Survey." Washington, DC: Department of Commerce. Available at http://www.census.gov/population/www/socdemo/age/ppl–167.html, accessed April 22, 2007.

U.S. Bureau of the Census. 2002b, February. "Voting and Registration in the Election of November 2000." Current Population Report P20–542. Washington, DC: U.S. Census Bureau, Department of Commerce. Available at http://www.census.gov/prod/2002pubs/p20–542.pdf, accessed April 22, 2007.

U.S. Bureau of the Census. 2002c, July. "2002 Census of Governments: Government Units in 2002." GC02(P). Washington, DC: U.S. Census Bureau. Available at www.census.gov/govs/cog/2002COGprelim_report.pdf, accessed April 22, 2007.

U.S. Bureau of the Census. 2003a, June. "The Hispanic Population of the United States: March 2002." Current Population Report P20–545. Washington, DC: U.S. Census Bureau, Department of Commerce. Available at http://www.census.gov/prod/2003pubs/p20–545.pdf, accessed April 22, 2007.

U.S. Bureau of the Census. 2003b, September. "Poverty in the United States: 2002." Current Population Report P60–222. Washington, DC: U.S. Census Bureau, Department of Commerce. Available at www.census.gov/prod/2003pubs/p60–222.pdf, accessed April 22, 2007.

U.S. Bureau of the Census. 2005, April 8. "Voting and Registration in the Election of November 2004." Washington, DC: U.S. Census Bureau, Department of Commerce. Available at http://www.census.gov/population/www/socdemo/voting/cps2004.html, accessed April 22, 2007.

U.S. Commission on Civil Rights. 1970. "Mexican Americans and the Administration of the Justice in the Southwest." Washington, DC: U.S. Government Printing Office. U.S. Congress General Accounting Office.

U.S. Commission on Civil Rights. 1971–1974. Mexican American Education Study Reports Nos. 1–6. Washington, DC: U.S. Government Printing Office. U.S. Congress General Accounting Office.

U.S. Congress General Accounting Office. 2004, June. *Treaty of Guadalupe-Hidalgo: Findings and Possible Options Regarding Longstanding Community Land Grant Claims in New Mexico.* Report to Congressional Requesters. Available at www.ago.state.nm.us/pio/annrpt/2007_annual_report.pdf, accessed April 22, 2007.

U.S. Department of Labor, Bureau of Labor Statistics. 1995, May. *A CPS Supplement for Testing Methods of Collecting Racial and Ethnic Information.* Washington, DC: Department of Labor.

U.S. Equal Employment Opportunity Commission. 2005. *Annual Report on the Federal Work Force: Fiscal Year 2005.* Available at http://www.eeoc.gov/federal/fsp2005/fsp2005.pdf, accessed April 22, 2007.

U.S. Office of Personnel Management. 1999, July. *Hispanics in the Federal Government: A Statistical Profile.* Available at http://www.doctr.ost.dot.gov/documents/ycr/opm_diversity/hispanic.pdf, accessed May 17, 2007.

Vaca, Nicolas C. 2004. *The Presumed Alliance: The Unspoken Conflict between Latinos and Blacks and What It Means for America.* New York: Harper Collins.

Valle, Victor, and Rodolfo D. Torres. 2003. "Class and Culture Wars in the New Latino Politics." In Francisco H. Vázquez and Rodolfo D. Torres (eds), *Latino/a Political Thought: Politics, Culture, and Society* (pp. 167–94). Lanham, MD: Rowman & Littlefield.

Verba, Sidney, Kay Schlozman, and Henry Brady. 1995. *Voice and Equality: Civic Voluntarism in American Politics.* Cambridge, MA: Harvard University Press.

Verba, Sidney, and Norman Nie. 1972. *Participation in America.* New York: Harper and Row.

Vernez, G., and A. Abrahamse. 1996. *How Immigrants Fare in U.S. Education.* Santa Monica, CA: Rand.

Vigil, Ernesto. 1999. *The Crusade for Justice: Chicano Militancy and the Government's War on Dissent.* Madison: University of Wisconsin Press.

Vigil, Maurilio. 1996. *Hispanics in Congress: A Historical and Political Survey.* Lanham, MD: University Press of America.

Vigil, Maurilio and Roy Lujan. 1986. "Parallels in the Career of Two Hispanic U.S. Senators." *Journal of Ethnic Studies* 13:1–20.

Villahermosa, Gilberto. 2002, September 1. "America's Hispanics in America's Wars." *Army Magazine.* Available at http://www.ausa.org/webpub/DeptArmy Magazine.nsf/byid/CCRN-6CCS5U, accessed April 22, 2007.

Walker, Nancy E., J. Michael Senger, Franciso A. Villaruel, and Angela M. Arboleda. 2004. *Lost Opportunities: The Reality of Latinos in the U.S. Criminal Justice System.* Washington, DC: National Council of La Raza.

Washington Post, Kaiser Family Foundation, and Harvard University. 1999. *National Survey on Latinos in America.* Available at http://www.kff.org/kaiser-polls/3023index.cfm, accessed April 17, 2007.

Wax, Emily. 2001, July 7. "For Area Bolivians, Cherishing the Past, Looking to the Future." *Washington Post* T4.

Weber, David J. 2003. *Foreigners in Their Native Land: Historical Roots of the Mexican Americans.* Albuquerque: University of New Mexico Press.

Welch, Susan, and John R. Hibbing. 1984. "Hispanic Representation in the U.S. Congress." *Social Science Quarterly* 65:328–35.

Welniak, Ed, and Kirby Posey. 2005, June. "Household Income: 1999." Census 2000 Brief. Washington, DC: U.S. Census Bureau, Department of Commerce. Available at www.census.gov/prod/2005pubs/c2kbr-36.pdf, accessed on April 22, 2007.

Wenzel, James P. "Acculturation Effects on Trust in National and Local Governments among Mexican Americans." *Social Science Quarterly* 87:1071–87.

White v. Regester (1973), 412 U.S. 755.

William C. Velasquez Institute. 2002, November 7. "Massive Latino Vote in Texas Gives Support to Democrats." Available at http://www.wcvi.org/press_room/press_archive/2002/tx/exit_poll110602.html, accessed April 22, 2007.

Wrinkle, Robert D. 1997. "Mexican American and Anglo Attitudes toward Immigration Reform: A View from the Border." *Social Science Quarterly* 78:324–37.

Index